REFORM AND DEVELOPMENT OF PRIVATE INTERNATIONAL LAW

Sir Peter North, CBE, QC, MA, DCL, FBA

REFORM AND DEVELOPMENT OF PRIVATE INTERNATIONAL LAW

ESSAYS IN HONOUR OF SIR PETER NORTH

Edited by
JAMES FAWCETT

OXFORD
UNIVERSITY PRESS

OXFORD

UNIVERSITY PRESS

Great Clarendon Street, Oxford OX2 6DP

Oxford University Press is a department of the University of Oxford.
It furthers the University's objective of excellence in research, scholarship,
and education by publishing worldwide in

Oxford New York

Athens Auckland Bangkok Bogotá Buenos Aires Calcutta
Cape Town Chennai Dar es Salaam Delhi Florence Hong Kong Istanbul
Karachi Kuala Lumpur Madrid Melbourne Mexico City Mumbai
Nairobi Paris São Paulo Shanghai Singapore Taipei Tokyo Toronto Warsaw

with associated companies in Berlin Ibadan

Oxford is a registered trade mark of Oxford University Press
in the UK and in certain other countries

Published in the United States
by Oxford University Press Inc., New York

British Library Cataloguing in Publication Data

Data available

Library of Congress Cataloging in Publication Data

Reform and Development of Private International Law: Essays in Honour of Sir Peter North/
edited by J.Fawcett.
p. cm.
Includes bibliographical references and index.
1. Conflict of laws. I. North, P. M. (Peter Machin) II. Fawcett, J. J.
K7041.R44 2002
340.9—dc20   2002074283
ISBN 0–19–925008–1

1 3 5 7 9 10 8 6 4 2

Typeset in Garamond by
Cambrian Typesetters, Frimley, Surrey

Printed in Great Britain
on acid-free paper by
Biddles Ltd, Guildford and King's Lynn

EDITOR

Professor James Fawcett
University of Nottingham

CONTRIBUTORS

Professor Paul R Beaumont
University of Aberdeen

Professor Joost Blom QC
*The University of British
Columbia*

Professor Ronald A Brand
University of Pittsburgh

The Hon. Sir Lawrence Collins
Royal Courts of Justice

Professor Hans Ulrich Jessurun
d'Oliveira
*University of Amsterdam,
European University Institute
(Florence)*

Professor James Fawcett
University of Nottingham

Professor Ian F Fletcher
University College London

Professor Jonathan Harris
University of Birmingham

Professor Trevor Hartley
London School of Economics

Professor Ole Lando
Copenhagen Business School

Professor David McClean CBE
QC
University of Sheffield

Professor C G J Morse
King's College London

The Hon. Peter Nygh
University of New South Wales

Professor Kurt Siehr
University of Zurich

CONTENTS—SUMMARY

CONTENTS

TABLE OF CASES

Australia

Canada

European Court of Justice and Court of First Instance

France

Germany

Hong Kong

Italy

Luxembourg

Netherlands

New Zealand

Nigeria

South Africa

Switzerland

UK

USA

TABLE OF LEGISLATION

Table of EC Legislation

INTRODUCTION

James Fawcett

Sir Peter North has had and will no doubt continue to have a remarkable career combining service to his university, the University of Oxford, public service, and service to private international law. Service to his University started with a Tutorship in law and a Fellowship at Keble College in 1965. He went on to become the Principal of Jesus College in 1984, a post which he still holds, Pro- Vice Chancellor of the University from 1988–1993 and Vice-Chancellor from 1993–1997. He has been a member of the University's Hebdomadal Council from 1985 and a Delegate and Chairman of Delegates to Oxford University Press. Public service has included membership of an enormous range of committees and Chairman of, *inter alia*: the Road Traffic Law Review, 1985–1988; the Independent Review of Parades and Marches in Northern Ireland, 1996–1997; the Independent Committee for the Supervision of Standards of Telephone Information Services, 1999 to date. He has been showered with honours, all of which have been thoroughly well deserved: a knighthood in 1999, a CBE in 1989, an Honorary Bencher of the Inner Temple in 1987 and an honorary Queen's Counsel in 1993, a Fellow of the British Academy in 1990, Membre de l'institut de Droit International, a doctorate in Civil Law in 1976, and honorary degrees from the Universities of Reading, Nottingham, and Aberdeen.

A. The Contribution of Sir Peter North to Private International Law

Peter North has made an outstanding contribution over many years to private international law as a writer, teacher, and reformer of the law.

In the early days of his career, Peter North wrote books on *Occupiers' Liability* (1971) and *The Modern Law of Animals* (1972). But he is best known, in England and abroad, to students, practitioners, and judges, as the editor of *Cheshire and North's Private International Law*. His association with the book started with the eighth edition in 1970 and has continued through to the current, thirteenth, edition, in 1999. From the outset he has put his own distinctive imprint on the book, toning down some of Cheshire's more suspect theories in some areas whilst at the same time introducing his own theories in other areas. As the co-editor of the 11th, 12th, and 13th editions, I can say that Peter North is the perfect person to write with. He can always see when something that I have written needs to be altered but manages to convey this in such a tactful way that it does not appear to be a criticism. In between successive editions of Cheshire, there have been books on *The Private International Law of Matrimonial Causes* (1977), *Contract Conflicts* (1982), *Cases and Materials on Private International Law* (with J H C Morris 1984) and his magisterial General Course on Private International Law at the Hague Academy of International Law entitled 'Reform, But Not Revolution' (1990),[1] which was substantially reproduced in *Private International Law Problems in Common Law Jurisdictions* (1993). Some of his numerous articles were published as *Essays in Private International Law* in 1993.

After a teaching associateship at Northwestern University School of Law, Chicago and lectureships at Aberystwyth and Nottingham, Peter North became a Tutor in Law and Fellow of Keble College Oxford in 1965. He was one of a formidable trio of private international lawyers at Oxford at that time, the others being Dr John Morris and Peter Carter. Former Bachelor of Civil Law students still recall with awe the experience of attending seminars conducted jointly by these three. One of the beneficiaries of Peter North's teaching (on Roman law) was the young Tony Blair. Peter North was a visiting professor at Auckland in 1969 and at the University of British Columbia from 1975–1976. Appointment as a Law Commissioner in 1976 meant that his teaching for the Law Faculty and his college at Oxford had to cease. Nonetheless, since then he has supervised PhD students, given innumerable lectures in England and abroad, including a course of lectures at the Hague Academy of International Law in 1980 on 'The Development of Rules of Private International Law in the Field of Family Law'[2] and the General Course on Private International Law in 1990, and has regularly

---

[1] (1990–I) *Hague Recueil des cours* 9.
[2] (1980) *Hague Recueil des cours* 5.

acted as an external examiner. It was whilst he was acting in this capacity that I first met Peter North. I was still recovering from an illness. It was Friday the 13th, not an auspicious date for a PhD viva. However, I could not have been in safer hands. The questions were penetrating. They queried underlying assumptions that I had made. But all of this was done in the most courteous way. This was not someone who was out to prove how clever he was but someone who, rather gently, was trying to find out how clever I was. Others can testify to a similar experience.[3] As one would expect, he has always been helpful and encouraging to younger colleagues, giving up his time to advise them on new projects.

Law reform can take place at different levels, national, European, and international. Peter North has been highly active at each of these levels. He was a Law Commissioner, entrusted with Law Reform in England and Wales, from 1976 to 1984. During this time the Law Commission was particularly active in reviewing and reforming private international law,[4] dealing with topics as diverse as the choice of law rules in the Draft Non-Life Services Directive,[5] the recognition of foreign nullity decrees,[6] financial relief after foreign divorces,[7] polygamous marriages,[8] choice of law rules in marriage,[9] classification of limitation of actions in private international law,[10] the law on foreign money,[11] the law of domicile,[12] and tort choice of law.[13] No one who has read the Working Papers and Reports which Peter North played a key role in producing can fail to be impressed by their clarity, scholarship, and attention to the relevant policy considerations. Recommendations for statutory change[14] have in most cases been

---

[3] See Beaumont, below, p 10.

[4] See generally North, 'Private International Law: Change or Decay?' (2001) 50 ICLQ 477 at 480 et seq.

[5] Report by a Joint Working Group of the Law Commission and the Scottish Law Commission, 11 April 1979.

[6] Law Com No 137 (1984).

[7] Law Com No 117 (1982).

[8] Law Commission Working Paper No 83 (1982). See also Law Com No 146 (1985) after Peter North left the Law Commission.

[9] Law Commission Working Paper No 89 (1985); Law Com No 165 (1987). Peter North was the Joint Chairman of the Joint Working Party dealing with this topic.

[10] Law Com No 114 (1982).

[11] Law Com No 109 (1981), Law Com No 124 (1984).

[12] Law Commission Working Paper No 88 (1985); Law Com No 168 (1987). Peter North was the Joint Chairman of the Joint Working Party dealing with this topic.

[13] Law Commission Working Paper No 87 (1984).

[14] Sometimes the Law Commission recognized that no change in the law was called for. See, eg, choice of law rules in marriage, n 9 above.

implemented,[15] albeit not always in the form that Peter North may have wanted. The Parliamentary draftsman would have done well to listen to Peter North's advice on how the Private International Law (Miscellaneous) Provisions Bill should be drafted to deal with torts committed in England.[16] The exclusion of defamation from the new statutory rules[17] was also not something that he favoured.[18]

It was during his time at the Law Commission that Peter North became a member of the UK delegation to the EEC Working Group on the accession of the UK to the Brussels Convention on Jurisdiction and the Enforcement of Judgments in Civil and Commercial Matters.[19] The UK was joining an existing convention and so the scope for major changes in the convention was limited. The opportunity for influencing the shape of things to come is naturally much greater when you are there at the outset of a new project. This was the case with the draft Convention on the Law Applicable to Contractual Obligations, now the Rome Convention 1980. Peter North was on the UK delegation to the EEC Working Group on this new convention. There was no doubt in England as to the important role that he played in determining the eventual terms of this Convention. The Lord Chancellor during the passage of the UK implementing legislation said that 'The point about this Convention is that due to the negotiating skills of Dr Peter North and those associated with him, the principles of English conflict rules in relation to contract have been adopted'.[20] Being the modest man that he is, Peter North would no doubt treat this statement with a certain wry amusement.

Continuing in the same vein, Peter North has been a member and is now the Chairman of the UK advisory committee on the proposed Hague Convention on Jurisdiction and Recognition and Enforcement of Judgments in Civil and Commercial Matters. His skill in carrying out this job is attested to by Paul

---

[15] See, eg, the Foreign Limitation Periods Act 1984, the Private International Law (Miscellaneous Provisions) Act 1995 Parts I, II and III.

[16] See Proceedings of the Special Public Bill Committee, Oral Evidence by North *HL Paper* 36 (1995) at 39. Compare the solution adopted by the Parliamentary Draftsman, s 9(6) of the Private International Law (Miscellaneous Provisions) Act 1995.

[17] Private International Law (Miscellaneous Provisions) Act 1995, s 13.

[18] See Oral Evidence by North *HL Paper* 36 (1995) at 40.

[19] He was also a member of the UK delegation to the EEC Working Group on draft directives on insurance law.

[20] Hansard (HL) Feb 15 1990 vol 515, col 1489.

Beaumont in his essay.[21] It is a matter of regret that his other responsibilities have prevented Peter North from being a Member of the UK delegation to the Hague Conference. His knowledge, experience,[22] and diplomatic skills would have been of inestimable value during the protracted and still inconclusive negotiations on this most difficult of projects.[23]

B. The Reform and Development of Private International Law

It is particularly appropriate that this collection of essays should take as its theme the reform and development of private international law. This is not only because of Peter North's own undoubted contribution to the reform and development of private international law but also because this is a theme on which Peter North has frequently spoken and written. As recently as February this year he could be heard delivering a lecture at University College London entitled 'Developments in the Field of Jurisdiction and Recognition of Judgments', which gave a masterly overview of this topic and was full of insights. This will in due course appear in *Current Legal Problems* 2002.

The essays in this collection reflect the three different levels at which reform and development of private international law take place. Robin Morse discusses the trend towards legislation in English private international law. He analyses the criticisms that have been made of this and uses the example of tort choice of law to show that legislation can be appropriate as a method of development of private international law. Trevor Hartley draws our attention to an area of private international law, namely that relating to matrimonial property, which is entirely judge made. Ron Brand examines the extensive US case law on *forum non conveniens* and choice of court clauses. Joost Blom shows how quickly the judges, in this case in the Supreme Court of Canada, can develop private international law once they set their mind to it. Development by the judges is naturally influenced by theoretical concepts. Sir Lawrence Collins discusses the considerable influence of the concept of comity in modern private international law. Writers too have had their part to play in the development of private international law. This is the subject of the contribution by Ole

---

[21] See below, p 10.
[22] This includes experience of a failed draft UK/US Judgments Convention.
[23] See McClean, below, p 225.

Lando. Of course, development at the national level does not take place in isolation. Kurt Siehr looks at the impact of international instruments on national private international law and the problems that this throws up. Robin Morse reminds us that the trend towards legislation in private international law has come about partly because of the influence of international conventions that England has adopted.

A number of contributors discuss various aspects of the ever growing Europeanization of private international law. Ian Fletcher focuses on the EC Regulation on Insolvency Proceedings and its impact upon established law and practice in England and Wales. In my contribution I explain the difficulty in applying the Brussels I Regulation on Jurisdiction and the Recognition and Enforcement of Judgments in Civil and Commecial Matters in intellectual property cases. The Europeanization of private international law is not without its problems. Paul Beaumont examines questions of legal basis and external competence and the best way for the UK and Europe to be represented in issues of private international law globally, as well as providing a welcome technical analysis of the newly worded contract provision in the Brussels I Regulation. Hans Ulrich Jessurun d'Oliveira focuses on the uneasy relationship between the EU and private international law and the movement in the former towards eroding the latter. Developments within the EU are of considerable interest to those outside Europe. They form a possible model for reform in other contexts, as Peter Nygh shows when he compares declining jurisdiction under the Brussels I Regulation and the preliminary draft Hague Convention on Jurisdiction and Foreign Judgments in Civil and Commercial Matters.

Finally, some contributors have concentrated on aspects of the reform of private international law on a worldwide basis. Jonathan Harris discusses the Hague Convention on the Law Applicable to Trusts and on their Recognition 1985 during his examination of the trust in private international law. Not surprisingly there is much discussion in this book of the ambitious project that has been absorbing the Hague Conference for nearly ten years, namely a Hague Convention on Jurisdiction and Foreign Judgments in Civil and Commercial Matters. David McClean discusses the history of this project and some of the factors that have led to the present fairly unpromising situation, which is that the prospects of reaching agreement are not good. Ron Brand explains the difficulty in developing a convention on a global basis when the EU Member States are keen to adopt a convention which looks as much as possible like their existing law under the Brussels Convention scheme. Hans Ulrich Jessurun d'Oliveira goes further and examines the threat that the ever increasing Europeanization of private international law presents to the work of the Hague Conference on private international law. If the Hague Judgments Convention, at least in its present ambitious form, does fail where do we go from there? Ron Brand suggests a more modest goal at the Hague Conference, namely a choice of court plus recognition convention, a solution that appeals to Peter North.[24] David McClean suggests that Commonwealth countries explore whether common ground can be found for an intra-Commonwealth convention on jurisdiction and the recognition and enforcement of judgments in civil and commercial matters. Whatever the fate of the Hague Judgments Convention, the work undertaken at the Hague can still be used to good effect in the future. It can inform the discussion of what we should do in intellectual property cases in private international law, which is the main subject of my own contribution. The preliminary draft Hague Judgments Convention that has emerged also provides a possible model for the development of the law on declining jurisdiction, which is examined in Peter Nygh's contribution.

This collection of essays contributed by his friends and colleagues honours Peter North's remarkable career and outstanding contribution to private international law. All the authors share the wish that Peter North enjoys reading their thoughts on some aspect or other of this most fitting of themes, the reform and development of private international law.

---

[24] He said this in his lecture on 'Recent Developments in the Field of Jurisdiction and Recognition of Judgments' at University College London on 7 February 2002.

1

THE BRUSSELS CONVENTION BECOMES A REGULATION: IMPLICATIONS FOR LEGAL BASIS, EXTERNAL COMPETENCE, AND CONTRACT JURISDICTION

*Paul R Beaumont**

A. Introduction

It is a great privilege to be able to take part in a collection of essays paying tribute to Sir Peter North. I have appreciated his scholarship for many years but only in recent years have had the privilege of getting to know him in three contexts. First he was deservedly awarded an Honorary LLD by the University of Aberdeen, second he was the external examiner for a PhD thesis that I supervised, and third he has been the Chairman of the UK Advisory Committee on

* Professor of European Union and Private International Law and Head of the School of Law, University of Aberdeen. Member of the UK delegation in the Council of European Union Working Party on the Revision of the Brussels and Lugano Conventions 1997–1999, member of the UK delegation at the Hague Conference on Private International Law negotiating a

the proposed Hague Convention on Jurisdiction and Recognition and Enforcement of Judgments in Civil and Commercial Matters of which I am a member. In the first context Sir Peter was modest and charming. He was at the time Vice Chancellor of the University of Oxford but had no airs and graces, side, or arrogance. He was genuinely delighted to receive the honorary degree, particularly because it was given as part of the celebrations of the installation of his old University friend Lord Wilson of Tillyorn as Chancellor of the University of Aberdeen. In the second context he gave the candidate a good viva. He subjected the arguments to rigorous scrutiny but accepted that the candidate's views were tenable even when he disagreed with them. The thesis was approved with no corrections and formed the basis, with significant deletions and additions, for an Oxford University Press monograph in private international law.[1] The third context is the one in which I have been working with Sir Peter in a more sustained way. We were both members of the committee from its first meeting in May 1997[2] and Sir Peter succeeded Lord Saville as chairman of the committee the following year when Lord Saville began chairing the Bloody Sunday enquiry in Londonderry. Sir Peter North is an excellent chairman. He reads the papers thoroughly, has an outstanding command of the issues, does not dominate the meeting, makes sure that he gets the views of all those present, allows a free flowing discussion without letting the meeting stray from the point, asks members of the UK delegation at the Hague (including me) penetrating questions, tries to help the committee to identify the national interest, has astute political antennae, and, above all, endeavours to help the members of the delegation to be able to do their job. This paper could have been about the proposed Hague Convention but the negotiations are still in

Jurisdiction and Judgments Convention from 1996 to the present and member of the UK delegation in the Council of European Union Committee of Civil Law (Brussels I) which negotiated the Brussels I Regulation, 44/2001 [2001] OJ L12/1, 1999–2000. Consultant to Scottish Executive Justice Department and the Lord Chancellor's Department. The views in this paper are those of the author and should not be taken as representing those of the UK Government or the Scottish Executive. Some of the issues in this paper were discussed by the author in the 'Interplay of Private International Law and European Community Law' in C Kilpatrick, T Novitz, and P Skidmore (eds), *The Future of Remedies in Europe* (Oxford, Hart, 2000) 167–190 and a full analysis of the Brussels and Lugano Conventions is provided in *Anton and Beaumont's Civil Jurisdiction in Scotland: Brussels and Lugano Conventions* (2nd edn, Edinburgh, W Green/Sweet & Maxwell, 1995).

[1] P R Beaumont and P E McEleavy, *The Hague Convention on International Child Abduction* (Oxford, Oxford University Press, 1999). This book is widely cited in the courts of countries outside the UK.

[2] See P R Beaumont, 'A United Kingdom Perspective on the Proposed Hague Judgments Convention' (1998) XXIV Brooklyn Journal of International Law 75 at 77–78.

progress and other contributors to this volume are dealing with that subject. It is, however, legitimate to focus on the Brussels I Regulation because the Advisory Committee that Sir Peter chaired was used by the UK Government to give advice on the negotiations of the revision of the Brussels and Lugano Conventions that led to an agreed text in April 1999 that formed the basis of the Brussels I Regulation. Also Sir Peter was part of the UK team that negotiated the 1978 Accession Convention whereby the UK, Denmark, and Ireland became parties to the Brussels Convention.

In July 1999 the Commission[3] proposed a new Council Regulation on jurisdiction and the recognition and enforcement of judgments in civil and commercial matters (known as Brussels I) which was given its first consideration in the Council of the European Union Committee on Civil Law on 20–21 September 1999.[4] The Amsterdam Treaty came into force on 1 May 1999 and with it a new Title IV of the EC Treaty that provided a possible legal basis for a new Regulation. However, there was a political vacuum in the Commission caused by the resignation of the college of Commissioners in March 1999.[5] In an astonishing sign that the disgraced Santer Commission had learnt nothing from its forced resignation in March 1999 it ignored its self-imposed and public commitment not to 'take fresh political initiatives'[6] until a new Commission had been appointed. In addition to introducing the proposed Brussels I Regulation it had already, on 4 May 1999, introduced a proposed Brussels II Regulation on jurisdiction and the recognition and enforcement of judgments in matrimonial matters and in matters of parental responsibility for children of both spouses based on the content of the Brussels II Convention and a proposed Directive based on the Service Convention.[7] All of this substantiates the view of the Committee of Independent Experts that the Santer Commission did not have a well developed sense of political responsibility.[8] The officials in the Commission should have waited until the Prodi Commission was in place and had time to think about the implications of important new legislative proposals in the field of private international law

---

[3] See COM (1999) 348 final.

[4] See Document 10742/99 JUSTCIV 124 which indicates that the Commission proposal was not actually received in the Council until 7 September 1999.

[5] See S Weatherill & P Beaumont, *EU Law* (3rd edn, London, Penguin,1999), pp 1059–1064.

[6] ibid, 1062.

[7] COM (1999) 220 and 221.

[8] See S Weatherill and P Beaumont, *EU Law* (3rd edn, London, Penguin, 1999), pp 1059–1064.

before introducing them. The college of Commissioners should have considered the merits of the alternative legal basis of Article 293 (ex 220) EC for the revision of the Brussels Convention. The impatience of Commission officials and the Santer Commission indicates a dangerous lack of political accountability.

B. Legal Basis

Title IV of the EC Treaty, in particular Article 65 of the EC Treaty which requires unanimity in the Council, is the legal basis for new private international law initiatives[9] including the Commission proposals on Brussels I and II and Service. The reasoning in the Commission's explanatory memorandum accompanying the draft Brussels I Regulation for choosing this legal basis is rather weak. The sound arguments are that there is an advantage in transparency in having a Regulation rather than a Convention because there is no implementing legislation[10] and the Regulation comes into force on the same day in all the Member States bound by it (1 March 2002) whereas ratification of a Convention amending the Brussels Convention will occur at different times in different Contracting States and may be delayed for a long time in some States.[11]

---

[9] See P Beaumont, 'Treaty of Amsterdam–Community Competence in Private International Law' (1999) 48 ICLQ 225–9; C Kohler, 'Interrogations sur les sources du droit international privé européen après le traité d'Amsterdam' (1999) 88 *Revue Critique de droit international privé* 1–30; O Remien, 'European Private International Law, the European Community and its Emerging Area of Freedom, Security and Justice' (2001) 38 Common Market Law Review 53–86; and J Israel, 'Conflicts of Law and the EC after Amsterdam. A Change for the Worse?' (2000) 7 Maastricht Journal of European and Comparative Law 81–99.

[10] See recital 6 to the Brussels I Regulation. But even this argument is two edged because lawyers in individual countries may find a primary statute like the Civil Jurisdiction and Judgments Act 1982 which implemented the Brussels Convention in its own terms in Schedule 1 more accessible and with a higher impact threshold than a Community Regulation. In any case the Regulation will require some implementing legislation and Member States secured a gap of fifteen months between the Regulation being agreed in December 2000 and its entry into force on 1 March 2002. The UK Order in Council (the Civil Jurisdiction and Judgments Order 2001, SI 2001 No 3929) makes it clear which courts in the United Kingdom (English and Welsh, or Northern Irish, or Scottish) have jurisdiction when the Brussels I Regulation allocates jurisdiction to the UK. The UK Government decided not to reproduce the Regulation in UK legislation, even for information, because it is directly applicable.

[11] See pages 4 and 5 of COM (1999) 348 final. This latter point is a definite advantage of a Regulation over the Convention but it must be weighed in the scales against the disadvantages.

The Commission also argued that opting for a 'Regulation enables the Court of Justice to ensure that it is applied uniformly throughout the Member States'.[12] The Commission neglected to point out that the Court of Justice is better able to ensure uniformity of the Brussels Convention than the new Brussels I Regulation. The former has a 1971 Protocol which allows all appellate courts to refer cases on the interpretation of the Brussels Convention to the European Court of Justice and requires courts of last resort to refer. On the other hand Article 68(1) of the EC Treaty removes the right of appellate courts to refer cases on the interpretation of any act adopted under Title IV and retains only the mandatory reference for courts of last resort. This unfortunate loss of judicial protection for people domiciled in Member States bound by the Brussels I Regulation and the removal of the opportunity for a Sheriff Principal, or the Inner House of the Court of Session, or the English Court of Appeal to refer these issues to the European Court of Justice, could have been avoided if the revision of the Brussels Convention had been concluded on the basis of the original legal basis, ie, Article 293 (ex 220) EC. This legal basis, which was the preferred legal basis of the UK, would also have avoided problems of variable geometry that are inevitable if one relies on a legal basis in Title IV. Denmark has an opt out Protocol from Title IV of the EC Treaty and cannot selectively opt in.[13] Thus the Brussels I Regulation does not apply to all fifteen EU Member States and therefore the Brussels Convention (and the 1971 Protocol allowing references to the ECJ) remains in place for Denmark and for other Member States when dealing with Danish domiciliaries.

A further advantage of using Article 293 of the EC Treaty as the legal basis would have been to act in good faith[14] with the Lugano States (Iceland, Norway, and Switzerland). Those States expected that the long parallel revision negotiations on the Brussels and Lugano Conventions which began in 1997 would have ended in 1999 with the signing of amending treaties for both Conventions at the same time. Instead the Lugano States have ignominiously been told to wait until the Brussels I Regulation is concluded and then fresh negotiations with them will be conducted under conditions not yet well established because of the doubts about who will be competent to conduct those negotiations. Clearly the EU Member States not bound by the Regulation (just

---

[12] ibid, 5.
[13] See [1997] OJ C340/101.
[14] The relevance of this principle to Community law was confirmed by the Court of First Instance in Case T-115/94 *Opel Austria GmbH v Council* [1997] ECR II-39, paras 89–94.

Denmark) will be competent but will the other Member States be represented by the Commission, or will they be there together with the Commission negotiating on the basis of a mixed competence between the Community and those Member States? Formal negotiations with the Lugano States have still not commenced at the time of writing in December 2001 and the Commission is yet to prepare a draft mandate for these negotiations. A legal basis in Article 293 would also have had the advantage of retaining external competence in these matters in the hands of the Member States of the EU rather than creating exclusive competence for the EU or mixed competence between the EU and the Member States bound by the Regulation. If the EU Member States have external competence it preserves the existing balance within the Hague Conference on Private International Law and avoids the common law orientated UK and Ireland being swallowed up in a civil law orientated EU voice. It allows Member States to choose independently whether to ratify a Hague Convention and not be forced to wait until all the Member States agree, if ever, to ratify.[15]

Furthermore it allows Member States to reduce the injustice against people not domiciled in one of the Member States of applying the exorbitant rules of jurisdiction and the requirement to recognize judgments from other Member States based on such rules by concluding conventions with one or more third States under Article 59 of the Brussels Convention. Such Conventions can no longer be entered into by Member States due to Article 72 of the Brussels I Regulation but existing Conventions still apply, see Part D below. There are other external problems generated by creating some Community competence in this area. What do you do about amending all the specialist conventions on maritime, transport and other matters that are given priority over the Brussels Convention by Article 57? The nightmare scenario is that every time one of those conventions is amended in the future there will need to be substantive negotiations in the EU to see if an amendment can be made to the Brussels I

---

[15] This problem might be overcome if the EU were to take an enlightened federal view like that adopted in Canada (where Canada can ratify a Hague Convention on behalf of those provinces and territories who want it) and the UK (where the Convention could be ratified by the UK for Scotland, or Northern Ireland, or England and Wales) and permit the use of the standard federal clause in Hague Conventions to allow those Member States to ratify a Hague Convention who want to, rather than wait until the whole of the EU is ready to adopt it. The present approach is that anything falling within Community competence can only be ratified by all the Member States (except Denmark) or none. This means that in external competence the Community is much more centralized than some enlightened federal states and even unitary states with devolved governments.

Regulation. This is because Article 71 of the Brussels Regulation, the replacement for Article 57 of the Brussels Convention, only applies to conventions to which the Member States are already parties, whereas under the Brussels Convention the Contracting States were happy not only to recognize existing specialist conventions but to permit the liberty to each other to conclude specialist conventions in the future on 'particular matters' which would trump the Brussels Convention rules on jurisdiction and still benefit from that Convention's rules on recognition and enforcement.[16]

C. Jurisdiction Rules

The substantive changes in the jurisdiction rules from the Brussels Convention for the new Regulation are based on the political agreement reached in the Council Working Party on the Revision of the Brussels and Lugano Conventions in April 1999.[17] They include a new uniform definition of the domicile of a legal person.[18] This is extremely useful as most cases under the Regulation will be against legal rather than natural persons. Plaintiffs can choose to sue legal persons at their principal place of business, or their central administration or their statutory seat. 'Statutory seat' is further defined for the UK and Ireland as meaning the registered office, or where there is no such office the place of incorporation, or where there is no such place the place under the law of which the formation took place. This last clause was drafted to deal with Scottish partnerships. They have legal personality but do not have registered offices or places of incorporation. So a partnership formed under Scots law can be sued in Scotland even if the partnership deed was signed abroad.

(1) Contract

The most hard fought change, after protracted negotiations, is to the contract jurisdiction. Article 5(1) of the Brussels Convention confers jurisdiction, 'in matters relating to contract', on the 'courts for the place of performance of the

---

[16] For background on the conventions on particular matters referred to in Art 57 of the Brussels and Lugano Conventions see *Anton & Beaumont's Civil Jurisdiction in Scotland*, (2nd edn, Edinburgh, W Green/Sweet & Maxwell, 1995), pp 65–69. Already in the course of 2001 the Committee of Civil Law of the Council of the European Union has spent considerable time discussing negotiating mandates in relation to maritime and nuclear conventions that are in the process of amendment to try to ensure consistency with the Brussels I Regulation.

[17] See JUSTCIV 60. See also recital 5 to the Brussels I Regulation.

[18] Brussels I Regulation, Art 60.

obligation in question'. This means that it is the obligation relied on by the plaintiff that constitutes the basis for establishing jurisdiction.[19] If the plaintiff is pleading more than one obligation then it is the principal obligation in question that must be looked to in order to determine jurisdiction and the court for the place of performance of the principal obligation is able to deal with the other obligations raised by the plaintiff as well.[20] If, however, the obligations relied on by the plaintiff are of equal standing and the places of performance of those obligations are in two different jurisdictions then the case has to be split between those jurisdictions.[21] This splitting of jurisdiction troubled some of the representatives of the Contracting States in the revision of the Brussels and Lugano Conventions. They were also concerned by the fact that the obligation in question might be the payment of money and that this generated only a very minor factual connection between the dispute and the courts taking jurisdiction because that country was the place of payment. The other problem was that the 'place of performance' had to be determined in accordance with the law selected by the choice of law rules of the country hearing the jurisdiction dispute.[22] This requirement was not always adhered to by national courts and imposed a complex process at a very early stage in litigation.[23] The UK

---

[19] Case 14/76 *De Bloos v Bouyer* [1976] ECR 1497. The Court said at para 11 that 'the word "obligation" in the article refers to the contractual obligation forming the basis of the legal proceedings'.

[20] Case 266/85 *Shenavai v Kreischer* [1987] ECR 239. The Court said at para 19 that in the 'case of a dispute concerned with a number of obligations arising under the same contract and forming the basis of the proceedings commenced by the plaintiff . . . the court before which the matter is brought will, when determining whether it has jurisdiction, be guided by the maxim *accessorium sequitur principale*; in other words, where various obligations are at issue, it will be the principal obligation which will determine its jurisdiction'. This dictum was applied by the House of Lords in *Union Transport Group v Continental Lines SA* [1992] 1 WLR 15.

[21] See Case C-420/97 *Leathertex v Bodetex* [1999] ECR I-6747, [2000] I L Pr 273. The Court said at para 40 and in the ruling that 'the same court does not have jurisdiction to hear the whole of an action founded on two obligations of equal rank arising from the same contract when, according to the conflict rules of the State where that court is situated, one of those obligations is to be performed in that State and the other in another Contracting State'.

[22] See Case 12/76 *Tessili v Dunlop* [1976] ECR 1473, 1485 affirmed by Case C-440/97 *Groupe Concorde* [1999] ECR I-6307, [2000] ILPr 626.

[23] For evidence for this view see Advocate General Colomer's Opinion in *Groupe Concorde*, ibid paras 44–58 and in P R Beaumont, 'Jurisdiction under the Brussels Convention in Contract, Tort, Delict and Quasi-Delict' in D L Carey Miller and P R Beaumont (eds), *The Option of Litigating in Europe* (London, UKNCCL, 1993), 13, 18. However, one of the factors influencing the European Court of Justice's decision in *Groupe Concorde* not to change the rule it had established in *Tessili* despite the advice of Advocate General Colomer was that a review of the Brussels Convention was under way at that time (see para 21 of the Court's judgment in *Groupe Concorde*).

Government after consultation[24] was quite happy with the existing Article 5(1) and therefore argued for the status quo.

After a great deal of discussion on Article 5(1) in the Council Working Party throughout 1998 revolving around the status quo (a position favoured by about one third of the States), abolition (favoured by another third) and a move towards a solution based on the notion of the 'place of performance of the characteristic obligation' (taken from the notion of characteristic performance in the Rome Convention and supported by the remaining third) a meeting took place in Helsinki in January 1999 between Finland, Switzerland, and the UK. At that meeting the UK undertook to consider carefully a compromise proposal as follows:

> A person domiciled in a Contracting State may, in another Contracting State, be sued:
>
> 1. in matters relating to a contract, in the courts for the place of performance of the obligation in question if the plaintiff can show on a *prima facie* basis that its own principal obligation has been fulfilled

The UK would have been willing to go along with the text because it basically preserved Article 5(1) of the Brussels Convention with a good faith proviso. The plaintiff would have to demonstrate on the face of his pleadings that he had fulfilled his part of the contractual bargain. However, the compromise did not go far enough for some of the Member States who favoured abolition of a contract rule of jurisdiction or the characteristic obligation solution and the Bureau[25] of the Brussels and Lugano Revision Working Party did not table it at the first meeting in February 1999 of the Council Working Party revising the Brussels and Lugano Conventions. Instead at least one influential member of the Working Party focussed attention on the payment obligation as being the only obligation which poses major problems in the application of Article 5(1) and suggested some modest changes to Article 5(1) that dealt only with the place of payment. These were then turned into concrete drafts and considered in the UK by the Hague Advisory Committee, chaired by Sir Peter North, as a sounding board before the crucial final meeting of the Working Party in April 1999 when a text on Article 5(1) had to be agreed.

---

[24] See *The Operation of the Brussels and Lugano Conventions*, a Consultation Paper issued by the Lord Chancellor's Department and the Scottish Courts Administration in April 1997 and prepared by P R Beaumont and P E McEleavy.

[25] Made up of the representative of the Member State holding the Presidency of the Council, the past and future Presidents and the permanent members, Gustav Moller (Chairman), Monique Gemetti-Greiner (Vice Chairman), and Fausto Pocar (Rapporteur).

The two options were:

Option 1

A person domiciled in a Contracting State may, in another Contracting State, be sued:

1. in matters relating to a contract, in the courts for the place of performance of the obligation in question. However, this does not apply when jurisdiction would be based only on the place of performance of the payment obligation under the contract, unless that place is expressly stipulated in the contract

Option 2

A person domiciled in a Contracting State may, in another Contracting State, be sued:

1. in matters relating to a contract, in the courts for the place of performance of the obligation in question. However, this does not apply when jurisdiction would be based only on the place of performance of the payment obligation under the contract, unless the plaintiff can show that he has performed his principal obligation under the contract

The UK consistently argued that it favoured the status quo but was willing to look at proposals that preserved its strengths. The strengths of Article 5(1) of the Brussels Convention are:

(1) The real link between the particular contractual dispute and the jurisdiction that is ensured by referring to the 'obligation in question' rather than the characteristic obligation.
(2) The accumulated wisdom from the European Court's case law on the existing Article 5(1) which gives it a certainty that any new concept lacks.
(3) The holistic treatment of contract jurisdiction rather than dividing it up into types of contracts which then leads to classification problems.
(4) Giving a choice of forum for the plaintiff—a meaningful alternative to the defendant's domicile.

Both options 1 and 2 met the four points above. However, option 1 weakened the fourth point unless the parties have the foresight to specify the place of payment. If they have that foresight they might be capable of agreeing an exclusive jurisdiction clause in which case Article 17 of the Brussels Convention, now Article 23 of the Brussels I Regulation, rather than Article 5(1) is applicable. However, option 2 had the weakness that it would have introduced an element of uncertainty because the plaintiff would have to argue what constitutes the principal obligation in question and demonstrate that he has performed it. The concept of principal obligation in question is, of course, already relevant whenever more than one contractual obligation is put in issue by the plaintiff.[26] However, in option 2 the plaintiff even when simply relying on the payment obligation (perhaps in a simple debt collection case) has to demonstrate what is his principal obligation under the contract and that he has performed it.

The UK was willing to go along with a compromise along the lines of these proposals but neither of them proved to be the basis for a unanimous agreement in the Working Party. There was no doubt that the focus of the negotiations for some Contracting States was on achieving a significant change to Article 5(1) and neither of these proposals went far enough. A solution eluded the negotiators until the eleventh hour. The text of Article 5(1) of what is now the Brussels I Regulation was produced like a rabbit out of the hat on the very last day of the work of the Brussels and Lugano Working Party. Had it not been acceptable then a united position could not have been maintained between the Brussels and Lugano States. This would have had the consequence that the 14 Title IV EC Treaty Member States would have been free to negotiate a contract jurisdiction and that parallelism with the Lugano Convention could only have been maintained by Denmark and the Lugano States accepting as a *fait accompli* whatever the 14 would have negotiated on their own. The new text is as follows:

A person domiciled in a Member State may, in another Member State, be sued:

1. (a) in matters relating to a contract, in the courts for the place of performance of the obligation in question;
   (b) for the purpose of this provision and unless otherwise agreed, the place of performance of the obligation in question shall be:
   —in the case of the sale of goods, the place in a Member State where, under the contract, the goods were delivered or should have been delivered,
   —in the case of the provision of services, the place in a Member State where, under the contract, the services were provided or should have been provided,
   (c) if subparagraph (b) does not apply then subparagraph (a) applies

The text went further towards the advocates of characteristic obligation than the previous compromise proposals. It moves to a system where in simple sale of goods contracts and simple provision of services contracts it is the place of performance of the characteristic obligation that has jurisdiction. This means

---

[26] See Case 266/85 *Shenavai v Kreischer* [1987] ECR 239.

that in sale of goods contracts and service contracts the only place which can have Article 5(1) jurisdiction is the place where the goods were delivered or should have been delivered or the place where the services were provided or should have been provided unless an alternative place of performance, eg, the place of payment, is expressly chosen by the parties or the place of delivery is in a non-Member State. The old Article 5(1) Brussels Convention rule, that focuses on the place of performance of the obligation relied on by the plaintiff in the proceedings, is retained in Article 5(1)(a) and it applies by virtue of Article 5(1)(c) where the place of delivery of the goods or provision of the services is outside a Member State, where party autonomy has intervened to specify the place of performance, to complex contracts involving more than just the provision of goods and services, and to other contracts which do not involve the delivery of goods or the provision of services. The scope of the party autonomy left by the phrase 'unless otherwise agreed' in Article 5(1)(b) of the Brussels I Regulation is not clear. The UK delegation were of the view when agreeing this compromise that it meant that if the parties expressly stated the place of performance in the contract the courts of that place would still have jurisdiction under Article 5(1)(a), and Article 5(1)(b) would not be applicable, if that was the place of performance of the obligation being relied on by the plaintiff in the action before the court and that that place had a real connection with the true substance of the contract. This view is reinforced by recital 14 to the Brussels I Regulation which states that 'The autonomy of the parties to a contract . . . must be respected' and would keep alive the European Court of Justice's case law that allows the parties to choose the place of performance for the purpose of Article 5(1) of the Brussels Convention unless the place chosen was a fictitious rather than real place of performance.[27]

Had the UK not agreed to the new Article 5(1) it would have meant that a deal could not have been done on all the other parts of the Brussels and Lugano Revision and this would have been very bad for the EU's relations with the Lugano States and would have opened up the whole negotiation again in the framework of preparing the Brussels I Regulation. Concessions were made in that Article 5(1)(b) does introduce classification problems into Article 5(1)

---

[27] See Case 56/79 *Zelger v Salinitri* [1980] ECR 89; and Case C-106/95 *Mainschiffahrts-Genossenschaft E G (MSG) v Les Gravières Rhénanes Sarl* [1997] ECR I-911. In the latter case at paras 30 and 31 the European Court require the chosen place of performance to have a real connection with the true substance of the contract and this is reiterated by the Court in *Groupe Concorde*, ibid, para 28. In that paragraph in *Groupe Concorde* the Court of Justice emphasizes the 'important position' accorded to the 'intention of the parties'.

and it can remove the real link between the particular contractual dispute and the jurisdiction hearing the case. The latter happens when a plaintiff is relying on an obligation in a sale of goods contract other than the obligation to deliver the goods and the place of performance of the obligation being relied upon is not in the same place as the delivery of the goods. However, this alternative obligation will usually be the payment obligation and parties can protect themselves by agreeing the place of payment.[28] Where the alternative obligation is not a payment obligation then one is probably into the realms of a complex contract which can not be classified as a sale of goods contract and therefore Article 5(1)(b) is not applicable and the old Brussels Convention rule is preserved by Article 5(1)(c) referring one back to Article 5(1)(a). In such cases the plaintiff is able to pursue the obligation in question in the place of performance of that obligation.

It is interesting to speculate as to what difference the new provision would make to cases decided under Article 5(1) of the Brussels Convention. *Barry v Bradshaw*[29] is a decision of the English Court of Appeal in a fairly straightforward contract for the provision of services. Mr and Mrs Barry were domiciled in Ireland and instructed an accountant who was also domiciled in Ireland to deal with their tax affairs. The Barrys sued the accountant in England for failing to secure capital gains tax retirement relief in England but the accountant argued that the English courts had no jurisdiction because the place of performance of the obligation in question was Ireland. In this case a lot turned on the pleadings because there was no evidence as to the terms on which the accountant was engaged. The accountant was, according to the plaintiff retained to 'represent, conduct and settle' their tax affairs and that this required the accountant to ensure that the Barrys were represented at a hearing of the General Commissioners of Inland Revenue in England on 15 December 1995. The accountant's failure to do so was the principal obligation in question in the case. This view was upheld by the English Court of Appeal. If we were applying Article 5(1) of the Brussels I Regulation to this case we would have to ask under Article 5(1)(b) 'what is the place in a Member State where, under the contract, the services were provided or should have been provided?' The answer would be that most of the services were provided in Ireland but that the particular service in dispute

---

[28] To be on the safe side drafters of international contracts will want to have an exclusive jurisdiction clause or failing that a place of payment clause that expressly confers jurisdiction on that place for any dispute over the payment under the contract.

[29] [2000] I L Pr 706.

'should have been provided' in England. If Article 5(1)(b) is interpreted in accordance with a characteristic obligation theory then the characteristic obligation in this case was the provision of services in Ireland (all the advice and work on the Barrys' tax affairs was done there) and therefore the English courts would not have jurisdiction under Article 5(1) but if one simply applies the wording of Article 5(1)(b) there is no reason not to say that the obligation in question is the provision of the service of making sure that the Barrys' capital gains tax relief was properly argued in England before the General Commissioners of Inland Revenue and that therefore England has jurisdiction as the place where the services should have been provided. In the absence of a report on the meaning of Article 5(1)[30] and a decision of the European Court it is impossible to be sure how the case would be decided. Since only the House of Lords is in a position to ask the European Court for a ruling on the issue it may be some time before there is any legal certainty.

In the famous *Groupe Concorde* case we have the benefit of the fact that Advocate General Colomer proposed an autonomous definition of place of performance based on the notion of the 'place where the obligation characterizing the legal relationship in question was or is to be performed' and applied it to the facts of the case.[31] In this case there was a contract for the carriage of goods from France to Brazil and Advocate General Colomer decided that the port of destination specified by the bill of lading, Santos in Brazil, must be deemed to be the place of performance. This is clearly the result that would flow from the application of the new Article 5(1)(b) if the port of destination was a Member State. However, that provision would not apply to the facts of the *Groupe Concorde* case because the port was not in a Member State and one would be back to Article 5(1)(a) and a determination, in accordance with the substantive law applicable under the conflict rules of the court seised, of the place of performance of the particular obligation in question.

In another recent English Court of Appeal case decided on the basis of Article 5(1) of the Brussels Convention the place of performance of the obligation in question was in issue in relation to payment under letters of credit. The English

---

[30] This is something that would have happened had the legal basis remained Article 293 EC and Professor Fausto Pocar would have written the report which he was preparing in 1999 when the decision was taken to change the legal basis and adopt a Regulation. This action precluded the publication of a report. Eventually when the Lugano Convention is amended we may get the benefit of Professor Pocar's report.

[31] Case C-440/97 *Groupe Concorde* [1999] ECR I-6307 paras 107–109 of the Opinion.

Court of Appeal decided that the English courts had jurisdiction as the obligation in question was the obligation to pay and London was the place of payment.[32] Had the Brussels I Regulation been applicable the result would surely have been the same because this was not a contract that falls within either of the indents in Article 5(1)(b). It would not be helpful to categorize a financial contract where one party is giving a financial guarantee to another as a contract for the provision of services. The same argument is true in relation to commercial agency contracts like the one in issue in *Leathertex*[33] and in relation to reinsurance contracts like the one in issue in *The Ethniki*.[34] Such cases would still be decided in the same way as they were under Article 51 of the Brussels Convention by applying Article 5(1)(a) of the Brussels I Regulation.

Perhaps most interesting of all is the English Court of Appeal decision in *MBM Fabri-Clad Limited v Eisen-Und Huttenwerke Thale AG*.[35] This was a case concerning the sale of goods by a German company to an English company. The English company argued that the obligation in question was the delivery of the goods in England in conformity with the contract whereas the German company argued that the principal obligation in this contract was the design, manufacture, and making available of the goods in Germany. The judge at first instance accepted the German company's argument because the breaches relied upon did not relate to the failure in the delivery of the goods to England but rather in the failure of the design and manufacture of the goods in Germany. However, the English Court of Appeal overturned his decision on the basis that the principal obligation was to deliver the goods in England in conformity with the contract and that the fact that the acts and omissions that led to the failure to supply the goods in conformity with the contract took place elsewhere is not material. The result here is exactly the one that would be arrived at by applying the first indent of the new Article 5(1)(b) of the Brussels I Regulation but it is arrived at by applying the rule now contained in Article 5(1)(a). Thus if the Court of Appeal were right that in a contract for the design, manufacture, and supply of goods it is always the supply which is the principal obligation, even when the defect is in design or manufacture, then introducing the place of delivery of the goods as the characteristic obligation in Article 5(1)(b) changes

---

[32] *Crédit Agricole Indosuez v Chailease Finance Corporation* [2000] I L Pr 776.
[33] Case C-420/97 *Leathertex v Bodetex* [1999] ECR I-6747.
[34] *Anonymous Greek Company of General Insurances "The Ethniki" v AIG Europe (UK) and others* [2000] I L Pr 426, CA.
[35] [2000] I L Pr 505.

very little. It will make a difference to cases where the plaintiff is simply trying to recover a money debt and has to go to the place of delivery of the goods to sue for it unless the place of payment is designated in the contract. It will also be material if the plaintiff is relying in his pleadings only on the failure to design or manufacture the goods properly.

(2) Other Changes to Grounds of Jurisdiction

Other changes to the Brussels Convention jurisdiction rules include a tort jurisdiction for threatened wrongs;[36] a codification of the interpretations by the European Court of Justice of the co-defender[37] and submission[38] jurisdictions in the Brussels Convention; minor tidying up of the insurance jurisdictions;[39] extension of the protective jurisdiction for consumers[40]; a new protective section on individual employment contracts;[41] a compromise between the Lugano and Brussels solutions on the exception to the exclusive jurisdiction of

---

[36] Brussels I Regulation, Art 5(3).

[37] ibid, Art 6(1), based on Case 189/87 *Kalfelis* v *Schröder, Münchmeyer, Hengst & Co and others* [1988] ECR 5565.

[38] ibid, Art 24, following the European Court of Justice's interpretation of Art 18 of the Brussels Convention in Case 150/80 *Elefanten Schuh* v *Jacqmain* [1981] ECR 1671 by omitting the word 'solely' from the English text.

[39] ibid, Arts 9(2) and 14 which depart from the wording in the former Arts 8(2) and 12A of the Brussels Convention. Indeed the Commission's proposal in Art 14 departed from the text agreed by the Council Working Party in April 1999 (see Art 12A of Document 7700/99 JUST-CIV 60 which combined the old Art 12A on large risks with specific references to the definition of large risks in certain Community insurance directives) by only referring to the insurance directives. This would have had the effect of making it more difficult to enter into an exclusive jurisdiction clause in certain large risks contracts not covered by the directives (eg, offshore oil and gas). It is highly surprising that the Commission should attempt to depart from the substance of the agreement in the Council Working Party. It is a regrettable sign of institutional self assertion. Normally a Commission proposal for a Regulation or Directive can only be amended by the Member States acting unanimously (see Art 250(1) (ex 189a(1)) EC). However the position is less clear in the context of measures introduced under Title IV of the EC Treaty in the five year period after 1 May 1999 because Art 67(1) does not give the Commission the sole right of initiative. Any Member State could make a counter proposal. So in this situation one of the Member States with voting rights in the Brussels I Regulation might put forward its own proposal based on Art 12A of the Council Working Party agreement and get the support of the other Member States. In fact by the time of the second meeting of the Committee on Civil Law (Brussels 1) in November 1999 the Commission put forward two options (the JUSTCIV 60 solution and its own solution which it had put forward in its first draft of the Regulation). The Committee unanimously approved the JUSTCIV 60 version and it has been retained in the final version.

[40] ibid, Arts 15 and 16 (ex Arts 13 and 14 of the Brussels Convention).

[41] ibid, Arts 18–21 (a consolidation and extension of the employment provisions in Art 5(1) and the last para of Art 17 of the Brussels Convention).

the place where the immovable property is situated for short term tenancies of immovable property;[42] a minor change to the exclusive jurisdiction over legal persons;[43] an express statement in the provision on prorogation that parties can choose to give non-exclusive jurisdiction to the courts of a Member State and a statement dealing with agreements entered into by electronic means;[44] a clarification of the meaning of the provision on related actions;[45] and— perhaps most significantly—a new provision providing for a clear date at which a court is first seised for the purpose of *lis pendens*.[46]

D. External Relations

Article 59 of the Brussels Convention has been retained in Article 72 of the Brussels I Regulation only for agreements already entered into by Member States with third States. Member States bound by the Regulation can no longer negotiate on their own with a third State or third States to enter into a recognition and enforcement convention with those States which would have the effect of no longer requiring the Member State to recognize and enforce a judgment given in another Member State bound by the Regulation based on an exorbitant ground of jurisdiction. The haste shown by the Commission in proposing the draft Regulation and its omission of an ongoing equivalent to Article 59 of the Brussels Convention, even for a transitional period,[47] indicates that the Commission would like the Community to have exclusive external competence in matters covered by the Brussels I Regulation as quickly as possible so that the Commission can negotiate on behalf of the Community at the Hague Conference on Private International Law and in any future bilateral

---

[42] ibid, Art 22(1) (ex 16(1) of the Brussels Convention).

[43] ibid, Art 22(2) (ex 16(2) of the Brussels Convention). The minor changes are that the seat of the legal person is to be determined by the private international law rules of the forum and the insertion of the word 'of' just before 'decisions of their organs'. This was to clarify an issue that was contentious in *Newtherapeutics Ltd v Katz* [1991] Ch 226, 244–245; see *Anton and Beaumont's Civil Jurisdiction in Scotland* (1995), p 149.

[44] ibid, Art 23 (ex 17 of the Brussels Convention). The old Art 17(4) of the Brussels Convention which gave an advantage to the stronger party to a choice of court clause has been deleted.

[45] ibid, Art 28(2) (ex 22(2) of the Brussels Convention).

[46] ibid, Art 30 (not in the Brussels Convention but it was Art 23 bis in the Council Working Party agreement of April 1999).

[47] Something held to be legally possible by the Council Legal Service in its Opinion of 17 March 1999, Doc 6683/99 JUR 99 JUSTCIV 48 at 9.

negotiations. However, one argument for mixed competence is that the Brussels I Regulation does not cover the recognition of judgments from non-Member States and this is a matter covered in any negotiation with a third State or States. Although mixed competence would retain a role for the Member States, alongside the Commission, in any negotiations at the Hague and with third States it would prevent the ratification of any agreement reached in the Hague by individual Member States who are party to the Regulation unless all such Member States agree to ratify the agreement.

At the time the Brussels I Regulation was concluded the Commission and Council agreed not to determine the question of external competence but rather to negotiate at the Hague on the basis of the Commission and Council speaking to a Council-agreed negotiating mandate. Member States remain free to speak on matters not covered by the mandate and to speak in support of those matters covered in the mandate. This pragmatic solution is the best that can be achieved at present at the negotiation stage. It was utilized in the Hague Diplomatic Session on the Hague Jurisdiction and Judgments draft Convention in June 2001. The Swedish Presidency of the Council spoke effectively to the Council mandate alongside the Commission. However, as the mandate was fairly extensive the room for Member States to contribute to the dynamic of negotiations was limited. The lesson that can be learned from that negotiation is the need to have a fairly flexible mandate so that the team of Council Presidency, Commission, and Member States can creatively respond to ideas being put forward by third States. However, the EU is locked into a requirement of having to get all fourteen Member States to agree to a particular outcome if any of the fourteen States are to be free to ratify the resulting Convention. So the flexibility in the negotiations is needed to be able to make compromises to do deals but all will be in vain if even one of the fourteen does not accept the deal when it reflects on it, until the Community revises its approach to external competence and allows Member States to ratify at least any international instruments arising from negotiations in the appropriate international institution for that field.

If the IGC in 2004[48] is to achieve anything useful in the field of external com-

---

[48] The Laeken Declaration of the European Council of 15 December 2001 prepares the ground for the 2004 IGC by setting up a Convention on the Future of Europe. The Declaration has the positive message that 'Europe needs to shoulder its responsibilities in the governance of globalization' but the Declaration has nothing to say explicitly about the division of external competence between the Union and the Member States. In relation to the division of compe-

petence it must escape from the outdated absolutism[49] that suggests that Community law must be the same in all Member States and therefore Member States cannot be free to ratify multilateral treaties that affect the operation of Community law in any way unless all the Member States agree to do so. The purity of Community law uniformity should be sacrificed, as it was to achieve the internal market where the doctrine of minimum harmonization was the key to success, in order to get a greater measure of global harmonization and equity. Much Community rhetoric focuses on how unacceptable it is for the Community to be paralysed in its internal decision making by one or two dissenting States, especially in an enlarged Europe, but the Community can be the source of paralysis in international negotiations by not being willing to move away from a fortress Europe in order to achieve international agreement due to the wishes of some Member States and the Commission. The Community is more concerned with removing barriers to the recognition and enforcement of judgments within Europe than to ensuring that in an international agreement fair rules of jurisdiction apply to people from non-EC Member States by preventing the recognition and enforcement in one Member State of judgments based on exorbitant grounds of jurisdiction against those people given in another Member State.

---

tence between Member States and the Union the Declaration is flatly contradictory (no doubt to keep the centralizers and decentralizers happy at the same time in a typical Union fudge) in that it says that this can lead 'to restoring tasks to the Member States' . . . 'while respecting the "acquis communautaire" ' unless the centralizers have won again and pulled the wool over the eyes of the decentralizers. The word 'tasks' was probably carefully chosen to reflect the idea of leaving more of the 'day-to-day administration and implementation of the Union's policy' to Member States while not returning any competences to the Member States which would inevitably have the effect of diluting the *acquis communautaire* to some extent, particularly if external competence is regained. One has to hope that the Convention and the Member States will tackle the issue of external competence and not assume that the division of internal and external competence has to be the same. No comfort can be taken from the Commission whose White Paper on *European Governance* launched in 2001 prior to the Laeken European Council says that 'The link between European and global governance should lead to the Union speaking more often with a single voice.' (Luxembourg, Office for Official Publications of the European Union, 2001), 55 and 50. It is not surprising, but rather sad, that the Commission wants to be that single voice for Europe more often. No thought is given to the idea that Europe can be a blockage to global agreement because it operates as a rather inflexible unit nor to the idea that the Commission as a relatively small bureaucracy is only suited and skilled to represent the Community and its Member States in a few areas and that private international law is not one of them.

[49] For a good example of the Court of Justice avoiding absolutism in the doctrine of supremacy of Community Law see its treatment of different prescription and limitation periods in Member States in Cases C-10–22/97 *Ministero delle Finanze v IN Co GE'90 Srl and others* [1998] ECR I-6307, discussed in S Weatherill and P Beaumont, *EU Law* (3rd edn, London, Penguin, 1999), pp 436–7.

If the IGC in 2004 adopts the Canadian or UK model for external competence and allows the EC to ratify a measure that will take effect in only some Member States initially but will hopefully, but not necessarily, be ratified by others in due course it will do a great service for the future of the Hague Conference on Private International Law and hopefully a number of other international institutions. It will be necessary to ensure that the decision to ratify by the EC could be taken by a qualified majority in the Council provided that it is recognized that individual Member States are free to decide whether to ratify the Convention for themselves. Community law would be more nuanced. For those States that have ratified the Convention Community law would accept that the Convention would take priority over the internal Community rules whenever a party from a non-EC Member State is involved and for those States that have not ratified the Convention the internal Community rules would continue to apply to their full extent. Such a solution would enable real flexibility in the international negotiations, taking advantage of the wide expertise available to the Member States and restoring the Community to its place as an encourager of good global solutions rather than being sidetracked into defending the *acquis communautaire* and institutional prerogatives and powers. The problem with this solution is that it does not allow a minority of Community States or even a majority smaller than a qualified majority in the Council to innovate internationally.

A radical solution would be to remove external Community competence completely from at least the private international law parts of Title IV of the EC Treaty. Thus the Community would have competence to legislate internally but the Treaty would make it clear that external competence remained with the Member States and that the *ERTA* doctrine of parallelism does not apply.[50] This has much to commend it. After all the Member States have not conferred external competence on the Community in Title IV of the EC Treaty. Any external competence is derived from a doctrine of the Court of Justice that was

---

[50] Case 22/70 *Commission v Council* [1971] ECR 263. A vast amount is written on Community external competence but for a good introduction see D McGoldrick, *International Relations Law of the European Union* (London, Longman, 1997) and for an orthodox treatment of external competence in the field of private international law see C T Kotuby, 'External Competence of the European Community in the Hague Conference on Private International Law: Community Harmonization and Worldwide Unification' (2001) XLVIII Netherlands International Law Review 1–30.

developed at a time of much greater judicial activism.[51] This solution would give complete freedom to Member States to negotiate with third States bilaterally or multilaterally and if the issues concern at least one party from that third State the international agreement would take priority over the internal Community rules.

A less radical solution, and one unlikely to be of much practical value unless it is drafted very permissively, would be to learn from the idea of closer cooperation in Article 11 of the EC Treaty to permit States to engage in closer global cooperation in private international law as long as at least eight Member States are willing to ratify a global agreement at the Hague. Closer cooperation has not yet worked as a model for deeper European integration but it might have some merit as a model for some EU States working together for global integration. Those EU States would continue to apply Community internal rules to all matters internal to the Community but would apply the international Convention rules whenever a party from a Convention State other than an EU State is involved and no party from an EU State who is not a party to the Convention is involved.

E. Scope

The substantive scope of the Brussels I Regulation is set out in Article 1 and is the same as Article 1 of the Brussels Convention.[52] The territorial scope is different in that the Brussels I Regulation does not apply to Denmark. The Brussels Convention will remain in force for cases involving Danish domiciliaries.[53]

F. Conclusion

Hopefully Sir Peter North will find it interesting to see the big picture of legal basis and external competence questions and the best way for the UK and

---

[51] There is a massive literature on judicial activism by the Court of Justice but for a brief introduction and references to further reading see S Weatherill and P Beaumont, *EU Law* (3rd edn, London, Penguin, 1999), pp 193–201 and 1074–1075.

[52] See *Anton and Beaumont's Civil Jurisdiction in Scotland*, Chap 3.

[53] See recitals 9, 21 and 22 to and Art 1(3) of the Brussels I Regulation.

Europe to be represented in issues of private international law globally alongside the small picture of a technical analysis of the old and new rules for contract jurisdiction in the Brussels Convention and Regulation. His career has
combined high level public service, indeed a quasi-political role, with erudite
scholarly writings on the policy issues and technical aspects of private international law. In a modest way this chapter seeks to echo this interesting combination and the present writer seeks to inadequately follow in Sir Peter's
footsteps in his own work.

2

REFORM OF PRIVATE INTERNATIONAL LAW BY JUDGES: CANADA AS A CASE STUDY

*Joost Blom**

A. Introduction

The 1990s saw a complete overhaul of the basic principles of Canadian private international law. The entire process was initiated and carried out, not by legislatures, but by judges. No other system of private international law has experienced a judicial re-invention of its foundations that was so rapid. By comparison, the 'revolution' in the United States was a slow-motion affair.

The lead actor in this drama was the Supreme Court of Canada, and its position in the Canadian legal system explains why the court's activity had such immediate and overwhelming effect. Unlike the Supreme Court of the United States, which sits at the apex of the federal, but not the state, judicial system,

* Faculty of Law, University of British Columbia. The author would like to acknowledge his great debt to Sir Peter North as teacher and scholar, and the happy association that the UBC Law Faculty has had with Sir Peter North over many years, including his two well-remembered stays with us as visiting professor.

the Supreme Court of Canada is the court of last resort in all matters, federal or provincial, arising in any Canadian court, whether provincial or federal.[1]

For the most part, the rules of private international law fall within the legislative sphere of the provinces.[2] An issue of private international law that is taken to the Supreme Court of Canada is, by virtue of the court's role at the head of the legal system of every province, potentially binding in all provinces, not just the one in which the case arose. An important qualification is that the court's decisions in private international law cases from Quebec, whose private law is a civil law system, are not usually binding in the other provinces, whose law is based on the common law,[3] and vice-versa. Hence the court's re-fashioning of the rules of private international law was at once effective in all the common law provinces, from which the cases in question came, and to some extent even in Quebec.[4]

After describing, in broad outline, the nature of the wholesale reform of Canadian (common law) private international law that has taken place since 1990, I will suggest some comparisons that may usefully be drawn between law reform as carried out by courts and by legislatures.

B. Conflicts Revolution, Canadian-Style

(1) The Common Law Background

As is well known, the Canadian political identity is strongly marked by the fact that the nation was born, not out of a revolution, but by the well-timed exercise of legitimate authority. The same is true of the 'new' principles of private international law, which were imposed from the top down rather than as

---

[1] Supreme Court Act, RSC 1986, c S-26, s 3. The Federal Court of Canada has a jurisdiction that is narrowly confined to certain federal matters. In only some of these, the main ones being federal taxation and review of federal administrative tribunals, is its jurisdiction exclusive. However, it should be noted that under s 96 of the Constitution Act 1867 it is the federal government that appoints the judges of the superior courts (meaning essentially the trial courts of plenary jurisdiction and the appellate courts) of every province.

[2] Constitution Act 1867, s 92(13), 'property and civil rights in the province'

[3] The common law 'provinces' should be understood to include the three northern federal territories, Yukon, the Northwest Territories, and Nunavut (formerly the eastern part of the Northwest Territories), whose private law is also based on the common law.

[4] Because of the constitutional implications of the court's decisions, most strikingly in *Hunt v T & N plc* [1993] 4 SCR 289, 109 DLR (4th) 16, which turned on the permissible effect to be given to a Quebec statute in the courts of British Columbia.

a consequence of irresistible agitation at the lower levels. Before *Morguard Investments Ltd v De Savoye*[5] was decided in 1990, there was no widespread sense that the Canadian common law system of private international law was fundamentally unsound (although this may testify more to our complacency than to the true state of affairs). The rules were mostly drawn from English precedent, with minimal adaptation to Canadian circumstances. Few areas had been changed by statute. The most notable of these areas was the recognition of divorces. The recognition of divorces within Canada was eliminated as an issue by the federal Parliament's exercise, after more than a century of hesitation, of its power to set up a divorce law that was effective throughout the nation.[6] The recognition of foreign divorces was eased by federal legislation that a divorce must be recognized in Canada if either party was ordinarily resident for one year in the country that granted the divorce, a rule that takes care of practically all meritorious cases.[7]

(2) Enforcement of Foreign Judgments

It was in the area of the recognition of civil judgments that the revolution was set off. Whether a judgment came from a Canadian or a truly foreign court, the English common law recognition rules applied. The only bases for recognition and enforcement were service of process on the judgment debtor while present in the country (or province) of the original court, and consent to the original court's jurisdiction (the judgment debtor having commenced the action in the court as plaintiff, or having attorned to the court's jurisdiction by voluntarily entering an appearance in the proceeding,[8] or having previously agreed to submit to the court's jurisdiction).[9] The rules took no account of the widespread exercise by Canadian and foreign courts of jurisdiction over defendants who neither were present in the jurisdiction nor consented to be sued there, but against whom the plaintiff made a claim that had substantial connections with

---

[5] [1990] 3 SCR 1077, 76 DLR (4th) 256.

[6] Divorce Act, SC 1967-68, c 24, replaced in 1986 by the Divorce Act, RSC 1985, c 3 (2nd Supp). Before the enactment of the 1968 statute, divorce law differed from one province to another, Quebec courts could not grant divorces, and the recognition in a province of a divorce granted elsewhere in Canada was a matter determined by the English recognition rules. The English rules did not work well in their original setting, and worked extremely badly in the Canadian one.

[7] Divorce Act, RSC 1985, c 3 (2nd Supp), s 22.

[8] Canadian courts seem to prefer the term 'attornment' to the, in England, more usual 'submission'.

[9] *Emanuel v Symon* [1908] 1 KB 302, CA. For the Canadian cases, see J-G Castel, *Canadian Conflict of Laws* (4th edn, 1997), pp 273–278.

the jurisdiction. In common law jurisdictions, including the Canadian common law provinces, the procedure for commencing an action against such defendants is service *ex juris*. Typically it is available only in cases where the facts giving rise to the cause of action are linked in a defined way to the territory of the forum. Examples are where the action is based on a tort committed in the jurisdiction or a breach of contract in the jurisdiction.

In the *Morguard* case, already mentioned,[10] two mortgage lenders had commenced foreclosure proceedings in the Alberta Court of Queen's Bench in relation to lands in Alberta. The borrower had formerly lived in Alberta but had moved to British Columbia. He was served with process there under the Alberta rules for service *ex juris*,[11] but chose not to appear in the proceedings. Judgment was given against him in default. There was a deficiency after sale of the lands, and the lenders sought to enforce the Alberta judgment by bringing an action on the judgment in the British Columbia Supreme Court. The enforcement action would fail according to the traditional rules, because the defendant had not been present in Alberta at the time the action was commenced, and he had not submitted or agreed to submit to the Alberta court's jurisdiction. The lenders would have to bring a fresh action in British Columbia on the original personal obligation.

That a mortgage debtor should be able to force a creditor to bring two actions, one in the province in which the lands were situated to obtain foreclosure, and then a second in the debtor's home province to get a judgment for the deficiency, offended against common sense. The situation might be tolerable if an international boundary was involved, but as between two Canadian provinces it seemed wholly irrational. The trial judge refused to apply the traditional rules, and so did the British Columbia Court of Appeal. The latter held that a judgment from another Canadian court should be enforced wherever the original court took jurisdiction in circumstances in which a British Columbia court would also have had jurisdiction.[12] The Supreme Court of Canada affirmed the decision, but placed it on broader grounds.

La Forest J, who gave the judgment for a unanimous court, went back to first principles or, more precisely, chose to articulate the first principles in a new

---

[10] [1990] 3 SCR 1077, 76 DLR (4th) 256.

[11] Service *ex juris* was available because the claim was in respect of a breach of contract in Alberta and the foreclosure proceeding related to land in Alberta.

[12] [1988] 5 WWR 650, BCCA.

way. The following passages in his judgment are worth quoting at some length, because they have been a starting point for all subsequent thinking, judicial and otherwise, about Canadian private international law.

> [The enforcement of foreign judgments at common law], it was thought, was in conformity with the requirements of comity, the informing principle of private international law, which has been stated to be the deference and respect due by other states to the actions of a state legitimately taken within its territory.[13]
>
> . . .
>
> For my part, I much prefer the more complete formulation of the idea of comity adopted by the Supreme Court of the United States in *Hilton v Guyot* 159 US 113 (1895), at pp 163–4 . . . :
>
> ' "Comity" in the legal sense, is neither a matter of absolute obligation, on the one hand, nor of mere courtesy and good will, upon the other. But it is the recognition which one nation allows within its territory to the legislative, executive or judicial acts of another nation, having due regard both to international duty and convenience, and to the rights of its own citizens or of other persons who are under the protection of its laws'. . .
>
> In a word, the rules of private international law are grounded in the need in modern times to facilitate the flow of wealth, skills and people across state lines in a fair and orderly manner.[14]
>
> . . .
>
> [W]hat must underlie a modern system of private international law are principles of order and fairness, principles that ensure security of transactions with justice.
>
> This formulation suggests that the content of comity must be adjusted in the light of a changing world order.[15]

La Forest J gave three reasons why the old rules for the enforcement of foreign judgments needed to be re-framed. One was that the concerns that underlay the English courts' attitude in the nineteenth century towards foreign judgments— the difficulties that English defendants would face if they were forced to defend actions in foreign lands and the dubious quality of justice in some of these lands—were out of place in the modern world of easy, rapid transportation and communication, and a high degree of economic and social integration among

---

[13] [1990] 3 SCR 1077, 1095, 76 DLR (4th) 256, 268.
[14] ibid, 1096 SCR, 268-69 DLR.
[15] ibid, 1097 SCR 269 DLR.

states. 'Accommodating the flow of wealth, skills and people across state lines has now become imperative'.[16] The second was the difference between international and inter-provincial enforcement. 'The considerations underlying the rules of comity apply with much greater force between the units of a federal state, and I do not think it much matters whether one calls these rules of comity or simply relies directly on ... reasons of justice, necessity and convenience . . .'[17]

The third reason was explicitly grounded in the Canadian constitution.

> [T]he English rules seem to me to fly in the face of the obvious intention of the Constitution to create a single country. This presupposes a basic goal of stability and unity where many aspects of life are not confined to one jurisdiction. A common citizenship ensured the mobility of Canadians across provincial lines . . . [S]ignificant steps were taken to foster economic integration. One of the central features of the constitutional arrangements incorporated in the *Constitution Act, 1867* was the creation of a common market . . .

> These arrangements themselves speak to the strong need for the enforcement throughout the country of judgments given in one province. But that is not all. The Canadian judicial structure is so arranged that any concerns about differential quality of justice among the provinces can have no real foundation. All superior court judges—who also have superintending control over other provincial courts and tribunals—are appointed and paid by the federal authorities. And all are subject to final review by the Supreme Court of Canada . . .[18]

> . . .

> [T]he rules of comity or private international law as they apply between the provinces must be shaped to conform to the federal structure of the Constitution.[19]

Applying the idea of comity as being both fundamental to private international law and conditioned by the Canadian constitution, La Forest J declared:

> [T]he courts in one province should give full faith and credit, to use the language of the United States Constitution, to the judgments given by a court in another province or a territory, so long as that court has properly, or appropriately, exercised jurisdiction in the action.[20]

---

[16] [1990] 3 SCR, 1098 SCR, 270 DLR.
[17] ibid.
[18] ibid, 1099–1100 SCR, 271 DLR.
[19] ibid, 1101 SCR, 272 DLR.
[20] ibid, 1102 SCR, 273 DLR.

The challenge was to define what determined whether a court's exercise of jurisdiction was proper or appropriate. The court cast no doubt on the propriety of the grounds that had traditionally been accepted as giving a court jurisdiction for the purpose of enforcing foreign judgments, namely, presence within the original jurisdiction or submission by agreement or attornment.[21] However, where the defendant was served *ex juris,* 'there must be some limits to the exercise of jurisdiction against persons outside the province'.[22] The Court of Appeal's 'reciprocity' approach, which asked whether the enforcing court could have taken jurisdiction in parallel circumstances, was rejected as lacking a uniform standard, which was essential at least in dealing with the problem within Canada.[23]

The court formulated this standard. It is worth observing that its formulation did not have the precision that would usually have been demanded of a statutory rule. The core idea, which La Forest J expressed in somewhat varying phrases, was that there must be a 'real and substantial connection' between the action and the province where the suit was brought.[24] La Forest J defended the lack of particularity in his test:

> It seems to me that the approach of permitting suit where there is a real and substantial connection with the action provides a reasonable balance between the rights of the parties. It affords some protection against being pursued in jurisdictions having little or no connection with the transaction or the parties. In a world where even the most familiar things we buy and sell originate or are manufactured elsewhere, and where people are constantly moving from province to province, it is simply anachronistic to uphold a 'power theory' or a single situs for torts or contracts for the proper exercise of jurisdiction.[25]

The Alberta foreclosure action indisputably met the 'real and substantial connection' criterion, and the default judgment was therefore enforceable.

---

[21] ibid, 1103–1104 SCR, 274 DLR.
[22] ibid, 1104 SCR, 274 DLR.
[23] ibid, 1104 SCR 275, DLR.
[24] La Forest J said of the case at bar that a 'more "real and substantial" connection between the *damages suffered* and the jurisdiction can scarcely be imagined' (emphasis added), ibid, 1108 SCR, 277 DLR. He also referred to a ' "real and substantial" connection between the jurisdiction and the *wrongdoing*' (emphasis added) (1106 SCR, 276 DLR, citing the test for the location of a tort that was used in *Moran v Pyle National (Canada) Ltd* (1973) [1975] 1 SCR 393, 43 DLR (3d) 239), a 'real and substantial connection with *the action*' (emphasis added) (1108 SCR, 278 DLR), and 'substantial connection with the jurisdiction where the action took place' (1109 SCR, 278 DLR).
[25] [1990] 3 SCR 1077, 1108-1109, 76 DLR (4th) 256, 278.

The impact of the *Morguard* decision was dramatic in several respects. To begin with, as a decision on the common law, it applied with full retroactive effect to all other cases. For many years, lawyers had frequently advised their clients that an action brought against the client in another jurisdiction should not be defended, since to defend the action was to attorn to the court's jurisdiction and so ensure that the resulting judgment would be enforceable against the client's assets elsewhere. Now, those who had followed their lawyers' advice, which had been correct on the law as it previously stood, were all at once declared to be liable on the default judgments that had been given against them in other provinces. As long as the claim on the judgment was not statute-barred it could be sued upon.[26]

The retroactivity of the new rule would surely have been unacceptable if the rule had been introduced by statute, but in a common law judicial decision it caused surprisingly little concern, in the courts or elsewhere.[27] A few years later, a litigant contended that the Supreme Court's decision, to be discussed below,[28] revamping the choice of law rule in tort should be applied prospectively only, and cited precedents from the United States Supreme Court. Huband JA, in the Saskatchewan Court of Appeal, said, 'In this nation, it would be an audacious step indeed for an appeal court to make a similar ruling with respect to a decision by the Supreme Court of Canada, which the Court itself declined to make'.[29]

---

[26] The *Morguard* decision did not affect the statutory regime for registration of extra-provincial judgments, which is embodied in uniform legislation in all Canadian provinces except Quebec. Since the jurisdictional grounds in the statutes reflect the pre-*Morguard* law, default judgments usually cannot be registered although they can, under *Morguard*, be enforced by bringing an action on the judgment: *Wilson v Hull* (1995) 128 DLR (4th) 403, Alta CA; *TDI Hospitality Management Consultants Inc v Browne* (1994) 117 DLR (4th) 289, Man CA; *Acme Video Inc v Hedges* (1993) 12 OR (3d) 160, CA.

[27] But see V Black and J Swan, 'Case Comment: New Rules for the Enforcement of Foreign Judgments: *Morguard Invesments Ltd v De Savoye*' (1991) 12 Advocates Q 489, 509-510. The technique of 'prospective overruling' of common law precedent was proposed, and rejected, in a case on the recognition of divorces: *Edward v Edward Estate* (1987) 39 DLR (4th) 654, Sask CA. The retroactive effect of the *Morguard* case was seldom disputed in subsequent cases and, where it was, the common law rule was affirmed without hesitation: *Beals v Saldanha* (1998) 42 OR (3d) 127, Gen Div, revd on other grounds (2001) 202 DLR (4th) 630, Ont CA; *87313 Canada Inc v Neeshat Oriental Carpet Ltd* (1992) 11 CPC (3d) 7, Ont Gen Div.

[28] See nn ff below and accompanying text.

[29] *Michalski v Olson* (1997) 123 Man R (2d) 101, CA, leave to appeal refused [1998] 1 SCR xi.

Another, perhaps more surprising, reaction to *Morguard* in the lower courts was to apply it, almost without question or qualification, to default judgments from the United States, the United Kingdom and other foreign countries.[30] Despite the heavy emphasis in *Morguard* itself on the constitutional parameters of the issue, the lower courts saw no reason to distinguish between Canadian judgments and truly foreign ones. Comity, even without a constitutional wind in its sails, was a sufficient reason to expose Canadian-resident judgment debtors to liability on judgments where the action had a real and substantial connection with the foreign country. Thus, for example, Canadian businesses that sell products to United States customers cannot complain if they are sued for defects in those products in their customers' home states.[31]

Only rarely in the reported cases does a default judgment fail to meet the sufficient connection test. One instance was where a British Columbia-based company, which had activities in Texas, sued another British Columbia resident in a Texas court for libel. The Texas court took jurisdiction on the basis that the allegedly libelous material had appeared on an Internet discussion group or bulletin board accessible by present and potential investors in the company who lived in Texas (or, of course, anywhere else).[32] The British Columbia Court of Appeal refused to enforce the judgment. The only connection with Texas put forward by the judgment creditor was 'the mere transitory, passive presence in cyberspace of the alleged defamatory material'. [33] This was not a real and substantial connection with Texas. Nor, indeed, did it amount to the 'minimum contacts' sufficient to support *in personam* jurisdiction under United States due process requirements. Comity therefore did not require recognition of the judgment.[34]

There can be little doubt that the Supreme Court's radical liberalization of the enforcement of foreign default judgments was for the most part a good thing. Within Canada it promotes the efficiency of the administration of justice by

---

[30] *Old North State Brewing Co v Newlands Services Inc* (1998) [1999] 4 WWR 573, BCCA; *Moses v Shore Boat Builders Ltd* (1993) 106 DLR (4th) 654, BCCA, leave to appeal refused [1994] 1 SCR xi; see further J-G Castel, *Canadian Conflict of Laws* (4th edn, 1997), p 282; J Blom, 'The Enforcement of Foreign Judgments: *Morguard* Goes Forth Into the World' (1997) 28 Canadian Business LJ 373.

[31] *Old North State Brewing Co v Newlands Services Inc* and *Moses v Shore Boat Builders Ltd*, ibid.

[32] *Braintech Ltd v Kostiuk* (1999) 171 DLR (4th) 46, BCCA, leave to appeal refused, [2000] 1 SCR vii.

[33] ibid, 62 (Goldie JA).

[34] ibid.

encouraging defendants to appear when they are sued in another province, and discouraging multiplicity of actions. In international cases it has the same effect, although it can be argued that by throwing their doors open in this way to foreign judgment creditors, the courts have deprived Canada of the chance to negotiate reciprocal concessions in other countries. Many of these countries have rules that are not as favourable to the enforcement of Canadian judgments as the Canadian rules are now to the enforcement of their judgments.

The main drawback of the way this reform has been achieved, however, is the uncertainty surrounding the application of the 'real and substantial connection' test. Every test gives rise to borderline cases, but this test has a particularly broad borderline, especially in international cases.[35] International litigation is an area where certainty as to whether a judgment will be enforceable is important. This is especially so in relation to a Canadian defendant that must decide whether to appear in the foreign proceedings. If the defendant guesses that the foreign judgment will be not enforced in Canada and decides not to appear, there can be a huge price to pay if the guess is wrong, namely, liability in Canada on a foreign default judgment.[36] When in doubt, the defendant will be pushed to defend, which means attorning to the jurisdiction of the foreign court and so losing any possible argument against enforcement of an eventual judgment. The foreign courts' reach into Canada is assisted, as it were, by the elasticity of the *Morguard* principle. It is this concern, as much as any other, that has prompted the Uniform Law Conference of Canada to engage in a project to draft a uniform Act on the enforcement of non-Canadian civil judgments.[37]

(3) Jurisdiction of Canadian Courts

The area of jurisdiction has felt the impact of *Morguard* in two ways. One is the creation of a constitutional threshold requirement for the valid exercise of judicial jurisdiction in cases with extra-provincial elements. Before *Morguard*,

---

[35] See Blom (n 30 above).

[36] In deciding whether to sue abroad, the plaintiff tends to have, financially speaking, less at stake. If judgment is obtained in default it is relatively inexpensive, even if enforcement may ultimately be denied in Canada. If the defendant appears in the action, the enforceability of the judgment is assured.

[37] J Blom, 'The Uniform Law Conference Project on the Enforcement of Non-Canadian Civil Judgments' in *From Territorial Sovereignty to Human Security: Proceedings of the 28th Annual Conference of Canadian Council on International Law, Ottawa, October 28-29, 1999* (2000) 118. See also V Black, 'Commodifying Justice for Global Free Trade: The Proposed Hague Judgments Convention' (2000) 38 Osgoode Hall LJ 237.

nobody had paid much attention to the question of how far a province could extend its courts' jurisdiction over cases with extra-provincial elements. Partly this low profile for the problem stemmed from the fact that jurisdictional rules in common law provinces are usually enacted indirectly through rules of court dealing with service of process, and so the issue could seem more a matter of court procedure than what it really was, the exercise of legislative power.

In *Morguard*, La Forest J directed attention to the constitutional implications of jurisdictional rules:

> The private international law rule requiring substantial connection with the jurisdiction where the action took place is supported by the constitutional restriction of legislative power 'in the province'.[38]
>
> . . .
>
> The restriction to the province would certainly require at least minimal contact with the province, and there is authority for the view that the contact required by the Constitution for the purposes of territoriality is the same as required by the rule of private international law between sister-provinces.[39]

Although, in that case, the court declined to pronounce definitively on whether such a constitutional restriction existed, the court said in a subsequent case that 'courts are required, by constitutional constraints, to assume jurisdiction only where there are real and substantial connections to that place'.[40]

This constitutional minimum requirement now enables defendants to dispute the existence of jurisdiction even if the rules of court, taken alone, would permit jurisdiction to be exercised. Some courts have come to use the phrase, 'jurisdiction *simpliciter*', to distinguish this issue from the one of *forum conveniens*, where the court has the right to exercise jurisdiction but chooses not to exercise it because there is a more appropriate forum for the action.[41]

---

[38] A reference to the Constitution Act 1867, s 92(14), 'administration of justice in the province'.

[39] [1990] 3 SCR 1077, 1109, 76 DLR (4th) 256, 278.

[40] *Hunt v T & N plc* [1993] 4 SCR 289, 328, 109 DLR (4th) 16, 44 (La Forest J). A similar statement was made by La Forest J in *Tolofson v Jensen* [1994] 3 SCR 1022, 1049, 120 DLR (4th) 289, 304.

[41] *Strukoff v Syncrude Canada Ltd* (2000) 80 BCLR (3d) 294, CA, leave to appeal refused (SCC, 24 May 2001); *Pacific International Securities Inc v Drake Capital Securities Inc* (2000) 194 DLR (4th) 716, BCCA; *Jordan v Schatz* [2000] 7 WWR 442, BCCA; *Furlan v Shell Oil Co* [2000] 7 WWR 433, BCCA; *Cook v Parcel, Mauro, Hultin & Spaanstra, PC* (1997) 143 DLR (4th) 213, BCCA, leave to appeal refused [1997] 2 SCR vii; *Craig Broadcast Systems Inc v Frank N Magid Associates Inc* (1998) 155 DLR (4th) 356, Man CA; *Oakley v Barry* (1998) 158 DLR (4th) 679, NSCA; *Lemmex v Bernard* (2001) 204 DLR (4th) 192, Ont Divisional Ct.

The practical significance of the growth of this constitutional doctrine has been modest, because, if the connections with the province are tenuous, a court would almost always have declined jurisdiction anyway on the ground of *forum non conveniens*. There is every sign, moreover, that if the court is persuaded that it is, under all the circumstances, the *forum conveniens*, it will find a sufficient real and substantial connection, even on relatively slight grounds.[42] It is also worth noting that the 'real and substantial connection' test has, so far, failed to impair the rule that mere transitory presence in the province gives the court jurisdiction, even if there is nothing else to connect the case to the province.[43]

The other area in which *Morguard* has affected the law relating to jurisdiction is *forum non conveniens*, especially as it figures in cases of *lis alibi pendens* and anti-suit injunctions. The emphasis on comity has encouraged Canadian courts to be less forum-centric in approaching the question whether they should insist on taking jurisdiction in the face of an action already under way in another province or country. The Supreme Court of Canada itself had to consider anti-suit injunctions in *Amchem Products Inc v British Columbia (Workers' Compensation Board)*.[44] The court held that an injunction should not have been granted in British Columbia, at the behest of a number of asbestos manufacturers, to restrain the Workers' Compensation Board of British Columbia from suing the manufacturers in Texas in respect of illness caused by their products to a large number of British Columbia workers' compensation claimants. The Texas court was said to have no doctrine of *forum conveniens*, and this had weighed with the courts below, which had held in favour of an injunction. The Supreme Court of Canada held this factor was irrelevant. The question was whether, supposing the issue had been raised before it, the Texas court could reasonably have concluded that it was a *forum conveniens* according to Canadian standards.

---

[42] *Duncan (Litigation Guardian of) v Neptunia Corp* (2001) 199 DLR (4th) 354, Ont SCJ, holding that the 'real and substantial' test should not be dogmatically applied if it would unjustly deny a local plaintiff access to the court (an Ontario resident sued his multinational employer in Ontario for injuries suffered by gas poisoning in the apartment his employer had supplied to him in China). Compare *Jordan v Schatz* [2000] 7 WWR 442, BCCA, which held that even if the action is statute-barred in the alternative jurisdiction(s), the mere presence of the plaintiff in the forum is not a real and substantial connection that supports jurisdiction *simpliciter*. See also *Oakley v Barry* (1998) 158 DLR (4th) 679, NSCA.

[43] *Teja v Rai* 2002 BCCA 16: *Ruwenzori Enterprises Ltd v Walji* 2000 BCSC 790. In *Teja* the court relied in part on La Forest J's confirmation in *Morguard* of the traditional grounds of jurisdiction (See n 21 above and accompanying text).

[44] [1993] 1 SCR 897, 102 DLR (4th) 96. See P Glenn, 'The Supreme Court, Judicial Comity and Anti-Suit Injunctions' (1994) 28 UBC L Rev 193.

> [W]hen a foreign court assumes jurisdiction on a basis that generally conforms to our rules of private international law relating to the *forum non conveniens*, that decision will be respected and a Canadian court will not purport to make the decision for the foreign court. The policy of our courts with respect to comity demands no less. If, however, a foreign court assumes jurisdiction on a basis that is inconsistent with our rules of private international law and an injustice results to a litigant or 'would-be' litigant in our courts, then the assumption of jurisdiction is inequitable and the party invoking the foreign jurisdiction can be restrained. The foreign court, not having, itself, observed the rules of comity, cannot expect its decision to be respected on the basis of comity.[45]

Since, under the circumstances, the Texas court could reasonably have held that it was *forum conveniens*, the issue of injustice to the asbestos companies did not arise. Had it arisen (ie had Texas been a *forum non conveniens* by Canadian standards), the court would have had to decide whether the personal or juridical advantages that each side sought to realize in its chosen forum were based on reasonable expectations that the party would have access to that forum. Only if a continuation of the foreign proceeding would deprive the asbestos manufacturers of legitimate advantages, based on reasonable expectations that claims against them would be brought in British Columbia, would the manufacturers have had the beginnings of an argument of injustice.[46]

The desirability, in the name of comity, of deferring to the acceptable exercise of jurisdiction by another court has altered the shape of argument in *lis alibi pendens* cases. In the past, the existence of parallel proceedings in another court was given no special weight in deciding whether an action brought locally should be stayed on the ground of *forum non conveniens*. Now, however, a party seeking to uphold an action in a second forum must meet, not only the argument of needless expense and inconvenience, but also the more potent argument that multiplicity of proceedings offends against comity.

The best example so far is *Westec Aerospace Inc v Raytheon Aircraft Co.*[47] A British Columbia firm had licensed computer software and hardware to a

---

[45] ibid, 934 SCR, 120–21 DLR.

[46] ibid, 933 SCR, 120 DLR. Even if that were so, the reasonable expectations of the other party to legitimate advantages in the other forum (albeit a *forum non conveniens*) would be weighed on the other side.

[47] (1999) 173 DLR (4th) 498, BCCA. The hearing of an appeal to the Supreme Court of Canada was adjourned on 25 January 2001 when it appeared that the Kansas court had given summary judgment, so that the issue of *res judicata* had superseded the jurisdictional argument (197 DLR (4th) 211n). The appeal was dismissed without reasons on 17 April 2001. See also *472900 BC Ltd v Thrifty Canada Ltd* (1998) 168 DLR (4th) 602, BCCA.

Kansas-based company that did no business in British Columbia. Disputes arose. The American company began an action in Kansas for a declaration that it was not in breach of contract, and the British Columbia company then brought an action in that province for damages for breach of contract. The British Columbia Court of Appeal held that the latter action should be stayed, notwithstanding that British Columbia was a *forum conveniens* for the proceeding. Kansas was equally a *forum conveniens*. The British Columbia firm had not established objectively by cogent evidence that there was some personal or juridical advantage that would be available to it in British Columbia that was of such importance that it would cause injustice to that firm to deprive it of the advantage.[48] To the argument that the court's approach would encourage a 'race to the courthouse' to get proceedings started first in one's own jurisdiction, the court replied that the race would be won only if the chosen jurisdiction was an appropriate forum.[49] It added that the alternative of a 'race to the courthouse' was a 'race to judgment' if parallel proceedings were allowed to continue, since each jurisdiction would be expected to recognize a judgment given in the other.[50]

To be sure, this shift in the courts' attitude to foreign proceedings and to their own jurisdiction is not unique to Canada, nor is it solely the consequence of the Supreme Court of Canada's innovations. The court in *Westec* cited as many English cases as Canadian ones, and *Amchem* itself relied heavily on a Privy Council decision.[51] However, it seems likely that the Supreme Court's recasting of the idea of comity, and making it a dynamic element of Canadian private international law, has hastened the process and made it more thorough.

(4) Choice of Law

It always seems to be tort cases that provide the opportunity for major rethinking of choice of law, and Canada is no exception to this rule. In *Tolofson v Jensen*[52] the Supreme Court of Canada heard consolidated appeals from a British Columbia and an Ontario case involving out-of-province automobile accidents. The actions were viable by the law of the province where they were brought, but both cases would fail if the court applied the law of the province

---

[48] (1999) 173 DLR (4th) 498, BCCA, paras 49–55.
[49] ibid, para 38.
[50] ibid, para 40.
[51] *Société Nationale Industrielle Aérospatiale v Lee Kui Jak* [1987] AC 871, PC.
[52] [1994] 3 SCR 1022, 120 DLR (4th) 289.

where the accident happened. In the British Columbia case, a passenger sued his father as driver, as well as the driver of the other car involved. The plaintiff and his father were British Columbia residents and the other driver was a resident of Saskatchewan, where the accident happened. The law of Saskatchewan would bar the action on limitation grounds and, as to the claim against the father, by a 'guest statute' requiring proof of gross negligence. In the Ontario case, passengers claimed against their husband and father as driver for injuries suffered in an accident in Quebec. Their claims would be barred under the law of Quebec, which bars all civil claims and applies a no-fault insurance scheme.[53] The Supreme Court of Canada held that the *lex loci delicti* should apply in both cases and to all the issues raised. This included the limitation rule, which it characterized, discarding long-standing precedent, as substantive in nature.

The Court's judgment was given, as in *Morguard*, by La Forest J. Once again he began with first principles:

> From the general principle that a state has exclusive jurisdiction within its own territories and that other states must under principles of comity respect the exercise of its jurisdiction within its own territory, it seems axiomatic to me that, at least as a general rule, the law to be applied in torts is the law of the place where the activity occurred, ie, the *lex loci delicti*. There are situations, of course, notably where an act occurs in one place but the consequences are directly felt elsewhere, when the issue of where the tort takes place itself raises thorny issues. In such a case, it may well be that the consequences would be held to constitute the wrong. Difficulties may also arise where the wrong directly arises out of some trans-national or inter-provincial activity. There territorial considerations may become muted; they may conflict and other considerations may play a determining role. But that is not this case . . .

> I have thus far framed the arguments favouring the *lex loci delicti* in theoretical terms. But the approach responds to a number of sound practical considerations. The rule has the advantage of certainty, ease of application and predictability. Moreover, it would seem to meet normal expectations. Ordinarily people expect their activities to be governed by the law of the place where they happen to be and expect that concomitant legal benefits and responsibilities will be defined accordingly. The government of that place is the only one with power to deal with these activities. The same expectation is ordinarily shared by other states and by people outside the place where an activity occurs. If other states

---

[53] In the Ontario case the passengers' claims against a Quebec resident, who drove the other car involved in the collision, had been discontinued but a claim over by the Ontario-resident defendant against the Quebec driver was still on foot.

routinely applied their laws to activities taking place elsewhere, confusion would be the result.[54]

These considerations justified removing from the tort choice of law rule the *lex fori*, which English and Canadian courts had long applied in tandem with the *lex loci delicti*.[55]

Although a rigid *lex loci delicti* rule was abandoned in the United States[56] and not adopted in the English statute on tort choice of law,[57] the court rejected any exception to the rule for domestic cases. La Forest J emphasized the 'extreme uncertainty' that a flexible exception would create.[58] He also thought that the desire for such an exception was often based on a dislike of the content of the *lex loci delicti*. It might be bad luck for a plaintiff to be injured in one jurisdiction rather than another, but—

> such differences are a concomitant of the territoriality principle. While, no doubt, as was observed in *Morguard*, the underlying principles of private international law are order and fairness, order comes first. Order is a precondition to justice.[59]

A flexible exception, he thought, was especially out of place in Canada's federal system.

> The nature of our constitutional arrangements—a single country with different provinces exercising territorial legislative jurisdiction—would seem to me to support a rule that is certain and that ensures that an act committed in one part of the country will be given the same legal effect throughout the country. This militates strongly in favour of the *lex loci delicti* rule.[60]

He went so far as to suggest, without deciding, that a province—and, by extension, its courts—had no constitutional power to attach substantive legal consequences to events occurring outside its borders other than the consequences dictated by the law of the jurisdiction where the events took place.[61]

---

[54] [1994] 3 SCR 1022, 1049-1051, 120 DLR (4th) 289, 305.

[55] *Phillips v Eyre* (1870) LR 6 QB 1, Ex Ch; *Boys v Chaplin* (1969) [1971] AC 356, HL; *McLean v Pettigrew* [1945] SCR 62, [1945] 2 DLR 65.

[56] *Babcock v Jackson*, 12 NY 2d 743, 191 NE 2d 279 (1963).

[57] Private International Law (Miscellaneous Provisions) Act 1995, ss 11–12.

[58] [1994] 3 SCR 1022, 1056, 120 DLR (4th) 289, 309.

[59] ibid, 1058 SCR, 311 DLR.

[60] ibid, 1064 SCR, 315 DLR. La Forest J cited Mason CJ's judgment in *Breavington v Godleman* (1988) 169 CLR 41, for the idea that choice of law must be uniform in a federal system.

[61] ibid, 1065–1066 SCR, 316–17 DLR These constitutional reflections are criticized by J-G Castel, 'Back to the Future! Is the New "Rigid" Choice of Law Rule for Interprovincial Torts Constitutionally Mandated?' (1995) 33 Osgoode Hall LJ 35.

Therefore, in cases involving torts committed in Canada, *Tolofson* leaves little room for escape from the *lex loci delicti*. In cases where the locus of the tort is indisputably within a province, such as automobile accidents, it is immaterial how extensively the facts are connected with another province.[62] So far there has been no reported case dealing with other torts in which the injury and the wrongful conduct occur in different provinces or in which, to use La Forest J's words, the wrong 'directly arises out of some trans-national or inter-provincial activity' so that the 'territorial considerations may become muted'.[63]

La Forest J left the door slightly ajar for the application of a flexible exception in international cases.[64] Aside from the fact that these do not raise the constitutional issues to which he gave weight, it is hard to see a principled reason for the distinction. The only one he adverted to was that an exception might be appropriate in an international convention dealing with choice of law, where Canada would obtain reciprocal benefits.[65] In any event the lower courts have eagerly grasped the chance to apply the *lex fori* in cases of Canadians suing each other in respect of automobile accidents that happened in the United States, where the location was virtually the only connection with the *lex loci delicti*.[66]

C. Conclusion: Pros and Cons of Judicial Law Reform

The Supreme Court of Canada's reform of Canadian private international law has been swift and far-reaching, leaving no part of the subject untouched. Change on this scale, and in such a short time, is almost unimaginable if pursued by legislative means. There would have to be commissions, working

---

[62] In *Leonard v Houle* (1997) 154 DLR (4th) 640, leave to appeal refused [1998] 1 SCR xi, an Ontario-resident victim was injured in Quebec in a collision with a van stolen in Ontario by an Ontario-resident thief, who, just before the accident, had driven across the border to escape the pursuing Ontario police. Quebec law applied. For a proposal to liberalize the rule, see J Walker, ' "Are We There Yet?" Towards a New Rule for Choice of Law in Tort' (2000) 38 Osgoode Hall LJ 331.

[63] See n 54 above and accompanying text.

[64] [1994] 3 SCR 1022, 1062-1063, 120 DLR (4th) 289, 314. The only exception he considered was in favour of applying the *lex fori*.

[65] ibid.

[66] *Wong v Wei* [1999] 10 WWR 296, BCSC; *Hanlan v Sernesky* (1997) 35 OR (3d) 603, Gen Div, affd (1998) 38 OR (3d) 479, CA; *Lebert v Skinner Estate* (2001) 53 OR (3d) 559, SCJ; *Wong v Lee* (2000) 50 OR (3d) 419, SCJ. One case, understood to be under appeal, held that an exception could be made even in inter-provincial cases in order to avoid injustice: *Lau v Li* (2001) 53 OR (3d) 727, SCJ.

groups, learned papers, draft legislation, commentary, lobbying by interest groups, revisions, a Bill, and then an Act—an Act in each of ten provinces, three territories and the federal jurisdiction if the changes were to be implemented nationally. Even if the process ran to a successful conclusion, the end product would almost certainly be less pervasive and sweeping than what the Supreme Court has wrought.

There are positive and negative sides to this exercise in judicial law reform, when compared with the legislative path. On the plus side, the dominant and maybe decisive consideration is that it could be done this way effectively, quickly, and on a national scale, whereas legislatively it may be doubted whether it could be done at all. The reforms also have the virtues of judge-made law. The new principles are responsive to testing by litigation, and capable of further development. A broad concept like comity, and the invocation of the need to accommodate the flow of wealth, skills, and people across state lines,[67] introduce dynamic, liberalizing elements into the judicial consideration of private international law issues.

The achievement, and these virtues, come at a price. One, as was noted earlier in relation to recognizing foreign judgments, is that if the rules are framed too loosely they promote uncertainty. On the other hand, if they are framed too rigidly, as was arguably the case in *Tolofson*, they are impossible to modify without taking another appeal to the Supreme Court of Canada. Some of the strengths of judicial law reform are also its weaknesses. The way rules are framed is driven by the exigencies of the dispute before the court, and the emphases that the judges in the Supreme Court choose to put on different aspects of the problem. Whether the court's formulation of the law gets the balance right is not tested until it is too late to do anything about it.

One further, arguably negative, aspect of these developments stems from the Supreme Court's wish to put constitutional underpinnings beneath Canadian private international law. If one likes the result one can point to this as a further thing that courts (or at least the Supreme Court of Canada) can do but legislatures cannot. The question must be asked, however, whether these developments have been entirely a good thing for either Canadian constitutional law or private international law.[68] The Supreme Court could have done practically

---

[67] *Morguard Investments Ltd v De Savoye*, [1990] 3 SCR 1077, 1096, 76 DLR (4th) 256, 270.
[68] See E Edinger, 'The Constitutionalization of the Conflict of Laws' (1995) 25 Canadian Business LJ 38.

all it did in respect of foreign judgments, jurisdiction, and choice of law without the constitutional reinforcement. *Morguard* had left the question open whether the obligation to give full faith and credit to the laws of other provinces had constitutional force, but the die was cast in *Hunt v T & N plc*. [69] It was on the basis of this obligation that a Quebec statute was held inoperative to prohibit the production of documents, situated in Quebec, for the purposes of court proceedings in British Columbia. The Supreme Court, again speaking through La Forest J, took pains to say that the principles enunciated in *Morguard* were 'constitutional imperatives, and as such apply to the provincial legislatures as well as to the courts'. [70] As was noted above, the Supreme Court suggested in *Tolofson* that even the *lex loci delicti* choice of law rule in tort might be constitutionally mandated. [71]

The disadvantage of giving private international law rules the status of constitutional imperatives is precisely that the provincial legislatures cannot change them. Innovation is stifled. The new rules bind the legislature of Quebec, which has always had its own system of private international law, along with those of the other provinces. It may be doubted whether the federal Parliament can change them, because they pertain to property and civil rights in the province. Even a constitutional amendment would be difficult because the new constitutional rules are not found in any provision of the constitution but are said to be inherent in the federal structure of Canada. Only the Supreme Court of Canada's authority to change the rules is certain. As a result, many of the basic principles of Canadian private international law may actually have been placed beyond the reach of legislative law reform. It seems that judicial law reform, for better or worse, has become the only option for important parts of Canadian private international law.

---

[69] [1993] 4 SCR 289, 109 DLR (4th) 16.
[70] ibid, 324 SCR, 40–41 DLR.
[71] See n 61 above and accompanying text.

3

FORUM SELECTION AND FORUM REJECTION IN US COURTS: ONE RATIONALE FOR A GLOBAL CHOICE OF COURT CONVENTION

*Ronald A Brand**

A. Introduction

At the end of 2001, negotiations at the Hague Conference on Private International Law for a Convention on Jurisdiction and the Recognition and Enforcement of Judgments had reached a critical stage, with doubts about the

* Professor of Law and Director, Center for International Legal Education, University of Pittsburgh. The author is a member of the United States delegation to the Special Commission negotiating the Convention on Jurisdiction and Foreign Judgments in Civil and Commercial Matters at the Hague Conference on Private International Law. The opinions expressed in this chapter are those of the author and should not be taken to represent the position of the United States government or any other member of the United States delegation. Valuable research assistance was provided by Michelle Saylor and Scott Jablonski.

road ahead.[1] The delegates to those negotiations had spent nearly a decade in an attempt to draft a treaty that would deal with both the rules of jurisdiction applied directly in the originating court and the rules governing recognition and enforcement of resulting judgments in the courts of another contracting state. A Preliminary Draft Convention completed in October of 1999[2] was revised under changed rules at the two weeks of Diplomatic Conference in June 2001.[3] The resulting Interim Text is replete with bracketed language and variations within many articles, making it a lengthy catalogue of negotiating positions, but not particularly useful in working toward a final Convention.

The confusing nature of the Interim Text made clear to many that the continuation of negotiations toward a comprehensive global Convention was an alternative unlikely to lead to satisfactory results. At the same time, the alternative of discontinuing the negotiations (either by suspension or complete default) was not a satisfactory option. Over the course of the negotiations delegations had identified both areas on which common ground did exist and issues upon which there was hope for successful compromise.[4] The course of the negotiations did allow two conclusions on which a more productive alternative could be based: (1) common ground in jurisdictional practice around the globe offered the possibility of a more modest convention that could achieve broad-based ratification; and (2) certain differences in jurisdictional

---

[1] This chapter was written in December 2001.

[2] Hague Conference on Private International Law, Preliminary Draft Convention on Jurisdiction and Foreign Judgments In Civil and Commercial Matters, adopted by the Special Commission on 30 October 1999 [hereinafter 'Draft Text']. Available at http://www.hcch.net/e/conventions/draft36e.html (visited 17 December 2001).

[3] Hague Conference on Private International Law, Commission II, Jurisdiction and Foreign Judgments in Civil and Commercial Matters, Summary of the Outcome of the Discussion in Commission II of the First Part of the Diplomatic Conference 6–20 June 2001, Interim Text [hereinafter 'Interim Text']. Available at http://www.hcch.net/e/workprog/jdgm.html (visited 17 December 2001).

[4] For discussions of a compromise/consensus approach, see R A Brand, 'Current Problems, Common Ground, and First Principles: Restructuring the Preliminary Draft Convention Text' in J J Barcelo III and K M Clermont (eds), *A Global Law of Jurisdiction and Judgments: Lessons from the Hague Convention* (forthcoming 2002) (containing papers presented at a symposium sponsored by Cornell Law School in Paris on 8 July 2000); R A Brand, 'Concepts, Consensus and the Status Quo Zone: Getting to 'Yes' on a Hague Jurisdiction and Judgments Convention' in C Charmody (ed), *Trilateral Perspectives on International Law* (forthcoming) (containing papers presented at a symposium sponsored by the American Society of International Law, the Canadian Council on International Law, and the Japanese Society of International Law in Ottawa, Canada, 24–25 October 2000); and R A Brand, 'Jurisdictional Common Ground: In Search of A Global Convention' in James A R Nafziger and Simeon C Symeonides (eds), *Law and Justice in a Multi-State World: Essays in Honor of Arthur T von Mehren* (forthcoming).

practice, as well as specific issues of jurisdiction unresolved in all legal systems, did not allow for clear and predictable legal rules in a global Convention. Thus, there existed the alternative of a Convention developed on a consensus basis, consistent with the original discussions of a 'mixed' convention approach, that would represent a very positive development in terms of private international law on a global basis.

In the discussion that follows, I begin with a brief overview of the negotiations at The Hague, indicating what I consider to be the problems that led to the difficult situation at the end of 2001. The next section provides an overview of US law on choice of court and *forum non conveniens*, as well as the interplay between these two areas of the law. I ultimately follow this with the suggestion that a more modest Convention than that exemplified in the 1999 and 2001 texts is both possible and likely to benefit parties to litigation throughout the world. This conclusion is based in part on issues concerning forum selection in US courts; issues important to both domestic and foreign litigants. While some have concluded that other States have little to gain from the United States in the negotiations (other than the prohibition of general 'doing business' jurisdiction—a politically unattainable result), I conclude that the current status of US law on choice of court and *forum non conveniens* demonstrates the significant benefits such a convention can offer to all parties to future litigation in the United States.

B. The Negotiations[5]

In May of 1992, Edwin Williamson, then Legal Advisor at the US Department of State, wrote to the Secretary General of the Hague Conference on Private International Law proposing the negotiation of a multilateral Convention on the Recognition and Enforcement of Judgments.[6] From the beginning of the discussions, the United States took the position that the product of the Hague Conference Special Commission should be a 'mixed' convention;[7] a position

---

[5] For a more detailed history of the negotiations, see R A Brand, 'Intellectual Property, Electronic Commerce and the Preliminary Draft Hague Jurisdiction and Judgments Convention' (2001) 62 U Pittsburgh L Rev 581, 582–586.

[6] Letter from Edwin D Williamson, Legal Advisor, US Department of State, to Georges Droz, Secretary General, The Hague Conference on Private International Law (5 May 1992) (*distributed with* Hague Conference document Lc ON No 15 (92)).

[7] A T von Mehren, *Recognition Convention Study: Final Report* 2.

supported by the original Hague Conference Working Group in that same year.[8]

Single (sometimes referred to as 'simple') Conventions on the recognition of judgments deal only with indirect jurisdiction and apply only to the decision of the court asked to enforce a foreign judgment. Thus, the recognizing court considers the jurisdiction of the court issuing a judgment in deciding whether to recognize the judgment of the originating court. Double conventions, like the Brussels and Lugano Conventions, not only deal with recognition, but also provide direct jurisdiction rules applicable in the court in which the case is first brought—thus addressing the matter from the outset and pre-empting the need for substantial indirect consideration of the issuing court's jurisdiction by the court asked to recognize the resulting judgment. The mixed Convention is a variation on the double Convention, providing rules for both jurisdiction and the recognition of judgments, but not purporting to be exhaustive in its lists of required and prohibited bases of jurisdiction. It does not cover the entire field, but rather leaves some bases of jurisdiction available under national law, although these bases are not subject to the convention's rules on recognition and enforcement of any resulting judgment.[9]

The benefit of a mixed convention in the negotiation process is that it allows the Hague Member States to build up a Convention from the status quo, and does not require agreement on a comprehensive set of jurisdictional rules that cover and connect the entire field of possibilities. It also allows the use of a consensus process likely to produce a convention acceptable to the largest number of states.[10] It therefore allows some areas of disagreement and experimentation to continue while at the same time locking in progress that can be achieved. A mixed Convention also allows certain issues that are unresolved in any single national legal system to remain outside the Convention and subject to later Conventions or protocols should an acceptable approach be developed. This is

---

[8] *Conclusions of the Working Group Meeting on Enforcement of Judgments*, Hague Conference on Private International Law Doc Lc ON No 2 (93), at 3 (4 January 1993).

[9] Under the mixed Convention approach, there would exist a list of required bases of jurisdiction and a list of prohibited bases of jurisdiction. Judgments founded on required bases of jurisdiction would be entitled to recognition under the Convention. Courts should not exercise jurisdiction founded only on bases on the prohibited list. For a few other situations, some exceptions to recognition would apply. Any jurisdictional basis not included on one of the two lists would be permitted, but a resulting judgment would not be entitled to recognition under the Convention. Instead, such judgments would be subject to review in the recognizing court in the manner applicable in the absence of a treaty.

[10] See Brand, *Jurisdictional Common Ground* (n 4 above).

particularly important in regard to jurisdiction for matters involving intellectual property rights and electronic commerce; matters for which no legal system has yet developed a satisfactory, fixed set of rules, and for which it would be presumptuous to believe a global solution could be found and then imposed by a treaty within the near future.[11]

While the negotiating process began with discussion of a mixed Convention, it was not until June of 1999 that the Special Commission voted specifically to adopt the mixed Convention model.[12] The intervening seven-year ambivalence of focus resulted in the primary development of double Convention language. Thus, even in the June 2001 Interim Text, which purports to follow a mixed Convention approach, the words often are those of a double Convention. Given that the negotiations prior to June 2001 were conducted by majority vote, and that fifteen of the Member States voting on specific Articles during the process were Member States of the European Union and others were states eager to become Member States of the EU, it is not surprising that the Draft and Interim Text language looks much like that of the Brussels and Lugano Conventions in force in the EU states. It also is not surprising that the EU states would prefer a Convention that looks as much as possible like the sets of rules they customarily apply in similar cases within their regional system. The problem is that such an approach has led to great difficulty in developing a Convention that will work on a global basis. In particular, the resulting text leads to many problems for the United States, which has a jurisdictional system based on constitutional limitations that result in a different focus than the rules of the civil law-oriented Brussels system.[13]

This heavy influence of the EU states resulted in a general focus on distinctions between the Brussels Convention system[14] and the approach to personal

---

[11] See Brand (n 5 above).

[12] *Preliminary draft Convention on jurisdiction and the effects of judgments in civil and commercial matters*, Adopted provisionally by the Special Commission, Hague Conference on Private International Law, Special Commission on International Jurisdiction and the Effects of Foreign Judgments in Civil and Commercial Matters, Working Document No 241 (18 June 1999).

[13] See, eg, R A Brand, 'Due Process as a Limitation on Jurisdiction in US Courts and a Limitation on the United States at the Hague Conference on Private International Law' (1999) 60 U Pittsburgh L Rev 661.

[14] The Brussels Convention is the most successful example of a regional approach to regulation of jurisdiction and enforcement of judgments: EC Convention on Jurisdiction and Enforcement of Judgments in Civil and Commercial matters, at Brussels, 27 September 1968, [1998] OJ C 27/1 (consolidated and updated version of the 1968 Convention and the Protocol of 1971, following the 1996 accession of the Republic of Austria, the Republic of Finland and

jurisdiction in the United States. While it can be an over-simplification, the basic difference between the US and European systems of jurisdiction is that the due process-oriented US approach results in a principal focus on the relationship between the forum state and the defendant.[15] *International Shoe*,[16] *World-Wide Volkswagen*,[17] *Asahi*,[18] and related decisions of the US Supreme Court require an analysis of the activity of the defendant within the forum state in order to determine whether the court has 'jurisdiction over the defendant'.[19] The European approach, on the other hand, focuses on the cause of action and its relation to the forum state. Thus, if a tort is committed in or has effects in the forum state, jurisdiction will exist in that state.[20] Similarly, if a contract is to be 'performed' in the forum state, jurisdiction will exist in that state.[21] A 'jurisdiction over the claim' approach focusing on the court/claim nexus is central to the Brussels I Regulation approach. US 'specific jurisdiction' takes account of both the court/defendant nexus and the court/claim nexus, by requiring that the cause of action 'arise out of' the activity of the defendant in the forum state.[22] Thus, it brings in the court/claim connection that is important in the

---

the Kingdom of Sweden) [hereinafter 'Brussels Convention']. On 1 May 1999, the Amsterdam Treaty became effective for the European Union Member States, and competence for coordination of internal rules on jurisdiction and recognition of judgments now lies with the Community institutions. The Council Regulation replacing the Brussels Convention was finalized on 22 December 2000, and became effective on March 1, 2002. Council Regulation (EC) No 44/2001 of 22 December 2000 on jurisdiction and the recognition and enforcement of judgments in civil and commercial matters, [2001] OJ L 12 [hereinafter 'Brussels I Regulation'].

[15] While Art 2 of the Brussels Convention and Brussels I Regulation provides that a person may always be sued in the courts of that person's state of domicile, the difficult issues arise not in this element of general jurisdiction, which exists also in the United States, but in the 'special' jurisdiction rules that follow, most all of which are based on a court-claim relationship rather than a court-defendant relationship. See Brand, *Jurisdictional Common Ground* (n 4 above).

[16] *International Shoe Co v Washington*, 326 US 310 (1945).

[17] *World-Wide Volkswagen Corp v Woodson*, 444 US 286 (1980).

[18] *Asahi Metal Industry Co v Superior Court*, 480 US 102 (1987).

[19] For a more detailed discussion of the application of the US Due Process Clauses to personal jurisdiction, see Brand (n 13 above) 664–689.

[20] Brussels I Regulation Art 5(3) (n 14 above).

[21] ibid, Art 5(1).

[22] The distinction between general and specific jurisdiction was first suggested in A T von Mehren and D T Trautman, 'Jurisdiction to Adjudicate: A Suggested Analysis' (1966) 79 Harvard L Rev 1121, 1144–1164. It was adopted by the US Supreme Court in *Helicopteros Nacionales de Colombia, SA v Hall*, 466 US 408 (1984). In *Helicopteros* the Texas long-arm statute at issue was specifically written to bring within the jurisdiction of its courts those foreign corporations 'doing business' in Texas. ibid, 413 n 7. (The statute was Texas Rev Civ Stat Ann, art 2031b (Vernon 1964 and Supp 1982–1983)). On specific jurisdiction, Justice Blackmun's opinion noted the following implications of the minimum contacts test of *International Shoe*: 'When a controversy is related to or "arises out of" a defendant's contacts with the forum, the

Brussels I Regulation approach and provides common ground on which to build. The problems are the level of difference at the extremes and the degree of willingness to accept the existence of those extremes outside the rules of the Convention (ie, within the area of permitted jurisdictional bases). This is fundamental to the question of how to proceed at the end of 2001. To the extent a more modest convention could benefit litigants from all nations involved in the negotiations, it would move the law beyond the status quo in areas where that is possible, while leaving the difficult areas for future evolution as legal developments permit.

The success of the New York Arbitration Convention has demonstrated the value of a very simple convention on choice of forum and enforcement of resulting decisions.[23] The lack of a similar Convention covering litigation creates an imbalance in favor of arbitration clauses in international commercial contracts, and at the same time demonstrates the value of a jurisdiction and judgments Convention that would go no further than recognizing choice of court clauses in business-to-business contracts, and providing for the recognition and enforcement of resulting judgments. Thus, it is not difficult to explain the rationale for a basic jurisdiction and judgments Convention. It may also be possible to imagine other areas in which basic agreement could be reached on additional jurisdictional bases without getting into more difficult jurisdictional terrain. For purposes of this chapter it is sufficient, however, to focus on the idea of a choice-of-court-plus-recognition Convention as the foundation for a more modest goal at the Hague Conference. Such a Convention has evi-

---

Court has said that a "relationship among the defendant, the forum, and the litigation" is the essential foundation of *in personam* jurisdiction.' 466 US at 414. Thus, specific jurisdiction requires that the cause of action in litigation 'arise out of,' and thus be directly related to, the activities of the defendant within the forum state. ibid, 415. The alternative is general jurisdiction: 'Even when the cause of action does not arise out of or relate to the foreign corporation's activities in the forum State, due process is not offended by a State's subjecting the corporation to its *in personam* jurisdiction when there are sufficient contacts between the State and the foreign corporation.' ibid, 414. Thus, so long as the contacts are 'continuous and systematic,' they may support jurisdiction even though the cause of action does not 'arise out of' those contacts. ibid, 414–415 (discussing *Perkins v Benguet Consolidated Mining Co*, 342 US 437 (1952), and *Keeton v Hustler Magazine, Inc*, 465 US 770, 779–780 (1984)). The *Helicopteros* Court found the cause of action at issue not to have arisen out of the contacts with Texas, thereby avoiding a discussion of specific jurisdiction. It then ruled that general jurisdiction did not exist under the Due Process Clause. 466 US at 418–419.

23 The United Nations Convention on the Recognition and Enforcement of Foreign Arbitral Awards, done at New York, entered into force 7 June 1959 (hereinafter 'New York Convention'). The text of the Convention, and information on its status, are available on the UNCITRAL website at http://www.uncitral.org/en-index.htm (visited 17 December 2001).

dent value, and avoids the problems of a comprehensive double Convention for the world. The following discussion of US law provides additional reasons for locking in the progress such a Convention would represent.

C. Choice of Court and *Forum Non Conveniens* in US Courts

The development of United States law on forum selection during the twentieth century witnessed concurrent evolution of two doctrines that do not necessarily bring consistent results, and which can bring to bear apparently inconsistent judicial policies. These doctrines also help explain the value of a global Convention favouring contractual choice of court clauses and subsequent recognition of the resulting judgments. Since the *Bremen* case in 1972,[24] US courts have tended to honour forum selection clauses in freely-negotiated contracts. With the Supreme Court's 1991 decision in *Carnival Cruise Lines*,[25] respect for choice of court clauses became, in the view of some commentators,[26] almost unquestioning in allowing the imposition of forum selection on weaker parties to a contractual relationship. At the same time, the development of the doctrine of *forum non conveniens* has allowed courts to decline to exercise jurisdiction even when it is otherwise available and venue is appropriate.

These doctrines come together when a motion is brought to stay or dismiss an action on grounds of *forum non conveniens* and there exists a choice of court clause in a contract between the parties. When the choice of court clause derogates from the forum court, that clause may be a factor weighing in favour of dismissing on grounds of *forum non conveniens* so that the case is tried in the chosen court. When that clause involves prorogation in favour of the forum court, however, its enforcement may run counter to an argument in favour of litigation in another court on the grounds of *forum non conveniens*. In this latter category of cases, respect for the chosen forum may come into conflict with the application of the doctrine of *forum non conveniens* in a manner that allows

---

[24] *M/S Bremen and Unterweser Reederei, GmbH v Zapata Off-Shore Co*, 407 US 1 (1972).

[25] *Carnival Cruise Lines, Inc v Shute* 499 US 585 (1991).

[26] See, eg, P J Borchers, 'Forum Selection Agreements in the Federal Courts After Carnival Cruise: A Proposal for Congressional Reform' (1992) 67 Wash L Rev 55; W W Heiser, 'Forum Selection Clauses in State Courts: Limitations on Enforcement After *Stewart* and *Carnival Cruise*' (1993) 45 Fla L Rev 361; J A Liesemer, 'Carnival's Got the Fun . . . and the Forum: A New Look at Choice-of-Forum Clauses and the Unconscionability Doctrine after *Carnival Cruise Lines, Inc v Shute*' (1992) 53 U Pittsburgh L Rev 1025.

courts to produce results that can be difficult to reconcile, particularly when viewed from abroad.

(1) Choice of Court in US Law

As in most countries, courts in the United States generally respect party autonomy in private commercial contracts and will uphold reasonable choice of forum clauses. This has not always been so evident in US law. Prior to 1972, US courts were reluctant to enforce clauses that would oust them of jurisdiction.[27] This changed when the Supreme Court ruled clearly in favour of upholding business-to-business choice of court clauses in a freely negotiated contract in *Bremen v Zapata Off-Shore Co.*[28] A German firm had contracted to tow an American company's oil-drilling rig from Louisiana to a point in the Adriatic Sea off the coast of Italy. When the rig was damaged in an accident in international waters, it was brought to Tampa, Florida, where the rig's owner brought an action in the Federal District Court against the owner of the tug, claiming both *in personam* jurisdiction over the owner and *in rem* jurisdiction over the tug.

Two contract clauses framed the analysis in the *Bremen* case. The first provided that the owner of the rig waived any right to hold the towing company liable for damage to the rig while at sea, even if such damage resulted from the negligence of the towing company or its employees.[29] Under the law at the time,

---

[27] See, eg, *Carbon Black Export, Inc v The Monrose*, 254 F 2d 297, 300301 (5th Cir, 1958), *cert dismissed*, 359 US 180 (1959) (stating that 'agreements in advance of controversy whose object is to oust the jurisdiction of the courts are contrary to public policy and will not be enforced.'). It has been said that this position rested on the rationale that '(1) the parties cannot by agreement in the contract alter the jurisdiction of the courts, and (2) such contractual stipulations are violative of public policy.' V Nanda, *The Law of Transnational Business Transactions* (1986), s 8.02[1][a]. Some commentators consider significant the distinction between conferring and ousting jurisdiction ('prorogation' versus 'derogation' in civil law terms). However, it has also been suggested that '[t]he real issue . . . is not whether the parties can by agreement 'confer' or 'oust' jurisdiction, but whether the selected or ousted court will exercise its own jurisdiction in such a way as to give effect to the intention of the parties'. G Delaume, *Transnational Contracts* (1986) s 6.01. cf *Bremen v Zapata Off-Shore Co*, 407 US 1, 12 (1972) ('No one seriously contends in this case that the forum-selection clause 'ousted' the District Court of jurisdiction over [the plaintiff's] action. The threshold question is whether that court should have exercised its jurisdiction to do more than give effect to the legitimate expectations of the parties, manifested in their freely negotiated agreement, by specifically enforcing the forum clause').

[28] *M/S Bremen and Unterweser Reederei, GmbH v Zapata Off-Shore Co*, 407 US 1 (1972). For a discussion of the pre-*Bremen* case law which often held choice of forum provisions void as against public policy, see M Gruson, 'Forum-Selection Clauses in International and Interstate Commercial Agreements' (1982) U Illinois L Rev 133, 138–47.

[29] 407 US 3 n 2.

this clause was likely to be enforced by a court in England,[30] but would be considered void as against public policy in the United States.[31] The second important clause provided that '[a]ny dispute arising must be treated before the London Court of Justice'. If this clause were upheld, requiring the US court to decline jurisdiction, then the waiver of liability clause would determine the outcome of the case.

The Supreme Court gave effect to the choice of court clause, stating that, '[t]he expansion of American business and industry will hardly be encouraged if, notwithstanding solemn contracts, we insist on a parochial concept that all disputes must be resolved under our laws and in our courts'.[32] Confirming that parties to an international transaction could select a neutral forum for the settlement of their disputes,[33] the Court stated that forum selection clauses 'are *prima facie* valid and should be enforced unless enforcement is shown by the resisting party to be unreasonable under the circumstances'.[34]

While the *Bremen* was a case in admiralty, both lower federal courts[35] and state courts[36] extended its rationale to non-admiralty cases. Deference to the parties' choice of forum was qualified only minimally when Chief Justice Burger noted that the agreement so enforced was 'unaffected by fraud, undue influence, or

---

[30] 407 US 8 n 8.

[31] 407 US 9 n 10. See, eg, *Dixilyn Drilling Corp v Crescent Towing & Salvage Co*, 372 US 697 (1963); *Bisso v Inland Waterways Corp*, 349 US 85 (1955).

[32] 407 US at 9.

[33] 407 US at 13. When the same dispute was litigated concurrently in the English courts, the English Court of Appeal sustained jurisdiction there under the choice of forum clause despite the fact that the transaction had no connection with England, noting that, 'in the absence of strong reason to the contrary', the discretion of the English court 'will be exercised in favour of holding parties to their bargain'. *Unterweser Reederi GmbH v Zapata Off-Shore Co* [1968] 2 Lloyd's Rep 158, 163, CA.

[34] 407 US 10.

[35] See, eg, *Coastal Steel Corp v Tilgham Wheelabrator Ltd*, 709 F 2d 190 (3rd Cir), *cert denied*, 464 US 938, 104 S Ct 349 (1983); *Crown Beverage Co v Cerveceria Moctezuma, SA*, 663 F 2d 886, 888 (9th Cir, 1981); *Staco Energy Prod Co v Driver-Haris Co*, 509 F Supp 1226, 1227 (SD Ohio 1981) (dictum); *Republic Int'l Corp v Amco Eng'rs, Inc*, 516 F 2d 161, 168 (9th Cir, 1975); *Shepard Niles Crane & Hoist Corp v Fiat, SpA*, 84 FRD 299, 305 (WDNY 1979) (dictum); *Hoes of Am, Inc v Hoes*, 493 F Supp 1205, 1209 (CD Ill, 1979); *Cruise v Castleton, Inc*, 449 F Supp 564 (SDNY, 1978); *Gaskin v Stumm Handel GmbH*, 390 F Supp 361 (SDNY, 1975).

[36] See, eg, *Abadou v Trad*, 624 P 2d 287 (Alaska 1981); *Volkswagenwerk, AG v Klippan, GmbH*, 611 P 2d 498, *cert denied*, 449 US 974 (1980); *Societe Jean Nicolas et Fils, JB v Mousseux*, 123 Ariz 59, 597 P 2d 541 (1979); *Smith, Valentino & Smith, Inc v Superior Court*, 17 Cal 3d 491, 551 P 2d 1206, 131 Cal Rptr 374 (1976); *Elia Corp v Paul N Howard Co*, 391 A 2d 214 (Del Super Ct 1978); *Green v Clinic Mawsters, Inc*, 272 NW 2d 813 (SD 1978); *Hi Fashion Wigs Profit Sharing Trust v Hamilton Inv Trust*, 579 SW 2d 300 (Tex Civ App 1979).

overweening bargaining power'.[37] Subsequent courts[38] and the Restatement[39] have interpreted *Bremen* to provide a presumption of validity for a choice of forum clause, with the party contesting the provision carrying the burden of proving grounds for an exception.

The exceptions to enforceable choice of forum provisions can be categorized as those cases (1) where enforcement of the provision would result in substantial inconvenience, or denial of an effective remedy,[40] (2) where there has been fraud, overreaching, or unconscionable conduct in contract relations,[41] or

---

[37] 407 US 12.

[38] See, eg, *Santamauro v Taito do Brasil Industria E Comercia*, 587 F Supp 1312, 1314 (ED La 1984) ('The burden is on the party resisting enforcement of the clause to prove that the choice was unreasonable, unfair, or unjust, or to show that the clause is invalid by reason of fraud or overreaching or that enforcement would contravene a strong public policy of this forum'.); *City of New York v Pullman, Inc*, 477 F Supp 438, 441 n 10 (SDNY 1979), *aff'd*, 662 F 2d 919 (2nd Cir, 1981), *reh'g denied*, 28 September 1981, *cert denied*, 454 US 1038, 102 S Ct 1038 (1982) ('Agreements entered into by knowledgeable parties in an arm's-length transaction that contain a forum selection provision are enforceable absent a showing of fraud, overreaching, unreasonableness or unfairness'.).

[39] *Restatement (Second) of the Conflict of Laws* (1971) s 80.

[40] 407 US 18. However,

> [W]here it can be said with reasonable assurance that at the time they entered the contract, the parties to a freely negotiated private international commercial agreement contemplated the claimed inconvenience, it is difficult to see why any such claim of inconvenience should be heard to render the forum clause unenforceable.

ibid, 16. This is basically the incorporation of the doctrine of *forum non conveniens*. However, it is important to note that courts have found that the existence of a valid forum selection clause does not prevent a transfer for *forum non conveniens* purposes under 28 USC s 1404(a):

> Congress set down in s 1404(a) the factors it thought should be decisive on a motion for transfer. Only one of these—the convenience of the parties—is properly within the power of the parties themselves to affect by a forum-selection clause. The other factors— the convenience of witnesses and the interest of justice—are third party or public interests that must be weighed by the district court; they cannot be automatically outweighed by the existence of a purely private agreement between the parties. Such an agreement does not obviate the need for an analysis of the factors set forth in s 1404(a) and does not necessarily preclude the granting of the motion to transfer.

Plum Tree, Inc v Stockment, 488 F 2d 754, 75758 (3rd Cir, 1973). When New York recodified its doctrine of *forum non conveniens* in 1984, it specifically provided that its courts cannot stay or dismiss an action on *forum non conveniens* grounds where the contract contains both a New York choice of forum clause and a New York choice of law clause and the transaction involved exceeds $1,000,000. NYCPLR s 327 (McKinney's 2001) (1984 NY Laws, Ch 421, NY Gen Oblig Law ss 5–1401 and 5–1402). This provision assures that New York courts will accept jurisdiction in accordance with the parties' choice in large transnational contracts.

[41] 407 US 15. The Supreme Court further developed the fraud exception in *Scherk v Alberto-Culver Co*, 417 US 506 (1974), when it stated:

(3) where enforcement would result in a violation of public policy or the transaction is otherwise unfair, unjust or unreasonable.[42] For the most part, these exceptions are relatively rare.[43]

Those familiar with Article 17 of the Brussels Convention and Article 23 of the newer Brussels I Regulation in the European Union will find important comparisons with US case law on business-to-business choice of court issues.[44] That provision in each instrument provides that where parties have agreed 'that a court or the courts of a Member State are to have jurisdiction to settle any disputes which have arisen in connection with a particular legal relationship, that court or those courts shall have jurisdiction'.[45] The same Article goes on to provide that '[s]uch jurisdiction shall be exclusive unless the parties have agreed otherwise'.[46]

This qualification does not mean that any time a dispute arising out of a transaction is based upon an allegation of fraud . . . the clause is unenforceable. Rather, it means that [a] . . . forum-selection clause in a contract is not enforceable if the *inclusion of that clause in the contract* was the product of fraud or coercion.

ibid, 519 n 14 (emphasis in original).

[42] 407 US at 15. The Court rejected Zapata's argument that the exculpatory clause contained in the agreement violated US public policy. ibid, 15–16.

[43] Commentators have divided these exceptions in different ways. See, eg, A E Covey and M S Morris, 'The Enforceability of Agreements Providing for Forum and Choice of Law Selection' (1984) 61 Denver LJ 837, 842 ('The primary limitations . . . are fraud, public policy, adhesion, statutory restrictions and inconvenience of the contractual forum.'); M Gruson, 'Forum-Selection Clauses in International and Interstate Commercial Agreements' (1982) U Illinois L Rev 133, 16385 (dividing the exceptions into the categories of (1) fraud, (2) bargaining relationship between the parties, (3) nature of the selected forum, (4) public policy of the forum, (5) statutory restrictions on forum-selection clauses, (6) inconvenience of the contractual forum and (7) other instances of unreasonableness). See also The Model Choice of Forum Act, s 3, which lists the following exceptions to enforcement of choice of forum clauses:

(1) the court is required by statute to entertain the action;
(2) the plaintiff cannot secure effective relief in the other state, for reasons other than delay in bringing the action;
(3) the other state would be a substantially less convenient place for the trial of the action than this state;
(4) the agreement as to the place of the action was obtained by misrepresentation, duress, the abuse of economic power, or other unconscionable means; or
(5) it would for some other reason be unfair or unreasonable to enforce the agreement.

W L M Reese, 'The Model Choice of Forum Act' (1969) AJCL 17, 292, 294.
[44] Brussels Convention and Brussels I Regulation (n 14 above).
[45] Brussels I Regulation Art 23 (above n 14).
[46] ibid.

There exist at least two important differences between the Brussels scheme for choice of court clauses and that existing under the common law in the United States. First, unlike the Brussels rule, US courts have not been willing to consider the allocation of authority to the chosen court to be either absolute[47] or exclusive.[48] Thus, the existence of a choice of court clause does not guarantee that the dispute may be resolved only in that forum, unless the clause expressly creates such exclusivity. In this respect, European courts go further in their respect for the chosen court. The other difference works the other way. US courts will uphold choice of court clauses in consumer contracts where European courts will not do so. The Brussels rule honours a choice of court clause in a consumer contract only if the agreement (1) is entered into after the dispute has arisen, (2) allows the consumer to bring proceedings in courts other than those otherwise available, or (3) provides for jurisdiction in the courts of the state that is the habitual residence of both the consumer and the other party.[49]

US law provides no such limitations on the enforcement of choice of court clauses for consumer contracts. In *Carnival Cruise Lines Inc v Shute*,[50] the Supreme Court upheld enforcement of a clause requiring disputes to be brought in the state courts of Florida. A Washington state consumer purchased a cruise ticket from a local travel agent for a trip off the coast of Mexico. The choice of court clause in fine print was on a cruise ticket that was not received until after the consumer had arranged and paid for the cruise. Justice Blackmun relied in part on an economic rationale, stating that 'passengers who purchase tickets containing a forum clause like that at issue in this case benefit in the form of reduced fares reflecting the savings that the cruise line enjoys by limiting the fora in which it may be sued'.[51] Thus, the Supreme Court made

---

[47] See, eg, *Sudduth v Occidental Peruana, Inc*, 70 F Supp 2d 691 (ED Tex, 1999) (denying defendant's motion to dismiss on *forum non conveniens* grounds in favour of the prorogated court, holding that the mandatory choice of court clause was invalid under *Bremen*); *Dentsply International, Inc v Benton*, 965 F Supp 574 (MD Pa, 1997) (refusing to enforce the mandatory choice of court clause in an employer contract holding that it was the result of unequal bargaining power).

[48] See, eg, *Steve Weiss & Co, Inc v INALCO*, 1999 US Dist LEXIS 8811 (SDNY) (stating that 'where parties only specify in a contract clause where jurisdiction is proper' the clause generally will not be enforced unless other language clearly identifies 'the parties intent to make jurisdiction exclusive'); *Hull 753 Corp v Flugzeugwerke*, 58 F Supp 2d 925 (ND Ill, 1999) (holding that a clause granting jurisdiction to German courts was not exclusive absent clear language that only German courts shall have jurisdiction).

[49] Brussels I Regulation Art 17 (above n 14).

[50] 499 US 585 (1991).

[51] ibid, 594.

clear the wide breadth of the *Bremen* policy favouring enforcement of choice of court clauses, encompassing even consumer contracts that contain no element of true negotiation.

(2) Forum Non Conveniens

The source of the doctrine of *forum non conveniens* is generally agreed to be Scottish jurisprudence, but it has a rich history in the US common law.[52] The concept was evident as early as 1801 in the United States in *Willendson v Forsoket*,[53] where a federal district court in Pennsylvania declined to exercise jurisdiction over a Danish sea captain sued for back wages by a Danish seaman, stating that '[i]f any differences should hereafter arise, it must be settled by a Danish tribunal'.[54] This dismissal was based on notions of justice and 'reciprocal policy',[55] looking very much like the modern approach to *forum non conveniens*. Other nineteenth and early twentieth century state and federal cases, while acknowledging the existence of jurisdiction, refused to decide cases between foreign parties, arising on foreign soil, and/or requiring the application of foreign law.[56]

---

[52] 'The earliest appearance of the words and the doctrine was in the late 1800s in a series of Scottish cases which set forth the established Scottish principle of permitting trial courts to refrain from hearing disputes when the purpose of justice would be better served by trial in another forum'. W Freedman, *Foreign Plaintiffs in Products Liability Actions: The Defense of Forum Non Conveniens* (1988). In Scotland, the origination of the concept traces to *MacMaster v MacMaster* (Judgment of 7 June 1833, Sess, Scot 11 Sess Cas, First Series 685), where it was held that the presence of estate assets in the forum was not an appropriate basis for suit against an absent foreign executor of a will. This was followed by *M'Morine v Cowie* (1845) Judgment of 16 January , Sess, Scot, & D Sess, Cas 270, in which it was held that the chosen forum was not 'proper' or 'appropriate.' For a Scottish description of the development in Scotland, see A E Anton, *Private International Law* (1st edn, 1967), 148–154.

[53] 29 Fed Cas 1283 (DC Pa 1801) (No 17,682).

[54] ibid, 1284.

[55] ibid.

[56] See, eg, *Canada Malting Co v Paterson Steamships, Ltd*, 285 US 413 (1932) (recognizing that discretion to decline otherwise valid jurisdiction was not exclusive to admiralty courts); *Slater v Mexican National RR Co*, 194 US 120 (1904) (affirming the lower court's decision to dismiss the case after reasoning that the events leading to the action occurred in Mexico and Mexican law would govern the action, even though the plaintiffs were United States citizens residing in Texas); *Collard v Beach*, 87 NYS 884 (1904) (stating 'the calendars of this state are congested, and it being difficult to administer speedy justice to litigants who are obliged to submit their controversies to our courts and have no other forum, it is eminently proper that we should refuse jurisdiction over actions for tort that properly belong in another forum'.); *The Infanti*, 13 F Cas 37 (SDNY 1848) (commenting that the court often 'discountenanced actions by foreign seamen against foreign vessels not terminating their voyages at this port, as being calculated to embarrass commercial transactions and relations between this country and others in friendly re-

Like the law on choice of court, US law on *forum non conveniens* now is anchored in a set of Supreme Court decisions that defines the parameters of the doctrine as it is applied in all US courts.[57] The 1947 case of *Gulf Oil v*

---

lations with it'.); *Johnson v Dalton*, 1 Cow 543, 548 (NY 1823) (stating that 'our courts may take cognizance of torts committed on the high seas on board a foreign vessel, where both parties are foreigners; but on principles of comity, as well as to prevent the frequent and serious injuries that would result, they have exercised sound discretion'.); *Gardner v Thomas*, 14 Johns 134, 137 (NY 1817) (stating 'there may be cases where the refusal to take cognizance of causes may be justified by the manifest public inconvenience and injury which it would create to the community of nations, and holding that this, where both parties were British and the suit arose out of a tort committed on a British vessel at sea, was such a case for dismissal); *Mason v Ship Blaireau*, 2 Cranch 240, 264 (US 1804) (deciding that a case filed in federal district court in Maryland should be heard, but recognizing the courts prerogative to weigh 'public convenience' factors to decide whether to maintain jurisdiction where the parties where both foreign.); *Willendson v Forsokett*, 29 F Cas 1283 (D Pa 1801) (noting that 'it has been my general rule not to take cognizance of disputes between the masters and crews of foreign ships'.).

[57]   The Supreme Court has not provided a clear answer to the question of whether, under *Erie R Co v Tompkins*, 304 US 64 (1938), the *forum non conveniens* issue is a matter of state or federal law. See, eg, *Piper v Reyno*, 454 US 235, 248 n 13 (1981):

> In previous *forum non conveniens* decisions, the Court has left unresolved the question whether under *Erie R Co v Tompkins*, 304 US 64, 58 S Ct 817, 82 L Ed 1188 (1938), state or federal law of *forum non conveniens* applies in a diversity case. *Gilbert*, 330 US 501, 67 S Ct 843; *Koster*, 330 US 529, 67 S Ct 834; *Williams v Green Bay & Western R Co* (above), 326 US549 (1946), 558–559, 66 S Ct 288–289. The Court did not decide this issue because the same result would have been reached in each case under federal or state law. The lower courts in these cases reached the same conclusion: Pennsylvania and California law on *forum non conveniens* dismissals are virtually identical to federal law. See 630 F 2d at 158. Thus, here also, we need not resolve the *Erie* question.

While the doctrine of *forum non conveniens* developed first in state courts, federal courts generally have followed the rule that, because the doctrine is essentially a procedural venue rule, they are permitted under *Erie R Co v Tompkins*, 304 US 64 (1938) to follow the federal doctrine in diversity cases. Justice Scalia seems to have affirmed that rule in *American Dredging Co v Miller*, 510 US 443 (1998), where he referred to the doctrine as a federal procedural rule, stating that 'federal courts will continue to invoke jurisdiction in appropriate cases, whether or not the state in which they sit chooses to burden its judiciary with litigation better handled elsewhere'. ibid, 454. At the same time, however, the decision in *American Dredging* held that a state statute removing admiralty cases from a *forum non conveniens* analysis was valid and effective. ibid. 453. In federal question cases, of course, the *Erie* analysis is not a problem because both the substantive and procedural law to be applied are federal.

    Although many states have adopted the federal doctrine since *Gilbert*, other states have followed their own paths. For good discussions on state examples of *forum non conveniens*, see Karolyn King, 'Open Borders—Closed Courts: The Impact of *Stangvik v Shiley, Inc*' (1994) 28 USFL Rev 1113 and JW Joyce, 'Forum Non Conveniens in Louisiana' (1999) 60 Louisiana L Rev 293. For example, the Texas Supreme Court abolished its state doctrine on grounds that a state statute precluded such discretionary dismissals. *Dow Chemical Co v Castro-Alfaro*, 786 SW 2d 674 (Tex 1990). See also King (above 1124–1126). The Texas legislature responded by enacting legislation permitting state courts to apply the doctrine where foreign plaintiffs sue

Gilbert[58] was the first Supreme Court decision directly to address the question of 'whether the United States District Court has inherent power to dismiss a suit pursuant to the doctrine of *forum non conveniens*'.[59] A Virginia resident brought a suit in a federal district court in New York against a Pennsylvania corporation that was doing business in Virginia, alleging negligence resulting in an explosion and fire that destroyed the plaintiff's warehouse in Virginia. The district court dismissed the case under the doctrine of *forum non conveniens* on the grounds that the case would be better tried in Virginia. The Second Circuit Court of Appeals reversed, but the Supreme Court held that the doctrine did apply. Justice Jackson stated that, in US courts, 'the proposition that a court having jurisdiction must exercise it, is not universally true'.[60] He also found the doctrine of *forum non conveniens* to apply specifically when jurisdiction does exist, noting that it 'can never apply if there is absence of jurisdiction or mistake of venue'.[61]

Gilbert makes clear that *forum non conveniens* is a doctrine that gives the court substantial discretion when more than one forum is available for the trial of an action:

> In all cases in which the doctrine of *forum non conveniens* comes into play, it presupposes at least two forums in which the defendant is amenable to process; the doctrine furnishes criteria for choice between them.

> The principle of *forum non conveniens* is simply that a court may resist imposition upon its jurisdiction even when jurisdiction is authorized by the letter of a general venue statute . . .

> . . .

United States defendants for personal injuries suffered abroad resulting from violations of Texas or United States law. Texas Civ Prac & Rem Code Ann s 71.051(a) (West Supp 1994). This exception is more in line with the modern trend in federal courts to deter forum shopping by foreign plaintiffs in already crowded dockets. Another interesting example is Washington State, where the state Supreme Court has rejected the *Piper* premise that a foreign plaintiff's choice of forum is presumptively inconvenient. *Myers v Boeing Co*, 794 P 2d 1272 (Wash 1990). See also King (above 1127–1128). New York decisions have been read to eliminate the first prong of the federal analysis—proof of an alternative, appropriate forum—which is not considered to be an essential part of the test. See Joyce (above 310).

[58] 330 US 501 (1947).
[59] ibid, 502.
[60] ibid, 504 (quoting from the decision of Justice Brandeis in *Canada Malting Co, Ltd v Paterson Steamships, Ltd*, 285 US 413, 422 (1932)).
[61] ibid.

Wisely, it has not been attempted to catalogue the circumstances which will jus-tify or require either grant or denial of remedy. The doctrine leaves much to the discretion of the court to which plaintiff resorts, and experience has not shown a judicial tendency to renounce one's own jurisdiction so strong as to result in many abuses.[62]

Such discretion is to be used judiciously, however, and 'unless the balance is strongly in favor of the defendant, the plaintiff's choice of forum should rarely be disturbed'.[63] In exercising its discretion, the trial court is to weigh both pri-vate interest and public interest factors:

An interest to be considered, and the one likely to be most pressed, is the private interest of the litigant. Important considerations are the relative ease of access to sources of proof; availability of compulsory process for attendance of unwilling, and the cost of obtaining attendance of willing, witnesses; possibility of view of premises, if view would be appropriate to the action; and all other practical prob-lems that make trial of a case easy, expeditious and inexpensive. There may also be questions as to the enforcibility of a judgment if one is obtained. The court will weigh relative advantages and obstacles to fair trial. It is often said that the plaintiff may not, by choice of an inconvenient forum, 'vex,' 'harass,' or 'oppress' the defendant by inflicting upon him expense or trouble not necessary to his own right to pursue his remedy. But unless the balance is strongly in favor of the defendant, the plaintiff's choice of forum should rarely be disturbed.

Factors of public interest also have place in applying the doctrine. Administrative difficulties follow for courts when litigation is piled up in con-gested centers instead of being handled at its origin. Jury duty is a burden that ought not to be imposed upon the people of a community which has no relation to the litigation. In cases which touch the affairs of many persons, there is reason for holding the trial in their view and reach rather than in remote parts of the country where they can learn of it by report only. There is a local interest in hav-ing localized controversies decided at home. There is an appropriateness, too, in having the trial of a diversity case in a forum that is at home with the state law that must govern the case, rather than having a court in some other forum un-tangle problems in conflict of laws, and in law foreign to itself.[64]

In his dissent, Justice Black expressed favour for a court exercising jurisdiction if it exists, and for the proposition that any authority to do otherwise should emanate from the legislature. He characterized the majority's holding as a clear balancing of conveniences:

---

[62] ibid, 507, 508.
[63] ibid, 508.
[64] ibid, 508–509 (footnote omitted).

The Court does not suggest that the federal district court in New York lacks jurisdiction under this statute or that the venue was improper in this case. But it holds that a district court may abdicate its jurisdiction when a defendant shows to the satisfaction of a district court that it would be more convenient and less vexatious for the defendant if the trial were held in another jurisdiction.[65]

Thus, the development of the doctrine in the lower courts became fixed in the Supreme Court.

In *Koster v Lumbermens Mutual Co*,[66] decided the same day as *Gilbert*, the Court addressed questions about the application of the *forum non conveniens* doctrine regarding the relationship between the parties and the forum. This was a derivative suit brought by a policy holder of a mutual insurance company, alleging breach of fiduciary duties. The plaintiff filed suit in his home forum, the Eastern District of New York, against defendants from Illinois. Justice Jackson, again writing for the majority, recorded the deference courts should provide to the plaintiff's choice of forum:

> Where there are only two parties to a dispute, there is good reason why it should be tried in the plaintiff's home forum if that has been his choice. He should not be deprived of the presumed advantages of his home jurisdiction except upon a clear showing of facts which either (1) establish such oppressiveness and vexation to a defendant as to be out of all proportion to plaintiff's convenience, which may be shown to be slight or nonexistent, or (2) make trial in the chosen forum inappropriate because of considerations affecting the court's own administrative and legal problems.[67]

Despite this deference to the plaintiff's choice, the Court nonetheless held dismissal on *forum non conveniens* grounds to be appropriate since in a derivative suit the individual plaintiff acts on behalf of all similarly situated persons, and in a matter involving internal affairs of a corporation, the conveniences often weigh in favor of the forum in which the corporation is located. While such suits are not required to be resolved in the home forum of the corporation, 'the ultimate inquiry is where trial will best serve the convenience of the parties and the ends of justice',[68] and 'plaintiff was utterly silent as to any reason of convenience to himself or to witnesses and as to any advantage to him in expense, speed of trial, or adequacy of remedy if the case were tried in New York'.[69]

---

[65] 330 US 501 (1947), 512–513 (Black, J, dissenting) (citations omitted).
[66] 330 US 518 (1947).
[67] ibid, 524.
[68] ibid, 527.
[69] ibid, 531.

In 1948, Congress responded to the *Gilbert* and *Koster* decisions by enacting a venue provision that transformed the way in which federal courts handle problems of forum shopping and docket congestion in domestic cases. Section 1404(a) of Title 28 of the US Code provides that, '[f]or the convenience of parties and witnesses, in the interest of justice, a district court may transfer any civil action to any other district or division where it might have been brought'.[70] The result of this provision is that diversity cases involving citizens of the United States are now dealt with as venue-transfer cases, rather than under the doctrine of *forum non conveniens.*[71]

Two developments regarding jurisdiction have also served to limit the application of the doctrine. The refinement of the 'minimum contacts' due process analysis to limit the reach of long-arm statutes through cases such as *International Shoe, World-Wide Volkswagen,* and *Asahi,*[72] means that many cases in which arguments of inconvenient forum can be made are disposed of on jurisdictional grounds.[73] In addition, the impact of the Supreme Court's decision in *Shaffer v Heitner,*[74] has limited *in rem* jurisdiction over a non-resident defendant having scarce connections with a forum.

In 1981, the Supreme Court decided *Piper Aircraft Co v Reyno,*[75] further defining the modern doctrine of *forum non conveniens* in US courts. A wrongful death action was brought in a California state court by Scottish plaintiffs against defendants from Ohio and Pennsylvania, based on an airplane crash in Scotland. The action was removed to a federal district court, then transferred under section 1404(a) to Pennsylvania. The plaintiff admitted forum shopping in order to get more favourable laws regarding liability, capacity to sue, and

---

[70] 29 USC s 1404(a).

[71] See, eg, J Bies, 'Conditioning Forum Non Conveniens' (2000) 67 U Chicago L Rev 489, 499.

[72] See nn 16–18 above and accompanying text.

[73] See J Duval-Major, 'One-Way Ticket Home: The Federal Doctrine of Forum non conveniens and the International Plaintiff' (1992) 77 Cornell L Rev 650, 663 ('The doctrine of *forum non conveniens* has diminished in importance given the modern development of the "minimum contacts" test for personal jurisdiction. The increased reliance by courts on the 'minimum contacts' notion of personal jurisdiction, when taken in concert with modern applications of venue and subject matter jurisdiction, satisfies requirements of fairness and reasonableness embedded in the Due Process Clause of the Fifth Amendment. A proper personal jurisdiction inquiry should dispose of many cases in which the choice of forum is truly inconvenient'.).

[74] 433 US 186 (1977) (holding that jurisdiction over a non-resident defendant could not be based solely on statutory rule that intangible property of the defendant that is unrelated to the cause of action is located in the state).

[75] 454 US 235 (1981).

damages.[76] The district court granted a motion for dismissal based on *forum non conveniens*, and the Third Circuit reversed. In holding that the action of the district court was a proper application of the doctrine of *forum non conveniens*, the Supreme Court rejected the contention that substantial differences in substantive law should prevent such dismissal:

> The Court of Appeals erred in holding that plaintiffs may defeat a motion to dismiss on the ground of *forum non conveniens* merely by showing that the substantive law that would be applied in the alternative forum is less favorable to the plaintiffs than that of the present forum. The possibility of a change in substantive law should ordinarily not be given conclusive or even substantial weight in the *forum non conveniens* inquiry.[77]

Thus, 'dismissal on grounds of *forum non conveniens* may be granted even though the law applicable in the alternative forum is less favourable to the plaintiff's chance of recovery'.[78] This, however, does not prevent a difference in law from being a factor considered by the court. '[I]f the remedy provided by the alternative forum is so clearly inadequate or unsatisfactory that it is no remedy at all, the unfavourable change in law may be given substantial weight; the district court may conclude that dismissal would not be in the interests of justice'.[79]

Justice Marshall's opinion for the majority in *Piper* noted that the development of the section 1404(a) transfer rules were drafted 'in accordance with the doctrine of *forum non conveniens*', but that the district court's discretion to dismiss is in fact more substantial under the transfer statute than under the common law doctrine.[80] Thus, the relocation of a case within the federal system is more flexible than is dismissal for purposes of litigation outside the United States.

In refining the *forum non conveniens* analysis, the *Piper* decision makes clear that consideration begins with the determination that an adequate alternative forum exists.[81] If it does, then the court must apply the private interest and public interest analysis set out in *Gilbert*.[82] The *Piper* majority read *Koster* to require that the 'plaintiff's choice of forum is entitled to greater deference when

---

[76] 454 US 235 (1981), 239.
[77] ibid, 250.
[78] ibid, 250.
[79] ibid, 254.
[80] ibid, 253.
[81] ibid, 254 n 22.
[82] See above n 64 and accompanying text.

the plaintiff has chosen the home forum',[83] thus justifying more favourable treatment of a resident or citizen plaintiff than of a foreign plaintiff. This distinction, however, was not based on the nationality of the party so much as on the determination of convenience in applying the private factor test of *Gilbert*:

> When the home forum has been chosen, it is reasonable to assume that this choice is convenient. When the plaintiff is foreign, however, this assumption is much less reasonable. Because the central purpose of any *forum non conveniens* inquiry is to ensure that the trial is convenient, a foreign plaintiff's choice deserves less deference.[84]

---

[83] 454 US 256.

[84] ibid. The idea that lesser weight should be given to the forum choice of a non-resident first appeared in *Swift & Co Packers v Compania Colombiana del Caribe*, 339 US 684, 697 (1950), when the Court stated that the '[a]pplication of *forum non conveniens* principles to a suit by a United States citizen against a foreign respondent brings into force considerations very different from those in suits between foreigners'. Most recently, in *Iragorri v United Technologies*, 24th F 3d 65 (2nd Cir 2001), the Second Circuit Court of Appeals rendered an *en banc* decision in which it explained its rationale for the difference in treatment of domestic and foreign plaintiffs in the *forum non conveniens* analysis. In that opinion, the Court stated:

> Based on the Supreme Court's guidance, our understanding of how courts should address the degree of deference to be given to a plaintiff's choice of a US forum is essentially as follows: The more it appears that a domestic or foreign plaintiff's choice of forum has been dictated by reasons that the law recognizes as valid, the greater the deference that will be given to the plaintiff's forum choice. Stated differently, the greater the plaintiff's or the lawsuit's bona fide connection to the United States and to the forum of choice and the more it appears that considerations of convenience favor the conduct of the lawsuit in the United States, the more difficult it will be for the defendant to gain dismissal for forum non conveniens. Thus, factors that argue against *forum non conveniens* dismissal include the convenience of the plaintiff's residence in relation to the chosen forum, the availability of witnesses or evidence to the forum district, the defendant's amenability to suit in the forum district, the availability of appropriate legal assistance, and other reasons relating to convenience or expense. On the other hand, the more it appears that the plaintiff's choice of a US forum was motivated by forum-shopping reasons—such as attempts to win a tactical advantage resulting from local laws that favor the plaintiff's case, the habitual generosity of juries in the United States or in the forum district, the plaintiff's popularity or the defendant's unpopularity in the region, or the inconvenience and expense to the defendant resulting from litigation in that forum—the less deference the plaintiff's choice commands and, consequently, the easier it becomes for the defendant to succeed on a *forum non conveniens* motion by showing that convenience would be better served by litigating in another country's courts.

The Second Circuit had invited the US Attorney General to file an *amicus curiae* brief on this issue, including comments on 'how, if at all, the question presented is affected by treaty obligations of the United States, including any treaty obligations concerning reciprocal access to courts by nationals of other countries'. ibid, n 2. The Justice Department declined the request, but provided some comment in a letter in response to the request. ibid.

Some courts have applied a domestic plaintiff standard to foreign plaintiffs from countries

One of the problems defendants raised in the *Piper* case was the inability to im-
plead potential third-party defendants who would be available in a Scottish
court.[85] While this was not unfair, it was considered burdensome, and '[f]ind-
ing that trial in the plaintiff's chosen forum would be burdensome, however, is
sufficient to support dismissal on grounds of *forum non conveniens*'.[86]

The most recent pronouncement by the Supreme Court on the modern doctrine of *forum non conveniens* came in *American Dredging Co v Miller*.[87]
Writing for the majority, Justice Scalia stated that the doctrine 'is nothing more
or less than a supervening venue provision, permitting displacement of ordinary rules of venue when, in light of certain conditions, the trial court thinks
that jurisdiction ought to be declined'.[88] He emphasized that the doctrine has
developed in response to court administrative and private litigant problems
that often result from a plaintiff's misuse of venue. Thus, the doctrine serves to
discourage plaintiffs from forum shopping.[89] 'The discretionary nature of the
doctrine, combined with the multifariousness of the factors relevant to its application . . . make uniformity and predictability of outcome almost impossible'.[90] This lack of uniformity is accepted because the doctrine serves as a
procedural rule, and not as a substantive rule affecting the primary conduct of
litigants.[91]

The *Gilbert-Koster-Piper* factors remain the foundation of the *forum non con-*

---

that are party to a Treaty of Friendship, Navigation and Commerce (FCN Treaty) with the
United States, which consistently include a provision requiring non-discriminatory treatment of
nationals of the other state in the courts. See, eg, *Irish National Insurance Company, Ltd v Aer
Lingus Teoranta*, 739 F 2d 90 (2nd Cir, 1984) (giving the foreign plaintiff's choice of forum the
same weight as that of a domestic plaintiff because the United States had such a treaty with
Ireland); *Petroquimica de Venezuela, SA v M/T Trade Resolve*, 823 F Supp 143, 150 (SDNY 1993)
('because such a treaty (FCN) exists between the United States and Venezuela . . . no discount
may be imposed upon the initial choice of a New York forum solely because certain plaintiffs are
Venezuelan corporations.'); *Roman v Aviateca*, US Dist LEXIS 21789 (1996) (not giving plaintiff equal access rights to the United States court because an FCN Treaty between the United
States and Nicaragua had been abolished). Cf *Murray v British Broadcasting Corporation*, 81 F 3d
287 (2nd Cir 1996) (refusing to give a foreign plaintiff's choice in forum the same deference as
a domestic plaintiff's choice even though an international convention provided that any copyright action would be governed by the laws of the jurisdiction in which a plaintiff sought relief).

[85] ibid, 259.
[86] ibid.
[87] 510 US 443, 453 (1998).
[88] ibid.
[89] ibid, 450.
[90] ibid, 455.
[91] ibid.

veniens doctrine in US courts. Thus, the analysis begins by considering whether an adequate alternative forum exists.[92] If it does, then the court considers the private interest[93] and public interest factors set out in *Gilbert*.[94] A plaintiff's choice of a forum with more favourable law is not dispositive, and a foreign plaintiff's choice generally is given even less deference than that of a domestic plaintiff.[95] A court often will impose conditions on a defendant asserting a *forum non conveniens* defence in order to ensure that the foreign forum is in fact available.[96] Conditions may include submitting to service of process and jurisdiction in the alternative forum, waiving any statute of limitations defences, agreeing to be bound by any judgments rendered by the alternative forum, and compliance with special rules on the production of evidence and witnesses.[97]

Two additional considerations that may come into play in a *forum non conveniens* analysis are the existence of related proceedings abroad and forum selection clauses. While the existence of related proceedings abroad is an important factor,[98] it is not alone dispositive in a *forum non conveniens* analysis.[99] The second consideration is the focus of the remainder of this chapter.

---

[92] See *Re Silicone Breast Implants Liability Litigation*, 887 F Supp 1469 (ND Ala 1995) (dismissing actions brought by some foreign plaintiffs against various United States-based manufacturers for harm caused from defective breast implants, but retaining a New Zealand plaintiff's action because a New Zealand statute prevented a remedy in her home forum); *Bhatnagar v Surrendra Overseas Ltd*, 52 F 8d 1220 (3rd Cir, 1995) (holding that excessive delay in processing the action in the alternative Indian jurisdiction was extreme enough to render that forum inadequate).

[93] For a good example of the modern trend in assessing private interest factors, see *Baumgart v Fairchild Aircraft Corp.* 981 F2d 824 (5th Cir, 1993).

[94] See above n 64 and accompanying text.

[95] See above n 83. See also *Agyenka v American Motors Corp*, 622 F Supp 242 (EDNY 1985) (stating that a foreign plaintiff's choice of forum is given less deference than a domestic plaintiff's choice).

[96] See, eg, *Re Union Carbide Corp Gas Plant Disaster*, 809 F 2d 195 (2nd Cir, 1986), *cert denied*, 484 US 871 (1987) (granting dismissal on grounds of *forum non conveniens* while requiring the defendant to submit to the jurisdiction of the courts of India, to waive any statute of limitations defences, and to agree to discovery in India according to the Federal Rules of Civil Procedure).

[97] See D W Dunham and E F Gladbauch, 'Forum non conveniens and Foreign Plaintiffs in the 1990s' (1999) 24 Brooklyn J Int'l L 665, 690. Conditioning discovery on compliance with rules established by the dismissing court remains an area of dispute among various courts. ibid, 690–691.

[98] See, eg, W L Reynolds, 'The Proper Forum for a Suit: Transnational Forum Non Conveniens and Counter-Suit Injunctions in the Federal Courts' (1992) 70 Tex L Rev 1663, 1676 ('The presence of related litigation abroad is another powerful factor favoring dismissal. There are significant advantages in having all the parties interested in apportioning a limited source of recovery assert their claims in one forum, not only to avoid inconsistent factual findings, but also 'to spare the litigants the additional costs of duplicate lawsuits'.).

[99] ibid.

D. The Convergence of Choice of Court Clauses and the *Forum Non Conveniens* Doctrine

As the above discussion indicates, the US common law doctrines on enforcement of choice of court clauses and *forum non conveniens* have, for the most part, developed separately. More recently, however, courts frequently have addressed situations in which the two doctrines intersect. Enforcement of choice of court clauses represents respect by the court for the autonomy of the parties in structuring their legal relationships, including their choice to have a dispute settled in a specific forum. The doctrine of *forum non conveniens*, on the other hand, represents respect for the discretion of the trial court in assessing conditions of convenience and justice to determine whether existing jurisdiction should in fact be exercised. Thus, the two doctrines may not always lead to consistent results.

This possible clash of doctrinal purposes is further complicated by the multiple conditions that may exist at the intersection of the two doctrines. This may be demonstrated by comparison with the Brussels I Regulation rules addressing choice of court and alternative fora. The Brussels rules (at least in business-to-business cases) are rather simple. Article 23(1) of the Brussels I Regulation provides a simple and direct rule:

> 1. If the parties, one or more of whom is domiciled in a Member State, have agreed that a court or the courts of a Member State are to have jurisdiction to settle any disputes which have arisen or which may arise in connection with a particular legal relationship, that court or those courts shall have jurisdiction. Such jurisdiction shall be exclusive unless the parties have agreed otherwise. Such an agreement conferring jurisdiction shall be either:
>
>   (a) in writing or evidenced in writing; or
>   (b) in a form which accords with practices which the parties have established between themselves; or
>   (c) in international trade or commerce, in a form which accords with a usage of which the parties are or ought to have been aware and which in such trade or commerce is widely known to, and regularly observed by, parties to contracts of the type involved in the particular trade or commerce concerned.

Thus, parties not only may select one forum in which jurisdiction otherwise exists over another forum in which jurisdiction otherwise exists, they may create jurisdiction in a forum that might not otherwise have jurisdiction. Further, once that jurisdiction is established, it is exclusive and no other forum governed by the Regulation may exercise jurisdiction in the case. This rule has certain benefits in terms of predictability of application. It is simple and direct. The related doctrines in US law have rather different, though equally legitimate, purposes.

(1) The Possibilities

In the United States, respect for choice of court clauses extends to cases in which a pre-determined choice of court clause would not be possible under the Brussels I Regulation.[100] At the same time, however, the nuances of the US common law approach can complicate the analysis. First, there is more than one category of choice of court clause possible. An exclusive choice of court clause[101] may lead to the same results as under the Brussels I Regulation, if, under the *Bremen* analysis, there is no substantial inconvenience, fraud, or public policy reason for a contrary result.[102] Because there is a presumption of non-exclusivity, however,[103] the certainty this analysis brings may be limited. Moreover, clauses may not be limited to exclusive and non-exclusive clauses. Courts have interpreted certain choice of court clauses to be non-exclusive, but accompanied by a waiver of the right to challenge jurisdiction and venue when an action is brought in the chosen court.[104] In these situations, the application of the clause may depend on which party gets to the court first, and which court it chooses.

The existence of a choice of court clause may also affect the application of the *Gilbert-Koster-Piper* factors for purposes of the *forum non conveniens* doctrine. A clause that derogates from the forum court will weigh in favour of dismissal, while a clause selecting the forum court will weigh against dismissal as part of the balancing of private and public interest factors.[105]

---

[100] Articles 17 and 21 of the Brussels I Regulation prevent pre-determined choice of court clauses in consumer contracts and individual contracts of employment.

[101] Courts often use the term 'mandatory' clause to refer to an exclusive clause in US courts.

[102] See above nn 41–43 and accompanying text.

[103] See below nn 106–107 and accompanying text.

[104] See below nn 125–127 and accompanying text.

[105] While some courts consider the balancing of the *Gilbert* private and public interest factors a single step in the *forum non conveniens* analysis, others see them as two separate steps. In the latter group of courts, some have held that the existence of a choice of court clause makes unnecessary the private factor balancing, but does not prevent a public interest balancing that can result in denial of enforcement of the clause. See, eg, *Re Hilliard*, 533 N E 2d 543, 545 (Ill App Ct 1989) (denying *forum non conveniens* motion based on choice of court clause, stating that '[i]f both parties freely entered into the agreement contemplating such inconvenience should there be a dispute, one party cannot successfully argue inconvenience as a reason for rendering the

The combination of the choice of court and *forum non conveniens* doctrines creates the possibility of at least six different basic factual relationships, with conceivable further variations on each of them. This can be demonstrated in the following chart:

	Forum Non Conveniens Status	
	prorogated court	derogated court
Choice of Court Clause		
exclusive clause	1	2
non-exclusive clause (with waiver of right to contest)	3	4
non-exclusive clause	5	6

While this chart demonstrates the multiple possibilities at the intersection between choice of court and *forum non conveniens*, it also begs the question of whether location of the case in a certain box within the chart provides an indication of the likely ruling on a motion to dismiss based on *forum non conveniens*. A purely intuitive analysis is likely to lead to the following results depending on the box into which a case falls:

(1) One would assume that a prorogated court presented with an exclusive choice of court clause (box number 1) would focus on the *Bremen* analysis and uphold the clause, denying a motion for dismissal on the grounds of *forum non conveniens*.

---

forum clause unenforceable.' See also W W Heiser, 'Forum Selection Clauses in State Courts: Limitations on Enforcement After Stewart and Carnival Cruise' (1993) 45 Florida L Rev 361, 397 ('The parties [to a choice of court clause] should be viewed as having given up their respective private interests for the most convenient forum in the event of litigation in exchange for whatever benefits each obtained in return for the concession'.).

(2) It would seem likely that a derogated court faced with an exclusive choice of court clause (box number 2) and a motion for dismissal, should grant that motion on either or both of the *Bremen* factors (honouring the choice of court clause) or the doctrine of *forum non conveniens* (considering the choice of court clause as a factor weighing in favour of sending the case to the prorogated forum).

(3) A non-exclusive choice of court clause combined with a waiver of a right to contest jurisdiction, venue and appropriateness of the chosen forum, when addressed by the prorogated court (box number 3), should bring a result similar to that in box number 1: application of the *Bremen* analysis to uphold the clause, denying a motion for dismissal on the grounds of *forum non conveniens*.

(4) A non-exclusive choice of court clause combined with a waiver of a right to contrast jurisdiction, venue and appropriateness of the chosen forum, when addressed by the derogated court (box number 4) will not necessarily bring the same result as that in box number 2; the waiver of the right to contest having the suit brought in the prorogated forum has no certain impact on the derogated court; there is no suit in the prorogated forum to contest because the right that has been waived has not been challenged. Thus, the existence of the non-exclusive choice of court clause is likely to be one of the factors (not necessarily a controlling factor) weighed by the court in the application of the doctrine of *forum non conveniens*.

(5) A prorogated court faced with a non-exclusive choice of court clause (box number 5) would seem less likely to decide to deny a motion for dismissal simply on a *Bremen* analysis. Here the case is more likely than a box number 1 case to proceed to a *forum non conveniens* analysis, with the non-exclusive clause being a significant factor in the application of the private interest balancing test.

(6) A derogated court faced with a non-exclusion choice of court clause (box number 6) would similarly seem less likely to decide to grant a motion for dismissal simply on a *Bremen* analysis than would be the case in a box number 2 case. Here, like in a box number 5 case, it would seem logical to proceed to a *forum non conveniens* anlaysis, with the non-exclusive clause being a significant factor in the application of the private interest balancing test.

Recent cases provide example of situations falling within some of these boxes. It is instructive to consider those decisions.

(2) The Case Law

The chart above may over-simplify the analysis by indicating that it is always easy to determine whether a clause is exclusive or non-exclusive. This is often discussed in US courts as the distinction between a mandatory and a permissive clause. The general US rule is that all choice of court clauses are non-exclusive unless it is clearly stated otherwise.[106] The rationale for this position has been stated as follows:

> To be mandatory, a forum selection clause must contain language that clearly designates a forum as the exclusive one.
>
> A permissive clause merely grants jurisdiction to the named forum, and does not preclude a cause of action from being brought elsewhere. If the court determines that a forum selection clause is not mandatory, that does not mean that the clause does not preclude a party from bringing suit in any jurisdiction where venue is proper. It simply means that the clause does not preclude a party from bringing suit in any jurisdiction where venue is proper. For a forum selection clause to be mandatory, the clause must clearly display the intent of the contracting parties to choose a particular forum to the exclusion of all other fora. Despite containing forceful words like 'shall,' the clause will not be deemed mandatory unless it is clear that the clause mandates the exclusive use of a particular forum.[107]

This general preference for interpreting choice of court clauses as non-exclusive provides some guidance, but is not always conclusive in all courts. At least one court would appear to find all choice of court clauses to be exclusive.[108]

Exclusive (Mandatory) Clauses

The interplay of an exclusive choice of forum clause with the doctrine of *forum non conveniens* is not a clear matter in US courts. A split in federal circuit courts demonstrates the positions on this issue. The Second Circuit has indicated that a federal district court should begin by applying the *Bremen* test to determine

---

[106] See, eg, *Steve Weiss & Co, Inc v INALCO, SPA*, 1999 WL 386653 (SDNY 11 June 1999) ('[i]n the absence of specific exclusionary language, this court will not assume an intent to confer exclusive jurisdiction on Italian courts').

[107] *Arguss Communications Group, Inc v Teletron, Inc*, 2000 WL 36936 at *6–7 (DNH 1999) (citations omitted).

[108] *Florida Polk County v Prison Health Servs, Inc*, 170 F 3d 1081, 1083–1084 (11th Cir, 1999) ('It is a venerable principle of contract law that the provisions of a contract should be construed so as to give every provision meaning,' and '[t]o read the forum-selection clause as permissive would render it surplusage, [but to] read the clause as mandatory—thus requiring all litigation arising out of the contract to take place in the [selected court]—gives the provision meaning'.).

the enforceability of a forum selection clause, and that a defendant's motion to dismiss on *forum non conveniens* grounds should be considered only if the court first finds that the parties did *not* form a contract with a valid choice of court clause.[109] The Fifth Circuit has taken a similar approach, rejecting a *forum non conveniens* challenge to an exclusive choice of court clause on the grounds that 'increased cost and inconvenience are insufficient reasons to invalidate foreign forum-selection or arbitration clauses'.[110] The Seventh Circuit has interpreted the *Bremen* language to mean that a choice of court clause is to be enforced unless the 'party challenging its enforcement can "clearly show that enforcement would be unreasonable and unjust, or that the clause was invalid for such reasons as fraud or overreaching", or that "trial in the [chosen] forum will be so gravely difficult and inconvenient that he will for all practical purposes be deprived of his day in court" '.[111] Thus, the Seventh Circuit finds an exclusive choice of court clause

> presumptively valid and enforceable unless (1) '[its] incorporation into the contract was the result of fraud, undue influence, or overweening bargaining power; (2) the selected forum is so gravely difficult and inconvenient that [the complaining party] will for all practical purposes be deprived of its day in court; or (3) [its] enforcement . . . would contravene a strong public policy of the forum in which the suit is brought, declared by statute or judicial decision'.[112]

The First Circuit, on the other hand, has ruled that a choice of court clause does not control the decision on a *forum non conveniens* motion to dismiss, but is 'simply one of the factors that should be considered and balanced' by the court in its *forum non conveniens* analysis.[113]

Despite this split in the Circuits (and recognizing that not all courts give clear consideration to whether the clause in question is exclusive or non-exclusive), the general approach to exclusive choice of court clauses is to enforce them,

---

[109] *Evolution Online Sys, Inc v Koninklijke PTT Nederland NV*, 145 F 3d 505, 509–10 (2nd Cir, 1998). See also *Sudduth v Occidental Peruana, Inc*, 70 F Supp 2d 691 (Ed Tex 1999), where the district court denied the defendant's motion to dismiss on *forum non conveniens* grounds only after determining that a mandatory choice of court clause was invalid under the *Bremen* standards.

[110] *Mitsui & Co (USA), Inc v Mira M/V*, 111 F 3d 33, 37 (5th Cir, 1997).

[111] *AAR International, Inc v Nimelias Enterprises SA*, 250 F 3d 510, 525 (7th Cir, 2001), quoting from *Bremen v Zapata Off-Shore Co*, 407 US 1, 15, 17 (1972). See also *Northwestern Nat'l Ins Co v Donovan*, 916 F2d 372, 378 (7th Cir, 1990) (holding that agreement to an exclusive forum selection clause waives objections to venue on the basis of cost or inconvenience to the party); *Heller Financial, Inc v Midwhey Powder Co*, 883 F 2d 1286 (7th Cir, 1989).

[112] *AAR International* (above n 111) 525, quoting from *Bonny v Society of Lloyd's*, 3 F 3d 156, 160 (7th Cir, 1993).

[113] *Royal Bed & Spring Co, Inc v Famossul Industria e Comercio de Moveis Ltda*, 906 F 2d 45, 51 (1st Cir, 1990).

either under the *Bremen* test or under a *forum non conveniens* analysis.[114]
Courts selected in such clauses have kept cases when faced with a *forum non conveniens* motion to dismiss,[115] and derogated courts have dismissed cases in
favour of the court selected in the clause.[116] Nonetheless, some courts have re-
fused to enforce clauses choosing another court in the face of a motion to dismiss based on *forum non conveniens*.[117]

[114] See, eg, *Mercier v Sheraton International, Inc*, 981 F 2d 1345 (1st Cir, 1992) (applying
forum non conveniens analysis despite apparent exclusive choice of court clause, but dismissing in
favor of the Turkish court named in the clause). When New York recodified its doctrine of *forum
non conveniens* in 1984, it specifically provided that its courts cannot stay or dismiss an action on
forum non conveniens grounds where the contract contains both a New York choice of forum
clause and a New York choice of law clause and the transaction involved exceeds $1,000,000.
NYCPLR s 327 (McKinney's 1987 Supp) (1984 NY Laws, Ch 421, NY Gen Oblig Law ss
5–1401 and 5–1402). This provision assures that New York courts will accept jurisdiction in accordance with the parties' choice in large transnational contracts.
[115] See, eg, *Heller Financial, Inc v Midwhey Powder Co*, 883 F 2d 1286 (7th Cir, 1989) (denying motion for dismissal or transfer under 28 USC s 1404(a)); *Poddar v State Bank of India* 79
F Supp 2d 391, 393 (SDNY 2000) (denying dismissal where clause created mandatory jurisdiction in courts in both India and the United States); *Cambridge Nutrition AG v Fotheringham*,
840 F Supp 299 (SDNY 1994) (enforcing New York choice of court clause despite motion to
dismiss brought by Spanish defendant for whom trial in New York was inconvenient).
[116] See, eg, *Royal Bed & Spring Co v Famossul Industria E Comercio de Moveis Ltda*, 906 F 2d 45
(1st Cir, 1990) (enforcing Brazilian choice of court clause in distributorship agreement under a
Bremen analysis); *Caribe BMW, Inc v Bayerische Motoren Werke Aktiengesellschaft*, 821 F Supp 802,
set aside, vacated and remanded on other grounds, 19 F 2d 745 (1st Cir, 1994) (finding German
choice of court clause valid and enforceable on a multi-factor analysis), *Bonny v Society of Lloyd's*, 3
F 3d 156 (7th Cir, 1993) (honouring English choice of court clause under *Bremen* analysis by dismissal of action under securities underwriting contract); *General Elec Co v G Siempelkamp GmbH
& Co*, 29 F 3d 1095 (6th Cir, 1994) (dismissing case on *forum non conveniens* challenge in favour
of German courts in accordance with choice of court clause in the sales contract); *Omron
Healthcare v Maclaren Exports*, 28 F 2d 600 (7th Cir, 1994) (applying *forum non conveniens* analy-
sis to enforce English choice of court clause in distributorship contract); *Aceequip, Ltd v Am Eng'g
Corp*, 153 F Supp 2d 138 (DC Conn 2001) (denying motion to dismiss in favor of Japanese court
when mandatory clause selected Connecticut forum); *Lawler v Schumacher Filgters Am*, 832 F
Supp 1044 (ED Va 1993) (enforcing choice of court clause in consultancy agreement naming
German courts as the chosen forum); *Hunter Distrib Co v Pure Beverage Partners*, 820 F Supp 284
(ND Miss 1993) (granting motion to dismiss for improper venue when faced with choice of court
clause naming Arizona courts); *TUC Electronics, Inc v Eagle Telephonics, Inc*, 698 F Supp 35 (D
Conn 1988) (dismissing case brought in Connecticut in face of New York state court choice of
court clause, applying combination of *Bremen* and *forum non conveniens* factors); *Santamauro v
Taito do Brasil Industria E Comercia Ltda*, 587 F Supp 1312 (ED LA 1984) (applying *Bremen* analysis to dismiss action on sales contract brought in Louisiana despite Brazilian choice of court clause);
Skyline Steel Corp v RDI/Caesars Riverboat Casino, LLC, 44 F Supp 2D 1337, 1338 (ND Ala 1999)
(sending case to chosen forum under 28 USC s 1404(a) transfer statute, but stating, 'the law of the
Eleventh Circuit is that forum selection clauses are virtually impossible to overcome by an application of the general principles of forum non conveniens'.).
[117] See, eg, *Sudduth v Occidental Peruana, Inc*, 70 F Supp. 2d 691 (ED Tex 1999) (refusing enforcement of clause requiring disputes to be brought in Peruvian courts where both parties were

Non-exclusive (Permissive) Clauses

While the Second Circuit relies strictly on a *Bremen* analysis when the choice of court clause is exclusive,[118] it applies a *forum non conveniens* analysis when addressing a non-exclusive choice of court clause. This is demonstrated in the case of *John Boutari & Son, Wines & Spirits, SA v Attiki Importers & Distribs*,[119] where the Second Circuit held that dismissal of an action on a distributorship contract on *forum non conveniens* grounds was erroneous, and the case should be tried in a US Federal District Court despite a Greek choice of court clause. The case was based in part on the finding that the clause was permissive and not mandatory. The Ninth Circuit applied a similar analysis to a case involving a clause selecting the Hong Kong courts, but affirmed a dismissal on grounds of *forum non conveniens*.[120]

Federal district courts have gone both ways when faced with a non-exclusive choice of court clause and a motion for dismissal on *forum non conveniens* grounds. While courts in Illinois[121] and Georgia[122] have enforced permissive choice of court clauses favouring foreign courts in the face of a *forum non conveniens* motion for dismissal, federal district courts in North Carolina[123] and

---

in the United States); *Pearcy Marine v Seacor Marine* 847 F Supp 57 (SD Tex 1993) (finding London choice of court clause to be unenforceable as a result of unequal bargaining power). Similarly, courts have found that the existence of a valid forum selection clause does not prevent a transfer for *forum non conveniens* purposes under 28 USC s 1404(a):

> Congress set down in s 1404(a) the factors it thought should be decisive on a motion for transfer. Only one of these—the convenience of the parties—is properly within the power of the parties themselves to affect by a forum-selection clause. The other factors— the convenience of witnesses and the interest of justice—are third party or public interests that must be weighed by the district court; they cannot be automatically outweighed by the existence of a purely private agreement between the parties. Such an agreement does not obviate the need for an analysis of the factors set forth in s 1404(a) and does not necessarily preclude the granting of the motion to transfer.

Plum Tree, Inc v Stockment, 488 F 2d 754, 757–58 (3rd Cir, 1973).

[118] *Evolution Online* (above n 109.

[119] 22 F 3d 51 (2nd Cir, 1994). See also *Blanco v Banco Industrial de Venezuela, SA*, 997 F 2d 974 (2nd Cir, 1993) (affirming a dismissal on *forum non conveniens* grounds even though New York was one of three jurisdictions named in a non-exclusive choice of court clause).

[120] *FIL Leveraged US Gov't Bond Fund Ltd v TCW Funds Management, Inc*, 1236 (Table), unpublished disposition, 1998 WL 476750 (9th Cir, 29 July 1998).

[121] *Hull, 753 Corp v Elbe Flugzeugwerke*, 58 F Supp 2d 925, 926 (ND Ill 1999) (enforcing non-exclusive clause favouring German courts).

[122] *Amermed Corp v Disetronic Holding, AG* 6 F Supp 2d 1371 (ND Ga 1998) (granting dismissal in favour of Swiss court selected in non-exclusive clause).

[123] *S & D Coffee, Inc v GEI Autowrappers*, 995 F Supp 607 (MDNC 1997) (denying dismissal in favour of English court named in non-exclusive clause).

Arizona[124] have refused motions to dismiss even where the clause called for the actions to be brought in foreign countries. The decision often seems to hinge on the weight given to the choice of court clause in balancing the private and public interest factors applied in the *forum non conveniens* analysis.

Non-exclusive Clauses With Waiver of Objections to Venue

In *AAR Int'l, Inc v Nimelias Exterprises SA*,[125] the Seventh Circuit addressed the interplay of the *Bremen* analysis with the *forum non conveniens* doctrine when a case was brought in the court designated by a non-exclusive choice of court clause and that clause was accompanied by 'unambigous language providing that the [party] shall not object to venue in [the chosen] court on the ground that such a court is an inconvenient forum'.[126] The court concluded that in such a case, 'the stricter standards announced in *Bremen* should control the analysis of [the] *forum non conveniens* motion',[127] and the traditional *forum non conveniens* analysis did not apply. Thus, the result was the same as if the clause had been exclusive.

The importance of the clause to the analysis

At least one commentator has stated that, in cases dealing with the convergence between choice of court clauses and the *forum non conveniens* doctrine, it makes 'little difference' whether the *Bremen* factors are applied or the case is analyzed under the *forum non conveniens* analysis.[128] This does not seem to hold true in all circumstances, however. The designation of the type of choice of court clause helps determine whether the court will focus on a *Bremen* or *forum non conveniens* analysis. This determination, in turn, has a substantial impact on the burden placed on each of the parties and the opportunity to challenge the trial court's decision on appeal. Under a *Bremen* analysis, the party seeking to avoid the choice of court clause has the 'heavy burden of showing not only that the balance of convenience is strongly in favour of trial in [the alternative forum] . . . but also that a . . . trial [in the chosen forum] will be so manifestly and gravely inconvenient to [that party] that it will be effectively deprived of a

---

[124] *Magellan Real Estate Inv Trust v Losch*, 109 F Supp 2d 1144 (DC Ariz 2000) (denying dismissal in favour of Ontario court named in non-exclusive clause).
[125] See above n 111.
[126] ibid, 525–526.
[127] ibid, 526.
[128] R K McLemore, 'Forum-Selection Clauses and Seaman Personal Injury' (2000) 25 Tulane Mar LJ 327, 350 ('The issue is essentially one of fairness and justice'.).

meaningful day in court'.[129] This appears to be a much more substantial burden than what is necessary to meet the *forum non conveniens* test, which requires a showing of an adequate alternative forum and a balancing of private and public interest factors. Moreover, on appeal, the question of enforceability of a choice of court clause is a question of law subject to *de novo* review,[130] whereas '[t]he *forum non conveniens* determination is committed to the trial court's sound discretion and may be reversed only when there has been a clear abuse of discretion'.[131]

Problems with categorization

Even if one can carefully catalogue each case to fit within the chart set forth above, that will not explain some US cases, or the opinions of some commentators. It has been suggested that '[u]sing *forum non conveniens* terminology, the parties lack the authority to contractually reallocate the various public interest factors, or those private ones of third parties not related to the contract'.[132] This approach would mean that no court could stop with the *Bremen* factors, and that the balancing required under traditional *forum non conveniens* analysis would always be necessary, even in the face of a valid, exclusive choice of court clause. The same author suggests that, at a minimum, 'the existence of a forum selection clause should remove the individual parties' convenience or inconvenience from the court's consideration of the various private and public interest factors'.[133] Even the cases that take this approach, however, often end up enforcing the choice of court clause.[134]

Some courts tend to ignore the *Bremen* analysis entirely, holding choice of court clauses unenforceable where 'enforcing the clause would "seriously

---

[129] *Bremen* (above n 24), 470 US 19.
[130] *AAR Int'l Inc* (above n 111), 250 F 3d 527.
[131] *Piper* (above n 75), 454 US 237.
[132] W W Heiser, 'Forum Selection Clauses in State Courts: Limitations on Enforcement after *Stewart* and *Carnival Cruise*' (1993) 45 Florida L Rev 361, 396.
[133] ibid, 397. See *Arthur Young & Co v Leong*, 383 NYS 2d 618, 619 (App Div) *appeal dismissed*, 390 NYW 2d 927 (1976) (stating that the existence of a choice of court clause 'obviated considerations of inconvenience to a party or a witness').
[134] See, eg, *Smith, Valentino & Smith, Inc v Superior Court*, 131 Cal Rptr 374, 551 P 2d 1206, 1209–1210 (Cal 1976) (enforcing Pennsylvania choice of court clause despite residence of plaintiff's witnesses in California); *Prudential Resources Corp v Plunkett*, 583 SW 2d 97, 99–100 (Ky Ct App 1979) (enforcing choice of court clause even where the party's witnesses would have to be presented by deposition since they would be unable to appear in person); *Hauenstein & Bermeister, Inc v Met-Fab Indus*, 320 NW 2d 886, 890 (Minn 1982) (enforcing choice of court clause where inconvenienced witnesses could submit testimony by deposition).

impair" ' the plaintiff's law suit.[135] Others acknowledge *Bremen* and *Carnival Cruise Lines*, but then go on to refuse enforcement to choice of court clauses by finding distinctions considered to justify such results.[136]

E. The Rationale for a Hague Convention Encompassing Choice of Court Jurisdiction

The current status of US law on both choice of court and *forum non conveniens* demonstrates the value of even a modest Hague convention on jurisdiction and judgments—not just for the United States, but for all of its potential treaty partners. The success of the New York Arbitration Convention[137] demonstrates the value of a convention that combines enforecement of choice of forum with enforcement of the resulting award. The lack of any such global set of rules for litigation disadvantages persons with legitimate reasons for preferring litigation over arbitration. The creation of such a convention would fill in this gap, thus creating greater certainty for the international commercial community and establishing a foundation upon which to build further judicial cooperation in the future.[138] It would also provide greater certainty for all parties to US litigation when a choice of court clause is involved.[139]

US law on choice of court differs from the mandatory and exclusive results of Article 23 of the Brussels I Regulation, and does not contain the limitations on such clauses in insurance, consumer, and employment contracts that are found in Articles 17 and 21 of the Regulation. US common law presents a presumption

---

[135] See, eg, *Morgan Trailer Mfg Co v Hydraroll, Ltd*, 759 A2d 926, 931 (Pa Super 2000).

[136] See, eg, *Walker v Carnival Cruise Lines*, 107 F Supp 2d 1135, 1140 (ND Cal 2000) (stating that the Supreme Court did not create a *per se* rule of enforcement of cruise line contract choice of court clauses, and holding that where the plaintiffs suffered severe physical disabilities, 'it is hard to envision circumstances which, in their totality, more clearly demonstrate the fundamental unfairness of enforcing a forum selection clause'.); *Corna v American Hawaii Cruises, Inc*, 794 F Supp 1005, 1011 (D Haw 1992) (refusing to enforce choice of court clause where plaintiffs only received their tickets with the clause two or three days before departure, and therefore did not have time to consider the option to reject the cruise contract without forfeiting several thousand dollars).

[137] New York Convention (above n 23).

[138] See R A Brand, 'Where To From Here? Prospects for a Hague Convention on Jurisdiction and the Enforcement of Judgments' (October 2001) 16 Int'l Arb Rpt 38.

[139] The limited focus of this chapter is not intended to suggest that a choice of court convention is all that is possible at The Hague. Rather it is meant to demonstrate that *at least* that much is possible in the current negotiations.

of non-exclusivity of choice of court clauses, combined with the *Bremen* analysis that allows courts to disregard even mandatory choice of court clauses in certain limited situations. The European approach focuses on efficiency, predictability, and minimal judicial discretion. The US approach (and that of most other common law states) gives up some efficiency and predictability in exchange for discretion to accomplish equity and fairness in individual cases. Whether one approach is better than the other does not matter so much at this point; what does matter is whether it is possible to bring the two systems closer together for the benefit of the global community.

Two parts of the 1999 Preliminary Draft and the 2001 Interim Text demonstrate the manner in which this divergence of approaches has so far been addressed at The Hague. The first is the combination of articles dealing with choice of court. Like the Brussels I Regulation, both Hague texts contain a general rule of exclusive jurisdiction for choice of court clauses.[140] The Preliminary Draft Text also contains a prohibition on pre-dispute choice of court clauses in employment contracts,[141] and both contain proposals for a prohibition on pre-dispute choice of court clauses in consumer contracts.[142] The Interim Text, however, reflects the very substantial concerns with this prohibition in consumer contracts, including numerous alternatives and variants and substantial bracketed text.[143] Much of the concern over the consumer contract rules relates to jurisdiction in electronic commerce; concerns not clearly resolved in any legal system at the current time, and upon which there is not likely to be global consensus. All that is clear from the Interim Text on these issues is that there is no certain path to a globally acceptable rule of jurisdiction on choice of court clauses that would be required by the Convention to exist in all Contracting States.

The other part of the two Hague texts dealing with the divergence of approaches discussed here consists of two companion articles representing a compromise on the application of rules of *lis alibi pendens* and *forum non conveniens* in various legal systems. While the Brussels approach includes a strict *lis pendens* rule, requiring a court second seised to defer to the court first seised in any matter,[144] the US approach is to allow parallel litigation and ultimately defer

---

[140] Draft Text Art 4; Interim Text Art 4.
[141] Draft Text Art 8.
[142] Draft Text Art 7; Interim Text Art 7.
[143] Interim Text Art 7.
[144] Brussels I Regulation Art 27 (above n 14).

through principles of *res judicata* and issue preclusion in favour of the first judgment. In other words, the Brussels system promotes a race to the courthouse, and the US common law system promotes a race to judgment. The US approach is, like that in most common law countries, tempered by the doctrine of *forum non conveniens*, which places discretionary authority in a trial court to defer to a foreign court earlier seised of the matter, or even to dismiss in favour of filing the case in a foreign forum not yet seised of the matter.

The Hague compromise approach is found in Articles 21 and 22 of the Interim Text, with Article 21 providing a modified *lis pendens* rule and Article 22 stating a modified *forum non conveniens* rule, with the two provisions working in tandem to allow the court first seised to decline jurisdiction under the Article 22 analysis. Thus, while the Convention would include a general rule of *lis alibi pendens*, deferring to the court first seised in most instances, this rule would be tempered by a variation on the *forum non conveniens* doctrine, allowing a court to dismiss in favour of a more appropriate forum in another state.

F. Conclusion

Articles 21 and 22 of the Hague Convention Interim Text indicate compromise on divergent aspects of differing legal systems regarding issues of *lis pendens* and *forum non conveniens*. The many brackets and variations in the articles dealing with choice of court, however, demonstrate the distance not yet travelled in The Hague in terms of bringing those systems together on very basic rules of jurisdiction. As long as the goal is a comprehensive convention, covering all aspects of jurisdiction in all civil matters not yet excluded by the rules of Article I of the Interim Text, that distance is unlikely to be narrowed. If, on the other hand, the goal is to achieve what is reasonably possible in order to move from the status quo to an improved global legal community, there may be hope. Global practice under the New York Arbitration Convention offers proof that a very basic choice of forum rule, accompanied by a corresponding rule on recognition and enforcement of the resulting award, can achieve dramatic success in the global community. The opportunity to accomplish the same for dispute settlement in the courts should not be dismissed simply because accomplishing much more is not possible.

Those who believe the only benefit of a jurisdiction and judgments convention for non-US states lies in getting the United States to agree to prohibitions on some of its basic rules of jurisdiction must understand first that such a goal is most likely politically unachievable, and second that there is benefit available from a more modest, but likely much more successful, convention that does for litigation what the New York Convention has done for arbitration. Such a convention could have a rule of exclusive jurisdiction based on party agreement in a choice of court clause in business-to-business contracts—similar in many ways to the rule now found in Article 23 of the Brussels I Regulation.

Current US law demonstrates that a Convention choice of court rule would add significant predictability in US courts. It would also facilitate improved planning opportunities for parties entering into contracts with US enterprises when those contracts contain choice of court clauses. The result would be a treaty obligation creating a single federal rule of respect for choice of court clauses in such cases that could not be departed from in federal or state courts in the United States.[145] This would be a substantial benefit for litigants from all countries in US courts, as well as for businesses wanting predictable contract provisions upon which successful commercial relationships can be developed.

---

[145] Under art VI of the US Constitution, that rule would be the supreme law of the land, preempting contrary state and federal law.

4

COMITY IN MODERN PRIVATE INTERNATIONAL LAW

*Lawrence Collins**

A. Introduction

In an unreported decision in the year 2000 Thomas J, sitting in the English Commercial Court, was concerned with a case in which a United States corporation was seeking in the United States an injunction to restrain arbitral and judicial proceedings in London, and a German corporation was seeking an injunction in London to restrain the United States proceedings. He refused the injunction restraining the United States proceedings, and said:[1]

> He [the United States district judge] will no doubt take into account . . . that he, as a judge of the United States Court, is being asked to exercise extraordinary extra-territorial jurisdiction over an arbitral tribunal sitting in London within

---

* LL.D (Cantab.), F.B.A. One of Her Majesty's Justices. Fellow, Wolfson College, Cambridge.
[1] See *General Electric Co v Deutz AG*, 270 F 3d 144, 161–162 (3d Cir 2001).

the jurisdiction of this Court. He will no doubt pay high regard to issues of comity, just as this Court has paid high regard to issues of comity in relation to the decisions made by him.

The purpose of this contribution is to re-open discussion of the role of comity in modern private international law, and to suggest that for historical reasons writers in the field have tended to neglect the influence of comity on the modern law. This writer hopes that he will be forgiven for venturing upon an area which is not among the primary interests of Sir Peter North, but seeks to excuse himself on the ground that some thoughts on a neglected area are intended as a sincere tribute to one whose contributions to the subject of private international law have been significant and original.

The litigation in which Thomas J made his remarks is reported in the United States as *General Electric Co v Deutz AG*.[2] The plaintiff, a New York corporation, had contracted with Moteren-Werke Mannheim AG, a German corporation with headquarters in Mannheim, Germany. The agreement provided that Moteren-Werke would design, and General Electric would manufacture, high horsepower diesel engines for locomotives. The contract also included a section in which Deutz AG, the parent company of Moteren-Werke, guaranteed the obligations of its subsidiary. The contract contained an arbitration clause providing for arbitration under the auspices of the International Chamber of Commerce in London. When the joint venture encountered difficulties, General Electric called upon Deutz to provide the additional funding necessary for the work to continue. The funding was not provided and General Electric commenced proceedings in the United States District Court for the Western District of Pennsylvania, asserting breach of contract claims against Deutz.

Deutz resisted the Pennsylvania proceedings on the ground that General Electric was bound by the arbitration agreement, and itself instituted arbitral proceedings through the ICC. In the US proceedings it was decided (by a jury!) that Deutz was not a party to the arbitration agreement, which applied only as between General Electric and Moteren-Werke, and not to the guarantee obligations. While the arbitral proceedings were still pending, Deutz applied for an injunction from the English court to restrain the US proceedings. Thomas J refused the injunction on the ground that it was doubtful that the arbitration agreement applied to the dispute. General Electric then obtained an injunction from the Federal Court in Pennsylvania to restrain further resort to the English

---

[2] 270 F 3d 144 (3d Cir 2001).

court, for example by appealing from any adverse decision of the arbitrators as to their jurisdiction, and from taking any further steps in the arbitration. Subsequently the arbitral panel held that it had no jurisdiction because Deutz was not a party to the arbitration agreement.

The Court of Appeals for the Third Circuit discharged the injunction granted by the District Court in Pennsylvania. It said that the case law of the Third Circuit required a 'serious concern for comity'. In parallel litigation, especially in international proceedings, 'the issue of comity is an important and omnipresent factor',[3] and in the light of these factors the case was not one which called for the extraordinary intervention of an injunction.

B. Comity: The Traditional View

The theory that comity is the basis of private international law has long been discredited. The thesis of this contribution is that the terms in which the theory was rejected by the leading textwriters have led modern writers to overlook the resurgence of the doctrine of comity, not as a basis for the system of private international law, but as a basis for the development of particular rules and attitudes in the resolution of international disputes.

The current edition of Cheshire and North[4] has this to say about comity:[5]

> In justifying this reference to a foreign law, English judges and textbook writers have frequently used the term *comity of nations,* 'a phrase which is grating to the ear, when it proceeds from a court of justice'.[6] Although the term has been often used, analysis of it reveals that it has been employed in a meaningless or misleading way. The word itself is incompatible with the judicial function, for comity is a matter for sovereigns, not for judges required to decide a case according to the rights of the parties. Again, if the word is given its normal meaning of courtesy it is scarcely consistent with the readiness of English courts to apply enemy law in time of war. Moreover, if courtesy formed the basis of private international law a judge might feel compelled to ignore the law of Utopia on proof that Utopian courts apply no law but their own, since comity implies a bilateral, not a unilateral, relationship. If, on the other hand, comity means that no foreign law is applicable in England except with the permission of the sovereign, it is nothing more than a truism. The fact is, of course, that the application of a

---

[3] At 160–161.
[4] *Private International Law* (13th edn 1999).
[5] ibid, 5.
[6] A quotation from Livermore, derived from de Nova.

foreign law implies no act of courtesy, no sacrifice of sovereignty. It merely derives from a desire to do justice.

That text dates essentially from the sixth edition in 1961, by which time Dr Cheshire had progressively strengthened his contempt for comity. He had begun in 1935 with this:[7]

> In justifying this reference to a foreign law, judges and text-book writers, following the theory of the great Dutch jurist, John Voet,[8] have frequently used the term 'comity', in order to indicate that they make the reference, not by compulsion, but from considerations of justice and of the mutual convenience of states. The fact that English judges have frequently adopted the same expression is a little unfortunate, for it is clear that our Courts admit evidence of an extraneous system of law, not because they are influenced by a feeling of courtesy to the foreign legislator, but because the foreign law is one of the essential facts in the case. The word 'comity' in this connection is meaningless if taken literally.

By the fourth edition in 1952[9] the expression was described as 'vague and ambiguous' and by the sixth edition in 1961 it had become 'incompatible with the judicial function'.[10]

Dicey[11] was no less contemptuous of the role of comity:

> Is, or is not, the enforcement of foreign law a matter of 'comity'? This is an inquiry which has greatly exercised the minds of jurists. We can now see that the disputes to which it has given rise are little better than examples of idle logomachy. If the assertion that the recognition or enforcement of foreign law depends upon comity means only that the law of no country can have effect as law beyond the territory of the sovereign by whom it was imposed, unless by permission of the state where it is allowed to operate, the statement expresses, though obscurely, a real and important fact. If, on the other hand, the assertion that the recognition or enforcement of foreign laws depends upon comity is meant to imply that, to take a concrete case, when English judges apply French law, they do so out of courtesy to the French Republic, then the term comity is used to cover a view which, if really held by any serious thinker, affords a singular specimen of confusion of thought produced by laxity of language.

So also Wolff[12] regarded the notion that the application of foreign law and

---

[7] 1st edn, 6.
[8] Voet the younger, who admitted foreign law *ex comitate*: see Westlake, *Private International Law* (7th edn Bentwich, 1925), 19–20.
[9] at 5.
[10] ibid.
[11] *Conflict of Laws* (1st edn 1896), 10.
[12] *Private International Law* (2nd edn, 1950), 15.

recognition of foreign rights did not depend on a legal obligation existing under public international law, but were acts of courtesy dictated by a *comitas gentium* as dangerous and erroneous.

What these writers were attacking was the theory, attributed to Voet the younger and to Huber[13] and Story,[14] that comity was the basis for the rules of private international law, and the supposed consequence that the application of foreign law, and the recognition of rights under foreign law, or the recognition of foreign judgments, depended on reciprocity. This is not the place for a discussion of whether Huber or Story meant what is attributed to them. It is sufficient to say for present purposes that it is now orthodox theory in common law and civil law countries that the basis of private international law lies in the domestic law of the forum,[15] and that while reciprocity has a role to play in some areas, particularly (but only in some countries and in certain types of foreign judgment) in the recognition and enforcement of foreign judgments, it is not an overriding principle of the conflict of laws. Writers in civil law countries take comity (courtoisie internationale) as simply one of the historical, and obsolete, bases for the recognition of foreign law.[16]

In the famous decision of the United States Supreme Court in 1895 in *Hilton v Guyot*[17] the views of Story were extensively quoted, and, for the (bare) majority Justice Gray said:[18]

---

[13] One of whose axioms was: 'The rulers of states arrange it by comity that the laws of each nation which are enforced within its boundaries maintain their validity everywhere, to the extent that the power or the laws of the other state and its citizens are not prejudiced' (this translation and the original Latin are in Yntema (1966) 65 Mich LR 9, at 26).

[14] 'The true foundation, on which the administration of international law must rest, is, that the rules, which are to govern, are those, which arise from mutual interest and utility, from a sense of the inconveniences, which would result from a contrary doctrine, and from a sort a moral necessity to do justice, in order that justice may be done to us in return': Story, *Conflict of Laws* (1st edn, 1834), 34. 'There is, then, not only no impropriety in the use of the phrase "comity of nations", but it is the most appropriate phrase to express the true foundation and extent of the obligation of the laws of one nation within the territories of another . . . The doctrine of Huberus would seem, therefore, to stand upon just principles' (ibid, p 37). See also Nadelmann, *Conflict of Laws: International and Interstate* (1972), 1 and 21; Watson, *Joseph Story and the Comity of Errors* (1992).

[15] See, eg, Beale, *Conflict of Laws* (1935, vol 1), 53–55.

[16] See, eg, Batiffol and Lagarde, *Droit International Privé* (vol. 1, 8th edn 1993), para 225; Loussouarn and Bourel, *Droit International Privé* (6th edn 2001), paras 93–94.

[17] 159 US 113 (1895). The views of Story on comity had been extensively discussed in *Bank of Augusta v Earle*, 13 US 519 (1839) by Taney CJ, when Justice Story was a member of the Supreme Court.

[18] At 163–164. See also the dissenting judgment of Chief Justice Fuller, at 233.

No law has any effect, of its own force, beyond the limits of the sovereignty from which its authority is derived. The extent which the law of one nation, as put in force within its territory, whether by executive order, by legislative act, or by judicial decree, shall be allowed to operate within the dominion of another nation, depends on what our greatest jurists have been content to call 'the comity of nations'. Although the phrase has been often criticised, no satisfactory substitute has been suggested.

'Comity', in the legal sense, is neither a matter of absolute obligation, on the one hand, nor of mere courtesy and goodwill, upon the other. But it is the recognition which one nation allows within its territory to the legislative, executive or judicial acts of another nation, having due regard to international duty and convenience, and to the rights of its own citizens or of other persons who are under the protection of its laws.

In *Hilton v Guyot* the Supreme Court approved the notion of reciprocity as a condition for the recognition and enforcement of judgments of foreign countries, but that has generally been abandoned in the United States,[19] although *Hilton v Guyot* continues to be cited routinely in cases involving foreign judgments.[20] In England, comity is often referred to in the context of the recognition of foreign judgments, but reciprocity is not a requirement.[21]

C. The Consequences

It might be thought that as a result of the abandonment of the comity doctrine as a basis for private international law, and as a result of the abandonment of reciprocity as a condition for the recognition and enforcement of foreign judgments, that comity would play very little part in the modern conflict of laws, and that *Hilton v Guyot* would no longer be regarded as a decision of any significance. Some of the textbooks recognize that judges refer to comity, but do not recognize that it is a concept of any significance. Read, in his classic work on *Recognition and Enforcement of Foreign Judgments*[22] says that comity as the equivalent of private international law became practically obsolete before the twentieth century, and was 'used only sporadically today as a euphemism'.

---

[19] See Scoles and Hay, *Conflict of Laws* (3rd edn 2000), Chap 24.
[20] For a recent example see *Int'l Nutrition Co v Horphag Research Ltd*, 257 F 3d 1324 (Fed Cir 2001).
[21] *Murphy v Sivajothi* [1999] 1 WLR 467 at 476. See, for the basis of recognition, *Adams v Cape Industries plc* [1990] Ch 433, CA.
[22] (1938), 53.

Scoles and Hay say of comity that 'references to it can still be found in judicial statements in the United States',[23] and they discuss *Hilton v Guyot* only in the context of reciprocity no longer being a condition for recognition and enforcement, although they recognise that foreign judgments are accorded recognition and enforcement 'as a matter of "comity".'[24]

What the texts do not reflect is that there are, quite literally, thousands of decisions in the field of the conflict of laws in the British Commonwealth and the United States which invoke the concept of comity. Nor is *Hilton v Guyot* a mere historical curiosity. In researching this paper, I have come across more than thirty decisions in the British Commonwealth in the last twenty years citing *Hilton v Guyot* on comity,[25] and more than 100 decisions in the United States in the same period. Comity may be a discredited concept in the eyes of the textwriters, but it thrives in the judicial decisions.

D. Jurisdiction in Public and Private International Law

The traditional use of the expression in the field of public international law refers to 'the rules of politeness, convenience and goodwill observed by states in their mutual intercourse without being legally bound by them'.[26] So in *Re St Mary the Virgin, Hurley*[27] Chancellor Peter Boydell QC in the Oxford Consistory Court granted a petition for the remains of a Brazilian national hero to be exhumed so that they could be re-interred in consecrated ground in Brazil. The petitioner was the Brazilian Ambassador, and the body was that of Hipolito Jose de Costa, who had founded in London the first uncensored Brazilian periodical. His writings materially contributed to the gradual transition of Brazil from a colony to an independent sovereign state, and following the declaration of independence in 1822 he was appointed Counsellor in London. Five years before that he had married an English lady, and when he died in 1823 transportation of his remains to Brazil was impractical because the sea journey then would have taken between three and four months, and he

---

[23] p 20.
[24] At 1150.
[25] See especially *Barclays Bank plc v Homan* [1993] BCLC 680; *CSR Ltd v Cigna Insurance Australia Ltd* (1997) 146 ALR 402; *Lipohar v R* (1999) 168 ALR 8; *Holt Cargo Systems Inc v ABC Containerline NV (Trustees of)* 2001 SCC 90.
[26] Oppenheim, *International Law* (9th edn Jennings and Watts, 1992), 51.
[27] [2001] 1 WLR 831.

was buried instead in a vault in Hurley church. Permission was granted for the exhumation on the ground, *inter alia,* that the principle of the comity of nations was persuasive towards the grant of permission. The Chancellor said:[28]

> . . . it is not every day that the remains of a national hero of a friendly sovereign state are to be found beneath the nave of a Berkshire church and . . . the principle of the comity of nations is, in my judgment, a relevant factor. This principle relates to the body of rules which sovereign states observe towards one another from courtesy or convenience, but which are not binding as rules of international law.

It was probably in a similar sense that in *Dallal v Bank Mellat*,[29] when deciding to recognize a decision of the US-Iran claims tribunal, Hobhouse J said that international comity required the English courts to recognize the validity of decisions of foreign tribunals whose competence was derived from public international law. He said that it would be anomalous and contrary to justice and comity if he were to decline to recognize the decision of the US-Iran claims tribunal in the Hague, which had been set up by two sovereign states. Considerations of comity applied with particular force since the Algiers Declarations, which were made to settle the hostages crisis, were part of an international agreement by which assets of Iran or Iranian national entities which were situated in foreign countries and were the subjects of claims were to be released and returned to Iran to set up a fund out of which awards made by the Tribunal would be satisfied.

But the expression is also used to refer to binding rules of public international law. In *Buck v Attorney General*[30] Diplock LJ said that the rules of comity were:

> The accepted rules of mutual conduct as between state and state which each state adopts in relation to other states and expects other states to adopt in relation to itself. One of those rules is that it does not purport to exercise jurisdiction over the internal affairs of any other independent state, or to apply measures of coercion to it or to its property, except in accordance with the rules of public international law.

He then went on to say that one of the most common applications of that rule was the doctrine of sovereign immunity. When comity is used in this sense, it no longer refers to mere courtesies. It is no doubt in the sense of binding rules of public international law that the expression is used in the cases on state im-

---

[28] At 834.
[29] [1986] QB 441 at 461–462.
[30] [1965] Ch 745 at 770.

munity. It was in this sense and in that context that Lord Denning referred to the 'comity of nations'[31] and that Cohen LJ referred to the 'principles of comity established by international law'.[32]

Similarly the rule that the English court should not normally make a determination that a foreign state is in breach of its international obligations to a third state is founded in comity in the sense of international law. In *Westland Helicopters Ltd v Arab Organization for Industrialization*[33] the principal issue was whether the Egyptian management of Arab Organization for Industrialization, an international organization of which Egypt and three Gulf State were members, could bring an action in England to lay claim to its assets. The right of the Egyptian management to sue depended in part on an argument that Egypt was entitled to appoint the management because the other Member States had been in breach of the treaty establishing the organization. It was held that to determine whether there had been a breach of treaty by the three Gulf states or by Egypt would be contrary to the principle of non-justiciability, because it would directly affect the rights of the international organisation to its assets and would indirectly affect the sovereign states which were members of it and 'comity precludes any such determination'.

So also, it is suggested, when the courts speak of comity in the context of jurisdiction over crimes which are partly committed or conceived abroad, they are talking about binding rules of public international law. Thus in *R v Treacy*[34] Lord Diplock said, in relation to the reasons for the geographical limitation on criminal jurisdiction:

> The only relevant reason is to be found in the international rules of comity which, in the absence of express provision to the contrary, it is presumed that Parliament did not intend to break. It would be an unjustifiable interference with the sovereignty of other nations over conduct of persons in their own territories if we were to punish persons for conduct which did not take place in the United Kingdom and had no harmful consequences there. But I see no reason in comity for requiring any wider limitation than that upon the exercise by Parliament of its legislative power in the field of criminal law.

---

[31] *Rahimtoola v Nizam of Hyderabad* [1958] AC 379 at 417.
[32] *Krajina v Tass Agency* [1949] 2 All ER 274 at 280.
[33] [1995] QB 282 at 294.
[34] [1971] AC 537 at 561–562. See also *Liangsiriprasert v US Government* [1991] 2 AC 225 at 251: 'Their Lordships can find nothing in precedent, comity or good sense that should inhibit the common law from regarding as justiciable in England inchoate crimes committed abroad which are intended to result in the commission of criminal offences in England', *per* Lord Griffiths. See also *Director of Public Prosecutions v Stonehouse* [1978] AC 55; *R v Doot* [1973] AC 807.

> There is no rule of comity to prevent Parliament from prohibiting under pain of punishment persons who are present in the United Kingdom, and so owe local obedience to our law, from doing physical acts in England, notwithstanding that the consequences of those acts take effect outside the United Kingdom.
>
> . . .
>
> Nor . . . can I see any reason in comity to prevent Parliament from rendering liable to punishment, if they subsequently come to England, persons who have done outside the United Kingdom physical acts which have had harmful consequences upon victims in England . . . Comity gives no right to a state to insist that any person may with impunity do physical acts in its own territory which have harmful consequences to persons within the territory of another state.

It is suggested that it is not accidental that similar language has been used, sometimes by the same judges, in relation to international civil jurisdiction. In 1886 Lord Coleridge said that Order 11 was enacted to bring English practice 'into accordance with well-settled rules of international law, or, at all events, comity'.[35] In *Vitkovice Horni a Hutni Tezirstvo v Korner*[36] Lord Radcliffe said that ordinary principles of international comity were invaded by permitting service out of the jurisdiction, and the courts should therefore approach with circumspection any request for leave to serve out of the jurisdiction. So also in *Tyne Improvement Commissioners v Armement Anversois SA, The Brabo*[37] Lord Normand said that the jurisdiction conferred by Order 11 was anomalous, and was a departure from the jurisdiction recognised by the comity of nations and an invasion of the sovereignty of the state within which leave to serve is granted. The idea being expressed here is not so much that the assumption of jurisdiction is contrary to international comity or international law, but that because in England jurisdiction depends on service of the proceedings, to authorize service in a foreign country may be a violation of the sovereignty of that country.

The same thought was expressed by Scott LJ in *George Monro Ltd v American Cyanamid*:[38]

> Service out of the jurisdiction at the instance of our courts is necessarily prima facie an interference with the exclusive jurisdiction of the sovereignty of the foreign country where service is to be effected . . . As a matter of international comity it seems to me important to make sure that no such service shall be allowed unless it is clearly within both the letter and the spirit of Or XI.

---

[35] *Field v Bennett* (1886) 56 LJQB 89 at 91.
[36] [1951] AC 869 at 882.
[37] [1949] AC 326 at 357.
[38] [1944] KB 432 at 437.

In *Mackender v Feldia AG*[39] Diplock LJ suggested that the jurisdiction claimed by the English court when it granted leave under Order 11 was 'a claim which conflicts with the general principles of comity between civilised nations'.

With the possible exception of the jurisdiction based on a contract being governed by English law, it can no longer be said that the jurisdiction claimed by English courts in civil litigation in relation to acts abroad is exorbitant. Nor, in the light of the bilateral and multilateral treaties concerning service abroad, can it be said that service abroad of English proceedings will (at least in the normal case) be an infringement of comity.[40]

E. Respect for Foreign Public Law

Thus far we have seen that comity is used to express concerns over the exercise of criminal jurisdiction in relation to acts committed in foreign countries, and also the service of proceedings in foreign countries, and the assumption of civil jurisdiction in relation to foreigners or to acts done abroad. The function of comity in this context is to ensure that there are limits to the jurisdiction of the forum to assert jurisdiction over acts taking place in the territory of another sovereign.

There are two rules supported by considerations of comity which have a different purpose. The first is the rule that the English court will not enforce a contract which was conceived to commit a wrongful act in a foreign country, even if otherwise the contract is valid by English law. The second is the rule (sometimes called the act of state doctrine) that the court will not rule on the validity of an act committed in a country where it is valid and authorized by law.

Comity played a major role in the two leading cases on the rule that it is contrary to public policy to enforce a contract made to break the laws of a friendly foreign state. Lawrence LJ said in *Foster v Driscoll*:[41]

> The ground upon which I rest my judgment that such a partnership is illegal is that its recognition by our courts would furnish a just cause for complaint by the

---

[39] [1967] 2 QB 590, 590, CA. See the same judge in *The Chaparral* [1968] 2 Lloyd's Rep 158 at 163, CA; *Amin Rasheed Shipping Corp v Kuwait Insurance Co* [1984] AC 50 at 65.

[40] But the position will be different if the foreign court considers that the proceedings are an infringement of sovereignty. Cf *Phillip Alexander Securities and Futures Ltd v Bamberger* [1996] CLC 1757.

[41] [1929] 1 KB 470 at 510.

United States government against our government . . . and would be contrary to
our obligation of international comity as now understood and recognized, and
therefore would offend against our notions of public morality.

In *Regazzoni v K C Sethia (1944) Ltd*[42] Viscount Simonds said:

> It can hardly be regarded as a matter of comity that the courts of this country will
> not entertain a suit by a foreign State to enforce its revenue laws. It is, on the
> other hand, nothing else than comity which has influenced our courts to refuse
> as a matter of public policy to enforce, or to award damages for the breach of, a
> contract which involves the violation of foreign law on foreign soil . . . Just as
> public policy avoids contracts which offend against our own law, so it will avoid
> at least some contracts which violate the laws of a foreign State, and it will do so
> because public policy demands that deference to international comity.

What the notion of comity is doing here is to express respect for foreign law,
and perhaps also the idea that assisting or encouraging a breach of foreign criminal law in the foreign country is in some way an invasion of its sovereignty, or
participation by the English judicial authorities in a crime in the foreign country. It was for that reason that in *Ispahani v Bank Melli Iran*[43] Robert Walker LJ
inclined to the view that the rule required not only that the contract be intended to break the foreign law, but also that it required that the prohibited acts
were to be carried out within the territory of the foreign state. That was because
'international comity is naturally much readier to accept that a country's laws
ought to be obeyed within its own territory, than to recognise them as having
exorbitant effect'.

In *Buck v Attorney General*[44] Diplock LJ linked the idea that to exercise jurisdiction over the affairs of a foreign state would be contrary to international law
and comity with the act of state doctrine by saying that for the English court to
pronounce upon the validity of a law of a foreign sovereign state within its own
territory would be to assert jurisdiction over the internal affairs of that state,
which 'would be a breach of the rules of comity'. The notion of respect for foreign law and foreign sovereignty also underlies the dictum of Scrutton LJ in the
famous case on the act of state doctrine, *Luther v Sagor*,[45] that it would 'be a serious breach of international comity, if a state is recognized as a sovereign independent state, to postulate that its legislation is "contrary to essential principles

---

[42] [1958] AC 301 at 318–319. See also *per* Lord Reid at 323.
[43] *The Times*, 29 December 1997, CA.
[44] [1965] Ch 745 at 770.
[45] [1921] 3 KB 532 at 558–559, CA.

of justice and morality".' The English Court of Appeal had relied on American authority, where it had been said that the rule rested upon 'the highest considerations of international comity and expediency'.[46] But in 1964 the United States Supreme Court abandoned international law and comity as the basis for the act of state doctrine,[47] and substituted as its basis the domestic doctrine of separation of powers, reflecting the strong sense of the judicial branch that its engagement in the task of passing on the validity of foreign acts of state may hinder the conduct of foreign affairs.[48]

F. Anti-suit Injunctions

Both in the Commonwealth and in the United States the courts have been sensitive to the charge that to grant an anti-suit injunction may be contrary to considerations of comity. It used to be emphasized that an anti-suit injunction was directed to the party and not to the foreign court. But it is well recognised that the foreign court might take a different view. In *Phillip Alexander Securities and Futures Ltd v Bamberger*[49] the Court of Appeal accepted that the conventional view was that an anti-suit injunction only operated *in personam,* with the consequence that the English courts do not and have never regarded themselves as interfering with the exercise of the foreign court of its jurisdiction. But in that case the German courts regarded the injunctions as an infringement of their sovereignty and refused to permit them to be served in Germany. Although comity was not referred to in terms in that case, it is clearly a recognition that an anti-suit injunction might be an interference with the sovereignty and jurisdiction of a foreign country.

The same point was made in *Barclays Bank v Homan*[50] where Glidewell LJ said that the judge in the foreign court might sometimes fail to appreciate the distinction between the restriction on the litigant and an interference with the exercise by the foreign court of its own jurisdiction. The point was proved when in the *Laker Airways* litigation Judge Harold Greene in the Washington DC federal District Court referred to Parker J's statement that the English injunction

---

[46] *Oetjen v Central Leather*, 246 US 297, 303–304 (1918).
[47] *Banco Nacional de Cuba v Sabbatino*, 376 US 398 (1964).
[48] See *W S Kirkpatrick & Co v Environmental Tectonics Corp Intl*, 493 US 400, 404 (1990) *per* Justice Scalia.
[49] [1996] CLC 1757 at 1789–1790.
[50] [1993] BCLC 680 at 700.

did not represent an interference by one court with proceedings in another, and said:

> With utmost respect, this court must differ. It can hardly be said that an order which . . . directs a party not to file further papers in this Court, as did the order of the British court . . . is anything other than a direct interference with the proceedings in this Court.[51]

It was no doubt with this decision in mind that in the final phase of this contest between the English and American courts, in *British Airways Board v Laker Airways Ltd*,[52] Lord Scarman said that an anti-suit injunction was, however disguised and indirect, an interference with the process of justice in the foreign court.

But comity considerations play a lesser role when the court enjoins breach of an arbitration or jurisdiction agreement. In the *Angelic Grace*[53] the Court of Appeal held that when an injunction was sought to restrain a party from proceeding in a foreign court in breach of an arbitration agreement governed by English law, the English court ought not to feel any diffidence in granting the injunction. In particular Leggatt LJ said[54] that he did not contemplate that an Italian judge would regard it as an interference with comity if the English court, having ruled on the scope of the English arbitration clause, then sought to enforce it by restraining the charterers by injunction from trying their luck in duplicated proceedings in the Italian court.

In England the most authoritative discussion of the role of comity in this context has been by Lord Goff in *Airbus Industrie v Patel*:[55]

> As a general rule, before an anti-suit injunction can properly be granted by an English Court to restrain a person from pursuing proceedings in a foreign jurisdiction in cases of the kind under consideration in the present case, comity requires that the English forum should have a sufficient interest in, or connection with, the matter in question to justify the indirect interference with the foreign court which an anti-suit injunction entails.

After drawing attention to reliance on comity considerations by the High

---

[51] *Laker Airways Ltd v Pan American Airways*, 559 F Supp 1124 at 1128 (DDC 1983).
[52] [1985] AC 58 at 95.
[53] [1995] 1 Lloyd's Rep 87.
[54] At 95.
[55] [1999] 1 AC 119 at 138 et seq.

Court of Australia[56] and by the Supreme Court of Canada[57] and by federal courts in the United States, he said that the case required the English court to identify, for the first time, the limits which comity imposed on the exercise of the jurisdiction to grant anti-suit injunctions. He preferred a solution which gave due recognition to comity, but, subject to that, maintained the traditional basis of the jurisdiction as being to intervene as the ends of justice might require.

Lord Goff, as Robert Goff LJ, had already subjected the American law to analysis in 1984,[58] and his speech in *Airbus Industrie* contains an elaborate discussion of the differing approaches which the United States federal courts have taken to the role of comity in anti-suit injunctions. There is a division of authority between the Circuits. There is what has been described as the laxer standard, under which the court will grant an anti-suit injunction if the foreign proceedings are vexatious or oppressive and cause inequitable hardship. This approach is adopted by the Fifth, Seventh, and Ninth Circuits, and involves consideration of the effect on the jurisdiction of a foreign sovereign as one factor relevant to the grant of relief, but requires evidence that comity is likely to be impaired.[59] The stricter standard (espoused by the Second and Sixth Circuits and the District of Columbia Circuit) requires the court to consider international comity and to grant an injunction only to protect its own jurisdiction or to prevent its public policies from being invaded.[60]

The *Laker Airways* litigation is a prime example of the operation of comity in modern commercial international litigation.[61] After the English courts had granted anti-suit injunctions to prevent the continuance by the liquidator of Laker Airways of his proceedings against the international airlines in the

---

[56] *CSR Ltd v Cigna Insurance Australia Ltd* (1997) 146 ALR 402 at 437–438.

[57] *Amchem Products Inc v Workers Compensation Board* (1990) 102 DLR (4th) 96.

[58] *Bank of Tokyo v Karoon* [1987] AC 45n.

[59] See especially the judgments of Posner CJ in *Philips Medical Systems International NV v Bruetman*, 8 F 3d 600 (7th Cir 1993); *Allendale Mutual Ins v Bull Data Systems*, 10 F 3d 425 (7th Cir 1993); and also *Kaepa, Inc v Achilles Corp*, 76 F 3d 624 (5th Cir 1996); *Seattle Totems Hockey Club, Inc v Nat'l Hockey League*, 652 F 2d 852 (9th Cir 1981). See also Collins, in *Current Legal Issues in International Commercial Litigation* (1997), 6–8.

[60] Especially *Laker Airways Ltd v Sabena Belgian World Airways*, 731 F 2d 909 (DC Cir 1984); *Gau Shan Co Bankers Trust Co*, 956 F 2d 1349 (6th Cir 1992); *China Trade & Dev Corp v MV Choong Yong*, 837 F 2d 33 (2d Cir 1987); *Republic of Philippines v Westinghouse Electric Corp*, 43 F 3d 65 (3d Cir 1995); *General Electric Co v Deutz*, 270 F 3d 144 (3d Cir 2001).

[61] For a full account see Collins, *Essays in International Litigation and the Conflict of Laws* (1994), 110–117.

United States, Judge Harold Greene in the District Court in Washington described the English injunctions as a direct interference with the proceedings in his court. It was in response to his remarks that Sir John Donaldson MR said:[62]

> . . . let it be said no less loudly and clearly that neither the English courts nor the English judges entertain any feelings of hostility towards the American antitrust laws or would ever wish to denigrate that or any other American law. Judicial comity is shorthand for good neighbourliness, common courtesy and mutual respect between those who labour in adjoining judicial vineyards.

Subsequently, when the Court of Appeals for the District of Columbia Circuit came to consider whether to uphold an injunction restraining Sabena from taking action in England to frustrate American proceedings, Judge Wilkey said that the court recognized

> that comity serves our international system like the mortar which cements together a brick house. No one would willingly permit the mortar to crumble or be chipped away for fear of compromising the entire structure.[63]

He said that comity was a complex and elusive concept: 'the degree of deference that a domestic forum must pay to the act of a foreign government not otherwise binding on the forum'.[64] He went on to say that the central precept of comity taught that, when possible, the decisions of foreign tribunals should be given effect in domestic courts, since recognition fostered international co-operation and encouraged reciprocity, thereby promoting predictability and stability through satisfaction of mutual expectations.

In this context he was talking about recognition of foreign judgments, where reciprocity is no longer a very fashionable basis for recognition. He then went on to talk about comity in a somewhat different sense when he said :

> but no nation can expect its laws to reach further than its jurisdiction to prescribe, adjudicate, and enforce. Every nation must often rely on other countries to help it achieve its regulatory expectations. Thus, comity compels national courts to act at all times to increase the international legal ties that advance the rule of law with and among nations.

---

[62] *British Airways Board v Laker Airways Ltd* [1984] QB 142 at 185–186.
[63] *Laker Airways Ltd v Sabena Belgian Airlines*, 731 F 2d 909, 937 (DC Cir 1984).
[64] ibid.

G. Extra-territorial Application of Legislation

The *Laker Airways* litigation involved the application of United States anti-trust law to international airline operations. Judge Wilkey said that it was often argued that the application of United States anti-trust laws to foreign nationals violated principles of comity. But allowing the conduct of the defendant to go unregulated could amount to an unjustified evasion of a United States law protecting a significant domestic interest. That was one context in which comity would not be extended to a foreign act. But if the anti-competitive aspect of the injury was not appreciable, and the actions of foreign governments denoted the existence of strong foreign interest, then comity might suggest a lack of congressional intent to regulate the alleged conduct, and comity might therefore have a strong bearing on where the application of a United States anti-trust law should go forward. But in the *Laker* case the violation of public policy vitiating comity was not that the evasion of a United States anti-trust law might injure United States interests, but rather that the United States judicial functions had been usurped, destroying the autonomy of the court. Comity ordinarily required courts of a separate sovereign not to interfere with concurrent proceedings based on the same claim, at least until a judgment was reached in one action. Although reciprocity might no longer be an absolute prerequisite to comity, American law had not departed so far from common sense that it was a reversible error for a court not to capitulate to a foreign judgment based on statutes, like the Protection of Trading Interests Act 1980, designed to prevent the court from resolving legitimate claims placed before it.

In *Hartford Fire Insurance Co v California* [65] it was held by a bare majority of the United States Supreme Court that the United States could exercise anti-trust jurisdiction under the Sherman Act in relation to allegations that London-based reinsurers had engaged in unlawful conspiracies to affect the market for insurance in the United States and that their conduct had produced substantial effects within the United States.

It was not in doubt that the Sherman Act applied to foreign conduct which was meant to produce and did in fact produce some substantial effect in the United States.[66] Cases at the appellate level below the Supreme Court had decided that

---

[65] (1993) 509 US 769.
[66] See 509 US at 796; *United States v Aluminum Co of America,* 148 F 2d 416 (2d Cir 1945); Restatement Third, *Foreign Relations Law,* s 415 (1987).

the courts could refuse to exercise jurisdiction under the Sherman Act if comity required that it should not be exercised.[67] In the *Hartford Fire Insurance* case, the English re-insurers argued that jurisdiction should not be exercised because the application of the Sherman Act to conduct which was lawful in England would lead to a conflict with English law and policy.

The majority held that it was unnecessary to decide whether there was a discretion not to apply the Sherman Act on comity grounds. That was because there was no true conflict between English law and United States law. Even if the conduct in England was consistent with United Kingdom law and policy, there was no conflict 'where a person subject to regulation by two states can comply with the laws of both'.[68] It was not argued by the English re-insurers that English law required them to act in some manner prohibited by the law of the United States, or that compliance with the laws of both countries was otherwise impossible. Consequently there was no conflict, and international comity was not involved.[69]

For the minority, Justice Scalia disagreed with the majority's position that comity involved the question whether the court should decline to exercise jurisdiction. He considered that the true question was whether the Sherman Act covered the relevant conduct. He accepted that the Sherman Act applied extra-territorially, but considered that the Sherman Act did not apply to cases in which its application would exceed the limits of customary international law. In considering Story's distinction between the 'comity of the courts' and the 'comity of nations', and concluding that only the comity of nations was relevant in his analysis, Justice Scalia is plainly treating comity in this context as equivalent to public international law. On that basis, and using the Restatement Third's analysis of the situations in which a state should refrain from prescribing law when the exercise of legislative jurisdiction is unreasonable,[70] Justice Scalia concluded that the exercise of legislative jurisdiction was contrary to international comity: the relevant activity took place primarily in the United Kingdom; the defendants were British corporations and British

---

[67] See especially *Timberlane Lumber Co v Bank of America, NT & SA*, 549 F 2d 597 (9th Cir 1976); *Mannington Mills, Inc v Congoleum Corp.*, 595 F 2d 1287 (3d Cir 1979); *Laker Airways Ltd v Sabena, Belgian World Airlines,* 731 F 2d 909 (DC Cir 1984).

[68] Citing Restatement Third, *Foreign Relations Law*, s 403, comment *e*.

[69] In *US v Nippon Paper Industries Co, Ltd*, 109 F 3d 1, 8 (1st Cir 1997) it was said: 'Comity is more an aspiration than a fixed rule, more a matter of grace than a matter of obligation. In all events its growth in the anti-trust sphere has been stunted by *Hartford Fire . . .*'.

[70] ibid, s 403(1).

nationals with their principal place of business or residence outside the United States. The United Kingdom had established a comprehensive regulatory scheme governing the London re-insurance markets, and had a heavy interest in regulating the activity. Consequently it was 'unimaginable that an assertion of legislative jurisdiction by the United States would be considered reasonable, and therefore it is inappropriate to assume, in the absence of statutory indication to the contrary, that Congress has made such an assertion'.[71]

H. Co-operation Between Courts

An important use of the comity concept is to express the desirability of co-operation between courts in the international context. Thus in *The Abidin Daver*[72] Lord Diplock said that the development in the law on staying of actions was 'that judicial chauvinism has been replaced by judicial comity to an extent which I think the time is now right to acknowledge frankly is, in the field of law with which this appeal is concerned, indistinguishable from the Scottish legal doctrine of *forum non conveniens*'.

But notions of comity do not require co-operation where the policy of the forum militates against it. The Supreme Court of Canada, in rejecting a universalist approach to international insolvency, said very recently:[73]

> In this appeal we are urged to adopt a 'universalist approach' to bankruptcies and insolvencies that affect more than one jurisdiction . . . The chaotic fact situation faced by the Trustees in this case, from Singapore to the Bahamas and Israel to New Zealand, is eloquent testimony to the need for judicial co-operation and international comity.

> . . .

> In *Morguard Investments Ltd v De Savoye*, [1990] 3 S.C.R. 1077, the Court expanded on the definition of international comity by noting that the twin objectives sought by private international law in general and the doctrine of

---

[71] 509 US at 819.
[72] [1984] AC 398 at 411. In the United States the *lis alibi pendens* doctrine has also been rooted in considerations of comity. In *Seguros del Estado, SA v Sci. Games, Inc*, 262 F 3d 1164 (11th Cir 2001) it was said that *lis alibi pendens* is a doctrine rooted in international comity which permits a court to refuse to exercise jurisdiction in the face of parallel litigation that is ongoing in another country.
[73] *Holt Cargo Systems Inc v ABC Containerline NV (Trustees of)* 2001 SCC 90. Cf *Society of Lloyd's v Meinzer* (2001) 55 OR (3d) 688 (Ont CA).

international comity in particular were order and fairness. This was reiterated in *Hunt v T & N PLC*, [1993] 4 SCR 289 at 325, and again in *Tolofson v Jensen* [1994] 3 SCR 1022, at 1058, where the Court gave pre-eminence to the objective of order . . .

But the Supreme Court of Canada rejected the universalist approach because the judge had been right, having acknowledged the importance of comity and international co-ordination in a proper case, to place primary emphasis on the fact that he was dealing with an *in rem* action by secured creditors against a ship which at the time of the bankruptcy the Federal Court had already arrested and he had already ordered appraised and sold.

Where, however, there is an interest in co-operation, comity will justify it. Under Article 24 of the Brussels and Lugano Conventions a court in a Contracting State may grant provisional or protective measures if a court in another Contracting State has jurisdiction over the substance of the matter. The question has arisen whether the English court will grant measures of a kind which the foreign court cannot or will not itself grant. The answer given by the Court of Appeal is that the English court may grant such relief. In *Credit Suisse Fides Trust SA v Cuoghi*[74] Millett LJ stated the underlying policy:

> It is becoming widely accepted that comity between the courts of different countries requires mutual respect for the territorial integrity of each other's jurisdictions, but that this should not inhibit a court in one jurisdiction from rendering whatever assistance it properly can to a court in another in respect of assets located or persons resident within the territory of the former.

In many cases on letters rogatory the courts have emphasized the considerations of comity inherent in the need for international judicial co-operation in obtaining evidence. Thus in *State of Minnesota v Philip Morris Inc*[75] Lord Woolf MR said:

> The approach of this court and other courts in this jurisdiction will be to seek to assist a foreign court wherever it is appropriate. For that reason the courts will seek to give effect to a Letter of Request wherever this is practical. Comity between jurisdictions demands no different an approach.

In *Soc Nat Industrielle Aerospatiale v US District Court*[76] the United States

---

[74] [1998] QB 818 at 827. See also *Refco Inc v Eastern Trading Co* [1999] 1 Lloyd's Rep 159 at 175.
[75] [1998] I L Pr 170 at 176. See also *Re International Power Industries NV* [1985] BCLC 128 at 130. For insolvency see *England v Smith* [2001] Ch 419, at 435, CA.
[76] 482 US 522 (1987).

Supreme Court, in considering whether a party seeking discovery/evidence from another party to the litigation, must resort first to the Hague Evidence Convention if the other party was abroad revealed a sharp divergence in the use of comity in that context. The question for the Supreme Court was whether French aircraft manufacturers who were being sued in the United States were obliged to give documentary discovery in the normal course of judicial proceedings in the United States. They argued that the effect of the Hague Evidence Convention was that the plaintiffs had to resort to the Convention and seek the documents through letters rogatory issued by the United States courts to the French court.

The majority rejected this argument. The Convention itself imposed no such role of first resort:

> Moreover, the concept of international comity requires in this context a more particularised analysis of the respective interests of the foreign nation and the requesting nation than [the defendants'] proposed general rule would generate.[77]

For the majority, comity 'refers to the spirit of co-operation in which a domestic tribunal approaches the resolution of cases touching the laws and interests of other sovereign states'.[78] The Court declined to hold as a blanket matter that comity required resort to the Hague Evidence Convention procedures without prior scrutiny in each case of the particular facts, sovereign interests, and likelihood that resort to those procedures would prove effective. The minority also rejected a blanket rule requiring first resort to the Hague Evidence Convention, but favoured a general presumption that, in most cases, United States courts ought to resort first to the Hague Evidence Convention procedures. In particular, the minority disagreed with the view of the majority that the concept of comity required an individualised analysis of the interests present in each particular case before a court decided whether to apply the Convention:

> Comity is not just a vague political concern favouring international co-operation when it is in our interest to do so. Rather it is a principle under which judicial decisions reflect the systemic value of reciprocal tolerance and goodwill . . . As in the choice of law analysis, which from the very beginning has been linked to international comity, the threshold question in a comity analysis is whether there is in fact a true conflict between domestic and foreign law. When there is a conflict, a court should seek a reasonable accommodation that reconciles the

---

[77] At 543–544.
[78] At 543, n 27.

central concerns of both sets of laws. In doing so, it should perform a tripartite analysis that considers the foreign interests, the interests of the United States, and the mutual interests of all nations in a smoothly functioning international legal regime.[79]

The minority thought that the Convention had already reconciled what might otherwise have been conflicting interests, and use of the Convention would advance those interests.

It is tempting to conclude that the difference between the majority and the minority had nothing to do with their views on the content of the concept of comity. The majority thought that in a particular case comity might require the court not to order discovery against a foreign party: the minority thought that comity involved a presumption that the competing sovereign interests of the United States and the country where the evidence was located could be accommodated by the Hague Evidence Convention procedures. But there was no attempt to analyse the elements of comity, and it is difficult to avoid the conclusion that it was simply being used as a label to justify conflicting results.

I. Conclusions

Almost a hundred years ago Lord Shaw of Dunfermline said:[80] '. . . the "comity of nations" is an expression which is familiar but necessarily indefinite. The attempts to fix it down into a set of rules of legal or binding effect, and the discussions which have accompanied such attempts, have been very fruitless'. It is possible to agree with this sentiment, but also to conclude that the use of the concept of comity in private international law, particularly in connection with the influence of public international law, is worthy of further research and analysis. The vast amount of material cries out for some synthesis, and this piece is intended as a modest step in that direction. What the author has endeavoured to show is that the material cannot, and should not, be dismissed as if it did not exist and had nothing to tell us about the function of private international law, the relations between legal systems, between courts and between public and private international law.

---

[79] At 555.
[80] *Lecouturier v Rey* [1910] AC 262 at 267.

5

THE EU AND A METAMORPHOSIS OF PRIVATE INTERNATIONAL LAW

Hans Ulrich Jessurun d'Oliveira

—God forgive me, he speaks Dutch fustian
Christopher Marlowe, Tragicall History of Doctor Faustus[1]

A. Introduction: Earlier Paradigm Switches

Although private international law has always been looked upon as an arcane subject—a characterization which the high priests celebrating its mysterious lore have seldom sought to deny—it has never ceased to be influenced by the outside world. The permeability of its body of rules and principles and indeed of its very structure has been repeatedly demonstrated over the centuries. The amazing change of paradigm brought about by the success, primarily on the continent to be sure, of volume VIII of von Savigny's *System des heutigen römischen Rechts*

---

* Professor Emeritus of Migration Law at the University of Amsterdam; former Professor of Comparative Law and Private International Law, European University Institute (Florence).
[1] The author is aware of the fact that 'Dutch' in this quotation in all probability means 'German', but he may be excused because of his descent, in the mother's line, from German families.

(1849) did not fall from the sky. It is the result, not only of the genius of the author, but of profound changes in society as well. I do not need to dwell too long on these well-known transformations. The instauration of the sovereignty of the people, the fall of the *ancien régime* and concentration of power in the bourgeoisie, the ideology of the enlightenment and its principles of freedom, equality, and a little solidarity, the industrialization, the professionalization, and bureaucratization of society and government, accompanied by new theories about the place and function of law, have all contributed to theories such as those of von Savigny.

It was a dramatic switch which he performed in focussing not on the interpretation of Statutes with a view to defining their personal-spatial scope anymore, but on the *objects* of legislation: legal relationships. The determination of their conceptual seat in order to connect them to a national legal system found its parallel in the emancipation of citizens from previous feudal, and *ancien régime* vertical relations. In hindsight, the preoccupation with the seat of a legal relationship and the abandonment of the text of local rules as the *sedes materiae* of private international law represented the equality of emerging nation states and was flavoured by considerations of public international law. The change of paradigm favoured solutions of a universal character, whereas the medieval postglossatorial masters were structurally bound to come out with unilateral solutions. The conflicts rules, using as they did and do a single connecting factor to link a legal relationship to a legal system, whether *lex fori* or a foreign law, formed a neutral and blind medium between legal orders, stressing in this way the sovereign equality of nations.

This method had its advantages. Ordering the legal aspect of society in a restricted number of forms and institutions, developing, on a mostly historical-dogmatic basis, a typology of legal phenomena enabled von Savigny and his followers to indicate for each instance of a typical legal relationship the key aspect: a characteristic of one or more actors such as domicile (and later on the continent nationality), the place where a crucial act took place, etc. General concepts, developed in the course of many centuries, and refined in universities and courts, a whole fabric of legal conceptualism, formed the infrastructure for the reasoned selection of these features which formed the bridge between substantive law and legal relationships on the one hand, and conflicts rules and the applicable law on the other. The method opened the possibility of convergence of conflicts rules in national legal orders, based as they were on common principles and concepts of Roman law.

Another advantage over Statute theory lay in its efficiency in dealing with the ever increasing number of similar cases, caused by the standardization of commercial activities in industrial society, a need to which the national codifications of civil law responded as well. These codes again reflected the equality of the citizens in the nation states. Post-revolutionary liberalism and ideas about the reduced role of the state paved the way for private dealings without much interference by the nightwatchman state.

With the rise of the welfare state and the regulatory omnipresence of the state in implementing social security, public health, consumer protection etc, civil law became intertwined with regulatory schemes and devices of all sorts in the twentieth century. Again, private international law underwent radical changes as a reflection upon the qualitative modifications of western societies, especially after the Second World War. This 'conflicts revolution', initiated in the USA, but which was hailed in Europe by many a scholar and digested in various ways in legal writings and case law, eventually took the more modest form of specific doctrines about how to deal with governmental inroads into the realm of civil law. Concepts such as *scope rules* developed, indicating written rules expressing the legislator's intent to cover a certain number of international dealings, answering to certain descriptions or requirements by its regulatory provisions. These scope rules were by their nature mostly unilateral in their appearance, indicating, eg, in which types of cases a currency regulation of a certain country, or an export permit system demanded application.

The concept of *directly applicable rules* found its way into the courts and even into legislation and international instruments. Here again, an inroad was sought into the regular unfolding of the system of private international law of identifying a case as an instance of a type, an institution, bringing it under the apposite conflicts rule with its characteristic connecting factor, and sending it to be governed by the applicable law. Coercive laws, originating in the *lex fori*, the *lex causae*, or even extraneous laws could tear the fabric of traditional private international law and lead to blatantly deviant results. Modern private international law has lost its unitary mode and shows a dual character: one concentrating in the Savignian way on citizens and their dealings, and the other incorporating the distinct and overriding interests of societies and states as a whole, including interests common to states, using techniques reminiscent of the old Statute theories.

Of course, the tools developed in order to define the applicability of regulatory rules issued by states and international organizations such as the EU appear to be much more sophisticated than the hermeneutic devices of the statutists. We are amused by the efforts made by medieval scholars, wrestling with the *consuetudo Angliae,* the law of primogeniture as expressed in various texts, possibly over-amused, and not without conceit. The attempt to distinguish Statuta as to their objectives into personal and real as part of the process of establishing their scope, of which we find already some roots in the works of Bartolus, is as such sensible. Teleological interpretation is nothing to joke about. But we chuckle about the method, which has been called *'rein verbal',*[2] or 'a very crude literal interpetation'.[3] If the local English Statute reads: *Bona decedentium veniant ad primogenitum* it is considered to deal primarily with the goods of the estate, whereas if the statute is phrased as *Primogenitus succedat etc* it is interpreted as being concerned primarily with the person of the heir. These features of the texts decide their scope. In the first case the Statute is territorial and governs only goods present within the territory of the local Statute whereas in the second case the personal character of the Statute could bring about certain extraterritorial effects, which depended in part on the Englishness of the *de cuius.* 'During five centuries this solution was ridiculed', writes Martin Wolff and he cites Bertrand d'Argentré (1519–1590) as having disqualified Bartolus and his followers by remarking *'pudeat*[4] *pueros talia aut sentire aut docere'.* ('It is a shame to teach students such nonsense').

I am not sure that this attitude is still fruitful. It would be better to place this method of interpretation of texts in its historical context, and to consider it not as whimsical clumsiness prevalent in a dark age, but as a way of dealing with important Latin texts which was firmly rooted in scholarly tradition in the early Renaissance. Texts as such had a much higher status in these centuries which rediscovered those bequeathed by the ancients. The *trivium* may have had its impact as well. In all events, it is important to keep in mind that, looming behind the Statuta and the demarcation lines amongst them, was the all encompassing firmament of Roman law, the *ius commune* of which the city states with their Statutes had succeeded in wrenching out exceptions to. These early manifestations of what we now call private international law owed their existence to the emergence of local inroads into the civil *ius commune*, which had

---

[2] Max Gutzwiller, *Geschichte des International-privatrechts, von den Anfängen bis zu den groszen Kodifikationen* (1977), p 37.
[3] Martin Wolff, *Private International Law* (1945), p 25.
[4] ibid.

not only to be defined in terms of horizontal demarcations amongst the various city states but also in terms of vertical, hierarchical dividing lines with an overarching legal system of which the political structure supporting it was gradually cracking and giving way to the rules of a new class: the citizens.

One of the most fascinating characteristics of the Savignian method is undoubtedly that it proved possible to cut its method loose from its ideological tenets and still keep a viable system to tackle cases with an international element. Savigny replaced the Roman *ius commune* by the Community of civilized Nations in order to safeguard a perspective of identical national conflicts rules on the basis of agreement about the seat of legal relationships, which in turn would be inspired by conceptions and principles derived from Roman law, although coloured by the *Volksgeist,* the national spirit, as expressed by the legal professions. This ideal was shattered by the rise of sovereign states which stressed their individuality and specificity, invented their own history, and took pride in diversity. The conflict rule as a neutral, abstract way of dealing with international cases came under pressure, as the identity of the concepts used in the conflicts rule exploded. The problem of characterization or qualification was one of the results. Babylon was introduced into a conflicts rule which was supposed to speak a common legal lingo. This situation challenged a basic tenet of the Savignian system: if the legal relationship (not the individual manifestation but the abstract model) forms the object of the conflicts rule, one wonders as to which law this legal institution owes its existence. The theory of characterization presupposes a meta-theory on private international law. Another symptom of this meta-theory forms the device of *renvoi.* The perceived conflict of conflict rules led to solutions which took account of divergences in a realistic fashion by trying to find ways to arrive, in the countries involved , at the same solutions, by referral, under certain conditions, to the foreign legal system, including its rules of private international law.

The atomization and cultural diversification of the legal systems, the continuing growth and relevance of the number of states brought about the rediscovery of the concept of public policy as a device to reject the graft of alien tissues of applicable law.

The pressures of public policy increased with the development of the welfare state. The body of law, previously seen as primarily a codification of rules sedimented during centuries of refinement, changed rapidly under the influence of the industrial revolution and the changing role of the state. Legal rules became more and more instrumental, less imbued with ethical principles for individual addressees than with efficiency and rationality in organizing social justice and taming wildlife in the economic jungle. The demarcation lines between private and public law on the continent became blurred. This development gave rise to the question whether the conflicts rule referred to private law only, or also to (semi)public law of the applicable legal system. At the same time one witnessed the emergence of the applicability of rules of legal systems which neither belonged to the *lex fori* nor the *lex causae,* inexplicable in the Savignian model, which only allotted some room for laws of the forum which were intended to advance the *publica utilitas.* These laws could have a political, or economic character, or could concern the maintenance of public order in the largest sense. Savigny gives as an example 'the many statutes which limit the acquisition of immovables by Jews'.[5]

Legislators tried their hand at social engineering : laws were enhancing rationality and efficiency in ordering social and economic life, and were seen to be serving specific goals and interests. This caused tensions with the mode of existence of conflict rules as impartial and blindfolded dispensers of formal justice among legal orders. The nature or essence of the institution or legal relationship as a frame of reference in selecting an applicable law through the intermediary of their respective seats, was replaced by ideas about the serving of relevant interests. This change of paradigm took place without many formal changes in the pattern of solutions afforded by private international law. On the surface, more or less the same rules applied, but their ideological content had changed dramatically. The seat of the marriage according to its nature was not important anymore, but the promotion of divorce. The seat of the relationship between parent and child was not the relevant issue, but the increase of possibilities for the child to receive maintenance. The seat of the contract was not the key question, but the acceptance of choice of law by the parties in order to streamline international trade. This injection of the originally dogmatic conflicts system with strong elements of furtherance of selected interests brought about some formal variations as well.

A well-known example is to be found in the Hague Conventions on the Law Applicable to Maintenance Obligations. Already in 1956, the first children's maintenance obligation convention declared that the law of the place of habit-

---

[5] Friedrich Carl von Savigny, *System des heutigen Römischen Rechts*, Achter Band, (1849), p 36.

ual residence of the child would apply, but if this law would deny any maintenance to the child involved, national conflicts rules of the forum would give the child a second chance. The 1973 Convention on Maintenance Obligations overall is an even more conspicuous serial killer of hopes of escaping maintenance obligations by offering the maintenance creditor a whole sequence of applicable laws, each coming into view if the previous one does not deliver the goods. The theory of the natural seat is exchanged for the theory of sitting pretty.

And what about the conflicts rule concerning the form of legal acts and legal transactions? Take the 1961 Hague Convention on the Conflicts of Laws Relating to the Form of Testamentary Dispositions. This convention unfolds in Article 1 a fan of at least eight connecting factors with one common goal: to allow testators to draw up wills valid as to form. Although this *favour* is cloaked in the form of a conflicts rule with multiple connecting factors, its aim is to achieve substantive justice, from which the Savignian system takes its distance. Or so it seems. What does Savigny say about the matter?[6] In accordance with the basic tenets of his system he indicates without any doubt in his mind the *lex causae* of each legal act as applicable to questions of form. But he is not blind to the 'enormous difficulties' which this rule may engender in cases where the act or expression takes place elsewhere. That is why he accepts a customary rule which had developed since the sixteenth century among jurists applying the law of the place of acting: *locus regit actum,* especially in the case of wills made out of town (the *lex causae* being for Savigny the law of the domicile of the testator). This customary rule responds to 'a recognized need' and should be followed. Here we find the Prussian scholar less dogmatic and more open to substantive considerations, be it in matters of form, than one would have thought. But the customary rule is not to elbow out the *lex causae,* applicable according to the Savignian lore. 'If one looks at the grounds for the introduction of our special rule, as favouring and facilitating, then one cannot be in any doubt to consider the rule as optional, and as offering a choice'.[7] Earlier writers had expressed the view that *locus regit actum* was exclusive, and did not allow for exceptions. Savigny bowed to the customary rule, but upheld the facultative applicability of the *lex causae* which followed from his general system. In other words: he did not integrate into his own system considerations concerning the interests involved and promotion of the efficiency of transactions, but he allowed their coexistence.

Nevertheless, the conflicts rule paradigm lent itself to injection with modern

---

[6] ibid, para 381–382.
[7] ibid, para 381.

approaches. The neutrality of conflicts law, concentrating upon concepts, not interests, geared to supporting equality among nations and nation states, could be cancelled and replaced by all kinds of substantive elements and considerations. Its formal attributes offered a mask behind which interest analysis in various shapes could take shelter.[8] The indirectness of its technique has made it available for solutions engendered by profound changes in western societies, especially after the Second World War.

Some observers, including this author, predicted the downfall of the conflicts rule system itself, as the premises for the Savignian paradigm shattered into pieces.[9] I was proven wrong: the conflicts rule is still with us, and is—so it seems—even more alive and kicking than twenty-five years ago. It is obviously so resilient that it can serve any master, a genie that can perform any trick, and can survive even conflicts revolutions raging on other continents, which has inflicted new conflicts, on the meta-level of conflicts of law.

This brings me to the subject of this essay. If it is true, as I suggested, that changes in society eventually bring about changes in legal structures and substance, can it then be maintained that the European Union as it is gradually developing into something we as yet do not know, is influencing the system of private international law as we know it? Does Blagojevic's thesis still hold good? He argued forty years ago in Marxist lingo: 'Dans toute étude historique du droit international privé ainsi qu'à l'occasion de la présentation de n'importe quelle théorie ou de n'importe quelle conception contenues dans le Droit international privé, il est nécessaire d'éclaircir chaque phénomène à la lumière des conditions et des circonstances du lieu et du temps où et comment ces phénomènes se sont manifestés'.[10]

---

[8] Cf Rudolf Wiethölter, Begriffs- oder Interessenjurisprudenz—falsche Fronten im IPR und Wirtschaftsverfassungsgesetz. Bemerkungen zur selbstgerechten Kollisionsnorm. In: A Lüderitz and J Schröder (eds), *Internationales Privatrecht und Rechtsvergleichung im Ausgang des 20. Jahrhunderts. Bewährung oder Wende? Festschrift für Gerhard Kegel* (1977), pp 213–263.

[9] H U Jessurun d'Oliveira, *De ruïne van een paradigma: de konfliktregel* (inaugural address University of Amsterdam) (1976).

[10] Borislav T Blagojevic, 'Théories des Statuts à la lumière de l'histoire générale de l'évolution de la société'. In: *De Conflictu Legum, Essays Presented to R D Kollewijn and J Offerhaus* (1962), pp 67–81 (69). The quotation can be translated as:

'In every study of the history of private international law, in this manner or on the occasion of presenting no matter which theory or no matter which conception contained in private international law, it is necessary to clarify each phenomenon in the light of the conditions and circumstances of the place and time where and how these phenomena manifested themselves.'

B. The EC and its Impact on Private International Law

The European Community and private international law have always been un-easy bedfellows.[11] How common is a common market if all transactions which imply freedom of movement of goods (including capital), persons, services are subjected to provisions of private international law which are not common to the Member States? Those national conflicts rules may result in the applicabil-ity, in the same case, of the law of country A or B, dependent on the place of the forum and its set of conflicts rules. Municipal systems of private law may differ as well, and the resulting diversity on two levels clashes with the idea of the commonality of the European Market. In the early days this contradiction did not matter so much and located itself at the periphery of European conscious-ness, which was very much occupied with discovering the identity of the EEC. Here the ECJ led the way in attributing to Community law the features of su-premacy, direct effect and (sometimes) exclusiveness. Sweeping statements were *en vogue* and called for, and are still reverberating: '*The EEC Treaty has cre-ated its own legal system which . . . became an integral part of the legal systems of the Member States and which their courts are bound to apply.*'[12] Previously the ECJ had already held that, considering the spirit, the general scheme and the word-ing of the Treaty '*the Community constitutes a new legal order of international law for the benefit of which the states have limited their sovereign rights, albeit within limited fields, and the subjects of which comprise not only Member States but also their nationals*'.[13] With the expansion and deepening of the Community the communicating vessels of Member States' legal orders and that of the Community shifted more and more towards the Community in an ongoing process of production of new versions of the Treaty and of unlimited secondary legislation. In the following paragraphs I intend to roughly indicate the devel-oping morphology of rules of private international law as they come into the sphere of influence of the E(E)C and the EU. Although the successive models also represent the general picture of historical evolution, in reality this succes-sion of events shows sometimes considerable overlap.

---

[11] In writing this essay I have been inspired by a host of articles on the subject. I would like to mention especially the following: Jona Israël, Europees internationaal privaatrecht, *NIPR* (*Nederlands Internationaal Privaatrecht*) 2001, 135–149; Erik Jayme/Christian Köhler, Europäisches Kollisionsrecht 2001: Anerkennungsprinzip statt IPR? *IP RaX* 2001, 501–514.

[12] Case 6/64 *Costa v ENEL* [1964] ECR 585.

[13] Case 26/62 *Van Gend en Loos v Nederlandse Administratie der Belastingen* [1963] ECR 1.

(1) Paracommunitarian Instruments

At the outset private international law and private law generally were barely affected by EC law. The general feeling was that the Community legal order was about administrative law and regulations. More or less as an afterthought Article 220 of the original Treaty summoned Member States (not even *the* Member States) 'as far as is necessary' to enter into negotiations with each other with a view to securing for the benefit of their nationals

> the simplification of formalities governing the reciprocal recognition and enforcement of judgments of courts or tribunals and of arbitration awards.

This kind invitation eventually led to the Brussels Convention on Jurisdiction and Recognition and the Enforcement of Judgments in Civil and Commercial Matters (1968), which, in its preamble, referred to Article 220 of the Treaty. As a *traité double*, dealing not only with recognition and enforcement, but with jurisdiction itself as well, it went beyond what was required by Articles 220. At the time, in l959, the Commission held the view that jurisdiction in civil and commercial matters lay firmly with the Member States but, as the effects of judgments were limited to the territory of the forum, there was a need for an instrument dealing with recognition and enforcement of judgments in these areas. This would improve legal protection and legal security in the common market. It is interesting to note that the Brussels Convention was negotiated mostly by specialists in private international law, as was the later Rome Convention on Contractual Obligations (l980).

The status of the Brussels Convention was ambiguous.[14] Did it form part of Community law or should it be considered as an ordinary convention, just like the conventions concluded under the Statute of the Hague Conference? As is shown clearly in the Preamble its umbilical cord rested in the womb of the Treaty. Its interpretation is a matter for the ECJ, but for the rest it was an international convention just like any other treaty. Nevertheless, the initiative stemmed from motives derived from the objectives of the EEC, and its uniform interpretation was secured or at least furthered by an EEC institution which itself would be influenced or inspired by those same objectives while dealing with issues of construction of the convention. Furthermore, only Member States could become party to the convention. New Member States had to accede successively to the Brussels Convention because this was consid-

---

[14] Cf Jan Kropholler, *Europäisches Zivilprozessrecht* (l998, 6th edn), p 26.

ered to form part of the *acquis (para)communautaire.* The preamble to the parallel Lugano Convention (1988) between Member States of the European
Community and those of EFTA did not even mention Article 220 of the Treaty
anymore, although both Conventions aspired to an identical content. The ECJ
is conspicuously absent as ultimate interpreter of the Lugano Convention,
which puts this instrument at an even greater distance from the Community.

The Rome Convention (1980) on the Law Applicable to Contractual
Obligations is even more loosely connected to the EC. No legal basis in
Community law is indicated in the preamble, where just a fleeting remark is
made on the desire to continue the work on unification of private international
law undertaken within the Community, with a specific reference to the
Brussels Convention. It was on a proposal of Benelux in 1967 that the
Commission initiated work on the unification of private international law
within the EC. The Benelux were keen on a decent burial of the Benelux
Uniform Law on pil and saw an opportunity in elevating their endeavours to
the level of the EC. Although substantively there was a connection with the
Brussels Convention, a legal basis for this unification of contract law was not
available. Thus, once again, the legal form which was chosen for the unification
was not a Community legal instrument, but a traditional convention. Likewise
there is no role for the ECJ in the interpretation of the provisions of the text. Its
powers to do so do not stem from the Treaty itself, and the Protocols to the
Rome Convention to enable the Court to take up this task have not received
enough ratifications to come into effect.

As to the contents of the Rome Convention, the provisions were drafted by
specialists on private international law and followed modern patterns ('characteristic performance', a Swiss invention) without any specific orientation towards the overall objectives of the EC. Nevertheless this Convention too was
considered to form part of the corpus of the *acquis communautaire*, although
clearly outside the Treaty framework. That the Convention with its conflicts
rules of universal application is situated outside the scope of the EC Treaty is
shown by the exclusion, in Article 1(3), of international insurance contracts
which cover risks that are situated in the territories of the Member
States, whether parties to the Rome Convention or not. In the same vein Article
20 states that

> This Convention shall not affect the application of provisions which, in relation
> to particular matters, lay down choice of law rules relating to contractual oblig-
> ations and which are or will be contained in acts of the institutions of the

European Communities or in national laws harmonized in implementation of such acts.

Clearly the Convention is not such an act of the EC institutions, but it is loosely and peripherally linked to its legal and institutional order.

(2) Scattered Provisions of Private International Law

In the meantime, we have had the privilege of witnessing the proliferation of a multitude of more or less hidden treasures of private international law in EC legal instruments, primarily directives on a wide variety of topics. This development tends to reduce the content and significance of the Rome Convention, as the latter gives in Article 20 priority to secondary community legislation. In this phase the legislative activity buzzed around the fundamental freedoms of the EC, especially the freedoms to provide and receive goods and services, and the free flow of capital. The private international law aspects involved in the freedom of movement of workers, or later, persons, drew less of the attention of the lawmaking institutions at the time. But many regulations and directives organizing the harmonization or coordination of national laws in the areas of provision of goods and services contained scattered conflicts rules.

A good example of the acts referred to in Article 20 of the Rome Convention are the various directives on non-life insurance law.[15] The exclusion of insurance contracts covering risks situated in Member States' territories from the Rome Convention (and by that token the inclusion in it of insurance contracts with extracommunitarian risks) was due to the ongoing work on secondary legislation in this area.

The direction of the play here is in the hands of Articles 57 on the freedom of establishment and 59 on the freedom to provide services and other provisions of the Treaty, especially those dealing with consumer protection, rather than in those of general principles of private international law. Some of the implications of this are as follows. The establishment of a common market of insurance products is the primary objective. Conflicts rules of the Member States as such are considered, because of their diversity, as a potential obstacle to this common market. They should not only be unified, but also framed in such a way as to promote or at least not stand in the way of free competition on the European insurance market. Even if a conflict rule allowing choice of law by

---

[15] Cf Fritz Reichert-Facilides and Hans Ulrich Jessurun d'Oliveira (eds), *International Insurance Contracts Law in the EC* (1993).

the parties is part of the legal order of all Member States, such a rule can lead to different results, as choice of law could refer to the laws of any (Member) State. If a common market does not necessarily imply common substantive rules, then at least unified conflicts rules indicating a specific legal order as applicable should be considered as a logical consequence. It should furthermore be kept in mind that the EC has jurisdiction in relation to the matter only insofar as the European Community is empowered to act, ie, in interstate intracommunitarian settings. This is presumably why the Rome Convention has excluded from its scope insurance contracts concerning risks situated in the Member States of the EC, the latter having powers to regulate these contracts. Once the EC has exercised its powers by legislating on insurance contracts with risks situated in the territories of Member States, it has gained implied powers to deal with insurance contracts at large in the international arena,[16] which have not been used up till now.

The tormented transition from a European common market towards a European internal market may be considered as the ideological quicksand on which the successive directives and regulations in many fields involving the provision of goods and services have been built. The Single European Act of 1986 which has introduced this internal market and defined it as comprising '*an area without internal frontiers in which the free movement of goods, persons, services and capital is ensured . . .*' stipulated its completion by the end of 1992.

What this goal of establishing such an internal market meant or implied for the existence of private international law is quite a mystery. Abolishing internal frontiers between the Member States is not only a matter of demolishing physical barriers, but the removal of (part of) the normative framework for which these barriers are the palpable expression: independent, more or less sovereign states with their own national legal systems. Harmonization and eventually unification of municipal legal orders are some of the tools for bringing about this internal market. Blurring demarcation lines between national legal orders involves changing private international law. Indeed, private international law as such can be perceived as a barrier in itself, as it is erected on the premise of the diversity of legal systems.[17] This diversity is logically inconsistent with the idea of an internal market without legal frontiers, as the latter implies homo-

---

[16] Case 22/70 *ERTA* [1971] ECR 263.

[17] Cf my dissertation *De Antikiesregel; een paar aspekten van de behandeling van buitenlands recht in het burgerlijk proces (1971)* (The non-selection rule; some aspects of the treatment of foreign law in civil proceedings).

geneous legal surroundings, but fully in tune with Article 6 of the EU Treaty, which purports to respect 'the national identities of the Member States'.

As practice and reality are obstinate and unruly characters this state of affairs has not yet been brought about. It proved to be not feasible to develop uniform substantive rules in the field; as a result the EC had to fall back on rules of private international law. Many interests, not necessarily convergent or common, are involved. As yet, the internal market is a market still divided in zones with different legal orders which need some sort of private international law to regulate the traffic. A good example of the silhouettes which loom up in this twilight zone is the succession of three non-life insurance directives of 1973, 1988 and 1992.[18] In these directives a number of provisions of private international law are dispersed. It is probably useful to tackle them by going backwards, starting from the third directive. The preamble of this third directive—itself already numbering thirty-three paragraphs, indicating the speed with which the subject is changing and its complexity—brings some amendments to the private international law part of the previous directives. The first amendment has to do with party autonomy. Paragraph 17 of the preamble states that

> whereas within the framework of an integrated insurance market policy holders who, by virtue of their status, their size or the nature of the risks to be insured, do not require special protection in the Member State in which a risk is situated should be granted complete freedom to choose the law applicable to their insurance contracts

This liberation from the chains of protection is brought about by Article 27 of the third Directive which reads:

> Art. 7(1)(f) of Directive 88/357/EC shall be replaced by the following:

> (f) in the case of the risks referred to in art.5(d) of Directive 73/239/EEC, the parties to the contract may choose any law.

In terms of transparency this two-step retrograde provision is not very outstanding. As one plods through the directives it turns out that the freedom to choose 'any law' is widened from the category mentioned under Article 5(d)(i) of the first directive to all categories listed there under Article 5(d). More insurance contracts listed as 'large risks' are brought under a primary regime of party autonomy as they are deemed to need no protection anymore. Insurance

---

[18] Dir73/239/EEC, Dir88/357/EEC and Dir92/49/EEC. To simplify matters even more, this threesome is flanked by a number of other directives.

contracts in the internal market, then, are divided into contracts involving large risks in which party autonomy is granted , because the policyholders are deemed to be capable of looking after themselves, and other insurance contracts, in which party autonomy is restricted, as policyholders are considered to be the weaker party being consumers or non-professional players on the market. This is a deviation from the system developed in the Rome Convention 1980, which distinguishes between consumer contracts, defined in Article 5 as concerning '. . . services for a purpose which can be regarded as being outside his trade or profession'.

Otherwise Article 7 of the second directive remains unchanged (although transplanting it to the third directive has been considered).[19] This two-page provision envisages various factual situations as to the place of the risk (as defined extensively in the Directive) and the habitual residence of the policy-holder which may or may not coincide. In most cases a restricted party autonomy to choose either law is allowed, and this freedom may even be extended, if the Member States which are connected with the case grant greater freedom of choice of the law applicable to the contract.There is an interplay between secondary community legislation and municipal private international law of the Member States, which necessarily leads to differentiation of regimes applicable to the contract, dependent on the extent to which the Member States allow the parties to choose the applicable law. In Section 3 of Article 7 the Directive refers to 'the general rules of private international law' of the Member States for matters covered but not regulated by the Directive. There is furthermore a wide variety of ways in which the provision in this Directive is implemented in the Member States. Some States, such as France, translated Article 7 into unilateral rules of private international law, others chose the multilateral form, whereas again some other countries primarily referred to the provision without copying it out. As to the general rules of private international law of the Member States which are to be applied as a stop-gap, many Member States have identified the Rome Convention as such. It is the Rome Convention,thrown out at the front door, then, which at the back door defines, eg, the freedom to choose another law and other issues not explicitly dealt with in the directives; its Article 1(3) is in practice partially revoked in this situation.

Article 7(2) of the second Directive takes its tune from Article 7 of the Rome Convention. Its first paragraph allows the application of mandatory rules of

---

[19] See Art 24 of the Proposal for a Third Non-Life Insurance Directive (92/C 244/02).

the forum, 'irrespective of the law otherwise applicable to the contract'; this corresponds to Article 7(2) of the Rome Convention.

The second sentence of Article 7(2) of the second Directive covers in its own way the situation described in Article 7(1) of the Rome Convention. Member States may stipulate that 'supermandatory' rules of the law of the Member State in which the risk is situated or of the Member State imposing the obligation to take out insurance shall be applied, whatever the law applicable to the contract. Here too, a motley cloak is thrown over the non-life insurance contract; far from harmonising existing rules in the Member States the Directive creates diversity and confusion.[20]

The matter has become even more complicated by Article 28 of the third Directive, which states, in effect, that the Member State in which a risk is situated shall not prevent a policyholder from concluding a contract governed by the rules of the home state of the insurer in a Member State as long as that does not conflict with legal provisions protecting the general good in the Member State in which the risk is situated. This concept of 'the general good' has been developed in the case law of the Court of Justice in order to allow Member States to maintain certain measures notwithstanding their infringement of the four fundamental freedoms, or the principle of freedom of competition. The criteria which the municipal measures must comply with in order to be acceptable under this doctrine are necessarily rather strict. This follows from the primacy of Community law. Conflicts lawyers are still sorting out the differences between mandatory rules of the forum, the supermandatory rules of other Member States, rules protecting the common good, and the public policy exception, all making inroads upon the *lex causae*. The conflict rules themselves, embraced in the directives, are double-barrelled and premised by complicated definitions of the connecting factors and other relevant words and phrases, such as 'situation of the risk', 'large risks', etc.

The case of the non-life insurance directives which consist primarily of detailed regulatory provisions but contain a few elements of private international law does not stand alone. There are many specific areas which have been dealt with

---

[20] See generally for the many doubts and laments raised by conflicts lawyers, the trade, and even representatives of the Commission: Reichert-Facilides/Jessurun d'Oliveira (eds) (above n 15). Patrick Pearson, present on behalf of the Commission at the Conference held at the European University Institute, considered Art 7 of the second directive as 'rather impenetrable for the layman', and 'hideously complicated', but suggested that the text was the maximum that could be achieved (p 6).

in the same manner, with the same complaints about their opacity. They seem to reflect the bewilderment in the community institutions about the place of private international law in a legal order which has the ambition to bring about an internal market without internal frontiers but encounters many barriers on its way to doing so, including national legal orders as aspects of the national identities of the Member States. The communitarian newspeak is perceived by conflicts lawyers all over Europe as gibberish and the proverbial sound and fury. It has proved extremely difficult to integrate private international law into the community legal order. No wonder that in the course of the Nineties new directions have been sought.

C. Amsterdam and After

The Amsterdam Inter Governmental Conference of 1996 introduced in the EU Treaty (Article 2, fourth indent) as one of the objectives the maintenance and development of the Union 'as an area of freedom, security and justice, in which the free movement of persons is assured . . .'. In Title IV of the EC Treaty concerning visa, asylum, immigration and other policies related to free movement of persons (the word order indicating the decreasing importance) Article 61 links the area of freedom, security and justice to 'measures in the field of judicial co-operation in civil matters' as provided in Article 65. This Article enumerates a set of measures which concern civil matters having cross-border implications, in other words matters pertaining to private international law. These measures are restricted, according to Article 65, by the proviso *'insofar as necessary for the proper functioning of the internal market'*. It remains to be seen, whether the measures taken or envisaged on this legal basis are indeed necessary for the proper functioning of the internal market as defined in the Treaty.

It has become increasingly clear that private international law has changed from an instrument of integration in the earlier phases of development of the Community into a manifestation of the shallowness of European harmonization. The survival of private international law indicates the existence of national legal orders of the Member States with their inherent diversity; it thus constitutes a nuisance and an embarassment. The deeper the penetration of Community law into the legal systems of the participating countries, the more pressure on private international law in the European context. This pressure leads to a number of strategies designed to change and erode the existing bodies of private international law. I mention the following tendencies:

(1) Communitarization of Existing Paracommunitarian Instruments

The communitarization of paracommunitarian conventions such as Brussels I (1968) and Brussels II (1998) in recent years is very significant in that this strategy not only implies introduction of specific forms of decisionmaking and eventually majority decisions, but also the extension of the self imposed tasks of the Community. Regulations of this kind are more exposed to the impact of the context of the Community legal order than the earlier conventions. The interpretation by the European Court of Justice of these documents will undoubtedly be influenced by the general principles of community law. Revisions of these regulations will enhance their inherently communitarian character.

In this connection a proposal may be mentioned, put forward by the European Group of Private International Law.[21] This proposal concerns in the first place Article 3 of the Rome Convention to which it adds a third paragraph reading as follows:

> 3. The fact that the parties have chosen the law of a non-Member State, whether or not accompanied by the choice of a tribunal of a non-Member State, shall not, where all the other elements relevant to the situation at the time of the choice are connected with one or more of the Member States, prejudice the application of the mandatory rules which are contained in or originate in acts of the institutions of the European Community and which are applicable in a Member State whose law would be applicable in the absence of a choice of law by the parties.

A few comments on these proposals, which anticipate the possibility of transforming the convention into a regulation, may be in order. First, one notices that mandatory rules of community law are explicitly mentioned as part and parcel of the otherwise applicable law which are choice of law proof. Parties may choose the law of a third country or of a Member State in which these mandatory rules have not been accepted, but if those are part of the law which would have been applicable if the parties would not have chosen such other law, they cannot be derogated from. A clear example of the communitarization of this text.

In the second place an interesting modification of the concept of a wholly internal case is proposed. If all other elements of the case are concentrated in one *or more* Member States, this case is considered, in this Community regulation,

---

[21] In its meeting of 15–17.9.2000 in Rome/Castelgandolfo, published, eg, in (2001) IPRaX, pp 64–66.

as internal to the Community. This is in line with the idea of the creation of an European area of justice without internal frontiers, but contrary to the concept of 'the internal case' which, up till now, is immune from Community law. It becomes more and more irrelevant to localize a case within a specific country; an intracommunitarian case showing elements in various Member States is put on the same footing as an internal case. This is a tremendous deviation from classical conflicts lore, which considers the distinction between internal and international as vital. Seen from the perspective of a European legal order, localization for the purposes of private international law loses much of its interest; the basic distinction seems to become that between community cases and extracommunitarian cases. As the European legal order absorbs the legal systems of the Member States and penetrates them deeper, further localization seems superfluous.

A second proposal concerns Article 7 of the Rome Convention for which a third paragraph is suggested:

> 3. Effect may only be given to the mandatory rules of a Member State to the extent that their application does not constitute an unjustified restriction on the principles of freedom of movement provided for in the treaty.

Here, as well, Community law with its four freedoms as the higher law is given precedence above mandatory rules of the *lex fori* (Article 7(2) or of a third country (Article 7 (1). It is of course problematic whether Article 65 of the Treaty can indeed form the legal basis for a regulation incorporating the Rome Convention, as the latter deals not only with intracommunitarian cases but also with cases which are linked, in part or as a whole, to the outside world. Can the text of the document be considered as 'necessary for the proper functioning of the internal market'? This is very doubtful. The same misgivings can be nursed concerning the eventual incorporation in such an instrument of provisions on the law applicable to non-contractual obligations. This has been proposed in the form of a draft convention by the same European Group of Private International Law (Rome II).[22] As the legal basis for an intracommunitarian regulation differs from a regulation concerning the private law relations with the outer world, the instruments have to be distinctly separated, and possibly diversified as to their content.

---

[22] See, eg, Marc Fallon, 'Proposition pour une convention européenne sur la loi applicable aux obligations non contractuelles' *European Review of Private Law* (1999), 1:45–68.

(2) Erosion into and Beyond Recognition

In implementing the Tampere conclusions the Commission has set itself a number of tasks while creating an area of freedom, security, and justice, including the approximation of substantive law in large parts of civil law, such as contract law and family law. This programme diminishes the need for (harmonized) private international law. Furthermore, viewed from the perspective of Community law, the nature of national rules as pertaining to civil law or administrative law has become irrelevant. The influence of community law on both branches of law, especially if they are considered to form a barrier against the internal market, is identical.[23] Under these circumstances the debate among conflicts lawyers concerning the distinction between public policy, mandatory rules, and supermandatory rules as in Article 7 of the Rome Convention loses its poignancy and becomes bleak indeed. The priority of Community law overshadows the nicety of the distinctions made.

This may be demonstrated in a somewhat unorthodox way. In the area of the fundamental freedom of movement of goods the ECJ has developed complex and dynamic criteria—in the absence of community regulation—for the assessment of the acceptability, under Community law, of national measures having effects equivalent to prohibited quantitative restrictions on the import of goods. One of the criteria of this 'rule of reason' laid down in *Cassis de Dijon*[24] and after is, that the measure has to be necessary to satisfy mandatory requirements relating to the effectiveness of a number of legitimate legislative purposes. If the country of origin of the goods has already put into place equivalent measures to protect this interest, the legislation of the importing country then becomes superfluous and unnecessary and by that token insufficient as a ground for derogation from the freedom of movement of goods. This line of thinking—which manifests itself in other areas as well—may have influenced the community in its measures to whittle down private international law as a barrier against the freedom of circulation of civil judgments; this freedom is seen both as an aspect of the freedom of movement of persons, and as conducive to the implementation of the concept of an internal market. The transplantation or the metaphorical use of the principle, that national rules of private international law have their equivalents in all Member States and are,

---

[23] Cf Jona Israel, 'Conflicts of Law and the EC after Amsterdam. A Change for the Worse?' (2000) *Maastricht Journal of European and Comparative Law* 81–99.
[24] Case 120/78 [1979] ECR 649.

by that token, superfluous seems to take root in the EC. One of the effects is the tendency to harmonize the systems of conflicts of law, and, in more recent times, to do away with conflicts of law altogether and to replace it by a system of mutual and informal recognition of judicial decisions originating from Member States. Recent developments in the area of criminal law, particularly concerning the international warrant which has to be recognized and implemented without any prior screening, point in the same direction.

A remarkable example of this trend to erode conflicts rules and reduce private international law in the context of the community to jurisdiction and recognition is the proposal for a regulation on jurisdiction and the recognition and enforcement of judgments in matters of parental responsibility.[25] This proposal, which seeks to find its legal basis in Article 65 of the Treaty, but which applies in all cases in the Member States (with the exception of Denmark) concerning parental responsibility, competes with the Hague Conventions on the Civil Aspects of International Child Abduction (1980) and on Jurisdiction, Applicable law, Recognition, Enforcement and Co-operation in respect of Parental Responsibility and Measures for the Protection of Children (1996). This fact alone suggests that the proposal is not only concerned with intra-communitarian cases, which means that it is not exclusively concerned with the freedom of movement of persons or the internal market, and furthermore that territorial instincts have been misguiding the legislative impulse to create yet another instrument for regional purposes in this field to the detriment of larger-scale instruments. This leads to a proliferation of international instruments which hampers the smoothness of handling cases with an international element instead of enhancing the much-vaunted efficiency of their processing. One may well wonder what exactly the relationship is between the establishment of an internal market, or the free movement of 'persons' in the community at that, and the free movement of judicial decisions concerning parental responsibility.

The Commission submits that a balance has to be struck between the best interests of the child on the one hand and the free circulation of decisions on the other hand. That is why it proposes to extend the principle of mutual recognition to *all* decisions concerning parental responsibility, beyond those envisaged in Regulation 1347/2000 (Brussels II) and which deal with parental responsibility in the context of divorce. To my mind this is a *non sequitur*. It is clear that

---

[25] Brussels, September 2001 COM (2001) 505 FINAL 2001/0204 (CNS).

no balance is struck at all, but that precedence is given to the free circulation of decisions. According to Article 3 of the UN Convention on the Rights of the Child 'in all actions concerning children . . . the best interests of the child shall be a primary consideration'.[26] This means that procedural arrangements concerning the rights of the children concerned are geared to their best interests, and that they are not to be balanced with the same weight as other interests or values. It is, therefore, insufficient to provide that a decision need not be recognized 'if this is manifestly contrary to public policy taking into account the interests of the child' (cf Article 15(2)(a)).

One of the underlying problems of such a regulation is the presumption that there exists common European ground in relation to family law and family relations, which is shared by, say, Greece and Finland. Perspectives on the best interests of the child, however, obviously vary widely in Europe and may result in invoking the exception of public policy in refusing recognition to culturally unacceptable decisions. Be that as it may, in the context of this essay attention may be drawn to the fact that this Proposal is devoid of any conflicts rule, just like its model, Regulation 1347/2000. Jurisdiction and recognition (without *exequatur*) are the key words, and the applicable law has become so irrelevant as not to be dealt with at all in the draft. Whatever the substantive rules applied in this area, eg, concerning the preliminary question as to who are the persons bearing parental responsibility, or to the measures themselves, the decisions produced by a local judge have to be carried out in the Community. I may be permitted to give an example. In the Netherlands, homosexuals are allowed to adopt children and have parental responsibility. The same goes for the lesbian spouse of a mother who gives birth to a child during the marriage. In the Netherlands, only one type of marriage is known: that between two adult partners of which the relative sex is irrelevant. Parental responsibility depends normally on the validity of this marriage, concluded by Dutch nationals or foreign partners as the case may be. Apart from the interference of public policy considerations in other Member States the Dutch marriage with its effects on parental responsibility has to be recognized in the community. The underlying idea of accepting diversity, ignoring conflicts rules, but stressing recognition and enforcement will, in these cases, be put to quite severe tests and pressures. It remains to be seen whether in this area, which is not remarkably characterized by harmonization of substantive law nor by unification of conflicts law,

---

[26] Cf Sharon Detrick, *A Commentary on the UN Convention on the Rights of the Child* (1999), p 85ff.

the stance of ignoring cultural diversity will work. It is not evident either that the trustworthiness of the judiciaries in the Member States is as great as one is liable to think about one's own judiciary. All judicial systems are piously thought to be equal, but some are more so than others, even in Europe.

Another important aspect of the erosion of the systems of private international law of the Member States may be perceived in the case law of the European Court of Justice concerning those conflicts rules. The Court has repeatedly held that those national conflicts rules and their effects—like all national measures—have basically to comply with the requirements flowing from the four fundamental freedoms. If national conflicts rules or their consequences are incompatible with those freedoms, they may only survive if they are in tune with the criteria as laid down by the European Court of Justice for justifiable inroads upon Community law: they must be justified by imperative requirements in the general interest, they must not be discriminatory, they must be suitable for securing the attainment of the objective which they pursue, and they must not go beyond what is necessary in order to attain it.[27] This case law reduces the scope for national conflicts rules both existing, and future, considerably.

(3) Imperialism

Articles 61 to 65 of the Treaty are extremely important in attributing competences to the EC in the field of judicial co-operation in civil matters having cross-border implications, 'insofar as necessary for the proper functioning of the internal market' , not only within the community, but in dealing with the outside world as well. As has been said thirty years ago in the *ERTA* case[28] *'each time that the Community, with a view to implementing a common policy envisaged by the Treaty, adopts provisions laying down common rules, whatever form these may take, the Member States no longer have the right, acting individually or even collectively, to undertake obligations with third countries which affect such rules.'*

This doctrine implies that since the Treaty of Amsterdam, the Community has taken over wheel and accelerator in private law and conflicts of law. The way in which the Community exercises this competence forms a threat to the functioning of other international organizations, such as Unidroit, the Council of Europe, and the Hague Conference on Private International Law. It has become

---

[27] See, eg, *Centros Ltd* Case C212/97, 9 March 1999 [1999 I 1459]; *Überseering BV* Case C-208/00 (not yet reported).
[28] Case 22/70 *Commission v Council (re ERTA)* [1971] 263.

clear that the EC means business in these organizations. As long as it is unable to become a party to these organizations it will orchestrate the activities of the Member States therein. This is, for instance, the case for the Hague Conference, which does not yet allow in its Statute of 1955 international organizations to become a member. For third countries, which are members of the Conference[29], it will be difficult to swallow the fact that they will have to negotiate in the future with an adamant bloc of fifteen countries—in the future considerably more—who speak with one mouth and will act upon instructions from Brussels. There are, furthermore, signs that the Community is determined to impose its own regimes in intra-community relations even though its members are or become parties to the Hague Conventions.

A few examples can be given. The drafting of a worldwide convention on jurisdiction and foreign judgments in civil and commercial matters may fail because of the exercise of the external competence by the EC in imposing as much as possible a system which is in tune with Brussels I. The United States has one vote, the EC disposes of fifteen votes. A shipwreck of this convention may prove to be disastrous for the existence of the Hague Conference itself, as the behaviour of the EC in this test case will set the tune for future negotiations.

The premature steps taken by the Commission to arrive at a Regulation on the Competence, Recognition and Execution of Measures concerning Parental Responsibility (including a French proposal on Rights of Access) intrude, as I suggested before, into several existing conventions concluded by the Hague Conference: especially those on the Civil Aspects of International Child Abduction (1980) and on Child Protection (1996) of which the latter is about to come into force. It seems that the Commission and the Council are deliberately steering a collision course with other international organizations which deal with private (international) law. Member States of the EU are not allowed anymore to individually ratify Hague Conventions on topics which are con-

---

[29] Cf A V M Struycken, Het Verdrag van Amsterdam en de Haagse Conferentie voor internationaal privaatrecht, *Weekblad voor Privaatrecht, Notariaat en Registratie*, (Special Issue on the European Union and Private International Law) no 6421, 11 November 2000. 735–745; H U Jessurun d'Oliveira, Den Haag tegen Den Haag, of EU tegen HC, *Nederlands Juristenblad* 2001, 1208; Charles T Kotuby, Jr 'External Competence of the European Community in the Hague Conference on Private International Law: Community Harmonization and Worldwide Unification', 2001 *NILR* 1–30; Harry Duintjer Tebbens, Ein Ziviljustizraum in der Europäischen Union—auf Kosten einer Aushöhlang der internationalen Zusammenarbeit in: Baur-Hansel (eds), *System Wechsel im Europäischen Kollisionsrecht* (C H Beck München, 2002) 171–192.

sidered to be covered by Article 65 of the Treaty. Negotiations are starting to make it possible for the EC to adhere to specific conventions or to become a member to the Hague Conference. 'Do the advantages to be gained from an independent approach at the regional level outweigh the disadvantages that come with the proliferation of instruments?'. This is the question raised in a recent memorandum issued by the Hague Conference.[30] The EU is not only disrupting the work of other international bodies, working on a larger scale than the EU or in a more specialized way, but is also trying to impose its own solutions on these bodies. These predatory activities may have deleterious effects for the Hague Conference and similar international organizations.

D. Concluding Remarks

In his authoritative and thoughtful contribution, twelve years ago, to a symposium in celebration of the 40th anniversary of the Centre of Foreign Law and Private International Law of the University of Amsterdam—which in retrospect turned out to be more of an epitaph as this Centre has fallen victim to the *Verelendung* caused by the austerity policy consistently pursued towards Dutch universities—Peter North answered the question : *'Is European Harmonisation of Private International Law a Myth or a Reality?'*.[31] He summed up the situation quite correctly at the time by remarking that the Hague Conference had been a major influence for common lawyers, but that, as far as EC initiatives were concerned, 'there is a feeling in the United Kingdom that the likelihood of further major private international law initiatives is not great'. In conclusion he forecasted that the influence of the Community would be 'a very gradual one and it may be a fairly limited one, given the extent of legislative change which has already taken place in the United Kingdom'.

How swiftly are things changing! Although, of course, the position of the United Kingdom and Ireland is governed by a Protocol granting the right to opt in or opt out of a number of Community instruments in this area, in practice the United Kingdom agrees regularly to participate, eg, in the parental re-

---

[30] Comments by the Permanent Bureau of the Hague Conference on the Proposal for a Council Regulation on Jurisdiction and the Recognition and Enforcement of Judgments in Matters of Parental Responsibility, presented by the Commission of the European Communities, 30 October 2001.

[31] *Forty Years On: the Evolution of Postwar Private International Law in Europe* (Kluwer Deventer 1990), pp 29–48.

sponsibility regulation. Generally, the competence of the EC on matters of private international law, though formally premised by this being necessary for the proper functioning of the internal market, has become unlimited, unless the ECJ shows the wisdom and the guts to put on the brakes. The Member States are flooded with a large number of measures, designed to eliminate conflicts law and introducing concepts geared towards a full faith and credit clause in the European judicial space. Given the goals of the EU, private international law will wither away, and will only be relevant in cases with an extracommunitarian element. In a way, my tribute to Peter North is offered as a follow-up, from a Dutch or continental perspective, to the answers he formulated to questions which are more than ever relevant to our common discipline. A discipline which he has served in his long and exemplary career in an outstanding fashion, even in the face of other important tasks such as chairing the Parades Commission in Northern Ireland.

6

SPECIAL RULES OF PRIVATE INTERNATIONAL LAW FOR SPECIAL CASES: WHAT SHOULD WE DO ABOUT INTELLECTUAL PROPERTY?

*James Fawcett**

A. Introduction

At the moment, one of the most problematic areas of private international law is that of jurisdiction in intellectual property cases where a claim for infringement of a right raises the issue of the validity of that right. The question of how jurisdictional rules operate in such cases has arisen in the context of the Brussels Convention on jurisdiction and the enforcement of judgments in civil and commercial matters, now the Brussels I Regulation,[1] and is now taxing minds

---

* Professor of Law, University of Nottingham. I am very grateful to Professors Trevor Hartley and Paul Torremans for their many helpful comments on this paper.
[1] This applies in all the EU Member States, apart from Denmark. The Brussels Convention will continue to apply in relation to defendants domiciled in Denmark.

at the Hague Conference on private international law during discussion of the Hague Judgments Convention. The problem that arises in both contexts is, in general terms, one of the interaction of different bases of jurisdiction. More particularly, under the Brussels I Regulation the problem is one of the interaction of the special rule for intellectual property cases raising the issue of validity of a patent, etc, which allocates exclusive jurisdiction to the Member State where the right was registered, and other bases of jurisdiction which are of more general application, in particular the basis of jurisdiction that a plaintiff can rely upon in a tort case. As far as the Hague Judgments Convention is concerned, the problem is more fundamental and raises the question of whether there should be any special rule of exclusive jurisdiction in intellectual property cases and, if so, how wide its scope should be, bearing in mind that the wider it is the more it cuts across other bases of jurisdiction, including the rule dealing with jurisdiction in tort.

B. Intellectual Property and the Brussels I Regulation

The application of the Brussels Convention in cases of intellectual property litigation was not thought out properly when the Convention was drafted and consequently the courts have had to struggle with the interaction of Article 16(4) (exclusive jurisdiction in proceedings concerned with the validity of a patent, etc) and other bases of jurisdiction, particularly Article 5(3) (matters relating to tort), in cases where an infringement claim raises the issue of invalidity. The Brussels I Regulation contains the same provisions, although Article 16(4) now becomes Article 22(4).

(1) The Nature of the Problem

Validity of a right

Some cases are concerned solely with the issue of validity of a right, for example there is a petition for revocation of a patent on this ground. In such a case the position is clear: Article 22(4) will apply. This states that the following courts shall have exclusive jurisdiction:

> in proceedings concerned with the registration or validity of patents, trade marks, designs, or other similar rights required to be deposited or registered, the courts of the Member State in which the deposit or registration has been applied

for, has taken place or is under the terms of a Community instrument or an international convention deemed to have taken place.[2]

This has to be read in conjunction with Article 25, which provides that 'Where a court of a Member State is seised of a claim which is principally concerned with a matter over which the courts of another Member State have exclusive jurisdiction by virtue of Article 22, it shall declare of its own motion that it has no jurisdiction'.

The Recitals in the Brussels I Regulation do not refer to any justification for the rules on exclusive jurisdiction as set out in Article 22. Nonetheless, by looking back at its predecessor, Article 16(4) of the Brussels Convention,[3] it is clear that there are two justifications for Article 22(4). First, this provision is based on the sovereign power of the forum, in that the grant of a national patent is an exercise of national sovereignty.[4] What is granted is a national right, granted under national laws and giving rise to monopolies which affect the public in the country of registration. This theme is also to be found in international conventions on intellectual property. Second, this particular head of exclusive jurisdiction can be justified in the same way as all the other heads of exclusive jurisdiction on the basis that it deals with '. . . matters which, because of their particular difficulty or complexity, require that the court having jurisdiction should be particularly familiar with the relevant national law . . .'.[5] According to the European Court of Justice, the courts of the Contracting State in which registration or deposit has been applied for are best placed to adjudicate upon cases in which the dispute itself concerns the validity of the patent or the existence of the deposit or registration.[6] The law applicable to the issue of creation of intellectual property rights is that of the State of registration or deposit.[7] The courts of the State in which registration or deposit occurred are best placed to try the case because they can understand best their own law. Looking at it the other

---

[2] European patents are dealt with by a separate provision in Art 22(4) which provides that 'Without prejudice to the jurisdiction of the European Patent Office under the Convention on the Grant of European Patents, signed at Munich on 5 October 1973, the courts of each Member State shall have exclusive jurisdiction, regardless of domicile, in proceedings concerned with the registration or validity of any European patent granted for that State'.

[3] See generally Fawcett and Torremans, *Intellectual Property and Private International Law*, pp 15–16.

[4] See the Jenard Report, [1979] OJ C59/36.

[5] AG Lenz in Case 220/84 *As-Autoteile Service GmbH v Malhe* [1985] ECR 2267 at 2271. See also Case 73/77 *Sanders v van der Putte* [1977] ECR 2383.

[6] Case 288/82 *Duijnstee v Goderbauer* [1983] ECR 3663 at 3676.

[7] See Fawcett and Torremans, pp 487 et seq.

way round, patent laws are different in different countries and the courts in a State other than the one in which registration or deposit occurred are going to find it difficult to understand the law of that State.

Infringement

There are also cases, and this is less common, which are concerned solely with the issue of infringement without the issue of validity being raised at all.[8] Again the position is clear. Actions for the infringement of patents, etc are governed, not by Article 22(4), but by the other bases of jurisdiction in the Brussels I Regulation.[9] In particular, an action for infringement is a matter relating to tort, delict or quasi-delict and, accordingly, falls within the scope of Article 5(3),[10] which provides that

> A person domiciled in a Member State may, in another Member State, be sued:
> . . . in matters relating to tort, *delict* or *quasi-delict*, in the courts for the place where the harmful event occurred or may occur;

According to Recital (12) of the Regulation special jurisdiction, as an alternative to jurisdiction in the defendant's domicile, is 'based on a close link between the court and the action or in order to facilitate the sound administration of justice'. Special jurisdiction is also designed to give the plaintiff an alternative forum to the defendant's domicile in which to sue. This comes out particularly noticeably in relation to the tort rule of special jurisdiction. The tort rule in the Brussels Convention was interpreted widely so that the place of the harmful event was interpreted to encompass both the place of the event giving rise to the damage and the place where the damage occurred.[11] The latter alternative was added because, in an appreciable number of cases, the place of the event giving rise to the damage would be the same as the domicile of the defendant.[12]

---

[8] See, eg, *Plastus Kreativ AB v Minnesota Mining and Manufacturing Co* [1995] RPC 438 (a patents case); *Pearce v Ove Arup Partnership Ltd* [1999] 1 All ER 769, CA (a copyright case).

[9] The *Duijnstee* case, n 6 above, at 3677. This follows the Jenard Report, n 4 above, at p 36. See also *Molnlycke AB and Another v Procter & Gamble Ltd and Others* [1992] 1 WLR 1112 at 1117; *Chiron Corp v Evans Medical Ltd and others* [1996] FSR 863 at 866; *Pearce v Ove Arup Partnership Ltd and others* [1997] 2 WLR 779 at 785, reversed but not on this point [1999] 1 All ER 769, CA; *Fort Dodge Animal Health Ltd and Others v Akzo Nobel NV and another* [1998] FSR 222. Neither is an action for a declaration of non-infringement within this provision: the *Chiron* case, above, at 866–867.

[10] For England see the *Molnlycke* case, n 9 above, at 1117; the *Pearce* case, n 9 above; the *Fort Dodge* case, n 9 above. For France see *Wegmann v Societe Elsevier Science Ltd* [1997] I L Pr 760, Cour de Cassation. For Germany see *Re Jurisdiction in Tort and Contract (Case I ZR 201/86)* [1988] ECC 415.

[11] Case 21/76 *Bier BV v Mines de Potasse D'Alsace SA* [1976] ECR 1735.

[12] ibid, at 1747.

Infringement raising the issue of validity

But what if the validity of a patent, etc is raised during the course of an action for infringement, or it is plain that it going to be put in issue? This raises two questions. The first is a narrow initial question. Is the court with infringement jurisdiction precluded from trying this issue when the patent, etc is registered in another Member State? The issue of validity can arise during the course of infringement proceedings in a number of different ways: as a defence to infringement, the obvious point being that a person cannot have infringed an invalid intellectual property right that should never have been granted in the first place; during a counterclaim for revocation; and during separate revocation proceedings in a separate Member State. This complicates things and in theory the answer to this narrow question might differ depending on the way in which it arises. The second question is a broader one concerning the intellectual property litigation as a whole. Is it possible to concentrate the trial of the infringement claim and the validity issue in one Member State or must the two aspects of the intellectual property litigation be split between two different States? In other words, if a Member State is not precluded from trying the infringement claim, can it also try the issue of invalidity or must the two issues be split between different courts in different Member States? On the other hand, if it is precluded from trying the issue of infringement, can the court with exclusive jurisdiction in relation to validity also try the issue of infringement? It is going to have to have a basis of jurisdiction in relation to infringement. If it has no such basis, again the issues will have to be split between the courts in different Member States.

(2) The Present Law

The answers to both of the above questions are uncertain,[13] with different answers coming from the English and the Dutch courts.

Are the courts precluded from trying an infringement claim where validity is in issue?

The English solution

There are two English cases which have held that the courts of a Member State

---

[13] For possible interpretations of the provisions in the Brussels Convention see Wadlow, *Enforcement of Intellectual Property in European and International Law*, paras 3–114 to 3–151.

are precluded from trying an infringement action where validity is in issue. The first of these is *Coin Controls Ltd v Suzo International (UK) Ltd and Others*.[14] The case concerned an action brought in England for the infringement of three European patents: a European patent (UK); a European patent (Spain); and a European patent (Germany). It was plain that validity was to be put in issue. Laddie J held that, as far as the Spanish and German patents were concerned, the English court had no jurisdiction, not only in relation to the validity part but over the whole of the claim, that is including the infringement part. This was on the basis that the claim was 'principally concerned' with validity within the meaning of Article 19 of the Brussels Convention, the predecessor of Article 25 of the Brussels I Regulation, with the result that the English court had to declare of its own motion that it had no jurisdiction. Laddie J said he could see no reason to give a narrow linguistic interpretation to the words 'principally concerned', and that 'something which is a major feature of the litigation is not incidental and is therefore a matter with which the action is principally concerned'.

This decision was expressly affirmed by the Court of Appeal in *Fort Dodge Animal Health Ltd and Others* v *Akzo Nobel NV and Another*,[15] which raised the same point as the *Coin Controls* case but in a rather different context. An infringement action was brought in the Netherlands by a Dutch company and its wholly owned subsidiary against, *inter alia*, three companies domiciled in England in respect of a European patent (UK). Subsequently, these defendants, the appellants in the English proceedings, petitioned the English Patents Court for revocation of this patent. They also intended to rely in the Dutch proceedings on the defence that the patent was invalid if the alleged infringing acts fell within the ambit of the claims. The appellants argued before the English Court that the only court which had jurisdiction to determine whether the appellants had infringed the UK patent was the English Patents Court. It followed that the prosecution of the claim in the Dutch courts was vexatious and should be restrained by injunction. The Court of Appeal held that the infringement claim brought before the Dutch courts was principally concerned with the validity of the UK patent and, therefore, by virtue of Articles 19 and 16(4) of the Brussels Convention the claim fell within the exclusive jurisdiction of the UK Court. In this case the issue of validity arose in both the context of separate revocation proceedings in another Contracting State and in the

---

[14] [1999] Ch 33.
[15] [1998] FSR 222.

context of a defence to the infringement proceedings. However, it seems clear that the result would have been exactly the same if the issue had arisen solely in the context of separate revocation proceedings.

These authorities have been criticised on the basis that they are incompatible with the language used in Article 19 of the Brussels Convention.[16] This only applies where a court is seised of a 'claim' which is principally concerned, etc. But is a 'claim' concerned with a defence thereto?[17] Moreover, where invalidity is raised as a defence can it really be said that the claim is 'principally' concerned with validity? The Court of Appeal in the more recent case of *Re Polly Peck International Plc (No 2)*[18] held, in a different private international law context,[19] that the word 'principally' meant 'chiefly' or 'for the most part'.[20] A claim for infringement to which invalidity is raised as a defence cannot be said to be chiefly concerned with validity. It is only by adopting an unnatural interpretation which equated principally concerned with 'not arising incidentally' that Laddie J was able to say that the claim was principally concerned with validity. The implicit decision in *Fort Dodge* that the result would have been exactly the same if the issue of validity had been raised solely in the context of separate revocation proceedings brought in another country took things even further. This gave an extraordinarily wide interpretation to Article 19 since it accepted that a Dutch claim for infringement was principally concerned with validity when this matter was not even raised in the Dutch proceedings but was only raised by separate revocation proceedings brought in another Contracting State.

Moreover, both decisions mean that a defendant can block the trial of an action for infringement by raising the issue of validity if the action is brought in a Member State other than the one where the patent, etc is registered and can do this at any time if allowed to plead invalidity at a late stage of the proceedings.[21]

---

[16] Fawcett and Torremans, pp 203–206.
[17] See Fawcett and Torremans, p 203; Wadlow, paras 3–93 to 3–96.
[18] [1998] 3 All ER 812 at 828, CA.
[19] This was in the context of s 30(1) of the Civil Jurisdiction and Judgments Act 1982.
[20] This was said in the Court of Appeal to be consistent with the approach in the *Fort Dodge* and *Coin Controls* cases, which clearly it is not.
[21] See Wadlow, *Enforcement of Intellectual Property in European and International Law*, para 3–91.

The Dutch solution

The Hague Court of Appeal in *Expandable Grafts Partnership* v *Boston Scientific BV*[22] adopted a very different solution. The appellants had sought injunctions from the Dutch court to prevent infringing acts not only in the Netherlands but also in certain of the other countries in respect of which either the European patent had been granted, or various national patents subsisted. The respondents took the position that the European patent at issue in the proceedings was granted wrongfully and instituted nullity proceedings in a great number of countries. The respondents argued that this meant that the Dutch courts no longer had jurisdiction because of Articles 16(4) and 19 of the Brussels Convention. This argument was rejected by the Court of Appeal of the Hague. The Court pointed out that these were infringement actions. 'With respect to these actions the jurisdiction of the courts does not cease to exist by operation of the law as soon as nullity actions are instituted. For it is the opinion of the Court of Appeal that the jurisdiction issue must be decided on the basis of the claim stated in the summons'.[23] The claim stated in the summons was in relation to infringements. However, the Court went on to accept that the institution of nullity actions may have consequences for the hearing of the infringement actions. 'Unless it is immediately clear that a nullity action cannot be deemed to be meant seriously, in the case of *main proceedings on the merits* the court which is asked to pronounce judgment on the infringement issue will have to adopt a cautious attitude towards the infringement action and in principle will have to stay the infringement proceedings until the foreign court has pronounced judgment on the nullity isssue'.[24] The same degree of caution had to be exercised in the case of interim infringement injunctions and the Dutch Court refused to grant the injunctions sought.

This Dutch decision has been welcomed.[25] In its favour is the fact that it does not strain the language of the Brussels Convention in the way that the English decision does. At the same time it is sensitive to the importance of the issue of validity, pointing out the 'fact that infringement and nullity are indissolubly linked with each other, since it is impossible to infringe a patent that is null and

---

[22] [1999] FSR 352; followed by the same Court in *Boston Scientific BV v Cordis Corp* [2000] ENPR 87.
[23] [1999] FSR 352 at 361.
[24] ibid.
[25] See, eg, Dutson [1998] LMCLQ 505 at 507; (1998) 47 ICLQ 659 at 667–668; Karet [1998] IPQ 328.

void'.[26] The staying of the Dutch infringement proceedings until the foreign court has pronounced judgment on the nullity issue fully acknowledges the importance of this issue.

Can the infringement claim and validity issue be tried before the same court?

The English solution

Can the court with exclusive jurisdiction in relation to validity also try the infringement claim? The Court of Appeal in the *Fort Dodge* case referred to the English court having exclusive jurisdiction over infringement.[27] This extends Article 16(4) to encompass infringement claims in the situation where such a claim raises the issue of validity. This is not consistent with the wording of that provision. Nor does it comply with the principle adopted by the European Court of Justice in relation to Article 16 that this should be interpreted in the light of its purpose and place within the scheme of the Convention, which has resulted in it being given a narrow interpretation.[28] Article 16(4) must be and has been interpreted restrictively.[29] Moreover, the Jenard Report makes it clear that infringement is excluded from the scope of Article 16(4). This may be referring to infringement where this arises on its own but, given that infringement commonly raises validity, it is more likely that such a case is also intended to fall outside Article 16(4). The courts in other EC Member States have not adopted this startling interpretation.

If, as seems likely, this interpretation of Article 16(4), is wrong, this still leaves the possibility that the courts of a Member State where a patent, etc is registered, have non-exclusive jurisdiction over infringement under some other basis of jurisdiction. Often the courts of the Member State where a patent etc is registered will have a basis of jurisdiction to try the infringement claim,[30] thereby allowing the concentration of litigation in relation to both infringement and validity in the same Member State, and often in the same court. In the *Fort Dodge* case, the English courts, which had exclusive jurisdiction in relation to the revocation

---

[26] [1999] FSR 352 at 361.
[27] See n 9 above, at 745.
[28] See Blumer at the WIPO Forum on Private International Law and Intellectual Property held at Geneva January 2001 in his paper on 'Patent Law and International Private Law on both sides of the Atlantic' at p 12.
[29] See the Nygh and Pocar Report, Prel Doc No 11, p 67 n 111.
[30] See Fawcett and Torremans, p 206.

proceedings in respect of a European patent (UK), also in fact had jurisdiction to try a claim for infringement by virtue of Article 2 of the Brussels Convention, the defendant being domiciled in England. But there is no guarantee that the Member State with validity jurisdiction will have infringement jurisdiction. Having to work within the limitations of the existing rules restricts what the courts can do and it is not possible to adopt an approach which always ensures that trial of the infringement claim and the validity issue are concentrated in the courts of the same State. In the situation where the court with validity jurisdiction does not have infringement jurisdiction, the infringement claim and validity issue will have to be split between the courts of different Member States. The plaintiff will be forced to bring an action for a declaration of validity in the Member State with validity jurisdiction under Article 22(4) and then bring the infringement claim in another Member State, with no risk of a defence of invalidity being raised.

The Dutch solution

The effect of the decision of the Court of Appeal of the Hague in the *Expandable Grafts* case is that the infringement claim and nullity issue will be subject to separate hearings. The Court accepted that this was far from ideal and that it was desirable for both issues to be tried before the same court. However, this was barred by Article 16(4). In other words, the court with infringement jurisdiction could not try the validity issue because this was subject to the exclusive jurisdiction of the foreign State of registration. This still leaves the question, which is answered above, of whether the court with validity jurisdiction could also try the infringement claim.

A ruling from the European Court of Justice

The Court of Appeal in the *Fort Dodge* case concluded that the matter of whether the infringement claim, in respect of which the issue of validity was raised, relating to the UK patent, came, by reason of Article 16(4) of the Brussels Convention, within the exclusive jurisdiction of the UK Patents Court was not '*acte clair*' and that a ruling should be sought from the European Court of Justice.[31] A ruling is also needed on the question whether the Courts of the State in which the patent is not registered are precluded from trying the infringement claim when this depends on the validity of the patent. A reference

---

[31] In the meantime, the Court was not prepared to grant an injunction restraining the respondents from continuing with the Dutch proceedings.

was not made to that Court in the *Fort Dodge* case.[32] However, these questions were referred to the European Court of Justice in the case of *Boston Scientific Ltd, Boston Scientific International BV and Scimed Life Systems Inc v Cordis Corporation and Cordis (UK) Ltd*,[33] which involved the same issues as the *Fort Dodge* case.[34] Subsequently though this case has been removed from the register[35] and the uncertainty that exists under the present law remains.

C. The Hague Judgments Convention

The Hague Judgments Convention provides an opportunity to start from the beginning, to decide what should happen in intellectual property cases and to provide solutions that are not available under the Brussels I Regulation. In particular, it is possible to concentrate the whole of the intellectual property litigation, that is the infringement claim and the issue of validity, before the courts of a single State.

As is mentioned elsewhere in this book,[36] the fate of the Hague Judgments Convention is uncertain, for reasons unconnected with intellectual property. However, even if a much less ambitious convention emerges, which does not deal with intellectual property, the considerable amount of work that has been carried out in relation to intellectual property and private international law will not have been wasted effort. For it helps to answer that most basic question: what should we do about intellectual property? This is highly relevant when it comes to possible future reform of the Brussels I Regulation. Moreover, it is not inconceivable that in the future there could be a separate convention, whether through the auspices of the Hague Conference or the World Intellectual Property Organization (WIPO), that deals solely with intellectual property and private international law.[37] The solutions put forward during discussion of the Hague Judgments Convention will then doubtless re-emerge.

---

[32] The Netherlands Court recognized that 99% of the alleged infringement was in the UK and therefore declined jurisdiction.

[33] Case C-186/00.

[34] For the questions referred see [2000] OJ C233/15.

[35] [2001] OJ C118/ 27.

[36] See Brand, above, at pp 51–53; McClean, below, p 256; Nygh, below, p 308.

[37] This was advocated by Dreyfuss and Ginsburg at the WIPO Forum on Private International Law and Intellectual Property in January 2001, where they set out a draft Convention on jurisdiction and recognition of judgments in intellectual property matters.

Before looking at the specific proposals put forward at the Hague in relation to intellectual property, it is necessary to put these in context by saying a little about the proposals in the preliminary draft Convention in relation to jurisdiction generally.

(1) Jurisdiction Generally

Preliminary drafts of the Hague Judgments Convention borrow extensively from what is now the Brussels I Regulation. The latest draft is contained in the interim text of June 2001, which emerged during Part One of the Nineteenth Diplomatic Session.[38] The bases of jurisdiction under the preliminary draft Convention are set out in Articles 3–16.[39] There is a general forum based on the principle that the plaintiff may bring suit in the courts of the defendant and which provides that a defendant may be sued in the courts of the State where the defendant is [habitually] resident.[40] However, unlike the Brussels I Regulation, this is not seen as some sort of fundamental jurisdiction with the result that all other jurisdictions must be seen as exceptions which must be narrowly interpreted.[41] This is followed by rules on choice of court,[42] contracts,[43] contracts concluded by consumers,[44] individual contracts of employment,[45] branches,[46] torts,[47] trusts,[48] and exclusive jurisdiction.[49]

A little more needs to said about both the tort rule and exclusive jurisdiction. The former has been influenced by the tort rule in what is now the Brussels I Regulation, as interpreted by the European Court of Justice. Article 10 of the preliminary draft Convention provides that

---

[38] All references in this paper to the preliminary draft convention are referring to this text. This contains a number of alterations to the preliminary draft convention of October 1999. The latter amended a preliminary draft convention provisionally adopted by the Special Commission on 18 June 1999. The Delegations felt that the Second Part of the Diplomatic Session could not be heard before the end of 2002 and should be prepared for by a further meeting of the Commission on General Affairs and Policy in early 2002.

[39] There are also provisions dealing with jurisdiction based on national law (Art 17) and prohibited grounds of jurisdiction (Art 18).

[40] Art 3(1).

[41] The Nygh and Pocar Report, Prel Doc No 11, p 28.

[42] Art 4.

[43] Art 6.

[44] Art 7.

[45] Art 8.

[46] Art 9.

[47] Art 10.

[48] Art 11.

[49] Art 12.

1. A plaintiff may bring an action in tort [or delict] in the courts of the State–

    (1) in which the act or omission that caused the injury occurred, or

    (2) in which the injury arose, unless the defendant establishes that the person claimed to be responsible could not reasonably foresee that the act or omission could result in an injury of the same nature in that State.

Perhaps not surprisingly, given its origin, this rule has been justified on the same grounds as the tort rule under the Brussels Convention. The Nygh and Pocar Report states that 'the courts of the defendant's forum are not always the best placed to ensure the sound administration of justice by comparison with the courts of the place where the tort or delict was committed'.[50] There is also a concern to provide an alternative to the defendant's forum.[51] Hence the need to give the plaintiff a choice between the forum of the place of the act and that of the place where its effects are felt,[52] a distinction which is spelt out in the text of the provision. Giving the plaintiff this option has been justified as follows.[53] First, it allows the plaintiff to choose the court that is best placed in the specific case to deal with the issues arising from the wrongful act. Second, when it comes to balancing the interests of the parties, it recognises that the position of the victim should be given preference over that of the party whose conduct was responsible for the injury. Allowing trial in the place of injury protects the plaintiff.[54] Third, the plaintiff is able to choose the court in the light of the law that will apply to his case.

The rules on exclusive jurisdiction are clearly modelled on the equivalent provision in what is now the Brussels I Regulation and cover most of the types of proceeding covered by that provision. The exclusive nature of these grounds of jurisdiction implies that if other courts are seised, nonetheless, they must automatically rule that they lack jurisdiction.[55] No explicit justification has been given overall for having exclusive jurisdiction rules under the preliminary draft Convention. The similarity of the particular heads of exclusive jurisdiction with the exclusive jurisdiction rules in what is now the Brussels I Regulation would suggest that the justification for each particular rule of exclusive jurisdiction is the same. This certainly seems to be the case as regards immovable property.[56]

---

[50] Prel Doc No 11, pp 57–58.
[51] ibid, p 58.
[52] ibid.
[53] ibid, p 59.
[54] ibid.
[55] The Nygh and Pocar Report, Prel Doc No 11, p 62.
[56] ibid, pp 64–65.

(2) Jurisdiction in Intellectual Property Cases

Jurisdiction in intellectual property cases has been identified as one of the more difficult topics under the Hague Judgments Convention and the Special Commission on the question of jurisdiction, and recognition and enforcement of foreign judgments in civil and commercial matters at its fifth meeting in October 1999 expressed the wish that an experts meeting be held to study further this topic. The experts meeting was duly held in Geneva 2001.[57] The lack of consensus reached by the experts at this meeting is reflected in the interim text of the preliminary draft Convention of June 2001, which questions whether intellectual property should even be included within the scope of the Convention[58] and, on the assumption that it is to be included, contains no less than three different proposals in relation to this matter. These will be examined below, when discussing more generally the possible approaches that could be applied in relation to intellectual property cases.

D. What Should We Do About Intellectual Property?

(1) The Possible Approaches

There are various approaches which could be adopted in relation to intellectual property and private international law, some of which have already been put forward in relation to the Hague Judgments Convention, others of which have not. Although many questions arise in relation to proposals dealing with intellectual property, such as precisely which rights should be included within the scope of such proposals,[59] I will concentrate on how each approach deals with validity, infringement and that 'most troublesome question',[60] namely the in-

---

[57] See the Report of the experts' meeting on the intellectual property aspects of the future Convention on jurisdiction and foreign judgments in civil and commercial matters, Geneva, 1 February 2001, Prel Doc No 13 April 2001. This meeting was timed to follow the WIPO Forum on Private International Law and Intellectual Property in January 2001.

[58] Art 12, paras 4–8 are all placed in square brackets. Footnote 80 of the annotated interim text of June 2001 acknowledges the disagreement over whether intellectual property should be included. For opposition in the US to the inclusion of intellectual property see Prel Doc No 13, p 10, note 2 and p 3. Objection has been made in the US to giving exclusive jurisdiction to the State of registration of a patent, etc It has also been argued in this book that it is presumptuous to think that a global solution can be found to intellectual property when no national system has developed a satisfactory, fixed set of rules, see Brand, above, at pp 54–55. For arguments for the inclusion of intellectual property see Prel Doc No 13, pp 9–10.

[59] The question whether copyright should be included is proving particularly problematic.

[60] The Nygh and Pocar Report, Prel Doc No 11, p 67.

teraction between infringement rules and validity rules. The possible approaches are as follows.

(a) The same approach as under the Brussels I Regulation

This would simply mean having a rule to deal with the issue of validity which allocates exclusive jurisdiction to the State of registration of the patent, etc. Nothing would be said at all about infringement, leaving this to come within other general bases of jurisdiction under the Convention. An early draft of the Convention contemplated this approach.[61] Whilst this would deal in a satisfactory way with validity or infringement on its own, when it comes to a claim for infringement raising the issue of validity this would involve all the uncertainty that exists under the present law but with no equivalent of the European Court of Justice to definitively resolve the matter.

(b) Giving the court with exclusive jurisdiction over validity an additional exclusive jurisdiction over infringement

This approach has been endorsed by the UK delegation at the Hague and an increasing number of delegations are switching over to support this view. It is described in the preliminary draft Convention as Alternative A and is set out as Article 12(4) and (5) in this draft. These provide that:

> 4. In proceedings in which the relief sought is a judgment on the grant, registration, validity, abandonment, revocation or infringement of a patent or a mark, the courts of the Contracting State of grant or registration shall have exclusive jurisdiction.
>
> 5. In proceedings in which the relief sought is a judgment on the validity, abandonment, or infringement of an unregistered mark [or design], the courts of the Contracting State in which rights in the mark [or design] arose shall have exclusive jurisdiction.

The effect of this provision is that, in a case of validity, exclusive jurisdiction is granted to the courts of the Contracting State of grant or registration or of the Contracting State in which rights in the mark arose. In a case of infringement on its own, this is treated exactly the same as validity with exclusive jurisdiction being given to the courts of the same Contracting State. In a case of infringement raising the issue of validity, whether as a defence, in separate revocation

---

[61] See the preliminary draft Convention adopted by the Special Commission on 30 October 1999.

proceedings or by way of a counterclaim, the court with exclusive jurisdiction in relation to the infringement will be in the same Contracting State as the court with exclusive jurisdiction in relation to validity. Indeed, it will often be the same court.

The arguments in favour of this approach are as follows. First, it provides a level of certainty that is lacking under the present law. By providing that the State with validity jurisdiction has exclusive jurisdiction over infringement it avoids even having to ask the question, that arises under the present law, of whether the State which would otherwise have infringement jurisdiction is precluded from trying that claim in the situation where the issue of validity is raised.

Second, it guarantees that the infringement claim and the validity issue are tried in the same State. It is desirable that the litigation in intellectual property cases is concentrated in a single State,[62] rather than being split up between different States, for the following reasons. First, it is not only inconvenient to the parties but also expensive to have to litigate in two different jurisdictions. Second, if you have two different courts in different States trying the infringement claim and the validity issue this could lead to different views on the width of the patent, etc. 'This would run counter to the concept that a patent which grants a monopoly with respect to a certain product or process, can have only one scope, and not a different scope for validity than for infringement. In addition, patent law involves considerations of public policy'.[63] Third, splitting the litigation can lead to practical problems. For example, the State with infringement jurisdiction may also have validity jurisdiction and may rule that the patent, etc is valid and then order the infringement to cease in the State of registration. There is then an attempt to enforce this order in the State of registration. But the courts of that State have previously held that the patent, etc is void. What happens then? The same problem can arise where the State with infringement jurisdiction has no validity jurisdiction and simply orders the infringement to cease in the State of registration. It is worth pointing out though that these practical problems can be met by co-ordinating the litigation. As the Dutch courts have shown, it is always possible to stay the infringement pro-

---

[62] See the *Expandable Grafts* case, n 22 above, at 361. This is also recognized by the fact that an additional Protocol to the European Patent Convention is being negotiated setting up a common international court which would hear infringement and validity issues in relation to European Patents. Participation before the common court would be optional for State parties to the European Patent Convention.

[63] Prel Doc No 13, p 4. This was the view of the UK and Australian Delegations.

ceedings pending a decision abroad on the question of validity. A fourth argument that has been put forward by the UK and Australian delegations at the experts' meeting[64] is that the questions of validity and infringement are closely linked and therefore should be tried in the same State, which in most States means the same specialized court. It is undeniable that validity and infringement are closely linked. Indeed, they have been described as being two sides of the same coin.[65] However, this does not necessarily mean that the trial of both matters should take place in the same State. If litigation is going to be concentrated in the same State this means in practice that it will have to be concentrated either in the State with validity jurisdiction or in the State with infringement jurisdiction. If the latter is chosen this effectively elevates infringement in importance over validity; conversely if the State with validity jurisdiction is chosen that will elevate this in importance over infringement. Whichever solution is chosen goes against the substantive law which does not regard one aspect as being more important than the other. It is submitted therefore that the close link argument is one that should operate not in favour of concentrating the litigation in a single State but, instead, in favour of splitting the litigation between the State with validity jurisdiction and the State with infringement jurisdiction. If this happens, the close link between infringement and validity justifies the staying of the infringement proceedings until the foreign court had decided the validity issue.[66]

Third, it avoids the spectre of a court trying the issue of validity of a right which is not registered there, something which it may find difficult to do. Moreover, there is a fear that, if foreign courts are able to determine the validity of rights not registered in their State, this may lead to corruption. Intellectual property rights can be of enormous financial value and the wider the range of States in which the issue of validity can be tried the more likely it is that a person is able to bring an action in a State in respect of which there are concerns that the judges are open to bribery.

The difficulty involved in determining the validity of a right registered abroad should not be exaggerated, at least in the European context. After all, the courts of an EC Member State are not precluded from trying actions for infringement

---

[64] ibid.

[65] *Chiron Corpn v Evans Medical Ltd and Others* [1996] FSR 863. See also *Organon Teknika Ltd v Hoffmann-La Roche AG* [1996] FSR 383 at 384; the *Fort Dodge* case, n 9 above.

[66] The *Expandable Grafts* case, n 22 above, at 361.

of a foreign copyright[67] by the fact that the creation of the right is put in issue. Moreover, provided that there is jurisdiction in relation to validity,[68] there is nothing to stop the court trying this issue as well, despite the fact that it is a foreign copyright. However, if the trial were to take place in the United States this could mean a jury determining the validity of foreign registered rights and it is questionable whether the members of a jury would be able to understand the highly complex technical issues involved. The fear of corruption is even harder to deal with. It is arguable that such a concern is not a legitimate consideration in the context of an international convention, where comity requires a respect for the ability of courts of other Contracting States. But when it comes to the quality of justice available abroad one must not be too unworldly and it has to be accepted that 'there are other parts of the world where things are badly wrong'.[69] The result is that, whilst the fear of corruption may not be expressed publicly at meetings of the Hague Conference, it is still likely to operate under the surface as a powerful influence on delegates in favour of giving the court with exclusive jurisdiction over validity an additional exclusive jurisdiction over infringement.

Fourth, it gives full effect to the exclusive jurisdiction rule in relation to validity and to the policy reasons justifying this rule. Exclusive jurisdiction in relation to validity can doubtless be justified on the same grounds as justify Article 22(4) of the Brussels Convention. Approach number (b) assumes that the maintenance of these policies is so important that they should apply even where validity is merely one part of the litigation, which has as its other part a claim for infringement.

Fifth, it protects the interest of the court in maintaining its business. Thus if a patent, etc is registered in Japan the Japanese courts will maintain their business in adjudicating on the validity of the right. Moreover, the Japanese courts will also have exclusive jurisdiction over the infringement claim, which in the absence of this provision they would not have had. Indeed, in the absence of this approach they might not have had any jurisdiction in relation to infringement let alone exclusive jurisdiction. The English courts in particular have reason to be concerned about the maintenance of their business. The English Patents Court has traditionally been a venue for patent litigation in cases where

---

[67] See the *Pearce* case, n 9 above.
[68] This would be under Arts 2, 5(5) or 6.
[69] *Muduroglu Ltd v TC Ziraat Bankasi* [1986] QB 1225 at 1248, CA.

the patent is registered in England. If foreign courts are able to try infringement actions in cases where the right is registered in England there is a fear that plaintiffs will take their patent litigation overseas, in particular to the Netherlands. Practitioners in England are concerned that under the present law the Dutch courts will become the European Centre for international infringement litigation. This has been triggered by the fact that the Dutch courts are prepared to grant cross-border injunctions in respect of foreign registered rights using their Kort-Geding Procedure.[70] However, the interest of courts in one State in protecting their business from being lost to the courts in some other State cannot be regarded as a strong interest. Indeed, it is questionable whether it is a legitimate interest at all in the context of an international convention.

There are though numerous arguments against this approach. First, it ignores entirely the fact that infringement is a tort and under the Convention the normal position is that a plaintiff can bring a tort claim in the State in which the act or the injury occurred.[71] The policies justifying this important rule of private international law are likewise ignored. Of particular concern is the fact that the plaintiff is not given a choice of fora in which to bring the infringement claim. The plaintiff does not even have the opportunity of bringing an action in the State of the defendant's residence, let alone the alternative under the tort rule of bringing proceedings in the place of the wrongful act or injury.

Second, it involves allocating jurisdiction in a tort case to the State where a patent, etc is registered. This involves breaking a fundamental principle in private international law that jurisdiction in tort is based on the idea of a meaningful connection with the State allocated jurisdiction. Under the Convention, and indeed under the Brussels Regulation as well, this connection is seen in terms of the person of the defendant being connected with a State or the defendant doing an act in a State or the defendant causing an injury there.[72] But if jurisdiction is allocated to the State where the right is registered what is the

---

[70] This is a shortened procedure reserved for provisional measures taken by the President of the court in urgent cases.

[71] This will not necessarily be the same as the State of registration of the right. For example, there could be a product which is manufactured in State A, where a patent has been registered. A very similar product is marketed in State B which infringes this patent. There is an act of infringement in B for the purposes of jurisdiction. When it comes to the applicable law, State B may apply the law of State A on the basis of the parties' common residence there (see Fawcett and Torremans, p 623). However, it is unlikely that there is actionability under the law of State A because the patent was infringed abroad.

[72] See generally, the Nygh and Pocar Report, Prelim Doc No 11, pp 58–59.

meaningful connection with that State? Certainly the *defendant* has no such meaningful connection with this State. The person of the defendant has no connection with that State and it is the plaintiff who has done the act of registering the patent in a State, rather than the defendant. What the defendant is likely to have done is to have infringed the patent in the State of registration[73] but it is submitted that this separate connection cannot justify allocating jurisdiction to the State of registration. The need for a meaningful connection is a very important consideration and, at one time, it appeared that it might prove a sticking point for at least one Member State of the Hague Convention. The United States at one stage said in relation to the then proposals in relation to intellectual property, one variant of which could lead to concentrating jurisdiction in the State where the right was registered, that it could not accept *in personam* jurisdiction in infringement cases over a defendant who had no relation with the jurisdiction.[74] However, since then it has come round to supporting approach number (**b**).

Third, patent disputes are arbitrable and it is therefore inconsistent to confer exclusive jurisdiction upon State courts.[75] However, this cannot be regarded as a strong point since, in practice, infringement disputes do not go to arbitration.

Fourth, it will often lead to a proliferation of actions. The parties have an interest in avoiding a proliferation of litigation. But this is the inevitable consequence of channelling all of a claim into the State where a right is registered. Intellectual property rights are normally registered in more than one State. Thus a patent may be registered, for example, in three different States, thereby creating three separate rights. If only the State where a right is registered has jurisdiction to try the infringement claim and invalidity defence it follows that, in order to protect his rights, the plaintiff will need to bring actions in three different States. Yet it may be the same defendant who has infringed all three rights. This problem will commonly arise with European Patents, where the multiplication of actions is inconsistent with the protection given to persons who wish to register their rights. A person by making just one registration can obtain European patents for a number of different States. Yet when it comes to litigation to protect those patents the claimant is forced to bring a series of different actions. This problem has been recognized in relation to European

---

[73] In a case of infringement of a trade mark over the internet the defendant may not have committed a positive act in the State of registration.

[74] Prelim Doc No 11, p 3.

[75] Prelim Doc No 13, p 5.

Patents and there is a proposal to introduce a common international court to deal with litigation relating to such patents. Whilst the problem may in the future be solved for European patents, it will remain for non-European patents. This proliferation of jurisdiction is obviously not fair to the plaintiff. Neither is it fair to the defendant who may well prefer to have trial of the infringement of all three patents in just one State. But this is not possible since the court with jurisdiction in relation to the patent registered in its State has no jurisdiction in relation to the other two patents.

Fifth, the width given to exclusive jurisdiction does not fit in with the general attitude towards, or the nature of the other rules of, exclusive jurisdiction. The background to the introduction of exclusive jurisdiction into the preliminary draft Convention is that 'it is far from certain that they [rules of exclusive jurisdiction] ought to be included in an international Convention, as in this context it might be argued that there is little practical value in arranging too rigid a distribution of State jurisdiction. For this reason, the Convention has limited the number and extent of the categories of exclusive jurisdiction, confining them to instances where they are found to be useful'.[76] The preliminary draft Convention allocates exclusive jurisdiction to three other types of proceedings. Each of these is drawn directly from what is now the Brussels I Regulation and is, as under that Regulation, very narrowly drawn. Thus the exclusive jurisdiction in relation to immovable property does not apply to all proceedings in relation to such property but only to proceedings which have as their object rights *in rem* in immovable property, thereby excluding the many proceedings which have as their object rights *in personam*. None of these other grounds of exclusive jurisdiction encompass a claim in tort. Moreover, when it comes to the other three grounds of exclusive jurisdiction, two are somewhat narrower than their Brussels I Regulation equivalent,[77] and the third is the same. It seems somewhat inconsistent then to have an exclusive jurisdiction in relation to intellectual property that is very much wider than the provision under the Brussels I Regulation.

Sixth, the wider the exclusive jurisdiction that is given in relation to patents, the greater the gap that opens up with the law on jurisdiction in relation to copyright. At the experts' meeting there was no support for giving exclusive jurisdiction in relation to copyright, not even in cases of validity of the

---

[76] ibid, p 64.
[77] ibid, pp 64–66.

right.[78] Whilst exclusive jurisdiction in relation to the issue of the validity of a patent, etc is well known, extending this to infringement is not and widens the gap with copyright even further. There is nothing wrong with having very different rules for patents, etc from those for copyright provided that this can be justified. But can it? Interestingly, one of the reasons given for not giving exclusive jurisdiction in copyright cases is that of avoiding the proliferation of litigation.[79] What is important in such cases is 'consolidating all the claims against a copier under different laws in one single court'.[80] But, as has been seen, the need to prevent the proliferation of actions also exists with patents, etc, particularly European patents.

Seventh, it deals badly with cases where infringement arises on its own, ie, the issue of validity is not raised. A possible argument that might be made in favour of extending an exclusive jurisdiction that applies in validity cases and in cases where infringement raises the issue of validity to cases of infringement on its own is that validity can always be raised in the future and indeed frequently is so raised.[81] However, it is submitted that such an argument is flawed. You cannot deal with jurisdiction on the basis of suspicions as to what defence might run.[82] The fact that the defendant can challenge validity does not mean that he will do so.[83] There is, of course, always the possibility that the issue of validity may be raised by some amendment to a claim form, but such a theoretical possibility should be ignored.[84] The courts should therefore only concern themselves with cases where the issue of validity has actually been raised, or at least it is clear that it is going to be put in issue.[85] Even in this situation, if it is immediately clear that the raising of the invalidity issue cannot be deemed to be meant seriously, shown by the fact that the arguments in favour of this are inadequate, then jurisdiction should be determined on the basis that there is a claim for infringement which does not raise the issue of invalidity.[86] Moreover, even if you accept that it is legitimate to look at what might happen, it still has to be asked whether the justifications for concentrating jurisdiction in the State

---

[78] Prelim Doc No 13, 7.
[79] ibid.
[80] ibid.
[81] The UK delegation regard the raising of this as almost inevitable, see Prel Doc No 13, p 4.
[82] The *Coin Controls* case, n 14 above, at 51.
[83] ibid.
[84] The *Chiron* case, n 9 above, at 872.
[85] The latter was treated in the *Coin Controls* case as being equivalent to actually raising the defence.
[86] See the *Expandable Grafts* case, n 22 above, at 361.

with validity jurisdiction, which apply where validity is actually raised, apply to the same extent in a case where it can only be said that validity might be raised. The spectre of a court trying the issue of the validity of a right registered abroad is not such a strong factor where there is only a possibility of validity being raised, rather than a certainty. The need to give effect to the validity rule and the policies underlying it is not as strong if there is merely the possibility of validity being raised, rather than a certainty. The need to protect the interests of the court in managing its business in relation to validity is likewise reduced in importance if there is only a possibility of validity being raised, rather than a certainty.

(c) Giving the State of registration exclusive jurisdiction for validity and non-exclusive jurisdiction for infringement

This too has been put forward as a proposal at the Hague Conference and is supported by the Swiss delegation. It is described as Alternative B and is set out in Article 12(5A). This proposal accepts that there should be exclusive jurisdiction in respect of proceedings that have as their sole object the registration, validity, nullity, or revocation of patents, trade marks, designs, or other similar rights. It then provides that

> 5A. In relation to proceedings which have as their object the infringement of patents, trademarks, designs or other similar rights, the courts of the Contracting State referred to in the preceding paragraph [or in the provisions of Articles [3 to 16]] have jurisdiction.

The effect of this proposal is that, in a case of validity on its own, exclusive jurisdiction is allocated to the State of registration. In a case of infringement on its own non-exclusive jurisdiction is granted to the courts of the Contracting State with exclusive jurisdiction in relation to validity. If the part in square brackets is included non-exclusive jurisdiction will also be granted to the courts of the State with jurisdiction under Articles 3–16. In a case of infringement raising the issue of validity it is unclear how this provision will operate. The same problem would arise as under the present law in the situation where the plaintiff seeks trial in State A, which has infringement jurisdiction, but the right has been granted or registered in State B which has exclusive jurisdiction over the validity of the right. Are the courts in State A precluded from dealing with the issue of validity?

The arguments in favour of this approach are as follows. First, it deals well with a case of infringement on its own. Provided that jurisdiction in an action for infringement is granted to all of the States with jurisdiction under Articles 3–16, an action for infringement is subject to the normal rules that apply to any other tort. Second, in an action for infringement that raises validity, litigation can be concentrated in one State, the State where the right is registered, if the plaintiff so chooses. The courts of this State will have exclusive jurisdiction over the validity issue but they are also given non-exclusive jurisdiction in relation to the infringement claim.

On the other hand, the following arguments can be made against this approach. First, in the situation where the plaintiff seeks to bring a claim for infringement, which raises the validity of the right, in a State other than the one in which the right is registered, it is unclear whether the proceedings have as their object the infringement of patents, etc. This uncertainty can be ended by adding a sentence spelling out that they do.

Second, in this situation if the proceedings are accepted as having as their object the infringement of patents, etc then the courts of the State with infringement jurisdiction will be able to try the infringement claim but, unless this also happens to be the State of registration, they will presumably not be able to try the validity aspect of the case because that will still be subject to the exclusive jurisdiction of the State of registration by virtue of Article 12 paragraphs 4 and 5. The result is that the litigation will be split between the courts of different States. However, this does not necessarily mean a lack of coordination in the litigation, as the Dutch courts have shown in the *Expandable Grafts* case.[87]

(d) An additional provision dealing with matters arising as an incidental matter

The preliminary draft Convention contains a third proposal described as Alternative A and B. It consists of three paragraphs and was drafted with the intention of it being used in conjunction with alternative A. However, it could be used in conjunction with alternative B. The first of these paragraphs, and the only one relevant to the present discussion, is set out in Article 12(6) and is concerned with matters arising as an incidental matter.[88] It provides that

---

[87] See n 22 above. This point was made by the Swiss, Finnish and Swedish delegations at the experts' meeting held at Geneva, Prel Doc No 13, p 4.

[88] Art 12(7) is concerned with the scope of intellectual rights encompassed within Art 12 and para (8) with the definition of a 'court' under this Article.

Paragraphs 4 and 5 shall not apply where one of the above matters arises as an incidental question in proceedings before a court not having exclusive jurisdiction under those paragraphs. However, the ruling in that matter shall have no binding effect in subsequent proceedings, even if they are between the same parties. A matter arises as an incidental question if the court is not requested to give a judgment on that matter, even if a ruling on it is necessary in arriving at a decision.

This is designed to allow a court with non-exclusive jurisdiction to decide on validity where this arises as an incidental question. For example, the validity of a patent, etc can be incidental to the lawfulness of the distribution of assets according to a will.[89] The validity of a patent, etc may in certain circumstances arise as an incidental question in license litigation.[90] Such cases will doubtless come within the definition of an incidental question, namely one that arises where the court is not requested to give a judgment on that matter, even if a ruling on it is necessary in arriving at a decision. This definition reflects the idea that where a decision on validity is being made as an incidental matter, the effect of the decision being limited to the resolution of the case between the parties, it is inadvisable to start allocating exclusive jurisdiction to the courts of a particular State.[91]

If approach number (c) above were to be adopted, would the addition of paragraph (6) end the uncertainty that exists under that approach in the situation where an infringement claim raises the issue of the validity of the right? If the issue of validity can be said to arise as an incidental question then validity is no longer a matter for the exclusive jurisdiction of the State of registration. But can validity be said to arise as an incidental question in an action for infringement? In principle, since infringement and validity are different sides of the same coin, it cannot be said that the latter question arises incidentally.[92] However, the definition of an incidental question raises the possibility that, in certain circumstances, the issue of validity can arise as an incidental question in the context of an infringement claim. For example, if validity is raised as a defence to an action for infringement the court is not requested to give a judgment on that matter, even if a ruling on it is necessary in arriving at a decision. On the other hand, if validity is raised in the same court as the infringement claim by way of a counterclaim for revocation, which is regarded under English law as a separate cause

---

89 Prel Doc No 13, p 6.
90 ibid.
91 See generally the Nygh and Pocar Report, Prel Doc No 11, p 67.
92 Prel Doc No 13, p 6.

of action, then this will result in a judgment and, seemingly, does not arise as an incidental question.

However, the addition of paragraph (6) to approach number (c) does not solve the problem of having to split the litigation between different States. In the situation where validity does not arise as an incidental question, unless the infringement action is brought in the State of registration, it will be necessary to split the litigation between different States since the State of registration will have exclusive jurisdiction over the issue of validity. Even in the situation where validity does arise as an incidental question, it may still be necessary to split the litigation since the State with infringement jurisdiction may not have a basis of jurisdiction which would allow it to try the issue of validity.[93]

(e) Giving the court with jurisdiction over infringement an additional jurisdiction over validity

The Nygh and Pocar Report has commented that, although infringement will often raise the issue of validity, this does not necessarily mean that the litigation must be focussed on the State of registration or deposit.[94] This raises the possibility of an approach, which has not been put forward at the Hague Conference, namely that of giving the court with non-exclusive jurisdiction over infringement an additional non-exclusive jurisdiction over validity.[95]

This approach means that in a case of validity on its own the action can be brought in any State with infringement jurisdiction, ie, the State of registration of the patent, etc and any State with jurisdiction under Articles 3–16. In a case of infringement on its own, again the action can be brought in any State with infringement jurisdiction. In a case of infringement raising the issue of validity, then the court with infringement jurisdiction is able to try the validity issue. However, this does not necessarily mean that the litigation will be concentrated in that State. Whether this happens will depend on how the issue of validity is

---

[93] It might be argued that where validity arises by way of a defence the court with infringement jurisdiction does not need a separate basis of jurisdiction to try this, provided no other State is given exclusive jurisdiction over this matter. See generally Wadlow, paras 3–132 to 3–134.

[94] The Nygh and Pocar Report, Prelim Doc No 11, p 67.

[95] The draft Convention on jurisdiction and recognition of judgments in intellectual property matters advocated by Dreyfuss and Ginsburg at the WIPO Forum of Jan 2001 provides in Art 8 that 'The issue of validity of a patent may be adjudicated in an infringement action brought pursuant to the rules of this Convention'.

raised. If it is raised as a defence to the infringement claim then the State with infringement jurisdiction will be able to rule on this matter. However, there is nothing to stop a defendant from bringing separate revocation proceedings in a State other than the one in which the infringement claim is brought. For example, the plaintiff may bring infringement proceedings in the State with jurisdiction under the tort head. The defendant may then bring revocation proceedings in the State where the patent, etc is registered. The result is that the litigation is split between different States. Alternatively, the defendant may bring separate revocation proceedings first by way of a pre-emptive strike. In this situation, unless the plaintiff subsequently brings the infringement claim in the same State, the result again will be that the infringement claim and the validity issue are split between different States.

This approach, like approaches (**b**) and (**c**), would have to be used in conjunction with Alternatives A and B, the additional provision dealing with matters arising as an incidental matter set out in approach number (**d**) above. That this is necessary can be seen from the following example. A court with infringement jurisdiction is faced with the defence that a foreign registered right is invalid and determines the validity of this right; this inevitably raises the question of what effect this determination will have abroad.

Approach number (**e**) is to a large extent the mirror image of approach number (**b**) so that many of the arguments in favour of the former are the arguments against the latter and vice versa. Thus the arguments in favour this approach are as follows.

First, it gives full weight to the fact that infringement is a tort and the normal position under the Convention is that a plaintiff can bring a tort claim in the State where the act or injury occurred. This gives full effect not only to the tort rule but also to the policies underlying it. It is an important consideration that the plaintiff in a tort case should be given a choice of fora and its importance is not lessened simply because validity of the patent, etc is in issue.

Second, it ensures that jurisdiction in tort is based on a meaningful connection with the State allocated jurisdiction, thereby upholding an important principle of private international law.

Third, by refusing to confer exclusive jurisdiction upon State courts it acknowledges that patent disputes are arbitrable.

Fourth, it avoids a proliferation of actions. This too is an important consideration

since it is in the interests of both parties. If the State with infringement jurisdiction is also given jurisdiction over the validity defence, regardless of where
the right is registered, a plaintiff who complains that a patent registered in three
different States has been infringed will only need to bring an action in one
State.[96] In the situation where there are multiple infringements in a number of
different States, the litigation in relation to all these infringements can be concentrated in the State of the defendant's domicile.

Fifth, it fits in with the other rules of exclusive jurisdiction under the
Convention, which are narrowly drawn, thereby upholding a basic principle of
private international law.

Sixth, when compared with the alternative of concentrating litigation in the
State where the right was registered, it reduces the gap between the treatment
of copyright and patents, etc.

There are then four arguments that can be made against this approach. First, as
has been seen, it does not guarantee that the trial of the infringement claim and
the validity issue are concentrated in the same State. The only way to guarantee this is to provide for exclusive jurisdiction for the infringement claim and
exclusive jurisdiction for the validity issue and to allocate this exclusive jurisdiction to the same State. Second, it raises the spectre of a court trying the issue
of validity of a right which is not registered there. Third, it gives no effect to the
exclusive jurisdiction rule in relation to validity and to the policies underlying
this rule. Fourth, it fails to protect the interest of the court in maintaining its
business.

(2) Which is the Best Approach?

The approach adopted should: provide certainty; concentrate the litigation in
a single State; give effect to both the exclusive jurisdiction rule and the policies
underlying it and to general bases of jurisdiction, including the tort rule, and
the policies underlying these; only give jurisdiction to a State with which there
is a meaningful connection; minimise the proliferation of jurisdictions; and fit
in with the basic principle of private international law that exclusive jurisdiction should be narrowly drawn. These are the relevant considerations when
choosing which is the best approach. However, it has been seen that none of the
possible alternatives will satisfy all of these considerations and each alternative

---

[96] For the desirability of this in relation to European patents see the *Expandable Grafts* case, n
22 above, at 361.

satisfies different considerations. The question therefore has to be: which approach best achieves overall the relevant considerations? Approach number (**b**) achieves these better than approaches numbers (**a**) and (**c**). The former is both certain and guarantees the concentration of litigation in a single State whereas the latter are both uncertain and lead to the litigation being split between different States. But there is of course an alternative to (**b**) in the form of approach (**e**). The advocates of approach number (**b**) appear to regard the concentration of the litigation in a single State as being not merely desirable but as being the sole or at least prime objective in intellectual property jurisdiction cases. Admittedly, if this were so, then approach number (**b**) would clearly be the best approach to adopt since this is the only approach that will guarantee this. However, this ignores the very obvious fact that, although the rules on jurisdiction for intellectual property have been examined at the Hague Conference as a separate topic, at the end of the day they will have to fit within the Convention as a whole and this is a Convention on private international law, not one on intellectual property which contains some private international law provisions. Any approach adopted must uphold basic principles of private international law that require a meaningful connection with a State that is allocated jurisdiction, give the claimant a choice of fora where there is a claim in tort and insist that exclusive jurisdiction is narrowly drawn. The big failing of approach number (**b**) is that it involves breaking these principles. This leaves approach number (**e**). This alternative is certain, ensures that basic principles of private international law are upheld and, whilst not guaranteeing that litigation is concentrated in one State, will, in certain circumstances, lead to this. It is this alternative that appears best to achieve overall the relevant considerations. It is therefore tentatively suggested that in cases of intellectual property the court with jurisdiction over infringement should be given an additional jurisdiction over validity.

E. What Should We Do About the Brussels I Regulation?

The Dutch Court of Appeal in the *Expandable Grafts* case acknowledged both the desirability of concentrating litigation of the infringement and validity issues in the same court and that this solution was barred by Article 16(4) of the Brussels Convention. The Court went on to say that, in the light of this, 'Amendment of the Conventions seems to be inevitable'.[97] We now have the

---

[97] See n 22 above, at 361.

Brussels I Regulation, which, although making numerous amendments to the Brussels Convention, contains the same provisions in relation to intellectual property litigation. However, this does not mean that the opportunity for changing the EC law for this type of litigation has gone for ever. Within five years of the entry into force of the Regulation, the European Commission is required to present a report on the application of the Regulation. This is to be accompanied, if need be, by proposals for adaptations to the Regulation.[98] What form should this amendment to the jurisdiction rules for intellectual property cases take? The approach that is best for the Hague Judgments Convention should be the one that is adopted for the Brussels I Regulation. When it comes to the Hague Judgments Convention it was suggested above that the litigation should be concentrated in the State with infringement jurisdiction. The arguments that have been set out above in favour of the adoption of this solution in the worldwide context of the Hague Convention are equally applicable in the European context of the Brussels I Regulation.

F. Conclusion

It is tentatively submitted that the best solution to the problem that arises in intellectual property cases where a claim for infringement of a right raises the issue of the validity of that right is that the State with infringement jurisdiction should be given an additional jurisdiction over the validity issue. Although various solutions have been proposed in the context of the Hague Judgments Convention, this is not one of them. Yet it leads to certainty, it ensures that basic principles of private international law are followed and, in certain circumstances, leads to the concentration of litigation in a single State. Not only does this appear to be the best solution in the worldwide context of the Hague Judgments Convention but it also appears to be the best solution in the European Community and, in due course, the Brussels I Regulation should be amended to so provide.

---

[98] Art 73 of the Brussels I Regulation.

7

A CULLING OF SACRED COWS—THE IMPACT OF THE EC INSOLVENCY REGULATION ON ENGLISH CONFLICT OF LAWS

*Ian F Fletcher**

A. Introduction

The entry into force of the EC Regulation on Insolvency Proceedings, from 31 May 2002, brought about numerous changes in the law and practice relating to insolvency in all the EC Member States, including the United Kingdom.[1]

---

* Herbert Smith Professor of International Commercial Law, University College London.
[1] Council Regulation (EC) No 1346/2000, of 29 May 2000: [2000] OJ L 160/1, Recital (32). Art 47 prescribes the date of entry into force. The Regulation applies to all Member States with the exception of Denmark: Recital (33). It is expected that special arrangements will be concluded—probably in the form of a convention between Denmark and the other fourteen

While some of those changes involve merely modest adjustment to existing procedures, others are of a more radical nature. Among these are a number whose effect is to reverse—or significantly recast—established rules and principles in the realm of English private international law. Although the changes are, strictly speaking, confined to those cases which fall within the ambit of the Regulation, they will almost certainly give rise to a wider consideration of the matters affected, to ascertain whether there are good reasons for maintaining a dissimilar treatment of cases on the basis that the Regulation is applicable to some, but not to others, by reason of the debtor's *modus operandi* at the time of the opening of proceedings. The purpose of this paper is to identify some of the more notable changes from the standpoint of English law, and to offer some thoughts on the advisability of retaining the previous rules for parallel application to cases outside the ambit of the Regulation.

B. The EC Regulation: Main Features

The Regulation on Insolvency Proceedings is the culmination of a protracted process of gestation, commenced as long ago as 1960, among the members of what was originally the European Economic Community. Article 220 of the EEC Treaty of 25 March 1957 committed the Member States to concluding arrangements for the simplification of formalities governing the reciprocal recognition and enforcement of judgments and awards. That somewhat modest and unspecific remit subsequently evolved into ambitious twin projects to introduce comprehensive regimes imposing direct rules of jurisdiction as well as virtually automatic rules for recognition and enforcement of judgments in civil and commercial litigation and in matters of insolvency. The latter topic was hived off into a separate project because of the special, collective character of insolvency proceedings. The civil and commercial litigation project progressed more rapidly and resulted in the Brussels Convention of 27 September 1968, afterwards much amended and expanded, which has been in force since February 1973.[2] The planned convention on insolvency matters never did

---

Member States—to enable the effects of the Regulation to be replicated under Danish domestic law.

[2] For an account of the Brussels/Lugano Convention, see, *eg,* Cheshire and North's *Private International Law* (13th edn. 1999), Ch 11. The Convention is replaced, as between all of the current Member States except Denmark, with effect from 1 March 2002, by Council Regulation No 44/2001, of 22 December 2000: [2001] OJ L 12/1.

enter into force in that form, but was rescued from oblivion by an initiative within the EC Council during 1999, whereby the final version of the Convention (completed in 1995) was converted into the form of a regulation, retaining intact the substantive provisions formerly accepted by all fifteen states.[3]

The twin projects commenced under the auspices of Article 220 EEC Treaty were thus concluded in different forms, and were completed within different periods of time. The underlying philosophy behind the two is strikingly similar, however. In each case, the simple mandate to improve the arrangements for recognition and enforcement of judgments within the Community was transcended, as a result of the application of a logical analysis derived from the fundamental principles on which the EEC, as a supranational organization, was seen to be based. The conditions necessary to enable the Community's internal market to function as intended could only be achieved through the elimination of competitive distortion caused by a variety of factors. Some distortion was attributable to economic, or fiscal, or regulatory practices pursued by individual States, while other kinds of distortion were caused through the differences between their domestic laws, further exacerbated by their divergent approaches to private international law. Only by progressive elimination of these variables—so the argument ran—could a fair and transparent internal market be established throughout the Community. The ongoing programme of gradual harmonization of substantive laws by means of regulations and directives represents one limb of this policy. But that programme has limitations, because the laws of third States remain untouched. To the extent that the choice of law processes under the Member States' individual rules of private international law could result in the selection and application of different laws substantively, the outcome of a case would remain dependent on the identity of the forum in which the proceedings were determined. Full uniformity of outcome was therefore seen to require the replacement of the separate national approaches to matters of conflict of laws. This required, first, the creation of a unified set of provisions governing the exercise of jurisdiction by national courts and authorities. In this way, the actual circumstances of the individual case, rather than a unilateral act of forum-shopping by the instigating party, would determine the forum for hearing the dispute. Then, by imposing a uniform code of

---

[3] The saga of the EC project for an insolvency convention is discussed in I F Fletcher, *Insolvency in Private International Law* (OUP, 1999), Chap 6. The work went to press before the events which resulted in the adoption of the finalized text in the form of a regulation.

choice of law provisions in place of the separate rules evolved by each State, a uniformity of outcome could be ensured in terms of the law selected and applied substantively. Only by this means could the system ensure that like cases were determined in like manner.

In the case of civil and commercial litigation, the above policy was ultimately realized by means of two conventions, the Brussels Convention already mentioned, and the Rome Convention of 19 June 1980 on the Law Applicable to Contractual Obligations.[4] The project for an insolvency convention represented an attempt to combine all aspects of the conflicts process within a single text, and this feature has been retained in the Regulation. Thus, Chapter I (Articles 1–15) defines the Regulation's scope of application, imposes direct rules of jurisdiction for cases falling within that scope, and prescribes uniform rules of choice of law which apply in all cases governed by the Regulation. Chapter II (Articles 16–26) establishes rules for recognition and enforcement throughout the Member States of judgments opening proceedings handed down by courts which have jurisdiction pursuant to Chapter I: such recognition is immediate and automatic, and can be resisted by another Member State only on the basis of a very restrictively worded provision in Article 26 utilizing the ground of public policy.[5] The remaining chapters include provisions which establish the conditions under which concurrent insolvency proceedings involving the same debtor may take place in different Member States, and how such proceedings are to be co-ordinated.[6]

(1) Key Principles of the Regulation's Application

The Regulation is self-limiting in its scope of application, in several ways. First, and most importantly, it only applies to proceedings where the debtor's *centre of main interests* (hereafter indicated in abbreviated form as 'COMI') is located in the Community.[7] No formal definition of COMI is supplied by the Regulation's substantive provisions, but Recital (13) to the text states that:

---

[4] Consequently, in non-contractual matters the Member States' rules of choice of law are presently unharmonized, so that the venue of proceedings can be a significant factor in terms of their outcome.

[5] The detailed provisions of the Regulation will not be examined in this paper. For a full account of these, see G Moss, S Isaacs, and I F Fletcher (eds), *The EC Regulation on Insolvency Proceedings* (OUP, 2002, forthcoming).

[6] Chapter II (Arts 27–38) governs so-called 'secondary insolvency proceedings', whose nature is briefly described below.

[7] Recital (14) to the Regulation.

> The 'centre of main interests' should correspond to the place where the debtor conducts the administration of his interests on a regular basis and is therefore ascertainable by third parties.

This statement will be of considerable importance when the Regulation is applied to actual cases, but of itself it provides no guarantee of certainty. Different courts could well reach different conclusions as to the location of the COMI, based on their separate evaluations of the same factual information. There is no procedure for resolving conflicts of jurisdiction, whether positive or negative, resulting from the conflicting conclusions of the courts of different States, which leaves the onus upon each national court to discharge its functions with meticulous regard to the intra-Community significance of its decision. The task of identifying the location of the debtor's COMI is assisted to some degree in the case of a company or legal person, because Article 3(1) establishes a rebuttable presumption that the registered office is the COMI in the absence of proof to the contrary. In cases to which the presumption applies, it will suffice for the petitioner to aver that the debtor's registered office is in the State in which proceedings are being initiated: the onus will be on any party who wishes to convince the court that it does not have jurisdiction, to adduce suitable evidence as to the true location of the debtor's COMI.

The Regulation is also self-limiting in terms of the types of proceedings to which it applies. Article 1(1) states that it applies only to *collective* insolvency proceedings which entail the partial or total divestment of a debtor and the appointment of a 'liquidator'.[8] A list of such proceedings, for each of the Member States, is supplied by Annex A.

The prescriptive principles for jurisdiction are contained in Article 3. There is a single factor, namely the location of the debtor's COMI, which determines competence to open insolvency proceedings which shall be internationally effective. Such proceedings can be referred to as 'main insolvency proceedings'. A subsidiary basis of jurisdiction is offered by Article 3(2), which allows insolvency proceedings to be opened in another Member State only if the debtor

---

[8] 'Liquidator' is defined in Art 2(b) to mean 'any person or body whose function is to administer or liquidate assets of which the debtor has been divested or to supervise the administration of his affairs', as listed in Annex C. The term thus bears a wider meaning than that which it has under English domestic law. Art 1(2) further excludes the Regulation from applying to insolvency proceedings concerning defined types of debtor. These are: insurance undertakings, credit institutions, investment undertakings which provide services involving the holding of funds or securities for third parties, and collective investment undertakings.

possesses an establishment in that other State. The term 'establishment', as defined by Article 2(h), denotes an established place of business maintained by the debtor: a mere presence of assets, or personal residential links including possession or ownership of residential property, does not suffice. Insolvency proceedings founded upon the presence of an establishment are restricted in their effects to the assets of the debtor situated in the territory of the State in question. Such territorial proceedings are termed 'secondary' proceedings when they take place concurrently with main proceedings opened at the COMI. The co-ordination of main and secondary proceedings is governed by Chapter III.

A uniform code of choice of law provisions is supplied by Articles 4–15 inclusive. The main rule, under Article 4, stipulates that the law applicable to insolvency proceedings and their effects shall be that of the Member State within whose territory the proceedings are opened (*lex concursus*), save as otherwise provided in the Regulation. The specific exceptions generated by Articles 5–15 are therefore of considerable importance, as they offer the sole means of escape from the consequences of application of the *lex concursus* with respect to assets and interests affected by the insolvency proceedings in question. Where it is possible to open both main and secondary proceedings, the *lex concursus* of the main proceedings applies to all assets save those which are situated in the State or States where secondary proceedings are opened. A bridging principle is supplied by Article 32(1) to the effect that any creditor may lodge his claim in the main proceedings and in any secondary proceedings. Thus the essential unity of the debtor's estate is maintained, and the concept of collectivity among creditors respected, subject to the concession that the process of distribution of assets comprised within a secondary proceeding will take place according to the rules of that *lex concursus*. This may prove advantageous for certain creditors whose claims would fare less well under the terms of the law governing the main proceedings, but the vital point of principle is that it is not permissible for the assets comprised in any secondary proceedings to be ring-fenced for the exclusive benefit of creditors who themselves are citizens or residents of the State in question.

Before examining the impact of the above rules on established principles, it is necessary to mention the significance of the Community Law dimension within which the Regulation takes effect. Under the by now familiar doctrines of direct applicability of EC regulations, and of the supremacy of Community Law when juxtaposed with conflicting provisions of national law, the

Regulation automatically has the force of law throughout the Member States as of 31 May 2002.[9] No legislative measures are necessary—or, indeed, are permissible—at national level to bring this into effect. On the other hand, it is the duty of every Member State to ensure that there is full compliance with the requirements of Community Law with regard to all legal and administrative processes which take place within its jurisdiction. Therefore, it is a prudent course for Member States to review the working of their insolvency laws and to take such measures as may be necessary to avert potential confusion or infraction resulting from the altered state of the law. This may be done by means of amendments to pre-existing provisions of primary or secondary legislation which, if left unaltered, could mislead parties as to the law's current effects.[10] In the case of legal rules or doctrines which rest on the authority of decided cases, however, the impact of the changes brought about by the Regulation will be less visible at first. Until an opportunity arises for a court to restate the law, parties will need to receive advice based upon the assumption that all previous authorities are subject to the overarching effects of the Regulation for any matters properly falling within its scope.

One final matter of some relevance, as will be seen, concerns a further principle established under Community law, namely the prohibition of any discrimination on grounds of nationality. This principle is expressed in Article 12 of the Consolidated EC Treaty of 1999 (effected by the Treaty of Amsterdam), and was formerly in force as Article 6 of the original EEC Treaty. In relation to the operation of the Regulation on Insolvency Proceedings, the effect of Article 12 is that a Member State is prohibited from applying its law in such a way that discriminatory effects are experienced by parties who qualify to be classed as 'nationals' of another EC State by virtue of the Treaty. In the

---

[9] See the definition supplied by Art 249 of the Consolidated EC Treaty of 1999 (formerly Art 189 of the EEC Treaty of 1957): 'A regulation shall have general application. It shall be binding in its entirety and directly applicable in all Member States'. For classic expositions by the ECJ of the doctrine of supremacy of Community law, see: Case 26/62 *Van Gend en Loos v Nederlandse Administratie der Belastingen* [1963] ECR 1; Case 6/64 *Costa v ENEL* [1964] ECR 585; Case 11/70 *Internationale Handelsgesellschaft v EVst fur Getreide und Futtermittel* [1970] ECR 1125; Case 106/77 *Amministrazione delle Finanze dello Stato v Simmenthal SpA* [1978] ECR 629. See also Case C-213/89 *R v Secretary of State for Transport, ex parte Factortame Ltd* [1990] ECR I-2433.

[10] In the United Kingdom, such amendments have been made using enabling powers under s 2(2) of the European Communities Act 1972 and under various sections of the Insolvency Act 1986. See the Insolvency Act 1986 (Amendment) (No. 2) Regulations 2002, S.I. 2002 1240.

case of natural persons, the status of being a 'national' of a Member State is derived from citizenship.[11] In the case of legal persons, Article 48 of the Consolidated Treaty (ex Article 58) provides that

> Companies or firms formed in accordance with the law of a Member State and having their registered office, central administration or principal place of business within the Community shall [for the purposes of the exercise of the right of establishment under Chapter 2 and of the freedom to provide services under Chapter 3] be treated in the same way as natural persons who are citizens of Member States.

We will next consider the impact of the foregoing principles upon established law and practice in England and Wales.[12]

C. The Impact of the Regulation on the Exercise of Jurisdiction in Insolvency Proceedings

(1) Jurisdiction to Open Proceedings Involving Companies

For the United Kingdom, according to Annex A, the following types of corporate insolvency proceedings are within the scope of the Regulation:

- Winding up by the court
- Creditors' voluntary winding up (with confirmation by the court)
- Administration
- Voluntary arrangements.

Hitherto, a sharp distinction has been maintained between the availability of the above procedures for companies formed and registered in England, and the conditions under which, if at all, they can be opened in a case where the company was not so formed. In the case of winding up by the court (also known as compulsory liquidation), section 117(1) of the Insolvency Act 1986 is but the latest in a series of statutory provisions to proclaim that

---

[11] See, eg, Art 39(2) of the Consolidated EC Treaty (formerly Art 48, EEC Treaty), on abolition of discrimination based on nationality between workers of the Member States.

[12] Although this paper does not address the position of either Scotland or Northern Ireland, it should be noted that the Regulation (and the provisions of the main EC Treaty) apply to the UK as a whole, as the Member State concerned. What is stated here regarding the required operation of insolvency law after May 2002 is therefore necessarily applicable, *mutatis mutandis*, to the other parts of the UK.

The High Court has jurisdiction to wind up any company registered in England and Wales.[13]

Judicial interpretation of the above provision has allowed the unqualified terms of section 117(1) to be applied even in cases where, apart from the fact of registration, the company has no functional links to this country. Thus, in an extreme case, even if the company never conducted any business in England, had no property here, and all its shareholders and directors were foreign nationals resident and domiciled abroad, the elemental fact that England was its country of incorporation enabled the company to be wound up here.[14] On the same premise, as an English-registered company it was eligible to undergo a voluntary winding up under Chapter II of Part IV of the Insolvency Act 1986, to enter into a voluntary arrangement under Part I of the Act, or to be the subject of administration order proceedings under Part II. In none of these matters was it formerly of relevance whether the company's affairs were managed in such a way as to furnish an operational nexus with this country: the sole criterion to be met was that the company must be 'a company' within the meaning of section 735 of the Companies Act 1985, which imposed the qualifying condition that the company must have been formed and registered under the present Companies Act or under defined, previous legislation.[15]

The operation of each of the types of insolvency proceedings mentioned in the preceding paragraph is now subject to the overarching effects of the Regulation. It is therefore impermissible for any of them to be opened as main proceedings in relation to a company whose COMI is in some other EC Member State apart from the United Kingdom.[16] If the company has an establishment in the UK, territorial proceedings could be opened, but if such proceedings are commenced after main proceedings have opened at the COMI, Article 3(3) imports the further limitation that the secondary proceedings must be winding up proceedings, thus narrowing the possibilities. As we have seen, Article 3(1) creates a presumption that the company's registered office is its COMI. This enables main proceedings to be opened in the company's state of incorporation unless

---

[13] See also s 117(2) of the Insolvency Act 1986, which confers a concurrent jurisdiction on the county court of the district in which the company's registered office is situated, in cases where the amount of the company's share capital does not exceed £120,000.

[14] *Reuss v Bos* (1871) LR 5 HL 176; *Re Tumacacori Mining Co* (1874) LR 17 Eq 534.

[15] Insolvency Act 1986, ss 73, 251 (final paragraph); Companies Act 1985, s 735(1),(3).

[16] If the company's COMI is within the UK, but not within England and Wales, the legislative provisions prescribing the circumstances under which proceedings can be opened within each part of the UK remain applicable.

the presumption is rebutted by evidence to show that it conducts the administration of its main interests on a regular and transparent basis at a location in some other Member State. Thus the former, unrestricted approach to the application of English insolvency procedures to English-registered companies has been attenuated in cases where the Regulation applies. However in cases where, although the COMI is not located within the UK, it cannot be shown to be located in any other Member State, the former law and practice remains applicable. This state of affairs is likely to continue indefinitely, because there is little likelihood that global arrangements governing insolvency jurisdiction will be concluded in the foreseeable future. Nor does it seem necessary or advisable for the UK to relinquish the jurisdictional control which its courts can exercise over companies which have been incorporated under this country's laws.

In the case of companies which have not been formed by registration under the laws of the UK, a more diverse policy has previously been applied towards the opening of insolvency proceedings. According to the Companies Act and the Insolvency Act, such companies are classified as 'unregistered companies',[17] a status which renders them ineligible to undergo either form of winding up—voluntary or compulsory—under Part IV of the Insolvency Act. Instead, Part V of the Act provides for the winding up of unregistered companies, and its provisions have been the subject of a fertile judicial development during the past fifty years.[18] A notable feature of the approach to exercising jurisdiction to wind up foreign companies is that it is not a requirement that the company has either conducted business, or had a place of business, in this country: a company can be wound up if it is found to have a 'sufficient connection' with this country.[19] A further aspect of the jurisdiction based on Part V is that it expressly precludes the voluntary winding up of an unregistered company, so that the only form of winding up available in the case of a foreign-formed company is a winding up by the court.[20] Additionally, foreign companies are considered, under the present terms of our legislation, to be ineligible to conclude a voluntary arrangement, or to be the subject of administration order proceedings, under Parts I and II respectively of the Insolvency Act 1986.[21]

---

[17] Insolvency Act 1986, s 220; Companies Act 1985, s 735.
[18] For an account of the evolving jurisprudence relating to the winding up of foreign companies under Part V of the Insolvency Act 1986, see I F Fletcher, op cit above, n 3, Chap 3, s 3.2.2.
[19] *Re Latreefers Inc* [2001] BCC 174 at 189, CA.
[20] Insolvency Act 1986, s 221(4).
[21] Cf *Re Devon and Somerset Farmers Ltd* [1993] BCC 410, distinguishing *Re International Bulk Commodities Ltd* [1993] Ch 77. See also G Moss (1993) 6 Insolvency Intelligence 19.

The impact of the Regulation in this area of the law is that the above propositions cannot be maintained in relation to any company which has its centre of main interests in another EC Member State. Regardless of the whereabouts of the company's state of incorporation, the fact that it currently has its COMI within the Community brings it within the ambit of the Regulation, and reserves to the State of the COMI an exclusive competence to open main insolvency proceedings. Only if the company has an establishment in this country can proceedings be opened in accordance with Article 3(2), and as we have seen these are restricted to the assets situated in the UK. In the absence of an establishment in England, no insolvency proceedings may be opened here.

A further effect of the Regulation is that, in the case of a company which has been formed in accordance with the law of another Member State, and which presently has its COMI in the UK, such a company, though classified as an unregistered company according to our domestic legislation, must be accorded parity of treatment with English-formed companies for the purposes of any type of insolvency proceedings which are listed in Annex A in relation to the UK. To do otherwise would be to contravene the principle of non-discrimination under Article 12 of the main EC Treaty, as mentioned above. Accordingly, any debtor which fulfils the criteria for being 'an EC national' must be permitted in another Member State to exercise legal rights under conditions equal to those accorded to persons who are nationals of that State. Since English-formed companies are eligible under the terms of the Insolvency Act to undergo either compulsory or voluntary winding up, or to enter into voluntary arrangements or to be the subject of an administration order, all of these possibilities must be available to a company which has a status equivalent to that of a natural person who is a national of a Member State. Strictly speaking, there is no necessity for English law and practice to be more extensively recast. It will continue to be lawful for our previous policy to be maintained in cases of companies whose COMI is outside the EC. Where such a company was also formed under the laws of a non-EC State, the position is entirely free from any Community Law concern. However, the position is rather less clear if the company, though having its COMI outside the EC, nevertheless qualifies to be treated as 'an EC national', for example because it was formed under the law of a Member State and has its registered office within the Community (even though that office happens not to be its COMI). To operate a discriminatory policy towards such companies, by comparison to the legal treatment of

English-formed companies, would contravene Article 12 of the EC Treaty, although it would not amount to an infraction of the Regulation.[22]

(2) Jurisdiction to Open Insolvency Proceedings Involving Individual Debtors

The jurisdictional code imposed by the Regulation applies also to the insolvency of individuals. According to Annex A, the types of proceedings which are within the scope of the Regulation are bankruptcy (or, in Scotland, sequestration) and individual voluntary arrangements. The two connecting factors already described—COMI and establishment—are applicable under Article 3 to determine competence to open main and secondary insolvency proceedings. However, in the case of the COMI there is no presumption as to its location in the way that is provided for companies by Article 3(1). It will therefore be incumbent on the party seeking to initiate insolvency proceedings relating to an individual as debtor to demonstrate that the proceedings are being commenced in the correct jurisdiction, having regard to the debtor's mode of conducting the administration of his interests on a regular, and objectively ascertainable, basis.[23] The use of the present tense in the drafting of Article 3(1) indicates that the vital question is the location of the COMI at the time when proceedings are to be opened. Similarly, if it is sought to open proceedings of a territorial nature, the party seeking to do so must demonstrate that the debtor has an establishment in the UK, within the meaning of Article 2(h). Again, the drafting of both the definition in Article 2(h) and the jurisdictional provisions in Article 3(2) employs the present tense. It is therefore arguable that secondary proceedings can only be opened in a jurisdiction in which the debtor's place of business is currently operational at the time the proceedings commence.

The above factors necessitate an alteration of English practice in the opening of proceedings involving individuals. Our insolvency legislation has traditionally allowed a bankruptcy order to be obtained on the petition of either the debtor or an unpaid creditor on the basis of the debtor satisfying any one of a range of alternative criteria which are deemed to constitute a sufficient nexus with this country. These criteria are currently listed in section 265 of the Insolvency Act

---

[22] By the Insolvency Act 1986 (Amendment) (No. 2) Regulations 2002 (above, n 10), amendments are imported into a number of sections of the Act of 1986, to indicate that they are to apply subject to the requirements of the EC Regulation including s 117 and s 221(4). The amendments have been limited to those necessary to ensure compliance with the Regulation.

[23] See Recital (13) to the Regulation, and comments above, section B.(1) (*Key principles*).

1986, and afford the possibility that a debtor can be the subject of a bankruptcy petition on the basis of existing or previous links of a somewhat tenuous nature, such as the fact of being domiciled in England and Wales (a status which carries no necessary requirement of residence or even personal presence within the jurisdiction).[24] Self-evidently, in the case of a debtor whose COMI is in another EC Member State no proceedings can be opened in England except where it can be shown that the debtor has an establishment here. Failing that, it will not be possible for proceedings to take place even though one or more of the criteria in section 265 are met. This applies even where the debtor personally seeks to petition for his own bankruptcy: the Regulation offers no ground on which an exception to the jurisdictional scheme of Article 3 can be made, even with the consent of all interested parties.

One uncertain point of interpretation concerns section 265(1)(c)(ii) of the Insolvency Act, which allows a bankruptcy petition to be presented where the bankrupt has carried on business in England and Wales at any time in the period of three years ending with the day on which the petition is presented. The concept of carrying on a business appears to correlate well with the Regulation's definition of an establishment. However, the drafting of this paragraph of section 265 imports a considerable flexibility with respect to the relevant time period: it would suffice if the debtor had previously carried on a business which has been discontinued by the date of the petition, provided that the business was being carried on at some time falling within the three-year reference period. It would appear that, where the Regulation applies, the use of the present tense in the drafting of Articles 2(h) and 3(2) precludes the opening of secondary proceedings in England if the alleged 'establishment' is constituted by a business which the debtor has ceased to carry on at some time prior to the date of the petition. There, however, is an element of uncertainty about this. This results from a particular doctrine founded on case law, and sanctified by the House of Lords in *Theophile v Solicitor General*,[25] to the effect that once a person has commenced carrying on business in England the business is considered to continue to be carried on until all debts incurred in the course of that business (including tax liabilities) have been settled through payment or formal

---

[24] Insolvency Act 1986, s.265(1)(a). The criteria offered as alternatives by s 265 are considered in detail in I F Fletcher, op cit above, n 3, Chap 2, s 2.1.

[25] [1950] AC 186, decided under s 4(1)(d) of the Bankruptcy Act 1914 (repealed). The doctrine has been reconfirmed as still applicable under the similar provision in s 265(1)(c)(ii) of the Insolvency Act 1986: *Re a Debtor (No 784 of 1991)* [1992] Ch 554.

arrangement. If this interpretation of the concept of 'carrying on business' is applicable to cases falling within the scope of the Regulation, the fact that unpaid debts remain after the cessation of active trading could supply the basis for finding that the debtor currently 'possesses' an establishment for the purposes of Article 3(2). This argument remains untested at present, and may in due course require a definitive ruling by the European Court of Justice to determine whether such a doctrine, arising from the jurisprudence of one Member State, can be accepted as a valid interpretation of one of the Regulation's key provisions, with Community-wide application. In support of such an extension of the meaning to be ascribed to the term 'establishment', it may be observed that it would otherwise be possible for a debtor to escape from the effects of insolvency law if, having carried on a business for a period in one Member State, he ceases trading and thereafter withdraws to another Member State whose laws do not enable insolvency proceedings to be opened in the case of an individual who is not engaged in trade.[26] It is submitted that, if such an individual cannot be answerable to the insolvency laws of the State in which he has formerly traded, an opportunity is created for the abuse of the Community Law rights of freedom of establishment and provision of services within the internal market.

D. The Proprietary Effects of Insolvency Proceedings

There is an inbuilt paradox in the approach of many national systems of law towards the subject of international insolvency. In line with the standard principles of private international law, it is commonly accepted that foreign insolvency proceedings, and any relevant judgments of foreign courts, cannot produce effects as of right with regard to parties and property that are subject to the jurisdiction of a separate, sovereign country. The extent to which foreign proceedings will be recognized, and effect given to them elsewhere, depends upon the separate application of the rules of private international law of each of the countries concerned. It is quite often the case, however, that the domestic law provisions governing insolvency proceedings are expressed in terms which claim universal effects in relation to all property of which the debtor is owner. This is true of English law, because the definition of 'property' in section

---

[26] Under the laws of a number of Member States—including Belgium, France, Italy, Luxembourg, Spain, and Portugal—an individual who is not engaged in commercial activity cannot be the subject of insolvency proceedings.

436 of the Insolvency Act 1986 includes the vital phrase 'wherever situated' in its description of the kinds of proprietary interest embraced by the term 'property' whenever used throughout the Act.

The claim to universality of effect in relation to property is especially problematic in cases where proceedings are opened on the basis of a relatively slight contact between the debtor and this country, for example where a foreign company is wound up by the court on the basis that it has assets in England which can be administered here.[27] If such a company also has assets in other countries, the effect of section 436 is that in the eyes of English law all such property is affected by the English winding up and it is the duty of the liquidator to take all practicable steps to retrieve and administer it for the benefit of the creditors. But, as Millett J (as he then was) perceptively observed in *Re International Tin Council,*[28] although in theory the effect of the English winding up order is worldwide it would be unrealistic to expect that international recognition will be forthcoming to the same extent as might be the case where the company is wound up in its own country. This presents a dilemma for the office holder, who must balance the duty to fulfil the statutory functions imposed on him as liquidator with the probability that costs would be wastefully expended in a vain attempt to claim foreign assets. The inelegant and unsatisfactory consequences of the present terms in which English law is framed were noted by the Court of Appeal in *Banco Nacional de Cuba v Cosmos Trading Corp*, in which Scott V-C commented that it would be desirable if the winding up by the English court of a foreign company could be limited to its activities and assets in this jurisdiction.[29]

Some of the concerns alluded to above are resolved for cases within the ambit of the Regulation, at least for the purposes of determining the intra-Community effects of insolvency proceedings. Article 16, within Chapter II, provides that any judgment opening insolvency proceedings handed down by a court which has jurisdiction under Article 3 shall be instantly and automatically recognized in all other Member States. This principle of extraterritorial effectiveness is reinforced by Article 17, which specifies that these effects shall be produced without any further formalities, and shall be co-extensive with the effects provided under the law of the State of opening proceedings, and by Article

---

[27] See references above, nn 17–20.
[28] [1987] Ch 419 at 446, aff'd [1989] Ch 309, CA.
[29] [2000] BCC 910 at 915.

18, which declares that the powers conferred on the liquidator by the law of the State of opening shall be exercisable in each of the other Member States (unless secondary proceedings are opened in the State in question). These principles are further reinforced by the general choice of law rules contained in Article 4, whereby the *lex concursus* shall determine such matters as the assets which form part of the estate; the respective powers of the debtor and the liquidator; the claims which are to be lodged; and the rules governing distribution of the estate.[30] Therefore, in cases where a debtor's COMI is in the UK, the Regulation reinforces the aspirations of our insolvency law to enjoy universality of effect. However, as we have seen, where English proceedings take place on the basis that the debtor has an establishment here, the terms of Article 3(2) (reiterated in Article 27) restrict the effects of such proceedings to assets of the debtor situated in the territory of the United Kingdom. This imports an automatic attenuation of the definition of 'property' contained in section 436 of the Insolvency Act, for cases which are governed by Article 3(2). To avoid giving rise to confusion, a modified definition of 'property' has been inserted in section 436. In the first instance, this is confined to dealing with the specific problem of ensuring that our law is compliant with the requirements of the Regulation.[31] In due course, however, it may be appropriate to conduct a more general review of the terms in which the definition of 'property' is cast, and to introduce a more flexible principle in relation to cases where England does not represent the debtor's 'home' jurisdiction. Where some other country can be said to constitute the appropriate forum for 'main' insolvency proceedings, the legitimate claims of such a jurisdiction to administer the bulk of the debtor's property should be suitably accommodated.

E. Foreign Fiscal and Public Liabilities as Provable Debts

Article 39 of the Regulation provides:

> Any creditor who has his habitual residence, domicile or registered office in a Member State other than the State of the opening of proceedings, *including the*

---

[30] Art 4(2)(b), (c), (g), and (i) of the Regulation (the entire Article is of great importance and deserves careful study).

[31] See the Insolvency Act 1986 (Amendment) (No. 2) Regulations 2002 (above, n 10), reg 18. The converse situation is also provided for, namely where the debtor's COMI is in the UK, but secondary proceedings are opened in another Member State on account of the presence there of an establishment. In such cases, the assets comprised in the secondary proceedings are carved out of the scope of the debtor's estate for purposes of the main proceedings.

tax authorities and social security authorities of Member States shall have the right to lodge claims in the insolvency proceedings in writing.[32]

This provision overturns, for cases falling within its scope, the long established exclusionary rule of English conflict of laws, whereby no action lies in England for the enforcement (either directly or indirectly) of foreign revenue laws.[33] The application of this rule to insolvency proceedings was specifically confirmed by the House of Lords as its *ratio decidendi* in the case of *Government of India v Taylor*.[34] Although the general provision on choice of law in Article 4 of the Regulation (referred to in the previous section) might at first sight appear to allow the *lex concursus* to control all aspects of the treatment of claims and distribution of the debtor's estate, including the vital question of whether certain species of claims are admissible to proof, the opening words of Article 4 state that its provisions apply '[s]ave as otherwise provided in this Regulation'. Therefore, the affirmative provision in Article 39 overrides any conflicting rule or practice under the law of any Member State, for the benefit of the tax authorities and social security authorities of other Member States. As there is no reference in Article 39, or elsewhere in the Regulation, to the rights of other public authorities to lodge proof for debts or liabilities claimed against the debtor (such as criminal fines or penalties), it will be necessary to classify the nature of any claims that are based upon the exception created by Article 39.

Although the rule affirmed by the *Taylor* case is no longer applicable whenever proceedings fall within the scope of the Regulation, the case remains good authority for all other situations. It may be anticipated that in due course the exclusionary rule itself may require to be reconsidered, because it can serve as the basis for denying recognition to a foreign liquidator or trustee in bankruptcy who has been appointed in proceedings in which the revenue authority of the foreign state is a significant (or, perhaps, the sole) creditor. Given that most insolvencies nowadays involve claims by fiscal authorities to some degree, a reappraisal of policy seems timely. Moreover, an emerging trend to remove the preferential status of revenue claims under national systems of insolvency should begin to allay concerns that the application of distributional rules favouring the fiscal authorities of the debtor's home jurisdiction would operate at the expense of ordinary English creditors, if assets situate here are turned

---

[32] Emphasis added.
[33] See Dicey and Morris, *The Conflict of Laws* (13th edn, 2000), Chap 5; Cheshire and North, op cit above, n 2, Chap 8, pp 108–110.
[34] [1955] AC 491.

over to the foreign liquidator to be administered according to the foreign law.[35] The global picture is still in a slowly evolving state however, and it would seem prudent to reserve a measure of discretion to English courts whether, and if so to what extent, to recognize the authority of foreign liquidators and trustees to repatriate property from this country for distribution according to the principles of the law under which they obtained their appointment.

F. Discharge of Obligations under Foreign Insolvency Proceedings

As already stated, English law applies the principle of universality in its assessment of the effects of its own insolvency proceedings. This applies not only to the proprietary effects considered in section D. above, but also to the effect of English proceedings upon obligations owed by the debtor at the time of commencement. In the estimation of English law, all such obligations as are provable in the proceedings are thereby discharged, leaving the proving creditors with such payment as may be forthcoming by way of dividend or under the terms of any composition or arrangement by which the proceedings are concluded. This is so irrespective of the law by which, according to the relevant choice of law rule, the obligation is governed.[36] Since English insolvency law regards all debts as provable in its own proceedings, regardless of their governing law, it has been accepted almost without question that all such obligations undergo the process of extinction which is an integral aspect of the insolvency process. It has never been considered to be necessary to refer to the governing law of the obligation (where it is the law of a foreign country) to confirm that the obligation is accepted to have been discharged. However, in a converse situation, where foreign insolvency proceedings have taken place under a law which similarly claims to result in a universal discharge of the debtor's obligations, English courts have consistently declined to consider such a discharge as

---

[35] Among the states which have recently abolished the preferential status formerly accorded to fiscal claims are Germany, Denmark, Sweden and South Africa. In the UK, paras 2.19–2.20 of the White Paper *Insolvency—A Second Chance* (July 2001, Cm 5234) signalled the government's intention to abolish Crown preference in all insolvencies as part of a range of reforms subsequently introduced in the Enterprise Bill 2002. See clause 242 of the Bill, as originally introduced

[36] See, eg, Insolvency Act 1986, s 281(1); *Royal Bank of Scotland v Cuthbert* (1813) 1 Rose 462; *Odwin v Forbes* (1817) Buck 57, PC. For further consideration of these issues, see I F Fletcher, op cit above, n 3, Chaps 2 and 3, ss 2.2, 2.5, 3.3, and 3.6.

having effect in relation to any obligation which is governed by English law. This is so regardless of whether the foreign proceedings themselves might be recognized by our law as having been opened in that forum which is the most appropriate according to international principles of jurisdiction. The unfortunate paradox is thus generated that English law may, in principle, consider that all the debtor's property at the time of opening the foreign proceedings has been legitimately appropriated for the purpose of satisfying creditors' provable claims, so far as is possible, yet it will be permissible for a creditor subsequently to bring proceedings in England to enforce any unpaid balance of an obligation which happens to have been governed by English law.[37] On the other hand, seemingly, the validity of the foreign discharge will be respected by English law in relation to provable obligations governed by the law of any other country.

The intellectual asymmetry of the above state of English law is difficult to defend, and has indeed received criticism.[38] However, it rests on a Court of Appeal authority which has remained unshaken for over 110 years, and has more than once been referred to with approval by the House of Lords when considering the effect of foreign legal proceedings on contracts governed by English law.[39] Now, it is submitted, the doctrine expounded by the Court of Appeal in 1890 in the *Gibbs* case[40] must be regarded as abrogated with respect to cases within the ambit of the Regulation. According to Chapter II, as previously indicated, when proceedings have opened in another Member State in accordance with Article 3, the law of the UK must accord recognition to the proceedings and, by Article 17, they produce the same effects in the UK as under the law of the State of opening (the *lex concursus*).[41] These provisions combine with the choice of law principle established by Article 4 in favour of the application of the *lex concursus,* notably paragraphs (e), (j), and (k) of Article 4(2). These specify that the law of the State of opening shall determine:

(e) the effects of insolvency proceedings on current contracts to which the debtor is party;

. . .

---

[37] *Gibbs v La Société Industrielle et Commerciale des Metaux* (1890) 25 QBD 399, CA.
[38] See, eg, Fletcher, op cit above, n 3, pp 105–110; F Piggott, *Foreign Judgments and Jurisdiction* (3rd edn, 1910) Part III, Book VI, pp 127–137.
[39] See *National Bank of Greece and Athens SA v Metliss* [1958] AC 509, at 523 *per* Viscount Simonds; *Adams v National Bank of Greece SA* [1961] AC 255, at 287 *per* Lord Denning.
[40] Above, n 37.
[41] See section B. above, text to n 5.

(j)   the conditions for and the effects of closure of insolvency proceedings, in particular by composition;

(k)   creditors' rights after the closure of insolvency proceedings.

The net effect of these provisions of the Regulation, where a debtor undergoes insolvency proceedings in a Member State whose law purports to confer a discharge from liabilities provable in the proceedings, is that English courts must accept that this discharge is fully effective in relation to any of the debtor's obligations which are governed by English law. Although, as has been emphasized before in this paper, there is no requirement under Community Law that we should amend our domestic law and practice for cases falling outside the ambit of the Regulation, the writer believes that it is desirable that this survival from the more chauvinistic era of the later nineteenth century should be revised in line with the spirit of internationalism that is characteristic of the present day. The English law of contract already accepts that a contract may be discharged on various grounds, including the occurrence of a frustrating event. Equally, it should be recognized that a contract whose governing law is English may be discharged through the insolvency of one of the parties to it, provided that the insolvency proceedings are opened in the jurisdiction in which the debtor's centre of main interests is located. This solution would be commercially appropriate, in that it would enable all parties to a contract to assess the potential consequences of the insolvency of any one of them. Moreover, by adopting a uniform approach for all cases irrespective of whether the Regulation is or is not applicable, a more stable and predictable legal environment would be produced.

G. Conclusion

The EC Regulation on Insolvency Proceedings has altered many established rules and principles of English (and UK) law relating to international insolvency. The changes themselves are rational in terms of the fundamental principles which govern the operation of the EC and its internal market. At the same time, by establishing a precedent for change in relation to matters which had long been treated as near-sacred, immutable features of the English tradition in cross-border insolvency, the Regulation may prove to be a useful catalyst towards a future, more general review of our approach to these issues.

8

THE TRUST IN PRIVATE INTERNATIONAL LAW

*Jonathan Harris**

A. Introduction

Amongst all the areas of private international law, that which relates to trusts is unique. Partly, this is because of the fundamental importance of the trust in many legal systems, principally those of the common law, and its total absence from the domestic law of most civil law States. Such a schism makes conflict of

---

* Professor of International Commercial Law, University of Birmingham.

laws problems inevitable. Of course, many of the most acute problems are faced by non-trust States, who may come into contact with the trust in an international context and be asked to recognize, and give some meaningful effect to, it in their jurisdictions.

Trust States tend to be very keen to secure the recognition of local trusts abroad. Increasingly, the international trusts world is a market place, where trust jurisdictions, particularly those offshore, compete to develop rules which are highly pragmatic and protective of the settlor's autonomy. However, the effectiveness of such rules would be very much compromised if their trusts were to be without effect[1] in non-trust States, especially as it is not easy to predict whether trust assets might subsequently become located in a non-trust State.

The Hague Trusts Convention[2] was a breakthrough initiative, unlike any attempted before or since at the Hague. It tackled both choice of law rules and the recognition of an institution with which many, if not most, of its Member States were unfamiliar.[3] In England, where the ambit of the Convention has been extended,[4] it is the dominant instrument concerning choice of law for trusts and is applicable to most express trusts and also the majority of constructive, resulting, and statutory trusts. The choice of law rules are highly pragmatic; they emphasize the 'obligation characteristic' of the trust, so that they have more in common with the choice of law rules of contract law than those for 'ordinary' property transfers. The recognition rules of the Convention facilitate recognition in both trust[5] and non-trust States of trusts otherwise incompatible with that State's domestic law.

But in stark contrast to this progressive legislation, certain aspects of the private international law of trusts in England are extraordinarily underdeveloped. The common law is particularly bereft of academic writing.[6] Moreover, the Hague

---

[1] Or of limited effect.

[2] The Hague Convention on the Law Applicable to Trusts and on their Recognition 1985, enacted into English law by the Recognition of Trusts Act 1987.

[3] At least in their domestic law.

[4] Recognition of Trusts Act 1987 s 1(2).

[5] An example being non-charitable purpose trusts, whose recognition may be required in England when such trusts are permitted by a foreign governing law: see below.

[6] 'Common-law writing and case law were both fumbling in the dark, and there had been a chorus of complaints about the deplorable state of the law:' M Lupoi, *Trusts: A Comparative Study,* translated by S Dix, (Cambridge, Cambridge University Press, 2001), p 331. Discussion of the common law principles includes: D Cavers 'Trusts *Inter Vivos* and the Conflict of Laws' (1930) 44 Harv LR 161; W Swabenland, 'The Conflict of Laws in Administration of Express

Convention applies only to the operation of trusts once brought into effect; it does not apply to their creation and constitution.[7] A distinction is drawn between the 'rocket-launcher' and the 'rocket'.[8] Whilst the Convention contains detailed 'rocket' rules, the choice of law rules which determine whether that 'rocket' was ever 'launched' are shrouded in uncertainty, particularly as regards the settlor's capacity to create the trust. Furthermore, when one passes to the choice of law rules applicable in equity and to such matters as resulting and constructive trusts, fiduciaries and tracing, or, indeed, to the characterization problems raised by the relationship between trusts and restitution, the law is still highly undeveloped. In the case of equitable claims, there is very little resembling a coherent set of choice of law rules at all.[9] The view that the justice meted out by an English court is bound up with English domestic law and that, accordingly, equity is not a proper subject for fully fledged choice of law rules, remarkably still attracts credibility today. Moreover, the influence of the historical legacy that 'equity acts in *personam*' continues to leave its mark, particularly on the law of jurisdiction.

The overall result is a curious mixture between, on the one hand, developed Hague Convention choice of law and recognition rules whereby private international law can foster the development of the trust in Contracting States and, on the other hand, areas of the private international law of trusts such as the creation of trusts and equitable claims which the conflict of laws has barely started to map. It is this bifurcation which will be examined in this chapter.

Trusts of Personal Property' (1936) 45 Yale LJ 438; W Land, *Trusts in the Conflict of Laws; Validity, Construction, Administration and Taxation of Trusts: What Law Governs* (New York, Baker, Voorhis & Co, 1940); P Croucher, 'Trusts of Moveables in Private International Law' (1940) 4 MLR 111; G Keeton, 'Trusts in the Conflict of Laws' (1951) 4 CLP 107; V Latham, 'The Creation and Administration of a Trust in the Conflict of Laws' (1953) 6 CLP 176; R Lafer and A Siegel, 'Trusts of Movables in the Conflict of Laws' (1961) NYULR 713; A Lowenfeld, 'Tempora Mutantur–Wills and Trusts in the Conflicts Restatement' (1972) 72 Col LR 382; A Wallace, 'Choice of Law for Trusts in Australia and the United Kingdom' (1987) 36 ICLQ 454. See also *American Restatement (2d) on the Conflict of Laws* (St Paul, Minn, American Law Institute, 1971), Chap 10.

[7] Article 4.
[8] 'The law designated by the Convention applies only to the establishment of the trust itself, and not to the validity of the act by which the transfer of assets is carried out': *Explanatory Report on the Convention on the Law Applicable to Trusts and on their Recognition by Professor Alfred Von Overbeck, Proceedings of the Fifteenth Session of the Hague Conference on Private International Law 1984, Book II—Trusts—Applicable Law and Recognition* (hereafter 'von Overbeck'), 370, para 54, p 381.
[9] See below.

B. The Hague Trusts Convention[10]

The Hague Trusts Convention is without doubt the most important source of detailed choice of law rules in trusts. Some key aspects of its scope, function, and significance will now be examined.

(1) Scope

The Convention, enacted into English law by the Recognition of Trusts Act 1987, applies to 'trusts created voluntarily and evidenced in writing'.[11] This is not a coherent category in English domestic law. Clearly, it covers the paradigm express trust. However, it seems also to cover, for example, the automatic resulting trust, and may also cover many instances where the constructive trust is imposed so as to reflect the will of the settlor.[12] In any event, the Convention has been extended in the United Kingdom to apply also to 'any trusts arising under the law of any part of the United Kingdom or by virtue of a judicial decision whether in the United Kingdom or elsewhere'.[13] This provision has the effect of imposing the Convention's choice of law rules on most trusts, save those which are governed by a law outside the United Kingdom and which cannot be said to 'arise' by judicial decision.[14] For many constructive and resulting trusts, it means that '. . . the applicable law . . . is "the law with which [such a trust] . . . is most closely connected".'[15] Indeed, given that the Convention appears to apply in England to all constructive and resulting trusts arising by the law of a part of the United Kingdom,[16] it is very curious that most cases where such trusts are in issue make almost no reference to the Convention in considering which law determines whether such a trust should be imposed.[17]

---

[10] Detailed discussion of the Convention can be found in J Harris, *The Hague Trusts Convention*, (Oxford, Hart Publishing, 2002).

[11] Article 3.

[12] Von Overbeck, para 51, pp 380–1. See further D Hayton, 'The Hague Convention on the Law Applicable to Trusts and on their Recognition' (1987) 36 ICLQ 260, 263–6.

[13] Recognition of Trusts Act 1987 s 1(2).

[14] This might exclude institutional constructive trusts and presumed resulting trusts not governed by the law of a part of the United Kingdom, since they are triggered by a set of facts and may be *affirmed* in an English court. They do not *arise* by the decision of the court.

[15] J-G Castel, *Canadian Conflict of Laws*, 4th edn (Toronto and Vancouver, Butterworths, 1997), p 551.

[16] And, depending upon how one interprets Art 3 and s 1(2), the Recognition of Trusts Act 1987, could be said to govern *all* such trusts, whatever law is applicable to them.

[17] Eg, *El Ajou v Dollar Land Holdings plc* [1993] 3 All ER 717, reversed on different grounds: [1994] 2 All ER 685; *Arab Monetary Fund v Hashim (No 9) The Times*, 11 October 1994; *Trustor AB v Smallbone*, unreported judgment of 9 May 2000, CA; *Kuwait Oil Tanker v Al Bader* [2000]

(2) Choice of Law Rules

The Convention's choice of law rules permit the settlor to choose the law which governs the trust.[18] However, it is a fundamental principle that the Convention does not introduce the trust into States which do not presently have it in their domestic law.[19] Accordingly, the settlor may not choose the law of a non-trust State to govern the trust.[20] If he does, the Convention does what it can to uphold the trust and provides that the law of closest connection[21] shall instead govern; only if that law does not provide for trusts does the Convention cease to be applicable.

In the absence of express choice, a trust is governed either by the law impliedly chosen by the settlor, or, in default, by the law of closest connection. That law of closest connection is ascertained from a list of implicitly hierarchical, but non-exhaustive factors, [22] of which the *situs* of the assets comes second to the place of administration designated by the settlor and must be considered alongside the place of residence of the trust and the place of fulfilment of the objects of the trust.[23]

It is striking how little importance the Convention apparently attaches to the law of the *situs*. As will be seen, this may partly be explained on the basis that the law of the *situs* should have a key role in deciding whether the trust was 'launched' in the first place. But more generally, the Convention exhibits a clear preference for an 'obligation' approach to the trust. This respects the settlor's autonomy, which is, after all, why express trusts[24] are brought into effect in the first place; it also ensures that English courts do not appear too unpragmatic in the global trusts community. But to an English lawyer, it tends to undervalue the fact that, in English law,[25] equitable interests are property

---

2 All ER (Comm) 271 (and see G Virgo, 'Interest, Constructive Trusts and the Conflict of Laws' [2000] RLR 122); *Grupo Torras v Al-Sabah* [2001] Lloyd's Rep Bank 36 (noted by J Garton (2001) 15 Trust Law International 93).

[18] Article 6. See also *Barton v Tod* [2002] EWHC 264 (ch), judgment of 20 February 2002.

[19] Von Overbeck, para 14, p 373.

[20] Article 6(2).

[21] As determined by Article 7.

[22] Von Overbeck, para 77, p 387. See also *Chellaram v Chellaram (No 2)* [2002] EWHC 632 (ch), [2002] 3 All ER 17 judgment of 16 April 2002, where Collins J ruled that Indian law governed a trust, even though none of the factors mentioned in Art 7 pointed to Indian law.

[23] Which are respectively listed third and fourth.

[24] Or so-called 'voluntary' trusts, the category described by Art 3.

[25] Although this is by no means the case in all trust States: see G Gretton, 'Trusts without Equity' (2000) 49 ICLQ 599.

interests enforceable against all but the *bona fide* purchaser of the legal estate for value without notice and that those rights may need to be enforced in the courts of the *situs*, especially if, for example, a person absolutely beneficially entitled seeks to terminate the trust and claim the property absolutely.[26] Those difficulties may be especially acute in relation to land, where the beneficiary might, for example, seek to occupy the land or force a sale thereof and where to do other than as the courts of the *situs* would do may prove ineffective.[27]

Then again, this pragmatism should not surprise us. Despite the reference in the Preamble to the trust 'as developed in courts of equity' and its description as 'a unique institution', the scope of the Convention, as laid down in Article 2, is far broader and not limited to common law trusts.[28] The division between legal and equitable rights is not a fundamental requirement under the Convention; still less that the beneficiary be regarded as beneficial owner. It suffices that the fund held by the trustee be treated as separate from his own personal assets, in the event of his bankruptcy, marriage, divorce, or death.[29] Moreover, the settlor's freedom to choose the governing law appears to represent the position at common law;[30] and in default, the law of the *situs* was not decisive.[31] Furthermore, in a competitive international trusts community, insistence upon application of the law of the *situs* can create insuperable problems, since assets may be, or may become, located in a non-trust State. Many such States have rules of forced heirship which prohibit or limit the transfer of assets on trust where the transfer is effected in order to defeat the entitlements of the settlor's family members, rendering trusts governed by the law of a trust State unduly vulnerable.

The pragmatism of the choice of law rules can also be seen in Article 8, which defines the scope of the governing law. Matters such as the trustee's capacity[32]

---

[26] This could happen if the law governing the trust has an equivalent to the English rule in *Saunders v Vautier* (1841) 4 Beav 115.

[27] See also J Harris, 'Ordering the Sale of Land Situated Overseas' [2001] LMCLQ 205, 213–4.

[28] See M Lupoi, 'The Shapeless Trust' (1995) 1(3) Trusts and Trustees 15.

[29] Although, as we shall see, even this fundamental aspect of the trust may not be required, given that Art 15 preserves the application of the mandatory rules designated by the forum's private international law rules in related areas of law.

[30] *Augustus v Permanent Trustee Company (Canberra) Ltd* (1971) 124 CLR 245.

[31] *A-G v Campbell* (1872) LR 5 HL 524; *Lindsay v Miller (No 1)* [1949] VR 13; *Iveagh v IRC* [1954] 1 Ch 364.

[32] Article 8(2)(a); or, at least, his capacity specifically to act as a trustee will be subject to the governing law. It may be that his capacity to receive property *at all* will fall outside the scope of the Convention as a preliminary matter.

and his ability to alienate the trust property are subject to the governing law,[33] even though one might tend to think of capacity rules as having a mandatory characteristic and hence not susceptible to party autonomy, and of alienation rules as concerning property transfers and hence a matter for the law of the *situs*.

C. The 'Recognition' of the Trust under the Hague Trusts Convention: The Position in Non-trust States

(1) What is 'Recognition'?

When one turns to the 'recognition' of trusts under the Convention, it is striking in one sense just how little the Convention requires of non-trust States. The fact that so few have ratified the Convention[34] may accordingly be due to misplaced fears; but it may also be because ratification may hardly seem worth the effort.

First, it is important to note that 'recognition' is not a complete step into the unknown for most non-trust States. Even outside the scope of the Convention, civil law States have been adept in accommodating the trust and it may be that they are sometimes given insufficient credit for this by trust States.[35] This is, of course, a very large subject and it is not proposed to address it here.[36] Suffice it

---

[33] Article 8(2)(d).

[34] Italy and the Netherlands being the sole mainland European non-trust States to have done so. However, a report commissioned by the Swiss government has recently recommended implementation of the Convention; see L Thévenoz, *Trusts in Switzerland. Ratification of the Hague Convention on Trusts and Codification of Fiduciary Transfers* (Zurich, Schulthess, 2001); see also D Hayton, 'Some Major Developments in Trust Law' [2001] Private Client Business 361, 369–70. In Luxembourg, a Bill was introduced on 14 December 2000 to implement the Hague Convention and was endorsed by the Luxembourg Chamber of Commerce on 14 March 2001 (see http://www.cc.lu/avis2001/2414wje.htm).

[35] See, eg, M Lupoi, *Trusts: A Comparative Study*, 156, n 304.

[36] See, eg, C de Wulf, *The Trust and Corresponding Institutions in the Civil Law* (Brussels, Emile Bruylant, 1965); D Hayton (ed), *Modern International Developments in Trust Law* (The Hague, Kluwer, 1999); D Hayton (ed) *Principles of European Trust Law* (The Hague, Kluwer, 1999); M Koppenol-Laforce, 'The Trust, the Hague Trusts Convention and Civil Law Countries: a Mission Impossible?' (1998) 3 Notarius International 27; M Lupoi, *Trusts: A Comparative Study*; F Sonneveldt and H van Mens, *The Trust—Bridge or Abyss Between Common and Civil Law Jurisdictions?* (Deventer, Kluwer, 1992); D Waters, The Trust in Civil Law Jurisdictions—the Dutch Experience (1999) 7 J Int Corp P 131; D Waters, 'The Concept Called "the Trust" ' (1999) 53 Bulletin for International Fiscal Documentation, 118; W Wilson (ed), *Trusts and Trust-Like Devices (United Kingdom Comparative Law Series, Vol 5)* (London,

to say for now that often non-trust States may 'translate' the trust into a concept known to them in their domestic law, such as a contract for the benefit of a third party,[37] agency, mandate,[38] or company.[39] Sometimes, States with no 'split' concept of ownership treat the beneficiary as the effective absolute owner,[40] in order to safeguard the trust fund from claims brought against the trustee personally. The idea that non-contracting non-trust States are helpless in the face of the trust is certainly without foundation.

Pursuant to Article 11, non-trust States which have ratified the Convention are required to recognize the trust. They should not do so by attempting to 'translate' the trust into the nearest civil law analogue; they must now recognize the trust *qua* trust. But what does the word 'recognition' actually mean? In point of fact, not very much. All Contracting States apply the Convention choice of law rules. If a trust is valid upon application of those rules, then it has the effects which the governing law decrees. However, this is always the case in the conflict of laws. We do not talk of 'recognizing' a contract in England. Nor does the word 'recognition' mean anything significant here. In particular, it would be extraordinary if it were to mean that a foreign trust *judgment* had to be recognized in England, even if the conditions of recogni-

---

Chameleon Press, 1981). A short summary by D Hayton of attempts to translate the trust into civil law jurisdictions may be found in J Glasson (ed) *International Trust Laws* (Bristol, Jordans, loose-leaf), Chap C3, pp 17–23.

[37] See the Swiss Federal Court's decision in *Harrison v Credit Suisse* ATF 96.II.79 JT 197.I.329, discussed by A Dyer and H van Loon, *Report on Trusts and Analogous Institutions*, Preliminary Document No 1, May 1982, *Proceedings of the Fifteenth Session of the Hague Conference on Private International Law 1984, Book II—Trusts—Applicable Law and Recognition*, 10, para 150, p 80; E Gaillard and D Trautman, 'Trusts in Non-Trust Countries: Conflict of Laws and the Hague Convention on Trusts' (1987) 35 Am J Comp Law 307, 315–6; see also the French Cour de Cassation's judgment of 20 February 1996, [1996] Dalloz-Sirey Jurisprudence, 390.

[38] Eg, *Faillité Four Seasons Overseas NV v SA Finimtrust* Trib d'arrondisement de Luxembourg, decision of 21 January 1971, [1972] *Revue Critique de Droit International Privé* 51, discussed by D Hayton in J Glasson (ed) *International Trust Laws*, chap C3 p 19 See also the Luxembourg Court of Appeal's decisions in *ABN Amro Bank SA v Trustees of the C (Jersey) Foundation* Case No 15430 (27 April 1994) and Case No 17370 *Trustees of the C (Jersey) Foundation v Internationale Nederlanden Bank (Luxembourg) SA* (22 May 1996), both discussed by P Kinsch, 'Trusts in a Civil Law Environment: Jersey Trustees may Sue in Luxembourg' (1996) 4 J Int Corp P 120, 121–3.

[39] See the Swiss decision in *OD-Bank in Liquidation v Bankrupt's Estate WKR* Case No FB920075, 98 Blätter für Zürcherische Rechtssprechung (1999) No 52, 225ss; noted E Paltzer, 'Trusts in Switzerland: some Recent Decisions of the Swiss Courts' (2000) 8 J Int Corp P 137.

[40] See, eg, the Italian decision in *Piercy v EFTAS*, Tribunal of Oristano, judgment of 15 March 1956, discussed by A Paton and R Grosso, 'The Hague Convention on the Law Applicable to Trusts and on their Recognition: Implementation in Italy' (1994) 43 ICLQ 654, 656–7.

tion of 'ordinary' foreign judgments were not satisfied, and even if the foreign court was jurisdictionally incompetent in the eyes of the State of recognition.[41]

(2) What Does Recognition Entail?

Furthermore, the scope of the 'recognition' required looks particularly weak when one looks at Article 11. This requires, in particular, that a Contracting State recognize that the trustee may sue or be sued in his capacity as a trustee.[42] Beyond that, matters are less clear. Both Articles 2 and 11 seem at first sight to require that the trust assets be treated as a separate fund not forming part of the trustee's personal wealth or available to his creditors. Shorn of that characteristic, it is difficult to imagine an institution as a 'trust' at all. Yet Article 15 preserves the right of the forum to apply the mandatory rules[43] of the State whose law the forum decrees applicable to related areas of law. Those areas include the transfer of title to property, security interests in property, the rights of creditors in matters of insolvency, and the protection in other respect of third parties acting in good faith. Moreover, the forum is free to apply its own international mandatory rules under Article 16. Could it be said that a rule of a given legal system that ownership must be undivided and that all assets owned by a person are accordingly treated as part of his personal wealth, is itself a mandatory rule capable of overriding Articles 2 and 11?

On one view, the answer to this is 'yes'; but this would strip the Convention of all usefulness and it is striking that it is not the attitude which non-trust States have adopted. The Netherlands, for example, reformed its domestic property law in order to accommodate the Hague Trusts Convention and the separation of trust assets from a trustee's personal wealth. Article 84, section (3) of Book 3, Dutch Civil Code lays down a general rule that upon a transfer of property from A to B, B becomes absolute owner of the property.[44] The legislation of

---

[41] Indeed, arguably the EC regime of enforcement of judgments contained in the Brussels I Regulation (Council Regulation (EC) No 44/2001 of 22 December 2000 on Jurisdiction and the Recognition and Enforcement of Judgments in Civil and Commercial Matters [2001] OJ L12/1) is far more radical, since it requires a Member State to recognize a judgment of another Member State in a civil and commercial trusts matter, and it does not seem to be a defence to recognition that the trust does not exist in the State of recognition. See below.

[42] Article 11(2). This is required irrespective of the provisions of the governing law.

[43] This is a reference to domestic mandatory rules of that State.

[44] D Hayton, 'The Netherlands Implementation of the Hague Trusts Convention' (1996) 5 J Int Corp P 127, 129. This is subject to a provision in the case of transfers into bank accounts to be held for the settlor's benefit, where 'the chose in action is not regarded as owned by B upon B's insolvency but is available only for A and not for B's creditors generally'. (ibid). See further M Koppenol-Laforce, *Het Haagse Trustverdrag*, (Deventer, Kluwer, 1997) 271–2.

1995 which implements the Hague Convention (the Wet Conflichtenrecht Trusts) makes clear that clause 84(3), Civil Code should not impede application of the Convention. It does this by effectively excluding Articles 15(1)(d) and (e) of the Hague Convention. Article 4 of the Wet Conflichtenrecht Trusts states that Dutch laws on transfer of property, security interests and creditor protection shall not prevent the recognition of a trust otherwise satisfying the Hague Convention's requirements.[45] There is a very strong case for saying that only States similarly prepared to accommodate the concept of a fund not forming part of the holder's personal wealth should ratify the Convention.

(3) Recovery of Trust Assets

A further uncertainty in the recognition provisions relates to following and tracing of trust assets. The Convention seems to provide that the law governing the trust shall determine whether trust assets can be recovered when mixed by the trustee with his own assets or alienated to a third party.[46] However, considerable uncertainty remains. For one thing, 'the rights and obligations of any third party holder of the assets shall remain subject to the law determined by the choice of law rules of the forum'.[47] The meaning of this phrase is not wholly clear, but seems only to invite a State to invoke the law of the *situs* to prevent recovery of trust assets from a third party who has purchased that property and thereby acquired title to it; it does not seem to allow a State to say that it does not allow trust assets to be recovered *at all* from third parties under any circumstances. In the Netherlands, however, Koppenol-Laforce and Kottenhagen argue that the beneficiary may be confined to a personal claim in respect of trust property situated within that State[48] and that '. . . the proprietary effects of the breach of trust will not be recognized in a non-trust country'.[49] Yet such an approach cannot be based on the non-recognition of the concept of a

---

[45] M Koppenol-Laforce and R Kottenhagen, 'The Institution of the Trust and Dutch Law' in *Netherlands Reports to the XVth International Congress of Comparative Law, Bristol 1998* (Antwerpen/Groningen Intersentia Rechtswetenschappen), section II A 3, p 137, 144. See also M Koppenol-Laforce, *Het Haagse Trustverdrag*, 271.

[46] Article 11(3)(d).

[47] ibid, second sentence.

[48] M Koppenol-Laforce and R Kottenhagen 'The Institution of the Trust and Dutch Law' 137, 148. They point out that, even within the Netherlands, there is a difference of opinion as to whether Dutch property law (and the protection that it affords to transferees of property) is compromised by the Wet Conflictenrecht Trusts 1995 (especially Article 4 thereof). See also M Koppenol-Laforce, *Het Haagse Trustverdrag*, 273–5.

[49] M Koppenol-Laforce and R Kottenhagen, ibid, 150. Compare the Luxembourg Court of Appeal's decision in Case No 15430 *ABN-Amro Bank Luxembourg SA v Trustees of the C (Jersey)*

constructive trust over property in the hands of any third party, since it is a key principle of the Hague Convention that Contracting States should not refuse to recognize a trust on the grounds that they do not know the trust, or a category of trust, in their legal system.[50] Article 11(3)(d) makes it clear that, in principle, trusts assets can be recovered from a third party and it would be unfortunate if this principle could be undermined by a domestic property rule of a Contracting State.

(4) Trusts Objectively Connected to Non-trust States

Article 13 permits non-trust States to refuse to recognize a trust if it has its closest connection with a non-trust State,[51] irrespective of whether that closest connection is with the forum.[52] This is another safety mechanism to ensure that the trust is not introduced into non-trust States though the back door. It ought not to be possible for a trust of which settlor, trustee, beneficiaries, assets, and place of administration are all situated in, for example, Italy to be entitled to recognition simply because the settlor chose English law to govern the trust.

There is, however, a big 'but' here. Article 13 is discretionary and it is very striking that Italian courts have not reached for it in respect of 'Italian' trusts governed by the law of a trust State.[53] The reversal of the 'natural order', whereby

---

Foundation (27 April 1994) (noted by P Kinsch 'Trusts in a Civil Law Environment: Jersey Trustees may Sue in Luxembourg' (1996) 5 J Int Corp P 120, 122), which 'makes it clear that the *lex situs* rule of the private international law of property cannot be used by third parties who have dealt with trustees to contest, in the event of proceedings being brought, the trustees' right to sue'. However, the case under discussion was concerned only with the capacity of trustees to sue in Luxembourg. The author goes on to suggest (at 123) that 'tracing remedies available to the beneficiary of an English trust would not be enforced . . . if they conflicted with the provisions of the *lex situs*'.

[50] Unless the governing law of that trust is a State which does not know the trust or the category in question (Art 5), or the conditions for exercising the discretion in Art 13 are met.

[51] Or indeed, with more than one non-trust State.

[52] In making this assessment, the choice of law clause, place of administration and habitual residence of the trustee are to be discounted.

[53] See, eg, *Casani v Mattei*, Tribunale di Lucca, reported in English in (1998/99) 1 ITELR 925. F Albisinni, 'National Digest for Italy', in J Glasson (ed) *International Trust Laws*, chap A51, p 18 comments that: 'To summarise, the conclusion of the Tribunal is the first and very clear judicial confirmation [that] . . . the Hague Convention, even if not intended to introduce the trust into domestic law of countries who do not have this institution, in fact eliminated the barriers to . . . [its] entrance in Italian law . . .'. See also M Lupoi, 'The Civil Law Trust' in R Atherton (ed) *the International Academy of Estate and Trust Law: Selected Papers 1997–9* (The Hague, Kluwer, 2000), Chap 4, pp 35, 46–9. See also the decision of the Milan Commercial Court of 27 December 1996, and the decision of the Genoese Commercial Court of 24 March 1997, both discussed by P Matthews (1998) 12 Trust Law International 104.

an institution not existing in domestic law is introduced for private international law purposes has led, and is continuing to lead, to the development of a domestic trust law in Italy. More and more trusts are being accepted in Italy with ever stronger Italian centres of gravity. Although such trusts tend to be governed by the law of a trust State, the trust is becoming accepted and there is every reason to think that it might lead to the development of a domestic law of Italian trusts.[54] Nor is this wholly surprising. Once the trust is admitted for private international law purposes, questions are likely to be asked as to why it is possible to achieve a certain result with a trust in Italy where there are some connections overseas, but impossible to do so in Italian domestic law.[55]

Accordingly, it can be said that the Convention *requires* little of non-trust States. However, both Italy and the Netherlands have thrown themselves into the spirit of the Convention; the result is that its 'full force' is felt in the Netherlands and that Italian law has gone further still to embrace the trust, virtually to the point of letting it into its domestic law.

D. Effects of Recognition under the Hague Trusts Convention on Trust States

At first sight, it might seem that the Convention does little of great significance in England. It largely consolidates common law choice of law rules and allows

---

[54] See further M Lupoi, 'The Civil Law Trust' in R Atherton (ed) *the International Academy of Estate and Trust Law: Selected Papers 1997–9*, Chap 4, pp 35, 46–7. Lupoi lists a number of other developments, including: the formation of a Consultative Group on Trusts ('*Consulta nazionale sui trusts*') under which the opportunities presented by the Convention have been considered; a Ministry of Finance report on taxation of trusts; rules to permit governmental officials to place assets on trusts governed by foreign law were adopted by the lower Chamber of Parliament; a Bill to provide for trusts (governed by the law of a trust State) for handicapped children; and, most significantly of all, another Bill on trust management which would *not* require the trust to be governed by a foreign law. There is also a new journal entitled *Trusts e Attività Fiduciarie*. See also D Hayton, 'The Development of the Trust Concept in Civil Law Jurisdictions' (2000) 8 J Int Corp P 159, 164; P Matthews, 'Italian Trust for Debenture Holders' (1997) 11 Trust Law International 20. But see M Graziadei, 'Trusts in Italian Law', in C Cumyn (ed) *La Fiducie face au Trust dans les Rapports des Affaires: Trust vs Fiducie in a Business Context* (Brussels, Bruylant, 1999), Chap E4, 286–7, who comments that Italian courts might yet use Art 13 in respect of trusts objectively connected with Italy but governed by a foreign law. See further P Matthews, 'Un Trust per l'Italiano' (1998) 12 Trust Law International 104; P Matthews, 'New Draft Italian Trust Law' (2000) 14 Trust Law International 33.

[55] See M Lupoi, 'Effects of the Hague Convention in a Civil Law Country' in *The Reform of Property Law* (Aldershot, Ashgate, 1997) pp 222, 227.

English trusts to benefit from recognition overseas. In sum, the Convention seems to provide benefit without burden. Such a view would be erroneous, however, even if some of the implications of ratification may not have been fully apparent at the time of ratification.

(1) The 'Shapeless' Trust

One problem is the description of the 'trust' in Article 2. It is very much broader than the common law trust. It refers to the relationship created by the settlor where assets have been placed under the *control* of the trustee. It goes on to state that 'title to the trust assets stands in the name of the trustee or in the name of another person on behalf of the trustee'. Unfortunately, 'control' is not at all the same as ownership and Article 2 might describe its 'trust' in a manner broad enough to cover cases of agency or mandate.[56] Assets might not be 'part of the trustee's own estate', but could be part of the settlor's own estate and 'controlled' by the 'trustee'. Furthermore, Article 2 provides that the trustee is accountable in respect of his duties to manage, employ, or dispose of the assets. However, it does not say *to whom* and presumably this could be the settlor.[57] Again, the reservation by the settlor of rights and powers to himself is expressly stated not necessarily to be inconsistent with the trust; but it is unclear how much power he can reserve to himself without the trust being considered a sham.

The result is what Lupoi calls a 'shapeless' trust, where the trustee need not be owner of the property and where title could remain in the hands of the settlor, who retains rights and powers and to whom the 'trustee' is accountable. Moreover, Lupoi suggests that very few countries would not have such a shapeless 'trust' in their domestic law and that, accordingly, very few are 'non-trust' States within the meaning of the Convention. The result is that an English court would be compelled to recognize such institutions under the Convention, even if they appear wholly alien to English domestic law. If this view is accepted, then the Convention has made a radical difference to English law and the scope of the Convention is wider than one might expect.

---

[56] M Lupoi, *Trusts: A Comparative Study*, p 334; but see D Hayton, 'The Developing European Dimension of Trust Law (2000) 11 KCLJ 48, 52.

[57] Although as M Lupoi rightly asks, 'How could an 'institution' be 'analogous' to the Anglo-Saxon trust if the trustee were to be accountable to the 'settlor'?': 'The Shapeless Trust' (1995) 1(3) Trusts and Trustees 15, 16.

(2) Obligation to Recognize Foreign Trusts Incompatible with English Domestic Law

Another important factor is the omission of Article 13 from the schedule to the Recognition of Trusts Act 1987. Presumably, English courts envisaged no difficulty in recognizing trusts governed by the law of a trust State, even if the trust was objectively connected to a non-trust State, or to a State not having the category of trust involved. But let us take the example of the STAR trust regime,[58] which originated in the Cayman Islands.[59] This allows a settlor to create a trust for objects or for a purpose. That purpose need not be charitable; non-charitable purpose trusts are given effect by an appointed 'enforcer', who has *locus standi* to enforce the trust should the trustees default in their obligations. In English domestic law, save in a few anomalous cases, non-charitable purpose trusts are void, there being no concept of an enforcer and, accordingly, nobody who can enforce them. Imagine now that an English settlor creates a trust for a non-charitable purpose. The trustees are English and the purpose is to be carried out in England, where the trust assets are located and the trust administered. The trust states that it is to be governed by the law of the Cayman Islands and that it shall be subject to the STAR regime. What is an English court to do? The answer is that it is not entitled to refuse to recognize the trust, because it has not enacted Article 13. If it had, it could have refused to recognise the trust, on the basis that the trust was objectively connected to England, and England was a State not providing for the category of trust involved.

An alternative might be for an English court to refuse to recognize a STAR trust on public policy grounds, pursuant to Article 18. Whether this Article should be invoked to deny recognition to such trusts is the subject of a forceful exchange between Duckworth and Matthews.[60] However, if the objection to

---

[58] See the Cayman Island's Special Trusts (Alternative Regime) Law 1997.

[59] On which, see A Duckworth, *STAR Trusts* (Saffron Walden, Gostick Hall, 1998); D Hayton, 'STAR Trusts' (1998) 4 Amicus Curiae 13; D Hayton, 'STAR Trusts' (1998) 8 Offshore Taxation Review 43; P Matthews, 'Shooting STAR: the New Special Trusts Regime from the Cayman Islands' (1997) 11 Trust Law International 67; A Duckworth, 'STAR Wars: the Colony Strikes Back' (1998) 12 Trust Law International 16; P Matthews, 'STAR: Big Bang or Red Dwarf?' (1998) 12 Trust Law International 98; A Duckworth 'STAR Wars: Smiting the Bull' (1999) 13 Trust Law International 158. See also A Duckworth, 'The New Frontier of Purpose Trusts': http://www.il-trust-in-italia.it/Congresso 1999/Duckworth%20New frontier. htm.

[60] P Matthews, (1997) 11 Trust Law International 67; A Duckworth, (1998) 12 Trust Law International 16; P Matthews (1998) 12 Trust Law International 98; A Duckworth, (1999) 13 Trust Law International 158.

non-charitable trusts is that they cannot be enforced, and if, by the governing law, someone can be appointed who *can* enforce the trust, it is very difficult to see why the trust should be denied recognition on public policy grounds.

If such trusts can be recognized in England when they are governed by a foreign law, but otherwise wholly connected to England, it might then be argued that private international law should act as a catalyst for reform of *domestic* law in England, just as it has in Italy. Why should *English domestic law* not also permit such trusts to be created and governed by English law, provided that they have an enforcer? There does not seem any manifest theoretical objection to such trusts once someone has *locus standi* to enforce them. Once again, one sees the atypical nature of the private international law of trusts, where private international law is capable of setting the agenda for domestic law reform.[61]

E. Creation of Trusts

Given the developed choice of law rules of the Hague Trusts Convention and the progressive nature of the Convention, it is curious that other areas of the private international law of trusts remain so undeveloped. Whilst we have detailed Convention rules for the *operation* of trusts, when one turns to look at the common law rules applicable to the *creation* of trusts in the first place, a mist of uncertainty descends. Very little is to be found in the books on the subject and the little case law that there is is inconclusive.[62]

Article 4 states that the Convention 'does not apply to preliminary issues relating to the validity of wills or of other acts by virtue of which assets are transferred to the trustee'. The difficulty is that the valid transfer of property to be held on trust involves a hybrid of 'ordinary' alienation of property and the 'specific' creation of a trust with that property. Although the details of the questions raised are beyond the scope of this chapter, it is this author's contention elsewhere[63] that a fundamental distinction must be drawn between those elements of a trust's creation which are common to all alienations of property, and those which are specific to the trust. If a settlor wishes to transfer his assets to a

---

[61] See further D Hayton, 'Developing the Obligation Characteristic of the Trust' (2001) 117 LQR 96, 100.
[62] See further J Harris, 'Launching the Rocket: Capacity and the Creation of *Inter Vivos* Transnational Trusts', in J Glasson (ed) *International Trust Laws,* Chap C2.
[63] ibid.

trustee to hold on trust for a beneficiary, then he is alienating his property every bit as much as if he is making an outright transfer to the 'trustee'. If either he lacks capacity to make that transfer according to the 'general' rules for property transfers, or legal title has not vested in the transferee by the law applicable to such transfers, then it is very difficult to see how a trust can be created. In order to deal with the property and exercise the powers of the legal owner in respect thereof, there is a very strong case for saying that the trustee must have acquired good title to it according to the law of the *situs*.[64]

If the settlor *can and has* transferred legal title to the trustee, the law of the *situs* ceases to have any legitimate interest in the precise mechanism by which the transfer is made. In particular, whether the settlor has capacity to create the trust structure with the property, and to alienate equitable title to the beneficiary[65] is a matter on which there seems no reason to deny the settlor autonomy, given that he will have already satisfied the 'mandatory' requirement of compliance with the law of the *situs* to alienate property at all. Accordingly, it is suggested that the question whether the settlor *can create the trust structure* and whether he *has* done so, should be a matter for the law governing the trust itself. This will also prevent the creation of a trust being struck down simply because the assets happen to be located in a State which does not have the concept of the trust.

In this author's view, similar distinctions should be drawn between other rules, depending upon whether they regulate property transfers in general, or trusts in particular. Hence, whilst a testamentary trust must be made in a will which is valid according to the law governing succession (because the requisite formalities do not relate specifically to trusts), the rule of English law that a declaration of a trust of land has to be in writing[66] relates specifically to trusts and should, accordingly be applied not because property is located in England, but only if the law applicable to the trust is English law, even if the property is located overseas.

Similarly, it is not possible to say whether, for example, foreign rules of forced

---

[64] Or the law of the place of the deceased's last domicile in the case of testamentary trusts of movable property.

[65] In the case of a common law trust.

[66] The Law of Property Act 1925, s 53(1)(b) states that 'a declaration of trust respecting any land or any interest therein must be manifested and proved by some writing signed by some person who is able to declare such trust or by his will'. See also *Barton v Tod* [2002] EWHC 264 (ch), judgment of 20 February 2002.

heirship should be treated as 'rocket' rules capable of being applied, where mandatory under Article 15, to override a trust to the extent that it infringes them, or 'rocket-launching' rules which prevent a trust ever coming into effect and which operate outside the Convention. Insofar as such rules strike down *any* disposition of property, they may be better regarded as preliminary matters outside the Convention; insofar as they merely limit the effectiveness of the trust, for example by declaring a portion of the trust invalid but not striking down the trust itself, they should be seen as 'rocket' matters not affecting the bringing into force of the Convention.

What is clear is that the views of this author can only be stated tentatively, because the English choice of law rules for the creation and constitution of trusts have such a long way to go to catch up with the Hague Convention's rules on the operation of trusts. They also lag far behind the rules of many offshore jurisdictions, which have sophisticated 'rocket' and 'rocket-launching' legislation which leave the English conflict of laws rules trailing in their wake.

F. Offshore Reaction

Offshore reaction to the Hague Trusts Convention (and reaction in the United States and Ontario) has been distinctly muted. In Ontario, concern was expressed about the rules applicable to a testamentary trust in the absence of choice, both as to the time at which this is assessed and the relative lack of importance seemingly attached to the testator's domicile.[67]

In the United States and offshore, the feeling in some quarters is that the Convention is nowhere near radical enough; that it is insufficiently protective of the settlor's autonomy, contains too may derogations and that it does not do enough to protect 'local' trusts from the claims of forced heirs. For some, the future for the private international law of trusts is extremely bold and pragmatic and gives full emphasis to the 'obligation' characteristics of the trust.[68]

In many offshore jurisdictions, English concern about subjecting a settlor's capacity to the law chosen by him to govern the trust is rejected. That law is used,

---

[67] M O'Sullivan, 'The Hague Convention on Trusts—Further Considerations' (1993) 2 J Int Corp P 65.
[68] See, in particular, J Schoenblum, 'The Hague Convention on Trusts: Much Ado about Very Little' (1994) 3 J Int Corp P 5.

even if capacity rules are traditionally thought to have a mandatory character, so that they cannot be freely evaded. It is common to provide that a trust governed by the local law will be valid if the settlor had capacity by the local law and that no other law may undermine that capacity.[69]

Perhaps the most important manifestation of the concern for 'insulating' local trusts is to be found with forced heirship. Many offshore States, far from seeking to preserve the application of mandatory rules of a foreign law, as does Article 15 of the Hague Trusts Convention, are anxious to ensure that such rules do not upset the apple cart. It is common to provide that no foreign law of forced heirship shall in any way undermine or affect the operation of a trust governed by local law.[70] Sometimes, it is even provided that no foreign *judgment* may undermine a trust governed by local law, even though in some cases States appear to have international obligations to recognize such foreign judgments.[71]

In this world where the settlor's autonomy is paramount, a State's private international law rules have to be 'competitive'. States such as the Cayman Islands do not want the strait-jacket of the Hague Trusts Convention and have snubbed it.[72] Since the Convention is open-ended,[73] their trusts might benefit from recognition in non-trust States; but they do not need to take on the burden of the Convention and its choice of law rules. On the other hand, the very individualized positions that they adopt may put their trusts on a collision course with the laws of other States, and their trusts may accordingly have greater difficulty in securing recognition overseas, particularly in States which do have forced heirship rules. 'Insular' choice of law rules can only protect a trust within the jurisdiction; outside the jurisdiction, they may harm the prospects for the trust's recognition.

---

[69] See, eg, section 90, Cayman Islands Trusts Law 1967 (1998 Revision), Part VII. See further J Harris, 'Launching the Rocket: Capacity and the Creation of *Inter Vivos* Transnational Trusts', in J Glasson (ed) *International Trust Laws*, Chap C2, pp 22–9.

[70] Eg, Cayman Islands 1998 Revision, s 91.

[71] Eg, Isle of Man Trust Act 1995, s 5(b)(ii).

[72] Although States such as the Isle of Man and Jersey which are bound by the Convention have still formulated pragmatic 'rocket-launching' rules. On one view, these undermine the spirit of Art 15, Hague Convention, which makes clear that mandatory rules of the law applicable to related areas of law are preserved.

[73] Although a State may decide to recognize trusts only when governed by the law of a Contracting State, pursuant to Art 21.

The difficulty is that the 'self-interest' approach and the fostering of the trust for private international law purposes in non-trust jurisdictions are largely contradictory. The Hague Trusts Convention is about compromise: it introduces the trust into non-trust States for private international law purposes, but provides various derogations to protect mandatory rules of designated States in related areas, and the forum's own mandatory rules and public policy. Moreover, it excludes a number of difficult issues from the Convention altogether and provides various derogations from the trust recognition principle. Put these ingredients together and you have a Convention which does not look too 'frightening' for non-trust States, but which is nonetheless a key first stage to the acceptance of the trust. Once it has gained a foothold into non-trust States, those that find its features positively advantageous may be tempted to introduce the trust into domestic law. But non-trust States will scarcely be encouraged to ratify the Convention if trust States themselves shun it or act with tepidity towards it. What is needed is a co-operative attitude from trust States, so that they accept the Convention's choice of law rules, with their limitation and derogations, and are prepared to recognize analogous institutions of non-trust States. That attitude is somewhat incompatible with the desire for a trust State to maximize its attractiveness in a competitive market.

G. Jurisdiction and Enforcement of Trust Judgments: The Brussels I Regulation

The trust also poses unique questions in the law of jurisdiction. The approach that has been taken under the EC regime[74] shares certain characteristics with the Hague Trusts Convention in playing down the *in rem* nature of the trust. In particular, a claim to assert a beneficial interest under a trust of land is not regarded as having as its 'object rights *in rem* in immovable property' for the purposes of Article 22(1) of the Brussels I Regulation.[75] This is despite the fact that a person who establishes absolute beneficial entitlement to land may be

---

[74] Under the Brussels Convention on Jurisdiction and the Enforcement of Judgments in Civil and Commercial Matters, as amended (enacted into English law by the Civil Jurisdiction and Judgments Act 1982). The Convention has now been replaced by Regulation (EC) No 44/2001 of 22 December 2000 ('the Brussels I Regulation') with effect from 1 March 2002: [2001] OJ L12/1. However, the trust provisions, and, presumably, the attitude to trusts displayed in the case law, are substantively unchanged.

[75] Case C-294/92 *Webb v Webb* [1994] ECR I- 1717. See also A Briggs, 'Trusts of Land and the Brussels Convention' (1994) 110 LQR 526; A Briggs (1994) 14 YEL 563.

able to terminate the trust and claim the property absolutely;[76] and that if the courts of the *situs* take a different view of his rights, any order delivered elsewhere might prove unenforceable.

On the other hand, the full 'obligation' characteristics of the trust are not recognized. A defendant domiciled in a Member State may normally be sued in that State.[77] However, he may also be sued 'as settlor, trustee or beneficiary of a trust created by the operation of a statute, or by a written instrument, or created orally and evidenced in writing, in the courts of the Member State in which the trust is domiciled'.[78] This provision applies to the internal relationship between the parties: 'as between the trustees themselves, between persons claiming the status of trustees and, above all, between trustees on the one hand and the beneficiaries of a trust on the other'.[79]

The place where a trust is domiciled is left to Member States to determine. Article 60(3) somewhat enigmatically states that 'in order to determine whether a trust is domiciled in the Member State whose courts are seised of the matter, the court shall apply its rules of private international law'. In the United Kingdom, section 45(3) of the Civil Jurisdiction and Judgments Act 1982 states that 'A trust is domiciled in a part of the United Kingdom if and only if the system of law of that part is the system of law with which the trust has its closest and most real connection'.[79a] This reference to the law of closest connection involves a kind of *forum conveniens* justification for jurisdiction, but one which is not highly pragmatic. A trust governed by English law is one over which the English court might not have jurisdiction; indeed, one or more non-trust Member States might alone have jurisdictional competence with respect to it.[80] In contrast, the proposed Hague Convention on Jurisdiction and the Recognition and Enforcement of Judgments in

---

[76] In English domestic law, he may do so under the rule in *Saunders v Vautier* (1841) 4 Beav 115.

[77] Article 2.

[78] Article 5(6). According to Collins J in *Chellaram v Chellaram (No 2)* [2002] EWHC 632 (ch), [2002] 3 All ER 17 judgment of 16 April 2002, Article 5(6) does not apply to constructive trusts.

[79] *Explanatory Report on the Brussels Convention, as amended by the United Kingdom, Irish and Danish Accession Convention, by Prof. Dr P Schlosser* ('Schlosser Report') [1979] OJ C 59/71, para 111.

[79a] This has now been re-enacted in sch 1, para 12, Civil Jurisdiction and Judgments Order 2001.

[80] Where the defendant is domiciled in an EU State other than the United Kingdom and the trust has its closest connection with the same or another such State. Even though the trust is stated to be governed by English law, the English courts would have no jurisdiction.

Civil and Commercial Matters[81] envisages that proceedings might be brought[82] in the place of principal administration of the trust, or the place with which the trust has its closest connection, or that where the settlor and all living beneficiaries are habitually resident,[83] or in the State whose law is applicable to the trust.[84] This last basis is particularly pragmatic: it ensures that a State designated by choice of law clause can apply its own law[85] and helps to 'insulate' it against the vagaries of the law of another State.

However, the EC regime[86] does give the settlor's autonomy a largely[87] free reign in that a choice of court clause for a Member State contained in the trust deed will be binding and, unless it states to the contrary, conclusive 'in any proceedings brought against a settlor, trustee or beneficiary, if relations between these persons or their rights or obligations under the trust are involved'.[88] But a number of important matters remain unresolved. For example, what if a purported express trust containing a jurisdiction clause fails in whole or in part and the settlor claims that the property is held on resulting trust for him? If the invalidity of the express trust is accepted by all parties, it might appear that any terms thereof are likewise either invalid, or at least irrelevant to litigation concerning a resulting trust. Again, what if a trustee of a written, express trust makes an allegedly unauthorized profit and is alleged to hold on constructive trust? Is he bound by the jurisdiction clause in the express trust?

More generally, it might be thought that there is something curious about Article 23(4), in that it will apparently govern litigation between trustee and beneficiary, even though neither party will ordinarily have executed the trust instrument. In litigation between trustee and settlor, the trustee may legitimately be deemed to have consented to the clause by agreeing to take on the role of trustee. What though of litigation between trustee and beneficiary? Curiously, *Parker and Mellows* suggest that, in the face of a foreign exclusive

---

[81] See the Interim Text of the proposed Hague Convention on Jurisdiction and the Recognition and Enforcement of Judgments in Civil and Commercial of June 2001 ('the Hague Judgments Convention'), available at http://www.hcch.net/e/workprog/jdgm.html

[82] In the absence of a choice of court clause.

[83] Provided that they are all resident in the same State.

[84] Article 11(2), interim text, Hague Judgments Convention.

[85] Even though the trust instrument contains no choice of court clause.

[86] And the Hague Judgments Convention regime: see interim text, Article 11(1).

[87] Subject to the rules protecting consumers, employees and insured parties.

[88] Article 23(4), Brussels I Regulation; compare draft Article 11(1), Hague Judgments Convention.

jurisdiction clause, 'it is inconceivable that the English courts would decline jurisdiction to hear proceedings brought by any beneficiary of a trust who had not executed the trust instrument where English law was specified as the proper law'.[89] Such a view cannot be correct for two reasons. First, the benefit received by a beneficiary will be subject to any terms or conditions of the trust instrument, which includes the jurisdiction clause. Secondly, Article 23(4) is clearly intended to extend the effect of jurisdiction clauses in the trust context beyond the scope of expressly consenting parties. Were that not the case, then it would be largely redundant, since jurisdiction clauses could simply be regulated by the 'general' jurisdiction clause rules of Article 23(1). As Schlosser explains, Article 23(1) was deemed insufficient to regulate trusts precisely because it is limited to bilateral agreements.[90]

Beyond these uncertainties there is something far more fundamental, both about the EC scheme and the proposed Hague Judgments Convention. It is clear that most trust judgments will fall within the scope of the Brussels I Regulation. It is equally clear that Member States *must* recognize and enforce such judgments. It would scarcely be appropriate for a Member State to deny recognition to trust judgments solely on the basis that the trust does not exist in that State's domestic law.[91] It follows that the effects of trust judgments are 'recognized' in a more material sense than under the Hague Trusts Convention.

Furthermore, the limited scope of Article 5(6) means that proceedings to create or affirm the existence of, for example, constructive trusts in civil and commercial matters may *have* to be brought in the State of the defendant's domicile. In other words, a non-trust State may have mandatory jurisdiction under the Regulation. The Brussels I Regulation, and before that the Brussels Convention, have a potentially radical effect on the cross-impact of trusts which does not seem to have received anything like the attention of the Hague Trusts Convention.

---

[89] A Oakley, *Parker and Mellows: Modern Law of Trusts*, 7th edn (London, Sweet and Maxwell, 1998), p 749.
[90] Schlosser Report, para 178. See also the Royal Court of Jersey's decision in EMM Capricorn Trustees Ltd v Compass Trustees Ltd (2002) 4 ITELR 34.
[91] Especially as the Regulation contains bases of jurisdiction relating to the trust.

H. Jurisdiction at Common Law

At common law, a number of provisions of the Civil Procedure Rules concern trusts.[92] Little in the form of an ideological attitude towards trusts can be gleaned from them. It is noteworthy that the criteria do not obviously entail a close connection with the trust.[93] There is, for example, no basis for service out of the jurisdiction that the law of closest connection to the trust is English law; nor that the trust is to be administered in England.[93a] In this respect, they provide less of a substantial connection than does Article 5(6), Brussels I Regulation.[94] On the other hand, in contrast to the Brussels I Regulation, there is a provision that, where English law is applicable, service out may be permitted, at least if the defendant is a trustee;[95] a view which is attractive in an international marketplace where it might be considered desirable that English courts should have control over English trusts. Moreover, any English judgment should qualify for recognition and enforcement under the Brussels I Regulation.[96]

Overall, it could be said that the rules on jurisdiction lack a certain coherence. In Europe, one might think it pivotal that English courts should have jurisdiction over English trusts, rather than the courts of non-trust States. The Brussels I Regulation's special jurisdiction provision relating to trusts seeks a close connection between the forum and the trust, but the limited scope of the Regulation's provisions may only succeed in forcing trust proceedings to take place in non-trust jurisdictions. The English common law rules contain a nod, but nothing more, in the direction of pragmatism. In neither case do the rules do enough to ensure that litigation concerning trusts governed by English law takes place in an English court.

---

[92] Specifically, CPR Part 6.20(11)–(15).

[93] Although in the case of constructive trusts and CPR Part 6.20(15), the fact that the liability allegedly arose from acts committed in England provides a substantial connection to the forum. However, the predecessor to this rule was interpreted broadly: see *ISC Technologies* v *Guerin* [1992] 2 Lloyd's Rep 430.

[93a] However, in the event of dépeçage, it will suffice fore the purposes of CPR Part 6.20(11) that English law is applicable either to the validity of the trust or to the administration of the trust: *per* Collins J in *Chellaram v Chellaram (No 2)* [2002] EWHC 632 (ch), [2002] 3 All ER 17 judgment of 16 April 2002.

[94] Of course, a claimant who wishes to obtain service out of the jurisdiction must also convince the court, *inter alia,* that England is the natural forum for the litigation: *Spiliada v Cansulex* [1987] AC 460; *Seaconsar Far East Ltd v Bank Markazi Jomhouri Islami Iran* [1994] 1 AC 438.

[95] CPR Part 6.20(11).

[96] At least if the matter is a civil and commercial one and not otherwise excluded from the scope of Art 1.

I. Equity, Constructive, and Resulting Trusts

This chapter is primarily concerned with the law of trusts and only a few words will be said about equity and private international law. In this area, the relevant questions are only starting to be asked. There are questions about whether equitable claims are the proper subject of choice of law rules at all. There are questions as to whether equity should rather be administered as part of the law of the forum; and of whether it is correct to say for private international law purposes that equity acts *in personam*, so that, even though equitable ownership may be at issue, the law of the *situs* should have little to say on the matter.

Remarkably, the law of the forum still seems to hold considerable sway in many matters, such as whether a fiduciary relationship exists.[97] Yet the idea that equitable claims should be regarded as so fundamentally different in character to legal claims that the subject should be wholly or partially immune from the choice of law process is hard to credit.

If it is decided that equitable claims should be subject to the choice of law process, there then follow complex questions of classification. Claims based upon knowing assistance in breach of trust, or knowing receipt of trust property, need to be classified and the outcome could be determinative of which law should be applied. When dealing with a claim that a defendant had dishonestly assisted a breach of trust in *Grupo Torras SA v Al Sabah*,[98] the Court of Appeal rejected the application of either restitutionary or tort choice of law rules. In an exercise of dubious coherence, the Court applied Spanish law as that of the place where the act upon which the defendant's alleged liability hinged had taken place. Having found that there was liability on the facts by that law, the Court assumed liability under English law. The result was a hybrid of application of the law of the forum, subject to demonstrating a basis of liability in Spanish law.[99] This is hardly a coherent characterization or choice of law process: the Court did not see the claim as restitutionary or tortious; but one is left wondering how exactly it did see the claim and what law it did apply.[100]

---

[97] The Federal Court of Australia in *Paramasivam v Flynn* treated the law of the forum as the governing law for 'general' breaches of fiduciary duty: (1998–99) 160 ALR 203. See also T Yeo, 'Choice of Law for Fiduciary Duties' (1999) 115 LQR 571.

[98] [2001] Lloyd's Rep Bank 36.

[99] See also *Arab Monetary Fund v Hashim (No 9) The Times*, 11 October 1994; *Kuwait Oil Tanker v Al Bader* [2000] 2 All ER (Comm) 271.

[100] See also A Briggs, 'Decisions of British Courts During 2000 Involving Questions of Public or Private International Law: B. Private International Law' (2000) 61 BYIL 434, 471–2.

Yet for the, admittedly different, exercise of jurisdictional allocation under the Brussels I Regulation, it has been held that knowing assistance and knowing receipt claims may both be treated as 'matters relating to tort',[101] with the result that jurisdiction is allocated to the place where the harmful event occurred.[102] It could be said that this is explicable on the basis that there is no special jurisdiction in restitutionary claims. However, the House of Lords in *Kleinwort Benson Ltd v Glasgow City Council*[103] appeared to consider that a claim needed to be based upon tort to fall within that Article, and that a claim based on unjust enrichment, even one contingent upon wrongdoing, would not fall within Article 5(3).[104] It may be that we are yet to hear the final word on these claims, particularly where knowing receipt is concerned.

In time, it may come to be generally accepted that claims based upon knowing receipt should be characterized as restitutionary and those for knowing assistance as akin to torts, both for jurisdiction and choice of law purposes. But at present, English courts seem uncertain as to whether and how to apply the *Dicey and Morris* choice of law rule which refers to restitution.[105] Instead, they seem inclined to refer to a foreign law to check that there is some form of liability but to return to English law to determine the consequences thereof.

Where claims involve the imposition or affirmation by a court of constructive and resulting trusts,[106] there is another large question to be answered. Once equitable claims become fully accepted as part of the choice of law family, how should a court approach a claim that the defendant holds property on a constructive or resulting trust? Irrespective of whether the proper basis of the cause of action is regarded as restitution or property, the fact remains that property rights

---

[101] For the purposes of Art 5(3).

[102] *Casio Computer Co Ltd v Sayo* [2001] EWCA Civ 661, *The Times*, 6 February 2001; *Dexter v Harley*, Ch D, *The Times*, 2 April 2001. Both cases are noted by T Yeo, 'Constructive Trustees and the Brussels Convention' (2001) 117 LQR 560.

[103] [1999] 1 AC 153. Although the case concerned a question of jurisdictional allocation within the United Kingdom, it was considered that the position would be the same for international cases involving more than one European State.

[104] T Yeo, 'Constructive Trustees and the Brussels Convention' (2001) 117 LQR 560, 564.

[105] L Collins (gen ed), *Dicey and Morris on the Conflict of Laws*, 13th edn (Sweet and Maxwell, 2000), chap 34, Rule 200. Rule 200(1) states that: 'the obligation to restore the benefit of an enrichment obtained at another person's expense is governed by the proper law of the obligation'. Rule 200(2) goes on to suggest that if the obligation arises in connection with a contract, its proper law is the law applicable to the contract; that if it arises in connection with a transaction concerning immovable property, its proper law is the law of the *situs*; and that in all other case, the proper law is the law of the place where the enrichment occurs.

[106] At least insofar as they fall outside the scope of the Recognition of Trusts Act 1987.

are ultimately in issue. Although the Court of Appeal in *Grupo Torras SA v Al Sabah*,[107] commented that it was unhelpful to classify a claim as one for a constructive trust, the fact remains that *all* trust cases, save where the defendant is made personally liable to account as a constructive trustee, have in common that the question of who owns what will have to be resolved. Whether the basis of the claimant's proprietary entitlement is descent of title or proprietary restitution, he may need to assert his rights in the *situs*; and a finding that he is absolutely beneficially entitled might entitle the claimant to terminate the trust and claim the property absolutely.[108] There is a coherent argument for saying that sometimes, the prime influence on which law should be applied is not the nature of the cause of action but the consequence of making out that cause of action.[109] In the context of resulting trusts, Stevens comments that, 'Even if the proprietary interest arises due to unjustified enrichment and through the mechanism of a trust, the justifications for applying the approach taken to proprietary interests generally remain'.[110] In other words, it *may* be appropriate to treat constructive and resulting trusts as raising common questions for the choice of law process. It is arguable that a characterisation exercise of putting issues in the right box, applying a choice of law rule and coming out with a defined answer can obscure the wood from the trees. It is appropriate to recognize that sometimes it is not the nature of the cause of action *but the interest that is ultimately being asserted* that is of greater importance. Accordingly, there is, at least, a persuasive case for asking whether, according to the law of the *situs*, a claimant can assert a proprietary interest[111] in assets within that jurisdiction.[112]

In sum, equitable claims should certainly be embraced within the choice of law community; but where constructive and resulting trusts are concerned, there is a stronger argument for starting with the question 'which law is it most appropriate to apply to equitable claims where a property interest is ultimately

---

[107] [2001] Lloyd's Bank Rep 36, 62.

[108] As he can in English law under the rule in *Saunders v Vautier* (1841) 4 Beav 115.

[109] J Harris, 'Anti-Suit Injunctions—a Home Comfort?' [1997] LMCLQ 413.

[110] R Stevens, 'Resulting Trusts in the Conflict of Laws' in P Birks and F Rose (eds) *Restitution and Equity, Volume 1: Resulting Trusts and Equitable Compensation* (London, Mansfield Press/LLP, 2000), p 147, 154.

[111] The law of the *situs* need not know the concept of a constructive or resulting trust, as long as it regards the claimant as having a property interest. Insofar as is feasible, English courts should accord to the claimant whatever property rights he would have by the law of the *situs*.

[112] It is argued that this is not inconsistent with the apparent lack of importance attributed to the law of the *situs* in the case of express trusts. As explained above, Hague Convention trusts must still be *created* outside the scope of the Convention; and it is argued that the law of the *situs* will play an important role in determining whether the settlor can and has alienated his property.

at stake?', rather than asking 'is the cause of action one in unjust enrichment, restitution for wrongdoing or property?'. Practical considerations, not the characterization process, may prove the key to finding suitable choice of law rules. Very often, those considerations will lead to the application of the law of the *situs*, rather than the law governing the causative event which gives rise to the claim. This will be particularly likely where a beneficial interest in immovable property is asserted, or in items of movable property all situated in a single jurisdiction.

J. Conclusion

At once, the trust shows private international law at its most progressive and its most regressive. The Hague Trusts Convention makes what are, in fact, fairly minor inroads into the law of non-trust Contracting States, but is a potential catalyst for much wider acceptance of the trust in the domestic law of those States. At the same time, the broad Convention understanding of the word 'trust' and the range of institutions which must be recognized under it in England may lead to a rethinking of aspects of the English domestic law of trusts. Even then, however, those whose prime mission is not to spread the gospel of the trust, but to compete within the global trusts market, reject the Convention as insufficiently pragmatic and protective of local trusts from the vagaries of foreign law. At the other extreme, equity is still the poor man of the conflict of laws and the process of integrating it is only just beginning. Not only do the answers not yet exist; there is a danger that we are still not posing all the right questions.

9

MATRIMONIAL (MARITAL) PROPERTY RIGHTS IN CONFLICT OF LAWS: A RECONSIDERATION

*Trevor C Hartley**

Matrimonial[1] property rights may be defined as property rights resulting from marriage. This essay is concerned with their international dimension, the choice-of-law problems that arise when a foreign element impinges on the situation. The leading cases almost all date from the nineteenth century. They are based on social attitudes so at odds with those of today that the legal rules laid down may no longer be acceptable. We shall reconsider them in the light of modern values. Such reconsideration is also necessary in view of the enormous changes that have taken place in the substantive law. Furthermore, academic discussion has hitherto been limited to disputes between the husband and the wife (or between one of them and the children claiming through the other). We shall consider whether the same rules should apply where creditors are involved.

* Professor of Law, London School of Economics.
[1] 'Matrimonial property', the normal expression in England, will be used in this essay; it means the same as 'marital property', the most common expression in the United States.

The questions to be discussed are as follows: first, whether the appropriate connecting factor should still be the husband's domicile; secondly, (assuming domicile of some sort is the test) whether a change of domicile after marriage should have the effect of changing the applicable law (the mutability theory says it does; the immutability theory says it does not); thirdly, whether immovable property (land) is subject to different rules from movable property; fourthly, whether modern kinds of matrimonial property rights should have different choice-of-law rules from the traditional kinds; and, finally, what happens when third parties are involved.

Our study will be divided into three parts: first, we will take traditional matrimonial property rights—the kinds of rights before the court in the leading cases—and reconsider how they should be dealt with; then we will look at the modern kinds of rights and decide what choice-of-law rules should apply to them; finally, we will deal with both these questions from the point of view of third parties.

A. Traditional Matrimonial Property Rights

Since the leading cases on matrimonial property in conflict of laws were decided in the nineteenth century, we must set the scene by saying something about substantive matrimonial property law at that time. Most systems of matrimonial property were then based on the assumption that the wife could not be trusted to manage her own affairs and that the husband was the natural head of the family. This meant that in practice he controlled her property as well as his own, though the legal theories on the basis of which this result was achieved differed from country to country. Let us first look at England.

(1) Substantive Matrimonial Property Law

The Common Law

The original position in the common law was that on marriage the husband became owner of the wife's personal property and gained extensive rights over her real property. However, this was to some extent balanced by his duty to support her and the fact that he was liable for her antenuptial torts and contracts.[2] This

---

[2] Bromley, *Family Law* (5th edn, 1997), pp 431–432.

system put the wife completely in the husband's power and it exposed her to the risk that he might abuse that power. However, equity gave her a measure of protection: if, before marriage, her property (or property given to her by her father) was settled on trustees 'for her separate use', it became her separate property, freed from the control of her husband. Extensive use was made of this device by the wealthier classes.

As social attitudes began to change, this system was seen as unacceptable. The solution adopted was to allow women to keep control of their property on marriage, so that the husband had no rights over it. The result was the system of separation of property, which was introduced by a series of statutes in the late nineteenth century of which the most important was the Married Women's Property Act of 1882. Under the new system, marriage had, in principle, no effect on the property rights of the spouses: each had his or her own property and could deal with it as seemed best.

In other common law countries, the law also evolved, though not always in the same way. In the United States, all but eight States[3] had matrimonial property systems based on the common law. They all responded to changing social ideas by modifying the traditional system to give the wife greater rights; only two[4] States, however, introduced complete separation of property along English lines.

Though the system of complete separation had many advantages for professional women or those with substantial property, it did nothing to help women who depended on their husbands for support. In time, English law took account of their needs; but this took place in the modern period and will be discussed in Part B, below.

Civil Law

Most of the major civil law countries applied some form of community of property. The basic idea behind the concept of community of property was that on marriage the property of the spouses was pooled and owned jointly. Property acquired after marriage also went into the joint estate. The best analogy is that of a partnership. Each spouse had an equal share in the joint estate, though in the past the husband was the manager. It is important to note that

---

[3] See n 8, below.
[4] North and South Dakota.

this was a community of both assets and liabilities: the debts of either party, both those contracted before marriage and those arising after it, were normally debts of the community. Both spouses were liable for them and the community property could be taken by creditors in satisfaction of those debts.

This is the general picture. The details varied from country to country. In some cases all the assets went into the community; in others, certain assets were excluded. Moreover, it was a common feature for the law to lay down several systems, possibly including separation of property, and to allow the spouses to choose among them. This was done by an antenuptial contract entered into by the parties, usually before a notary. In the absence of a choice, the law would specify which regime would apply. This system, which will be called the 'default regime', was usually the one regarded as the most popular.

French law was the system involved in the leading English case, *De Nicols v Curlier*,[5] decided by the House of Lords in 1899. At this time, the French Civil Code recognised a number of matrimonial regimes and gave the parties a choice among them. The choice had to be exercised by a contract concluded before the marriage and could not be varied afterwards. In the absence of such a contract, the default regime applied. Known in French as the *régime légal*, this was a community of movables and acquisitions. Under this system, the community consisted of all the assets of the spouses except immovables owned by each of them prior to marriage or subsequently acquired by gift or succession.[6] The result was that there were three distinct patrimonies or estates: the husband's separate property, the wife's separate property and the community, the latter being jointly owned in undivided shares by the two spouses.[7] The administration of all three was vested in the husband.

In theory, this system was more favourable to the wife than the original common law system, since community property was jointly owned. In practice, however, the result was more or less the same while the marriage lasted, since the husband controlled all the property—his, hers, and theirs. In this respect, it was less favourable to the wife than the system of separation of property which became established in England towards the end of the nineteenth century, since the latter system gave the wife control over her own property.

---

    [5] [1900] AC 21.
    [6] Amos and Walton, *Introduction to French Law* (3rd edn, 1967), p 255. There were certain other exceptions.
    [7] ibid, p 254.

In other civil law countries, different versions of the community-of-property system were to be found. Under Roman-Dutch law, for example, *all* the property of the spouses—both what they owned before marriage and what they acquired during marriage—went into the community. This became the default regime in South Africa, though spouses could choose separation of property by antenuptial contract.

Eight American States[8] adopted community of property, mainly on the basis of Spanish law. However, the systems found in these States have moved a considerable distance from the original community concept; there are also significant differences among the eight States themselves.[9] In these States, the concept of joint property has to some extent been replaced by the idea of one spouse having an interest in the property of the other.

(2) The Leading Cases

This is the background against which the leading cases were decided. The most important were three cases decided by the House of Lords in 1804, 1891, and 1899 respectively. We will consider movables separately from immovables.

Movables: Mutability or Immutability?

The first case (decided in 1804) was *Lashley v Hog*, an appeal to the House of Lords from Scotland.[10] It concerned Scottish matrimonial property law, under which, at the time in question, marriage had the effect of transferring all the wife's movables to the husband. They then became his property to do with as he liked. While the marriage subsisted, the wife had no rights over his property, but, on the death of the husband, the wife could claim a *jus relictae*, which entitled her to a third of his movables if there were children, or half his movables if there were none. This right could be defeated by an *inter vivos* transfer of property by the husband and was subject to the rights of creditors, but it prevailed over the terms of the husband's will. If the wife died first, she could pass her claim to a *jus relictae* to her successors: it remained inchoate while the husband

---

[8] Louisiana, Texas, New Mexico, Arizona, Nevada, California, Washington, and Idaho.

[9] See Harold Marsh, *Marital Property in Conflict of Laws* (University of Washington Press, Seattle, 1952), Chap II.

[10] (1804) 4 Paton 581; 2 Coop T Cott 449. For an analysis of the case, see Goldberg, 'The Assignment of Property of Marriage' (1970) 19 ICLQ 557 at 580–584.

lived, but, on his death, half or a third of his movables would go to her successors.[11]

In *Lashley v Hog*, the husband was of Scottish origin but domiciled in England at the time of the marriage. The wife was also domiciled in England. They married in England. After the marriage, the husband made a great deal of money. The couple then changed their domicile to Scotland. After the death of both parties, a dispute arose as to whether the wife, who had died first, had had a claim to his movable property as a *jus relictae*. The House of Lords held that she did, a ruling that might be thought to establish that the applicable law changes with each change of domicile. This is the mutability theory.

The second House of Lords decision, *Welch v Tennent*,[12] concerned only immovable property; consideration of it will be postponed for a moment. The third, and most important, case is that decided in 1899, *De Nicols v Curlier*,[13] the only one of the three that was an English appeal. It concerned a French couple who were married in France when they were both domiciled there. There was no marriage contract; so, according to French Law, the *régime légal* (community of movables and acquisitions) was applicable. After the marriage, they moved to England, where they became domiciled, and set up in the restaurant business. They were extremely successful and became wealthy, almost all of their property being in the name of the husband. He died first and left his estate in trust for the benefit of his wife during her life and to their daughter and her children on the death of the wife.

The wife brought proceedings claiming that, since they were married under a system of community of property, the whole estate was joint (community) property.[14] The community was terminated by the death of the husband, whereupon the wife was entitled to a half share. Under civil law concepts, this would not be by right of succession, but simply by reason of the fact that she had always had a (hitherto undivided) share in their joint assets. She therefore

---

[11] For a fuller discussion of Scots matrimonial property law, see Anton, 'The Effect of Marriage upon Property in Scots Law' (1956) 19 MLR 653; Eric M Clive, *The Law of Husband and Wife in Scotland* (2nd edn, 1982). For a succinct explanation of the principles relevant to the case, see Goldberg, above.

[12] [1891] AC 639.

[13] [1900] AC 21.

[14] The immovables would have been bought out of the profits of the business, as the couple had almost nothing when they came to England; consequently, the immovables too would have fallen into the community.

argued that half the assets went to her on this basis and that only half fell into the husband's estate: the will applied only to this latter half.

The initial proceedings were confined to the movables. A V Dicey, the original author of the well-known English text book on the Conflict of Laws, *Dicey and Morris*, was counsel for the child and grandchildren. They claimed that the English system of separate property applied, under which the wife would be entitled to nothing except what she had been given under the will. Dicey's argument was that, though the couple were married in community of property, the governing law changed to English law once they had acquired a domicile in England. Since all the property had been acquired after this date, French law was irrelevant. This contention was dismissed by the trial judge, who found in favour of the wife. His judgment was reversed by the Court of Appeal on the basis of *Lashley v Hog*. On a further appeal to the House of Lords, the Court of Appeal's judgment was reversed and that of the trial court restored.

Dicey had admitted that, if there had been a contract stipulating the matrimonial regime, it would have applied to property acquired after the change of domicile. He maintained, however, that, in the absence of a contract, the regime changed with the change of domicile. This argument was rejected by the House of Lords on the ground that, under French law, a couple who married without a contract were in exactly the same position as if they had married with a contract stipulating that the *régime légal* was to apply. The House of Lords consequently refused to draw the distinction urged by Dicey, namely that between a marriage subject to a contract and a marriage without one. *Lashley v Hog* was distinguished on the ground that a *jus relictae* was not a matrimonial property right, but a right of succession.[15]

This would seem to establish that the applicable law regarding matrimonial property rights is that of the domicile at the date of marriage and that subsequent changes of domicile have no effect (immutability theory). However, *De Nicols v Curlier* was confined to movables, and further proceedings were brought before Kekewich J regarding the immovables. This case, known as *Re De Nicols (No 2)*, did not go on appeal. In his judgment, Kekewich J held that the French law applied also to the immovable property; however, he did so on

---

[15] This was the view of Lord Halsbury; Lord Morris concurred and Lord Shand said that he agreed with Lord Halsbury's interpretation of the case (see p 38). Lord Macnaghten and Lord Bampton also distinguished *Lashley v Hog*, though the precise grounds on which they did so are not clear.

the basis that, under French law, couples who married without a contract specifying the matrimonial regime they wished to adopt were deemed to have entered into an implied contract in favour of the *régime légal*. He regarded this as the ground on which the House of Lords' decision was based. He held, therefore, that the husband and wife should be treated as if they had entered into an express contract, and he decided the case on this basis.

In view of this, it seems that there are two possible ways of reconciling *De Nicols v Curlier* with *Lashley v Hog*. The first is that accepted in *De Nicols v Curlier* itself, namely that *Lashley v Hog* did not concern a true matrimonial property right. On this basis, it could be concluded that the immutability theory is correct. If one accepts the interpretation put forward by Kekewich J, on the other hand, one could restrict *De Nicols v Curlier* to cases in which there is either an express antenuptial contract choosing the applicable regime or where, under the law of the domicile at the time of marriage, the parties are deemed to have entered into an implied contract. *Lashley v Hog* could then be regarded as applying in all other cases. The result would be that the matrimonial property regime would be immutable whenever there was a contract, express or implied, while the regime would change with each change of domicile (mutability) when there was no such contract.

Was the House of Lords justified in distinguishing *Lashley v Hog* in the way it did? Is a *jus relictae* a right of succession? Such a characterization is supported by the fact that a *jus relictae* may be defeated by an *inter vivos* transfer of property and is subject to the rights of creditors; it is rendered less certain, however, by the fact that, if the wife dies first, she can pass her *jus relictae* to her successors. This, it will be remembered, is what happened in *Lashley v Hog*. Nevertheless, it does seem that in *Lashley v Hog* itself the House of Lords considered that a *jus relictae* was a right of succession. The leading opinion in the case was given by Lord Eldon and, though his reasoning is sometimes hard to follow, his argument is that, if the husband dies first, the wife's claim will be one of succession; therefore, where the wife dies first, her right should be characterized in the same way.[16] In view of this, it was not unreasonable for the House of Lords to distinguish *Lashley v Hog* on this ground when they decided *De Nicols v Curlier*. In any event, since it was a Scottish appeal, *Lashley v Hog* was not binding on the House of Lords in *De Nicols v Curlier*.

---

[16] See 4 Paton at 615; 2 Coop T Cott. at 485. For a fuller discussion, see Goldberg, 'The Assignment of Property of Marriage' (1970) 19 ICLQ 557 at 580–584.

In spite of this, should the alternative solution adopted by Kekewich J in *Re De Nicols (No 2)* be preferred? It is suggested that it should not. First of all, it is not what the House of Lords itself said in *De Nicols v Curlier*. Dicey expressly argued that a distinction should be drawn between cases in which there was an antenuptial contract and those in which there was not. This argument was rejected. The House of Lords said that the parties were in the same position *as if* they had entered into a contract specifying that the *régime légal* was to apply; but this is not the same thing as saying the regime was immutable because they were *deemed* to have entered into such a contract.

The second objection to Kekewich's solution is that, according to him, everything depends on whether under the foreign law the default regime applies by virtue of an implied contract or whether it applies simply by operation of law. The objection to making this the crucial distinction is that in most legal systems of the French type the precise legal reason why the default regime applies in the absence of a contract is of no importance: nothing turns on the distinction between the theory that there is an implied contract and the theory that the default regime applies by operation of law. In view of this, the foreign legal system itself will often have no decided view on the question. French law is a case in point. When *De Nicols v Curlier* was decided, academic opinion in France did indeed favour the view that, in the absence of an express contract, the parties were deemed to have entered into an implied contract choosing the *régime légal*; today, however, academic opinion has swung round to the view that the *régime légal* applies by operation of law.[17] This was not the result of any change in the Civil Code or in the case law: it was just a different intellectual fashion. It need hardly be said that basing a rule of English conflict of laws on so tenuous and insubstantial a distinction in the foreign law is highly undesirable.

Moreover, the distinction makes no sense. If the parties to a marriage want the default regime to apply, they will not make a contract to select it: such a contract would be pointless, since—as far as they can tell—it will make no difference. They could hardly be expected to make a contract just to ensure that their matrimonial regime would be recognized in England. Why, therefore, should their choice of regime be treated as somehow less binding than that of a couple who wanted to adopt some other regime and therefore had to enter into an antenuptial contract in order to ensure that it applied to their marriage?

---

[17] Batiffol and Lagarde, *Droit International Privé* (7th edn, 1981–1983), vol II, sect 619; Planiol and Ripert, *Traité Pratique de Droit Civil Français* (2nd edn, 1957), vol VIII, sect 8 (pp 28–31).

For all these reasons, the mutability or immutability of the matrimonial regime should not depend on whether or not there was an antenuptial contract, express or implied. Since this is the only basis on which *De Nicols v Curlier* can be reconciled with the mutability theory, one must conclude that the immutability theory represents English law.

This is the view that Dicey himself took in the second edition of his book, which was published in 1908.[18] In the third edition, however, the Kekewich theory was adopted. This edition was under the joint authorship of Dicey and Berriedale Keith; it was published in 1922, a few days before Dicey's death at the age of 87. It is reasonable to assume that Berriedale Keith was responsible for the change. One can only speculate why he might have made it, but he may have felt that the English system of separate property was better than the civil law system and wanted to make it applicable to foreign couples who immigrated to England. Whether this was justifiable at the time is a matter on which opinions might differ. In *De Nicols v Curlier* itself immutability produced a fairer result: the wife had made a significant contribution to the success of the business[19] and it was reasonable that she should have had a share in the proceeds.[20]

The conclusion to be drawn from the above discussion is that, unless and until the House of Lords reverses its decision in *De Nicols v Curlier*, English courts are bound by authority to accept the immutability doctrine.[21]

Immovables

The other leading authority, *Welch v Tennent*,[22] was decided by the House of Lords in 1891 on appeal from Scotland. The parties were domiciled in Scotland. Before the marriage, which was without a contract and took place in 1877, the wife had owned immovables in England. After the marriage, she sold

---

[18] Rule 175(2) and pp 639–641 and 837.

[19] See the judgment of Lord Brampton at 38.

[20] In the 12th edition, Dicey and Morris reverted to the immutability theory: the author of the present essay was responsible for this change. This has been retained in the current (13th) edition when Mr Adrian Briggs took over responsibility: see Rule 148.

[21] This is the main theory on the Continent, though Switzerland is an exception. It is also the theory in South Africa. The United States, on the other hand, follows the mutability doctrine, though it does so in a modified form: if the parties change their domicile, the old law applies to property acquired before the change and to property acquired (after the change) with the proceeds of such property; the new law applies to other property.

[22] [1891] AC 639.

the immovables and the proceeds were paid to the husband. The parties subsequently separated and the wife claimed that, under Scottish law, she was entitled to reclaim the proceeds of the sale of the immovables. The House of Lords held, however, that the rights of the parties in the English immovables were governed by English law, as the *lex situs*; so the wife's claim failed.

This case stands for the proposition that matrimonial property rights in immovables are governed by the *lex situs*. The only way in which *Re De Nicols (No 2)* can be reconciled with it would appear to be on the basis of the theory put forward by Kekewich J in the case, namely the distinction between the situation where there is an express or implied antenuptial contract and where there is not. However, this distinction has already been rejected where movables are involved, and there is no logical reason why it should be accepted in the case of immovables. If the two cases cannot be reconciled, one has to choose between them. Since *Welch v Tennent* was an appeal from Scotland it is not, strictly speaking, binding on English courts, though it is strongly persuasive. It would, therefore, be possible for an English court not to follow it. In view of this, one can consider the two positions on their merits.

Should the law of the domicile or the *lex situs* determine the matrimonial property regime of the parties with regard to immovables? As we shall see below, there are good reasons why the *lex situs* should apply with regard to rules specifically applicable to the matrimonial home. There are also good reasons why it should apply where the rights of third parties are in issue. Where this is not the case, however, there is good reason why the matrimonial property regime of the parties should be different with regard to land owned by them outside their domicile. If an English couple buy a villa in Spain, there is no reason why it should be subject to Spanish matrimonial property law. Likewise, if a Spanish couple buy a flat in London, they would be surprised to learn that English matrimonial property law applied to it. To have different matrimonial property regimes applicable to different items of property is extremely inconvenient. Put in more general terms, the justification for applying the law of the domicile is that it is likely to reflect the values, attitudes and expectations of the parties. There is no reason why this should be the case with regard to the *lex situs* of any particular piece of land owned by them.[23] It is suggested, therefore, that an English court should refuse to follow *Welch v Tennent*: the law of the domicile should apply to immovables as well.

---

[23] As we shall see, different considerations apply to the *lex situs* of the matrimonial home.

Conclusions

The above discussion of the leading authorities suggests that the law of the domicile at the time of the marriage should determine the matrimonial property regime of the couple. This should apply to immovables as well as to movables.

(3) Whose Domicile?

The leading cases clearly state that it is the husband's domicile, not the wife's, that is applicable. However, it is no longer acceptable for the law to discriminate on grounds of sex; so the automatic preference for the husband's domicile must be reconsidered. There are also legal reasons for this. All the relevant cases were decided before it was possible for a wife to have a domicile separate from that of her husband. Thus, if one regards the relevant time as being immediately after the marriage, the wife's domicile would necessarily have been the same as that of the husband. Today, this is no longer so.[24]

It is also possible to argue that such discrimination is contrary to the European Convention on Human Rights. Article 14 of the Convention provides that the rights set forth in it must be secured without discrimination on grounds of sex, and Article 1 of the first Protocol provides for the protection of property. If one reads these two provisions together, one could argue that it is contrary to the Convention for a legal rule to determine matrimonial property rights by the law of the domicile of the husband alone.[25]

Taken together, these considerations make it justifiable to suggest that the existing case law should no longer be followed. Equal weight should be given to the domicile of *each* party. If the parties are domiciled in the same country at the time of the marriage, there will be no problem. If they are domiciled in different countries, one should look at all relevant factors in order to decide where the centre of gravity of the marriage lies. This should not be done mechanically. The purpose is to ascertain the legal system that the parties might reasonably

---

[24] Since 1 January 1974, the date on which section 1(1) of the Domicile and Matrimonial Proceedings Act 1973 came into force, it has been possible for a wife to have a separate domicile.

[25] The European Convention on Human Rights was given limited effect in UK law by the Human Rights Act 1998. Whether it has any direct effect on private law rights is controversial: see Wade, *Human Rights and the Judiciary* (Judicial Studies Board Annual Lecture for 1998), arguing that it does, and Buxton, 'The Human Rights Act and Private Law' 2000 (116) LQR 48, arguing that it does not. For a rejoinder, see Wade, 'Horizons of Horizontality' 2000 (116) LQR 217.

have expected to apply, equal weight being given to the expectations of both parties. Since we are assuming at this point in the discussion that there is no express or implied choice of law, this test must be applied objectively. Which country's legal system would a reasonable man or woman in the position of the parties have expected to apply? Henceforth, we will use the term 'matrimonial domicile' to indicate that country. We can, therefore, refine the statement of law made above by saying that the matrimonial property rights of the parties depend on the matrimonial domicile at the time of the marriage. Although this makes the law less certain, a degree of uncertainty cannot be avoided if the wife is to be given equal rights.

(4) The Role of Intention

In determining the matrimonial domicile, should one consider only the circumstances existing at the time of marriage, or should one also consider where the parties intend to establish their home after the marriage? The latter view, usually called the matrimonial home theory, has been championed by Cheshire and was linked to his theory regarding capacity to marry. It has the advantage of looking to the future, rather than to the past; however, it introduces a further element of uncertainty: what if the parties never actually carry out their intention? For this reason (in part), it has been rejected by the Appellate Division of the Supreme Court of South Africa (the highest court in that country) and by the High Court in England.

The South African case was *Frankel's Estate v The Master*,[26] a case in which the husband was domiciled in Germany and the wife in what was then Czechoslovakia. At the time of the marriage, they intended to establish their home in South Africa and did so four months later. Nevertheless, the Appellate Division held that their matrimonial property regime was determined by the law of Germany, the domicile of the husband at the time of marriage, not by that of South Africa, their intended matrimonial home.

The English case is *In re Egerton's Will Trusts*.[27] At the time of the marriage, the husband was domiciled in England and the wife in France, but they intended to settle in France after the marriage and did so two years later. In his judgment, Roxburgh J contrasted the view of Morris, the editor for many years of *Dicey and Morris*, with that of Cheshire. Morris preferred the actual domicile of the

---

[26] 1950 (1) SA 220.
[27] [1956] Ch 593.

husband[28] at the time of the marriage, except perhaps in a 'clear case' where they change their domicile very shortly after the marriage in pursuance of a pre-matrimonial intention to that effect.[29] Cheshire, on the other hand, considered that the law of the intended matrimonial home should apply.[30] Roxburgh J rejected Cheshire's view and preferred that of Morris. He held that English law applied.

These two cases establish that the intended matrimonial home has no general role to play. In both of them, however, the husband and wife were domiciled in different countries before the marriage. In both, the court automatically chose the husband's domicile. No consideration was given to the wife's domicile, the only question being whether the intended future domicile should replace the husband's domicile at the time of the marriage.

We said above that where the parties are domiciled in different countries, we must look to other factors to determine the matrimonial domicile. Should the intended matrimonial home have a role to play here? Surely it should if, as was the case in *In re Egerton's Will Trusts*, the parties intended to establish their home in the country in which one of them is domiciled. It is hard to think of a more decisive factor to tip the balance. If a French woman marries an English man and they agree to live in France, it is reasonable, in the absence of countervailing factors, to conclude that the matrimonial domicile is France. It is suggested, therefore, that if *In re Egerton's Will Trusts* were to come before the courts today, it should be decided in favour of French law.

The position is more difficult where, as in *Frankel's Estate v The Master*, the parties are domiciled in different countries, but do not intend to settle in either of them. Where the intended matrimonial home is neutral as between the two domiciles, it is much less likely to be decisive. There may be situations in which, as between the three countries in question, the intended home has the strongest claim, but this would be rare. It could be argued that, in *Frankel's Estate v The Master*, the parties intended to shake off the dust of both Germany and Czechoslovakia, and make a new life for themselves in South Africa. The year was 1933, when Hitler first came to power. However, even if they detested the philosophy of the Nazis, that does not mean that they rejected German

---

[28] Roxburgh J said (at 600) that it was 'indisputable law' that the wife's domicile was irrelevant.

[29] Dicey's *Conflict of Laws* (6th edn, 1949), p 541.

[30] G C Cheshire, *Private International Law* (4th edn, 1952), pp 491 et seq.

matrimonial property law. At the time, German law provided for a system of separate property, with the husband having certain powers of management over the wife's assets. There was nothing Nazi about this. It was based on social conceptions prevalent in Germany at the time. It originated in the German Civil Code of 1896 and remained unchanged throughout the Nazi period. It is surely more likely that the parties expected German or Czech law to apply than South African law, a system about which they probably knew nothing and which provided for an extreme form of community of property.

If the parties had been living in South Africa at the time of the marriage, they would almost certainly have entered into an antenuptial contract providing for separate property. This was normal for middle-class South Africans at the time. If they had consulted a lawyer, they would have been advised to do so. The matrimonial home theory would, therefore, have had the paradoxical result that the parties would have been saddled with a matrimonial property regime radically different from what they would have chosen if they had been domiciled in South Africa all along. For these reasons, the court was surely right in rejecting the application of South African law.

One can conclude, therefore, that, where the parties are domiciled in different countries at the time of the marriage and intend to establish their future home in one of those countries, their intention to do so may well tip the balance in favour of that country; in other cases, however, it will not normally be decisive.

(5) Antenuptial Contracts

The discussion so far has proceeded on the assumption that the parties did not enter into a contract before marriage specifying the matrimonial property regime they desired. There can be little doubt, however, that, in the absence of an express or implied agreement as to the applicable law, the law of the matrimonial domicile must determine the validity and effect of such a contract.[31]

(6) Choice of Law by Agreement

The next question is whether the parties can choose the applicable law by agreement. Where they enter into an antenuptial contract to choose the matrimonial property regime under which they wish to be married, there is no reason why

---

[31] See Dicey and Morris, *The Conflict of Laws* (13th edn, 2000), Rule 149(2) and the authorities cited in n 39.

they should not be able to choose the law to govern it.[32] An express choice of law would be rare, but it should often be possible to find an implied choice. Many legal systems lay down special formalities for such a contract—for example, it may have to be entered into before a notary—and if the parties choose the formalities of a particular legal system, they could normally be regarded as having intended that legal system to govern.

Can the parties choose the applicable law, even if they do not enter into an antenuptial contract? It is hard to imagine they would expressly choose the governing law without also choosing a particular matrimonial property regime, but if they did so, there is no reason why effect should not be given to it. Should an implied choice have such an effect? According to Roxburgh J in *In re Egerton's Will Trusts*, it should. Though he was unwilling to regard the parties' intention as to their future matrimonial home as indicating the applicable law, he would have been willing to uphold a 'tacit' contract as to the applicable law.[33]

Although this may be right in principle, the two examples he gave were, to say the least, hard to understand. The first was of two 'comparatively poor persons': the woman has a few national savings certificates and the man is a weekly wage earner. They decide to emigrate to Australia as soon as they are married and carry out this intention. In such a case, he said, a court might well infer that they intended their matrimonial property rights to be governed by the law of Australia. The second example was of an elderly and wealthy widower who marries a young wife. They decide to emigrate to South Africa, because of its warm climate, and do so immediately after marriage. Roxburgh J said that he could not imagine that any court would ever infer that they intended their matrimonial property rights to be governed by South African law. Although he did not explain why this should be so, the clear implication is that the elderly and wealthy husband would not want a legal system to apply that would allow his young wife to get her hands on his money. It need hardly be said that it is wrong for a court to indulge in speculation of this kind. It is suggested, therefore, that, in the absence of an antenuptial contract choosing the matrimonial property regime, the court should not hold that there is an implied choice of law unless it is clear that the parties actually considered the matter and were in agreement as to the applicable law.

---

[32] See Dicey and Morris, Rule 149(3) and the authorities cited in n 40.
[33] The evidence before him did not disclose the existence of any such contract.

B. Modern Matrimonial Property Rights

Up to now, we have been assuming that matrimonial property rights of the traditional kind have been in issue. These were focused on the effects of marriage on the ownership of property. The issue was whether one spouse became co-owner of some or all of the property that had previously belonged to the other. Today, this focus has become less sharp and there has to some extent been a bridging of the gap between community of property and separation. The dividing line between matrimonial property and maintenance (alimony) has also been blurred.

One of the major developments in the civil law has been the deferred community, a system largely pioneered in Scandinavia.[34] The basic principle is that the spouses keep their own property while the marriage subsists, but when it is terminated by death, divorce, or otherwise, their property is pooled and divided out equally.[35] The advantage of this is that it gives the economically weaker party a share in the other's success while avoiding the management problems that result from joint ownership. In principle, neither party has a property right in the other's assets until the marriage is terminated. Each can deal with his or her property without the consent of the other.[36]

If the relevant rules are fairly precise and if the community comes into existence more or less automatically on termination of the marriage, this could still be regarded as a matrimonial property system. As such, the law of the matrimonial domicile should be applied, even to immovable property. A more difficult question is whether the special features of the system make it appropriate to apply the matrimonial domicile at the date of termination of the marriage, rather than at the date of its celebration. In favour of the former, it could be argued that the parties' rights crystallize only on termination. However, the idea behind this system is that each party has some sort of right with regard to the other's property from the very beginning. The wife might have given up her career to look after the children on this understanding. In such a case, it might seem unfair that her rights could be defeated by a change of domicile.

---

[34] For a general discussion, see *International Encyclopedia of Comparative Law* (1971–), vol IV, Chap 4, pp 138 et seq (1980).

[35] This may be limited to property acquired during the marriage. If the marriage is of short duration, redistribution may be correspondingly limited.

[36] There may be exceptions: for example, the other spouse's consent may be required for transfers of immovable property. Moreover, if a party squanders his or her property, the other party may be able to obtain a court order.

In common law countries, the courts now have wide powers to transfer assets from one spouse to the other when the marriage is terminated by a decree of divorce or nullity. In some cases, the end result may be little different from that under a system of deferred community. However, the principle is different.[37] Such redistribution requires a court order; the court enjoys wide discretion; a matrimonial property contract may be disregarded; and the needs, resources and behaviour of the spouses are major considerations. At this point, we have crossed the line between matrimonial property and maintenance.[38] The *lex fori* is the applicable law.[39]

A spouse's right under English law to occupy the matrimonial home, originally granted by the Family Law Act 1996, is a property right since, if registered, it binds purchasers. It should, however, be regarded as an exception to the rule that matrimonial property rights, even over immovables, are governed by the law of the matrimonial domicile. The *lex situs* should be applicable. Any other solution would be impractical, since rights in foreign land could not be registered under the Act. Moreover, the matrimonial home is different from other immovable property, since, by its very nature, it is indicative of a significant link between the spouses and the country in which the property is situated. Thus, if a couple come to England for a limited period—for example, five years—and, therefore, retain their domicile in a foreign country, this fact should not prevent the wife from acquiring rights in the matrimonial home in England.

C. Third Parties

So far, we have been considering the situation where one spouse has a claim against the other, or where a third party, usually a child, has a claim against one spouse through the other—for example, where a child succeeds to the estate of the wife and claims that this consists of half the joint assets of both parties. This

---

[37] *International Encyclopedia of Comparative Law*, Vol IV, Chap 4, pp 130–131.

[38] In Case C-220/95 *Van den Boogaard v Laumen* [1997] ECR I-1172, the European Court had to distinguish between maintenance and matrimonial property for the purpose of Art 1(1) of the Brussels Convention. It concluded that if a court order for the transfer of property is designed to enable a spouse to provide for himself or herself, or if the needs and resources of each of the spouses are taken into consideration, the order is to be regarded as concerning maintenance (para 22 of the judgment).

[39] See Dicey and Morris, Rule 86(7) and the authorities cited in n 63. For a partial exception (foreign maintenance orders), see ibid, para 18–195.

has been the issue in all the decided cases. Now we must consider the position where the rights of third parties are involved.

One situation in which this could occur is where one spouse sells property to a third party, and the other spouse claims that the third party has not obtained a good title for some reason based on matrimonial property law—for example, because the property was jointly owned and could not be sold without the consent of both spouses. A second situation is where a creditor obtains a judgment against one spouse, or claims against the bankrupt estate of one spouse, and the other spouse claims that, for reasons of matrimonial property law, assets which appear to belong to the debtor are not in fact available to the creditors. The question is: which law decides the matrimonial property rights of the spouses when these are asserted against third parties?

To make the problem clearer we will give an example:

> At the time of their marriage H and W, both Shiite Muslims, are domiciled in Iraq. They marry there according to Shiite Muslim law, as applied in Iraq at the time. They subsequently become domiciled in England, where H builds up a business empire. He amasses a great deal of property, both movable and immovable, all in his name alone. He then goes bankrupt. His creditors claim that all the property in his name is available to satisfy his debts, but his wife says that their matrimonial property regime is governed by Shiite Islamic law, under which half of his assets belong to her. She says that these assets are not available to his creditors.

Is this a good argument, assuming that she can prove the foreign law?

Surely, it is not. As between husband and wife, the law of the matrimonial domicile at the time of marriage is an appropriate system because, as explained above, it is most likely to be the system under which they married. It gives effect to their expectations. For this reason it is fair to apply it to disputes between them. However, where third parties are involved the position is entirely different. There is no way in which it can be said that the application of that law upholds the reasonable expectations of the creditors when they decide to do business with the husband. How could they even know where the husband and wife were domiciled when they married? Even if, contrary to what was argued above, one took the view that the applicable law changes with each change of domicile, it would still be difficult for persons doing business with the husband to know where he and his wife were domiciled. Are they to be suspicious of everyone with a foreign accent or appearance? Must they then check on their domicile and determine under what matrimonial property regime they were married? That would be absurd.

The position is the same where the husband sells property that appears to belong to him. If the purchaser were bound by the matrimonial property rights of the wife, as laid down by the law of the matrimonial domicile at the time of marriage, he would again be faced with an impossible task in checking whether the husband can give him a good title. This would make it very difficult for people of foreign appearance to sell their movable or immovable property and could well cause racial prejudice in the housing market. Yet this would be the result if the rules proposed earlier in this essay were applied to third parties.

The solution is to apply the *lex situs* to determine the matrimonial property regime of the spouses, with regard to both movables and immovables, when the rights of third parties are involved. It might be thought wrong to apply different choice-of-law rules to decide the same issue, depending on the parties involved. However, this is the only way in which justice can be done both to the spouses and to third parties. Of course, this means that the rights of one spouse could be defeated if a third party claims an interest in the property—for example, if a couple married in community of property invest their joint money in foreign land and register that land in the name of one spouse only. However, many authorities maintain that, even as between the spouses, the *lex situs* should determine matrimonial property rights in land. This was rejected above except in the special case of rights that apply specifically to the matrimonial home. However, the rejection of the *lex situs* is possible only if it is restricted to disputes between the spouses. Where third parties are involved, the *lex situs* must be applied. The arguments in favour of the *lex situs* are just as strong when items of movable property—for example, securities—are concerned.[40] There too, third parties should not be required to make inquiries as to the domicile of the parties.

D. Summary

1. Matrimonial property rights are property rights resulting from marriage. Rights created by a court order on termination of a marriage are not matrimonial property rights if the court had extensive discretion in making

---

[40] This appears to be the position in the United States. There, the *lex situs* applies to immovables, even as between the spouses. In the case of movables, the law of the domicile normally applies as between the spouses, but the *lex situs* applies where the interests of third parties are concerned: see *Restatement Second, Conflict of Laws* (1971), Vol II, § 258, Comment *h* (p 112) and § 259, Comment *c* (p 114).

the order and if it was entitled to take into account the needs, resources and behaviour of the parties.

2. In proceedings between a husband and wife, or between a third party claiming through one spouse against the other, the following rules apply to determine the law governing the matrimonial property rights of the spouses—

   (a) Unless the parties have agreed on the law to be applied, the applicable law is that of the matrimonial domicile at the time of marriage.

   (b) The matrimonial domicile is the country with which the parties and the marriage are most closely connected, equal weight being given to the connections of each party. Where both parties are domiciled in the same country, this will normally be the matrimonial domicile. If they are domiciled in different countries, but intend to settle in one of them after the marriage, that country will normally be the matrimonial domicile.

   (c) Changes of domicile after the celebration of the marriage have no effect on the matrimonial property regime of the parties.

   (d) If the parties enter into an antenuptial contract, the law of the matrimonial domicile determines the validity of that contract.

   (e) Where there is an antenuptial contract, or even where there is no such contract, the parties may choose the applicable law by agreement. Such agreement may be express or implied, but, in the latter case, it must be clear that the parties considered the matter and were in agreement.

   (f) The above rules apply to both movable and immovable property, except that the *lex situs* governs matrimonial property rights that apply specifically to the matrimonial home.

3. In proceedings in which the rights of third parties are involved (other than where a third party claims through one spouse against the other), the *lex situs* determines the matrimonial property rights of the parties with regard to both movable and immovable property.

10

ON SOME WRITERS ON THE CONFLICT OF LAWS OF CONTRACTS

Ole Lando*

This article is about some writers on the conflict of laws of contracts. Most of them published their works between 1930 and 1960. The authors to be mentioned impressed me and influenced my writings.

I am a Dane, born in 1922. I took my Danish law degree in 1947. Since 1951 I have been writing about and teaching conflict of laws and comparative law. I still do it.

One day in the summer of 1944, when I lived in Sweden as a refugee, I saw in a law library an English book by G C Cheshire called *Private International Law*. I took it from the shelf and looked into it. It was about how English courts dealt with cases having a foreign element. It described these cases. One was about a Moslem who came from the Near East to London with his three wives. How did the courts react to such a ménage in a country where husbands had to content themselves with one wife? Another case was about two Englishmen who had made a contract for the smuggling of spirits into the United States during

* Professor of International and Comparative Law, Copenhagen Business School.

the time of prohibition. Was this contract enforceable? Both the cases and the way in which the author analysed them interested me. I also liked the subject.

Why? In the preface to the first edition of *Private International Law* Cheshire described his fascination with the subject,[1] '. . . of all the departments of English law, Private International Law offers the freest scope to the mere jurist'. Arthur Nussbaum, a German scholar now living in the United States[2] quoted the English writer Baty: 'There is a sweep and range in it which is almost lyric in its completeness . . . It is the fugal music of law'. Nussbaum also mentioned one of Germany's most brilliant authors on Private International Law, Franz Kahn, who published articles on the subject around 1900. Kahn did not hold any academic position nor did he ever act as judge in a lawsuit. Financially independent, he chose Private International Law as an avocation as others may choose philosophy or history. 'Such a thing', Nussbaum wrote, 'is unlikely among writers on procedure or real property'. He also mentioned its cosmopolitan trait, 'the world wide outlook, which it imports, and the international character of research and thought. The student feels himself, as it were, a member of an international community of learning. Frequently he will have to examine foreign legal ideas and will thereby obtain insight in the variety of and interplay of heterogeneous legal concepts and ideas all over the world'.[3]

In the fifties I began to prepare a thesis on the Conflict of Laws of Contracts.[4] The primary purpose was to suggest methods and rules to be adopted by the Danish courts. At that time there were few reported Danish cases on the subject and relatively little literature. Many issues were unsolved. In forming my view on what law is I was influenced by the Nordic realists. With some qualifications they agreed with the American justice Oliver Wendell Holmes, who had said the following: 'The prophecies of what the courts will do and nothing more pretentious are what we understand by law. In making the prophecy the lawyers are guided by the sources of inspiration which guide the courts, ie the statutes, customs, precedents, doctrine and the values, attitudes

---

[1] Preface to the first edition of Cheshire, *Private International Law* (1935), here quoted from Cheshire and North, *Private International Law* (19th edn, 1999), p v.

[2] Arthur Nussbaum, *Principles of Private International Law* (New York, 1943), preface.

[3] ibid.

[4] Kontraktstatuttet, (the law governing the contract) Copenhagen 1962. Later presentations of the subject are to be found in *The International Encyclopaedia of Comparative Law*, Vol III, Private International Law, Chap 24, Contracts (1976) and in Lando, 'The Conflict of Laws of Contracts, General Principles' (1987) 189 *Recueil des cours de l'académie de droit international* 225–447.

and ideals which govern a people and its judges. Bad laws and wicked laws are also law'.

However, a realistic view on what the law is does not prevent you from having an idealistic view as to how the law should be. Like several young colleagues I saw the choice-of-law rule as a means to achieve universal justice in the world of private law. The substantive laws of the countries were different, and we did not then consider whether this could be otherwise. Justice had to be established by way of choice-of-law rules. The ideal choice-of-law rule was an 'all-sided' one, which, based on certain criteria, gave foreign law the same scope of application as the law of the *forum*. We were 'universalists'. In a world that recently had been tormented by war, and now had established the United Nations to restore peace and justice on earth, universal choice-of-law rules would be a contribution to universal justice. The problems were, however, complicated. From the reported cases we could see that the situations containing foreign elements were manifold and complex. However, we believed that the refined techniques and stringent logic of the choice-of-law rules could solve the problems.

I spent the year 1955–1956 in the United States at the University of Michigan Law School in Ann Arbor. In addition to the American material on private international law the library held the literature and law reports of England, France, Germany, Italy and Switzerland. The books had been collected for Ernst Rabel who had prepared his four-volume work on the *Conflict of Laws, A Comparative Study*[5] in Ann Arbor. During my stay in Michigan professor Hessel E Yntema helped me generously, discussed my plans and read some of my first drafts.

A. The Early Writers

The early authors had shaped the modern ones, the modern authors stood on their shoulders so to speak. I had to give a short account of what they had written. However, not being a historian I had no profound knowledge of the society and ideology of the past, and I think that my description of the ancient writers came to suffer because of that.

---

[5] After Rabel's death in 1954 a second edition was prepared: see now Ernst Rabel, *The Conflict of Laws, a Comparative Study* (2nd edn) Vol I (1958), Vol II (1960), Vol III (1964). Vol IV (1950) never appeared in a second edition.

The glossators and post-glossators from the twelfth till the fourteenth century founded private international law as a science. They would apply the law of the place of contracting to contracts. The Frenchman Dumoulin from the sixteenth century had the merit of showing that the place of contracting could be fortuitous. If a man from Tübingen while on passage in Italy there sells his house in Tübingen you should apply the law of Tübingen and not that of the place of contracting. Ulrich Huber advanced the territoriality principle, a principle which has led to good and to bad rules. He based the application of foreign law on *comity,* a concept which arouses an association of courtesy, based on reciprocity. It is unclear what it means, but it is still invoked in some of the common law courts.[6]

Friedrich Carl von Savigny who in 1849 published Volume 8 of *System des heutigen römischen Rechts* pointed to the existence of an international community of nations having intercourse with one another. The more this intercourse expands the more desirable is it that in cases containing foreign elements the same legal relations may expect the same decision whether the judgment be pronounced in this state or that.[7] This is not comity but it brings benefits to all concerned, both individuals and states. Von Savigny was a universalist. He wanted the courts all over the world to 'ascertain for every legal relationship that law to which in its proper nature it belongs or is subject where it has its 'seat'.[8] This is an important principle even today.

Von Savigny had a considerable influence on the German courts and on courts in other countries. However, some of his reasoning was conceptual, and the application of some of the rules he advocated led to practical difficulties.

It is interesting to note how the legal arguments changed from the old to the modern authors. This may be illustrated by comparing the arguments which in 1849 von Savigny and in 1938 Henri Batiffol put forward in support of applying the law of the place of performance as the law applicable to contractual obligations.

Von Savigny argued that it was in the nature of the obligation that its seat must be at the place of performance. The obligation, he said, consists of an invisible relationship between two persons, in one of them it is an extension of his freedom,

---

[6] See Cheshire and North, above n 1, p 5.
[7] Friedrich Carl von Savigny, *System des heutigen römischen Rechts* Vol 8 (1849) §348, p 27.
[8] ibid, §348, p 28.

in the other it is a limitation of his freedom. For the creditor the obligation means power, for the debtor it means dependence. In determining the seat of the obligation one should have regard to the situation of the debtor because it is in the nature of the obligation that the debtor has to perform an act. The act which before the conclusion of the contract was merely an option and uncertain becomes, when the contract is made, compulsory and certain. The expectation of both parties is now directed towards this necessity and certainty, the doing of the act, the performance of the obligation. Therefore the place of performance is the seat of the obligation.[9] In favour of this solution von Savigny also invoked sources in Roman law.

When each of the parties to a contract has to perform in a different country two legal systems will apply to the contract. This von Savigny said, is in accordance with Roman law where a contract of sale was often concluded through two separate stipulations.[10] He succeeded in convincing the Germans to adopt this splitting. The courts practised it in many cases, and it led to strange and often inconsistent results.[11] In 1986 the Germans abandoned it in favour of the rules of the Rome Convention on the Law Applicable to Contractual Obligations (hereinafter the Rome Convention).

Batiffol agreed with von Savigny that the expectations of the parties are directed towards the fulfilment of the obligations, and that the fulfilment will occur at the place of performance. In the life of the contract the economically important part is its performance. It is not only the parties whose attention is directed to the place of performance, it is also there that third parties experience it. Where governmental interests are involved they are to be found at the place where the contract would manifest itself to the outer world.[12] His arguments savoured more of social realities than von Savigny's speculations on the 'nature' of the obligation.

Batiffol held von Savigny's idea of splitting the contract into two laws to be '*évidemment mauvaise*'. A choice of one was necessary and for this reason he chose the place of the performance of the principal, also called the characteristic obligation.[13] This is the one of the two parties' obligations which is paid for,

---

[9] ibid, § 369 p 201 and § 270, p 205.
[10] ibid, p 202.
[11] See Nussbaum, *Deutsches internationales Privatrecht* (Berlin 1932), p 218ff.
[12] Henri Batiffol, *Les Conflits de lois en matière de contrats, Étude de droit international privé comparé* (Paris, 1938) 86ff.
[13] See Art 4(2) of the Rome Convention on the Law Applicable to Contractual Obligations, which establishes a presumption in favour of the law of the place of business of the party who has to perform the characteristic obligation.

the thing or the right which is sold or leased, the service provided or the cover for a risk, etc.

B. Importance of the Case Law

Another change of attitude which occurred in the twentieth century dealt with the importance of the case law. Some of the earlier Continental professors had openly showed their contempt for the jurisprudence of the courts. In his famous text book on criminal law from 1810 the Austrian professor Anselm Feurbach had written: 'The author thinks that he has acted wisely in not entirely passing over the judicial decisions much though he hates that cushion of literary indolence, that support of blind arbitrariness.'[14] In a foreword to a textbook on private international law published in the early years of the twentieth century the Swedish professor Reuterskiöld confessed that he had not paid much heed to the court decisions. He had only used them as illustrations. The legal writing, he said, should be given at least the same rank as the decisions. In reality the latter were only a more or less correct application of the doctrine.[15] Before the First World War and even for some time after many Continental writers ignored the cases.

However, several Continental authors writing after the First World War began to study and to invoke the cases. The German writer Arthur Nussbaum[16] and the French writer Henri Batiffol[17] did so. Both felt it necessary to explain *why* they paid attention to the cases.

The court decision, Nussbaum said, 'is in fact more important than doctrine or principle. When deciding a case the judge feels his responsibility for the living individuals before him whom his judgment will affect economically and often also mentally. The problems of the case force themselves upon him with the power of the direct and immediate experience. The response which his sense of justice will give to this challenge will often lead the judge to the right result even though he does not arrive at a cognition of the pertinent arguments'.[18]

---

[14] Here quoted from Martin Wolf, *Private International Law* (2nd edn, Oxford, 1950), p 33.
[15] C A Reuterskiöld, *Handbok i svensk privat internationell rätt* (Stockholm, 1907), Preface.
[16] Arthur Nussbaum, *Deutsches Internationales Privatrecht* (Berlin, 1932).
[17] Henri Batiffol, above n 12, 81–103.
[18] Arthur Nussbaum, above n 16 in the Preface.

The last sentence reveals a feeling of superiority which may still be found among Continental University professors. Arthur Nussbaum was then a professor at the prestigious university in Berlin. In Nussbaum's mind the feeling of superiority was mixed with respect for the inarticulate judges' intuitive sense of justice.

Henri Batiffol was younger than Nussbaum and more modest. He had studied in the United States, and with Ernst Rabel in Berlin, and he was influenced by the case oriented common law writers and by the comparative method which Rabel advocated and applied. In his book from 1938 *Les Conflits de Lois en Matière de Contrats*, with the subtitle *Étude de droit international privé comparé*[19] Batiffol argued—and also showed—that a careful study of the case law of the United States, England, Germany, Italy, Switzerland and France would give the reader a better understanding of the problems than he would get by reading the theories of the authors. Like the common lawyers Henri Batiffol explained the positions of the courts and showed the trends. I admired Batiffol's comparative survey and analysis of cases. In my thesis I adopted the same approach.

C. Party Autonomy

On the freedom of the parties to choose the law applicable to the contract there was in the beginning of the twentieth century a real split between the Continental writers and the courts. The professors were against it. *La loi s'impose elle n'est pas choisie,* the law is a mandate, it is not to be chosen. The courts in England, France, and Germany did not follow the professors. In both decisions and dicta they gave effect to the choice of law by the parties and they even invoked the presumed intention of the parties.

Nussbaum would give effect to the parties' express choice of law. Since most of the substantive contract law consists of non-mandatory rules a conflict between rules of the chosen law and mandatory rules of the law which would have applied in the absence of the parties' choice seldom arose in practice. The conflicts that occurred were between the rules of the proper law of the contract and the public policy of the law of the forum, whether the parties had chosen that law or not. In these cases public policy should prevail.[20] When the parties had

---

19 Batiffol, above n 12, p 2.
20 Arthur Nussbaum, above n 16, p 215.

not made an express or tacit choice of law that law shall apply with which the contract has its closest contact and not that which the parties were presumed to have intended.[21] He was critical of the German courts' application of the presumed intention of the parties or the law of the place of performance. To determine the law of the closest contact he pointed to a number of presumptions for specific contracts and typical situations.[22] In some cases, notably after 1945, the German courts adopted his 'centre of gravity' approach and Nussbaum's presumptions even before the Rome Convention was enacted.[23]

It is a Continental tradition that in order to justify his existence a young academic writer must advance a theory. Being a Continental scholar Batiffol advanced a theory. In the case material he claimed to have discerned a common trend on which he could build a theory on the autonomy of the parties, which as mentioned, had divided the writers and the courts. He agreed with the French writers that the parties could not choose the law applicable to the contract. However, they could select the connecting factors, the place of contracting and notably the place of performance of the contract. In doing so and in pointing to the law that they wanted to apply the parties could *localize* the contract in a certain country and thereby indirectly influence the law applicable. Although he did not support the parties' freedom to choose the law he called his doctrine a theory on *la loi d'autonomie*.

Batiffol's opposition to this freedom was based on the assumption that *la loi s'impose,* that there is always a legal system and a rule of that legal system which operates upon the parties' acts when they do them. I do not agree. In fact, no legal system operates upon an international contract until a court applies that system. It is the forum country that decides which system of law applies. Its conflict of law rule gives effect to the parties' choice of law. Nor do I believe in the localization theory. In some French cases the courts had upheld French parties' choice of English law in situations where the contract had little or no contact with England. It was not localized in England.[24] The courts' reason for doing so was that French interests were at stake. The parties' freedom to chose the law applicable to an international contract enhanced French business.

---

[21] Arthur Nussbaum, above , p 221ff.

[22] ibid, p 217ff

[23] See Lando, *Contracts, The International Encyclopaedia of Comparative Law*, Vol III, Chapter 24 (1977), p 126ff.

[24] For example, Cass, civ, 27 Jan 1931, S 1933, I 41. For England see *Vita Food Production Inc v Unus Shipping Co* [1939] AC 277, PC.

However, since Batiffol was ready to accept that the parties had localized the contract in the country the law of which they had chosen, his theory very seldom brought him in real conflict with the jurisprudence. It was a diplomatic *via media* between the view of the 'autonomist' courts and that of the 'anti-autonomist' writers.

As Batiffol did, I found interesting trends in the case material, but some of them were rather depressing for an idealistic universalist. In all the countries the homeward trend of the courts was conspicuous. For example, it was remarkable to notice the great regularity with which the courts in England, France, Germany, and other countries found by various methods that it was the law of the forum which was presumably intended by the parties. The law of the forum, however, was not applied in every case, and in many of the countries no rules or even presumptions were established. I found that unsatisfactory too. In the cases I could not see any basis for a global theory like the one on *la loi d'autonomie*.

However, as already mentioned, Batiffol's method and handling of the subject matter was admirable. I met him in Paris in 1956 and later. I was impressed by his unpretentious manners, his common sense, and his enormous working capacity. He was a good diplomat and at the same time a very ethical person.

D. Dicey and Cheshire

In England the decided cases were the authority. The judges made the law and the authors tried to distil the rules from the cases. In order to get some knowledge of the substantive English contract law I read some articles, and a book, Cheshire and Fifoot, *Law of Contract*. It was as illuminating and well written as Cheshire's *Private International Law*. I soon came to cherish those substantive contract rules, which had stood the test in the courts. On the other hand, I also learned how much the unwritten common law had been steered by the accidents of litigation. The English courts had not addressed some of the issues in contract, which on the Continent were considered to be important. There was no authority, as the English said. I noticed the modest and almost self-effacing way in which some English jurists made their suggestions': *It is respectfully submitted that . . .*'. However, in private international law the situation was different. As Cheshire had said, 'Private International Law offers the freest scope to the mere jurist'. And the courts listened to the jurists. As Lawrence Collins has said, 'In the English conflict of laws the courts have been influenced by the opinions of jurists . . . to a far greater extent than in most other subjects'.[25]

In the eighteenth and nineteenth centuries the writings of continental jurists such as Ulrich Huber, and Carl Friedrich von Savigny were studied by the English judges. When in 1896 Albert Venn Dicey published the first edition of the *Conflict of Laws* the great author in the common law world had been the American Joseph Story. His *Commentaries on the Conflict of Laws*[26] had influenced the English courts. Story knew but was not impressed by the lofty ideas of the continental writers, and he had studied the precedents in the United States and England.

After Story Dicey took over. During the major part of the 105 years Dicey's book has existed, ie, in Dicey's lifetime, and after J H C Morris assumed the general editorship in the 1940s and Lawrence Collins in the 1980s it has been a leading work on private international law in England. It gave and gives a loyal account of the English law and suggestions as to what the law should be where it was still unsettled. However, Dicey and his successors did not attack the decisions of the English courts. Although J H C Morris did not favour party autonomy, in the edition of Dicey and Morris for which he was responsible as editor and—in the chapter on contracts in general—also as author[27] he stated that 'when the intention of the parties to a contract . . . is expressed in words this expressed intention, in general, determines the proper law of the contract'.[28]

Cheshire did not see his task as being a subordinate annotator of the court decisions. In his book on *Private International Law* he wanted to 'approach the more controversial subjects in a spirit of constructive criticism'. On several points Cheshire proposed to change the law and to fill in the gaps. And he was influential.

Cheshire agreed with Batiffol on the question of party autonomy[29] but acknowledged that the courts gave effect to the choice of law by the parties. Like other English writers he was critical of the English courts' reliance on the presumed intention.[30] In fact he and his colleagues succeeded in persuading the

---

25 In Dicey and Morris, *The Conflict of Laws* (13th edn, 2000), para 1–017.
26 The first edition dates from 1834 and the last from 1883.
27 See 'The Proper Law of a Contract, A Reply' (1950) 3 ILQ 197ff.
28 See Dicey and Morris, *The Conflict of Laws* (9th edn, 1973), Rule 146, sub-rule 1, 728.
29 Cheshire, *Private International Law* (4th edn), p 200.
30 Cheshire, *Private International Law* (5th edn, Oxford, 1960), p 208.

English courts to replace the presumed intention by an objective method under which it is the contacts of the parties and the contract that determine the applicable law. This is also the approach taken by the Rome Convention, which is now in force in the United Kingdom.[31]

I regret that I never met G C Cheshire. He was an eminent writer. His style was lucid, engaging and unpretentious. In the preface to one of the editions of his *Private International Law* he noted how baffling and sobering it sometimes is to read what one has written some years earlier. In the preface to one of the last editions which he published alone he wrote that 'old age has many regrets'. I agree on both points.

It is fortunate that after his death Cheshire's *Private International Law* has appeared in numerous new editions prepared by Sir Peter North.

E. Ernst Rabel

In the first half of the twentieth century Ernst Rabel was the great comparatist. His work on the sale of goods, *Das Recht des Warenkaufs* [32] introduced the comparative method as a tool for legal integration, which many lawyers use today. He predicted future developments and started research and a movement, which eventually led to a world law for international sales,[33] and to the later attempts at establishing general principles of contract law for Europe[34] and for the World.[35]

Before him private international law had been a national science. Each country had its own conflict rules and the concepts used were those of the forum country. This approach is still found among writers. Rabel, however, argued that a primary purpose of private international law is to provide predictability. The parties to an international contract must know which law will apply, and for this reason that law must be the same law wherever a suit is brought.

---

[31] See now Cheshire and North, above n 1, Chap 18, p 533ff.

[32] Vol I (Berlin, 1936), Reprinted 1957, Vol II (Berlin and Tübingen, 1958).

[33] The United Nations Convention on Contracts for the International Sale of Goods 1980, now in force in almost sixty countries.

[34] See Lando and Beale (eds), *Principles of European Contract Law*, Parts I and II (The Hague, 1999), xlviii and 561.

[35] See The Unidroit Principles of International Commercial Contracts, (Rome 1994), xx and 256.

The private international law should be unified. However, if your wish to unify the law, you cannot determine the meaning of the legal concepts you use by the law of the forum. You must give them a new meaning on the basis of a comparative research. 'If we disengage the conflict of law rules from the fetters of the *lex fori* then the comparative research will adapt them to each other'. [36] In Europe of today the Court of Justice of the European Communities is regularly doing what Rabel had said. It does it when it interprets Community legislation and the rules of the Brussels Convention on Jurisdiction and the Enforcement of Judgments in Civil and Commercial matters, which is now a Regulation. The Court will do it when it begins to give rulings on the uniform choice of law rules governing contracts and torts.

Rabel knew that he was not above reproach. He once wrote that in their explorations on foreign territory comparatists will come upon natives lying in wait with their poisonous arrows.[37] It seems as if Ernst Rabel himself had felt some arrows. And they were in fact let off. I have met natives of more than one country who have told me that, although they considered Rabel to be a great scholar, you should not rely on what he wrote about the conflict of laws of *their* legal system. The words of a French colleague: '*Méfiez vous de Monsieur Rabel!*' still ring in my ears. I wonder how justified this criticism was. In most countries there are several opinions. For practical reasons Rabel could only give one view of the law of a country. The natives who had shot at Rabel often belonged to another school than the author that he had relied on.

Large parts of Rabel's comparative study on the *Conflict of Laws*[38] were about contracts. In this work I found a rich material and also support for the parties' freedom to chose the law. Their choice, he said, will 'obviate the unpredictable findings of unpredictable tribunals and consolidate the contract under one law while negotiation is in course'.[39] However, I could not use Rabel's method as I used that of Batiffol. Batiffol went through the important specific contracts, sales, loans, transport, employment, insurance, etc, and through all the issues in contract, from its formation till its end. As far as he could, he gave for each of the contracts and each of the issues in contract an account of the position of the courts of the legal systems he had chosen to examine. Rabel, who took in

---

[36] See (1931) 5 *Zeitschrift für ausländisches und internationales Privatrecht* 241, 267. See on Classification, Cheshire and North, above n 1, Chap 3, p 35ff.

[37] (1951) 16 *Rabels Zeitschrift für ausländisches und internationales Privatrecht* 341.

[38] Above n 5.

[39] *The Conflict of Laws* Vol. II (2nd edn, 1960), 365.

many more legal systems than Batiffol, could not do that. In my view his presentation was not as instructive and well systematized as that of Batiffol.

Among other influential Continental writers one should mention the Swiss author Adolf Schnitzer who proposed to establish a presumption in favour of the law of the domicile or place of business of the party who is to perform the characteristic obligation.[40] The Swiss courts adopted this approach which also became an important principle in the Rome Convention which is now in force in all the countries of the EU.[41]

F. The Honest Americans and Their Dilemma. Cavers, Currie, and the Other Modernists[42]

The American cases and the modern American writers came to influence my attitude towards the conflict of laws. They showed me that the conflict of laws was, and will always be, in a crisis.

As we have seen, the European rules of private international law rely on the contacts of the legal relationship to decide the applicable law. In the USA, this was also the approach until the middle of the twentieth century. As regards contracts the majority of the courts applied the law of the place of contracting or the law of the place of performance. In doing so they had acted under the influence of the Dutch writers of the seventeenth century, in particular Huber and Voet, of the earlier English cases and of the American authors such as Joseph Story and Joseph Beale who adhered to the principle of territoriality. The first Restatement on the Law of the Conflict of Laws (1934) of which Beale had been the reporter had split the contractual problems into two parts. The formation, the interpretation and the validity of the contract was governed by the law of the place of contracting; the performance of the contract was governed by the law of the place of performance. This was in accordance with the dictum of Justice Hunt in Scudder v Union Bank of Chicago[43] decided by the US Supreme Court in 1875. According to Beale's dogmatic and authoritative writings these were the rules which were to be followed and which at that time most of the courts claimed that they followed.[44]

---

40 Schnitzer, *Handbuch des internationalen Privatrechts I & II* (4th edn, Basle, 1957).
41 See Cheshire and North, above n 1, Chap 18, p 533ff.
42 For a survey of the theories of these authors see Cheshire and North, above n 1, Chap 2.
43 91 US 406, 412–413 (1875).
44 Joseph Beale, *A Treatise on the Conflict of Laws* I–III (New York, 1935). The conflict of laws of contracts was examined in Vol II.

It was David F Cavers who started the 'American Revolution'.[45] In an article in the Harvard Law Review from 1933 he questioned whether the rules advocated by Beale and others were in reality the rules which the courts followed. In a careful analysis of American cases he showed that the courts of the United States had not allowed the elements of contact alone to determine the applicable law. Very often they considered the results which the application of the various laws would produce. A certain connecting factor was relied on because it gave the court the opportunity to apply the law of the state or the country to which it pointed, but this was not in fact an automatic application of a choice of law rule.[46] It was a choice of what the court thought was ' the better law'.

Classical examples were the two cases *Scudder v Union Bank of Chicago* mentioned above, and *Hall v Cordell* decided by the US Supreme Court in 1891. In the first case, the respondent Scudder had promised to honour a bill of exchange, which the plaintiff had intended to draw upon him. The promise was made orally and was given in Illinois, the bill was payable in Missouri. Under the law of Missouri the oral promise was not binding, by the law of Illinois it was binding. In a passage, which became famous Justice Hunt said. ' Matters bearing upon the execution, the interpretation and the validity of a contract are determined by the law of the place of where the contract is made'.[47] As the question turned upon the execution of the promise which had been given in Illinois the contract was held to be valid. Sixteen years later the same issue came before the Court in *Hall v Cordell*; this time, however, the connecting factors were reversed; the promise was made in Missouri and the draft was payable in Illinois. Speaking for the Court Justice Harlan said:' Nothing in the case shows that the parties had in view, in respect to the execution of the contract, any other law than the law of the place of performance'.[48] And thus the oral promise was enforced.

This glaring contradiction as Beale rightly called it,[49] showed how covert techniques were used to uphold interstate transactions in order to save *bona fide* contracts from invalidity or to pursue other policies. In the coming years many American courts continued to do so.

---

[45] See Cheshire and North, above n 1, p 23ff.
[46] David F Cavers, 'A Critique of the Choice-of-Law Problem' (1933) 47 Harvard Law Review 197–208.
[47] 91 US 406, 412–413 (1875).
[48] 142 US 116, 120 (1891)
[49] Joseph Beale, *The Conflict of Laws* (1935), II 1079.

The courts sometimes found that by a happy coincidence the existing conflict rule promoted justice as in *Scudder*, but when it did not, they established another rule in its place, as they did in *Hall*. They pretended to ask the question: Which is the decisive connecting factor? However, they knew that the real question was which substantive rule do we prefer? The same phenomenon we find in Europe, but as true Europeans we tend to sweep it under the carpet. Cavers, however, openly expounded it and so did later American authors.[50]

Cavers showed that the existing choice of law rules were unfit for solving interstate and international disputes. He revealed a crisis, which the American doctrine has not yet, and, it is submitted, may never overcome. Cavers and his successors[51] made many of the American courts analyse the governmental interests behind the substantive rules of law and consider the outcome of the various laws in conflict. The successors of Cavers among the modernists included Brainred Currie.[52] Currie proposed that the courts should examine the policies behind the rules on substantive law which were in conflict and assess the interests which respective states showed in having their rules apply. If this examination revealed a 'true' conflict, the law of the forum should apply. Many courts followed suit.

Cavers had uncovered the truth about the American case law, and most of the things he said about it, the *lex foris* and the rule-selection techniques also applied to the European jurisprudence. However, the approaches and rules he and his contemporaries tried to establish instead were not the same. Currie wanted to apply the law of the forum and Cavers tried to establish some principles of preference for contracts and torts which did justice to the parties. An attempt to strike a compromise between the various American theories was made in the Restatement of the Conflict of Laws, Second which was published in 1971, and in the new Book IV from 1991 of the Louisiana Civil Code. They contain both an' *approach*' which takes after the theories of Cavers, Currie and other modern writers, and *choice-of-law rules* which resemble the traditional rules. § 6 of the Restatement gives the American court several options.[53] It can

---

[50] See Lando, *Contracts, The International Encyclopaedia of Comparative Law*, Vol III Chap 24 (1977), p 138 and passim.

[51] Currie, *Selected Essays on the Conflict of Laws* (1963).

[52] See *The International Encyclopaedia of Comparative Law*, Vol III Private International Law, Chapter 24, Contracts (1976) and Lando, 'The Conflict of Laws of Contracts, General Principles' (1987) 189 *Recueil des cours de l'académie de droit international* 225–447.

[53] The 'approach' laid down in § 6 of the Restatement is called 'Choice of Law Principles' §6 provides:

pick and choose, as it thinks fit. There is no hierarchy in the considerations provided in § 6 (2).

The methods and rules, which the American Revolution introduces, are complicated.[54] Under a rule selection technique the application in space of each substantive rule will be determined separately. Today the courts in many states apply various versions of this method, and some have retained the old rules. So far they have not been able to agree upon clear criteria for the result selection, and the confusion is widespread. Symeonides says that the American conflict of laws is still continuing 'its quest for maturity'.[55] Will it ever reach it?

The rules of the traditional theory, Currie said, 'have not worked and cannot be made to work . . . But the root of the trouble goes deeper. In attempting to use rules we encounter difficulties that stem, not from the fact that the particular rules are bad . . . but rather from the fact that we have such rules at all. We would be better off without choice-of-law rules'.[56]

I found some truth in this statement. In the European cases we also find a covert result selective approach. In contract matters the *lex foris* appears to have abated after the coming into force of the Rome Convention, but it has not disappeared. Courts still tend to regard the law of the forum to be the better law. I found that if the courts choose a result selective approach they create unpredictability. If they select the law applicable by the contacts of the relationship they will often face substantive rules which they do not approve of. That will often lead them to apply 'the better law'. The refined techniques and stringent logic of the choice-of-law rules cannot solve these problems.

---

(1) A court, subject to constitutional restrictions, will follow a statutory directive of its own state on choice of law.

(2) When there is no such directive, the factors relevant to the choice of the applicable rule of law include
    (a) the needs of the interstate and international systems,
    (b) the relevant policies of the forum,
    (c) the relevant policies of other interested states and the relative interests of those states in the determination of the particular issue,
    (d) the protection of justified expectations,
    (e) the basic policies underlying the particular field of law,
    (f) certainty, predictability and uniformity of result, and
    (g) ease in the determination and application of the law to be applied.

[54] See also the criticism in Cheshire and North, above n 1, p 27.

[55] With these words Symeon Symeonides ends his article on 'Choice of Law in the American Courts in 1999' in The American Journal of Comparative Law Volume XLVIII (2000) 143, 180.

[56] Currie, *Selected Essays on the Conflict of Laws* (1963), pp 180,183.

Therefore I turned to another subject, the comparison and unification of the substantive law of contract which I found would better ensure that the parties will get 'the same decision whether the judgment be pronounced in one state or another'.[57] But that is another story.[58]

G. Conclusion

The development of the writings on private international law after 1930 reflects a general change of attitude among the writers. The authors and the courts went into a more respectful and fruitful dialogue with each other. Among the writers a realistic, pragmatic, and socially orientated reasoning replaced an abstract and speculative one. In these respects the common lawyers in England and the USA influenced the civil lawyers of the European Continent. Finally, comparative law came to assume a greater importance not only for the writers, but also for the courts and legislators on both sides of the Channel.

---

[57] von Savigny, above, n 7, p 27.

[58] See Lando, 'The Eternal Crisis', in *Festschrift für Ulrich Drobnig* (Tübingen, 1998), p 361ff, and Lando 'Some Features of the Law of Contract in the Third Millennium' (2000) 40 Scandinavian Studies in Law 343ff.

11

THE HAGUE CONFERENCE'S JUDGMENTS PROJECT

*David McClean**

One thing that Sir Peter North and I have in common is the fact that we owe our interest in the conflict of laws to John Morris, and especially to his lectures to BCL candidates in a notably unprepossessing lecture room in Magdalen College. Although Peter was never able to join the *Dicey and Morris* editorial team, the three of us did collaborate briefly in preparing the Conflicts title for *Halsbury's Laws*, and Peter wrote an affectionate memoir of John Morris for the Proceedings of the British Academy.

John Morris had a blind spot so far as the work of the Hague Conference on Private International Law was concerned, and Peter's own career as Law Commissioner, college principal, and vice-chancellor has prevented him from taking any direct part in the work of the Conference. Given the increasingly prominent role of common lawyers in work of the Hague Conference,[1] there must be a sigh of 'if only' in noting that fact.

---

* Professor of Law, University of Sheffield.
[1] For an historical survey, see David McClean, 'Common Lawyers and the Hague Conference' in *E Pluribus Unum: Liber Amicorum Georges AL Droz* (Martinus Nijhoff, 1996), pp 205–218.

But to stop there would be to underestimate Peter North's very real if indirect engagement with the activities in The Hague. As a Law Commissioner he was of course much concerned with the development of private international law, notably in the field of family law, and in his writings he was a critical commentator on the Hague Conference's work in this field.[2] His courses in the Hague Academy will have familiariszed him with the room in which most of the Conference's meetings are held. More recently, he has played an important part in formulating the policy which United Kingdom delegations have sought to advance. So it is not inappropriate for an essay in this volume to look at an aspect of the Conference's recent work.

The original plan was for this essay to analyse and comment upon some aspect of the Hague Convention on Jurisdiction and Foreign Judgments in Civil and Commercial Matters. Legal writers are sometimes at the mercy of events, and the plan proved incapable of execution for the simple but conclusive reason that no such Convention has been agreed. At the date of the submission of this text (December 2001), the Nineteenth Session of the Conference, the final act of which was expected to contain the agreed text of the Convention, stands adjourned. The Commission on General Affairs and Policy of the Conference is to meet in the first part of 2002, though the date has become uncertain, to review the prospects for the successful completion of the Judgments Project which has been a principal activity of the Conference since 1992. It seems at the very least doubtful whether the Project will come close to meeting the ambitious targets set for it.

So this essay, while not yet a *post mortem* examination, now has a more modest aim: to give an account of the process which has led to the present position, to offer some reflections on the problems which have beset it, and to suggest some implications for future action in English (and indeed Commonwealth) law. If it reads as a *cri de coeur* from a frustrated participant in the process at The Hague, so be it; but that should not conceal that same participant's admiration for the quality and sincerity of the work by Permanent Bureau and delegates alike in a most taxing exercise.

---

[2] See his Hague Academy lectures on 'Development of Rules of Private International Law in the Field of Family Law', *Recueil des cours*, Vol. 166, especially Chapter 4; and his Horace E Read Memorial Lecture on 'Hague Conventions and the Reform of English Conflict of Laws', first published in (1981) 6 Dalhousie LJ 417 and reprinted with additional material in his *Essays in Private International Law* (OUP, 1993), pp 225–256.

A. Previous Endeavours

Some of the more successful pieces of work undertaken by the Hague Conference concern the recognition and enforcement of judgments in the field of maintenance obligations. It was this that prompted the suggestion at the Ninth Session of the Conference in 1960 that a Convention should be prepared on the recognition and enforcement of judgments in civil and commercial matters generally. The United Kingdom was the lone abstention in an otherwise unanimous vote in favour of undertaking that work. The results are fully chronicled in the *Actes et Documents* of the Conference.[3] It proved impossible to complete the work at the Tenth Session in 1964, and several further meetings were necessary, the end-products being a Convention agreed in April 1966 and an Supplementary Protocol agreed in October of the same year. Both were eventually signed in 1971. Only three ratifications were received,[4] and the work must be regarded as unsuccessful.

B. Origins of the Judgments Project

The possibility of returning to the topic was suggested by the United States in 1992. In its commentary on the proposal[5] the Permanent Bureau of the Conference suggested two reasons for the failure of the 1971 texts: the complexity of those texts, with convention, protocol, and bilateral supplementary agreements; and the success of the Brussels and Lugano Conventions. In her 1997 report on *International Jurisdiction and Foreign Judgments in Civil and Commercial Matters*[6] Catherine Kessedjian (who took a major part in the subsequent work) argued that there was a more fundamental reason:

> If we consider the needs of litigants in international litigation, we see that although it is vital to secure for a judgment obtained in any one country effects in one or more other countries, the first priority is to ascertain which court has international jurisdiction to adjudicate initially on the merits of the case. This, we believe, is by far the most important question for litigants. A claimant wants to be able to take action speedily, in a court close to him and whose rules are famil-

---

[3] *Actes et documents de la Session extraordinaire, 13 au 26 avril 1966.*
[4] Those of Cyprus, the Netherlands (originally for the Kingdom in Europe; later also for Aruba), and Portugal.
[5] Preliminary Document No 17 of May 1992.
[6] Preliminary Document No 7 of April 1997.

iar to him, in order to protect the rights which he enjoys or thinks he ought to enjoy. As for the defendant, he does not want to have to defend the suit in a court far away from the centre of his personal or economic interests, and he wants the court dealing with the case to uphold his right to adversarial proceedings which respect to the fullest the right of defence. In our view, therefore, the issue is much more one of direct jurisdiction than of the recognition and enforcement of judgments.[7]

In other words, the 1971 Convention failed because, unlike the Brussels and Lugano texts, it was not a double Convention dealing with both jurisdiction and the enforcement of foreign judgments. A single Convention, limited to recognition rules, would not serve the perceived needs.

No-one can accuse the Hague Conference of rushing in to the Judgments Project. When the United States proposal was first considered by the Special Commission on General Affairs and Policy in June 1992, it decided to have the issues examined by an *ad hoc* Working Group which met in October of the same year. In effect, that Group reported favourably on the prospects for the work. Signs of trouble ahead could be detected in the discussion on the overall strategy.[8] The Group recognized the advantages of a double Convention, but felt that a full double Convention would be too ambitious. It canvassed the idea of a mixed convention, the nature of which was clarified as the negotiations continued over the ensuing years. It also took as a starting point the ideas developed in the Brussels Convention, but also looked at the notion of 'doing business' as a basis for jurisdiction. It would not be an exaggeration to say that those issues remained on the agenda of the Project for the following nine years.

C. An Exploratory Round

The Seventeenth Session of the Conference, held in 1993, decided to include the question of recognition and enforcement of foreign judgments in civil and commercial matters in the work programme of the Conference. There was still no time-scale for the work, and that matter and the whole question of the shape of a possible Convention was referred to another Special Commission, which duly met in June 1994.

---

[7] Para 8.
[8] The Group's Conclusions formed Preliminary Document No 19 of November 1992.

Its meeting began with statements from a spokesman of the parties to the Lugano Convention and from a delegation from a Brussels Convention party; each emphasized the exploratory nature of the meeting and expressed coded hesitations about the whole project. Other delegations expressed concerns about the level of damages in United States judgments, and gave voice to doubts as to the wisdom of tackling both contractual and other issues in the same text, and about the feasibility of a full double Convention. The mood of the meeting was interpreted, perhaps surprisingly, as showing strong support for a double Convention, and the rest of the meeting was largely devoted to an examination of acceptable grounds of jurisdiction. That discussion identified further difficulties: the acceptability of the notions, familiar from the Brussels text to some delegations, of protective jurisdiction (eg for consumers) and of exclusive jurisdiction, and the place of *forum non conveniens*. Delegations from outside Europe expressed alarm at the almost knee-jerk reaction of their European colleagues in defending the Brussels-Lugano text. However, the Chairman's summary at the end of the meeting indicated that the work should be aimed at a double Convention, drawing inspiration in principle from the Brussels-Lugano Conventions. The Special Commission asked for a further meeting at which issues could be considered in detail, and this was held in June 1996. Debate was resumed on some of the controversial issues, including *forum non conveniens*,[9] excessive or multiple damages,[10] and default judgments, but no attempt was made to identify ways of resolving those issues.

At the Eighteenth Session of the Conference held in 1996, it was decided to include the Judgments Convention on the agenda of the Nineteenth Session to be held in 2000. The preparation of the Convention was entrusted to a new Special Commission which met for the first time in June 1997. The Kessedjian report, already referred to, was the major paper before the meeting.

D. The Special Commission of 1997–1999

In some respects the June 1997 meeting was quite extraordinary. To the

---

[9] On the basis of a detailed paper by the Permanent Bureau, *Note on the Question of Forum Non Conveniens in the Perspective of a Double Convention on Judicial Jurisdiction and the Enforcement of Decisions*, Preliminary Document No 3 of April 1996.

[10] The subject of a further paper by the Permanent Bureau, *Note on the Recognition and Enforcement of Decisions in the perspective of a Double Convention with Special Regard to Foreign Judgments Awarding Punitive or Excessive Damages*, Preliminary Document No 4 of May 1996.

frustration of some delegates, who had already lived with the issues for five years, the process almost began again, on the basis that the 'real work' was now beginning. The top table, with support from a number of delegations, was still proclaiming the aim of a double Convention: the United States and others were already persuaded that this aim was unrealistic. It was decided to take no decision on major strategic matters, but to begin at the detailed end, in other words with relatively uncontroversial matters, presumably to enable the meeting to play itself in. The same tactical approach was taken on other occasions, to the frustration of many.

So, discussion began with jurisdiction over immovables (where the *lex situs* principle is readily agreed, but the precise scope of the rule is much more difficult), and over aspects of company law, and then moved to, of all things, intellectual property where the distinction between infringement and validity issues, if it exists at all, is profoundly difficult. It was ruled that certain issues such as *forum non conveniens* could not be discussed at that meeting, The chairman similarly refused to re-open the aim of a double Convention, even when the debate on exorbitant or excluded grounds of jurisdiction clearly raised the issue, and discouraged debate on excessive damages. However, on that matter the United States indicated that, contrary to earlier assurances, it could not in a global context contemplate the approach to the problem of excessive damages adopted in the abortive United Kingdom-United States bilateral Convention of 1978.

A first canter around the issues of jurisdiction in contract and torts took place, and the doing business ground was again discussed; the United States delegation was asked to prepare a paper on the subject. There was at least agreement on a general jurisdictional ground based on the habitual residence of the defendant.

At the end of the June 1997 meeting, the plan was for a further meeting in March 1998 to address the recognition and enforcement issues, *forum non conveniens* and related issues, and perhaps to identify by means of indicative votes the lists of authorized and prohibited grounds of jurisdiction. A preliminary draft Convention might be agreed in November 1998.[11] As will be seen, the programme slipped by twelve months, and two additional meetings were needed. Each meeting brings delegates (technically 'experts' in a Special

---

[11] See the paper *Preliminary Results of the Work of the Special Commission* published in September 1997.

Commission, supposedly less tied to briefs from their home Governments)[12] to The Hague for some two weeks.

The meeting in March 1998 made quite good progress in three days of discussion on the recognition issues.[13] In fact, generally speaking the recognition and enforcement issues were the easier to tackle, the controversial points being less threatening to the overall structure of the Convention. A discussion took place on *forum non conveniens* where a Swiss proposal seemed to suggest the possibility of a compromise solution, which was developed in proposals made later in the meeting, and on jurisdiction in contract and tort with no consensus being reached. There was further discussion of the doing business notion, a lengthy paper having been submitted by the United States delegation.[14] Many delegations continued to find the notion unacceptably vague, but were able to give no convincing answer to the repeated request from the United States for details of any cases in which the application of the United States approach had produced an unacceptable result.

The concerns of the United States delegation played a large part in the discussions. A second lengthy paper[15] addressed the constitutional understanding of Due Process as a limiting factor on the freedom of manoeuvre that delegation could enjoy. It demonstrated, for example, that the United States could not become a party to a Convention with a jurisdictional basis for actions in tort similar to that in Article 5(3) of the Brussels-Lugano texts, which points to the place where the plaintiff suffered damage, for in many cases brought on that ground the necessary 'minimum contacts' between the forum and the defendant would not exist.[16]

---

[12] This notion was more than usually unrealistic in these negotiations. The present author, attending as an Observer from the Commonwealth Secretariat enjoys a genuine freedom to make points, usually from a general common law perspective, which some delegations are inhibited from making.

[13] A full report of its work is to be found in Catherine Kessedjian's *Synthesis of the Work of the Special Commission of March 1998*, Preliminary Document No 9 of July 1998.

[14] Working Document No 64 of 6 March 1998, comprising a paper by Professor Paul R Dubinsky of New York Law School on 'The Reach of Doing Business Jurisdiction and Transacting Business Jurisdiction over non-US Individuals and Entities'.

[15] R A Brand, 'Due Process as a Limitation on Jurisdiction in US Courts and a Limitation on the United States at the Hague Conference on Private International Law', Working Document No 43 of 3 March 1998.

[16] The language is that of the leading case of *International Shoe Co v Washington* 326 US 310 (1945).

The limited progress made put more pressure on the November 1998 meeting, the aim of which was said by the chairman to be to produce 'some sort of text'. The Permanent Bureau had produced a new document, a Preliminary Draft Outline, which was essentially a compendium of the proposals contained in Working Documents submitted at the previous two meetings. The earlier Working Documents were set aside and the discussion continued on the basis of the Outline and a whole new flurry of Working Documents. There were also other specialist papers: one[17] by the co-rapporteurs (Peter Nygh and Fausto Pocar) examining the problem of securing uniform interpretation of any new Convention, in the absence of any equivalent of the European Court of Justice which can rule authoritatively on the meaning of the Brussels text; a detailed examination of the issues surrounding provisional and protective measures,[18] a paper on the United States approach to intellectual property issues,[19] and a paper from the International Association of Democratic Lawyers arguing for a jurisdiction to deal with infringements of human rights.[20] This latter issue was one which the delegates seemed to find difficult to handle, perhaps simply because of its unfamiliarity in the specific context with which they were dealing.

Progress was slow. The issue of the geographical scope of the Convention was postponed, but choice-of-court clauses took many hours of discussion.[21] Jurisdiction based on the appearance of the defendant also gave rise to unexpected difficulty, focused in part on the issue of the defendant's right to challenge the jurisdiction without being held to have submitted to it. Use was made of break-out groups on particular topics such as jurisdiction in contract. The informal group on contracts made a number of attempts to reach a compromise between the activity-based jurisdiction favoured by the United States and elements of the Brussels-Lugano texts on the presence of a branch or agency of the defendant: the group seemed determined to oppose reliance on the place of performance. Eventually some measure of agreement was reached on both contract and tort provisions. Another change of position by the United States

---

[17] Working Document No 94 of November 1998.

[18] C Kessedjian, 'Note on Provisional and Protective Measures in Private International Law and Comparative Law', Preliminary Document No 10 of October 1998.

[19] Curtis A Bradley, 'Adjudication of Transnational Intellectual Property cases under the proposed Judgements Convention', Working Document No 97 of November 1998.

[20] Paul R Dubinsky, 'Proposals of the Hague Conference and their Effect on Efforts to Enforce International Human Rights through Adjudication', Working Document No 117 of November 1998.

[21] The issues gave further difficulties even at the June 2001 meeting.

opened the door to compromise on the vexed issue of excessive and punitive damages. Hints of a possible compromise could be detected in the discussion of the *lis pendens* and *forum non conveniens* issues.

This was all quite encouraging, but the United States delegation made a lengthy intervention towards the end of the meeting drawing attention to the fact that the basic question of a double Convention had remained out of sight throughout the meeting, and reiterating the arguments which that delegation had consistently advanced ever since 1994 for a mixed Convention.[22] No decision was made, however, on this essential structural point. But at least the Drafting Committee was able to produce a partial draft text, to be used as the basis for discussion at an additional meeting of the Special Commission in June 1999.

That meeting reached some significant decisions. It adopted a slimmed-down provision on contracts, limited to contracts for the supply of goods and services; it rejected a general activity-based jurisdiction; and it finally agreed a compromise on *lis pendens* and *forum non conveniens*. New issues discussed included consumer contracts, trusts and maritime jurisdiction.

On the Monday of the second week, the chairman finally allowed discussion on the question of a double or mixed Convention. An overwhelming majority endorsed what had become the *de facto* position, that the draft Convention should be in the form of a mixed Convention. As a later document, the Explanatory Report to the 1999 Draft, puts it, this means that there are three types of provisions:

(1) a list of required jurisdictions whose judgments are entitled to recognition and enforcement in other Contracting States subject to conditions of due process, public policy, and the need to avoid inconsistent judgments;
(2) a list of prohibited jurisdictions which may not be exercised and, if by any ill chance a judgment is based upon any of them, such judgment shall not be recognized; and
(3) an undefined area (the 'grey area'), not falling within 1 and 2 above, where jurisdiction pursuant to national law may be exercised and where recognition likewise depends on the national law of the State addressed.

---

[22] See A von Mehren, "Enforcing Judgments Abroad: Reflections on the Design of recognition Conventions' (1998) 24 Brook JoIL 17.

The meeting achieved the preparation of the text of a preliminary draft Convention.[23] One further meeting of the Special Commission was held in October 1999 to finalize that text. It filled in some of the missing Articles, those on geographical scope, individual contracts of employment (on which the United States signalled that it found the inclusion of this matter difficult), multiple defendants, counter-claims, third party claims, authentic instruments, and settlements. It returned to the difficult matter of 'regular commercial activity' as a basis for jurisdiction, resorting to square brackets to indicate continued disagreement; adopted the same strategy over human rights actions; decided to exclude maritime jurisdiction from the scope of the Convention; and noted three variant proposals for a federal clause. On many matters a vote was taken, and the majorities were sometimes narrow. But a text emerged, published with a full Explanatory Report by Professors Nygh and Pocar.[24]

E. Preparations for the Diplomatic Session

The Nineteenth Session of the Hague Conference was to convene in June 2001, and the intervening period saw increasingly busy consultations. Some centred on the concerns of the United States. It was recognized that the Due Process standard, requiring a meaningful link between the forum and the defendant, has both positive and negative effects. Positively, it may give jurisdiction on the basis of the defendant having done business, been commercially active, in the relevant State: an activity jurisdiction. Negatively, it makes it difficult or impossible for the United States to accept some of the protective jurisdiction rules developed in Europe (which turn on a link between forum and plaintiff) or a jurisdiction based, without more, on the place of a tort. Related difficulties arise in the area of contracts. So far as the United States is concerned, business practice is relevant as well as legal approaches. The notion that a consumer should not be able to sign away his right to select a forum is readily accepted in Europe; it is directly contrary to US practice, and the business lobby in the United States seems unwilling to move on this issue.

---

[23] Working Document No 241.
[24] There is of course a considerable amount of other commentary, eg, A Bucher, 'Vers une convention mondiale sur la compétence et les jugements étrangers' (2000) *La Semaine Juridique* 77.

The very length of the negotiating process meant that new issues had arisen, notably the phenomenon of electronic commerce. There was much discussion as the suitability of traditional notions (such as place of performance) for at least some types of e-commerce transactions, such as those wholly performed on-line. The notion that a consumer could sue in his own country, wherever that might be, was a matter of particular concern, for businesses advertising products on web-sites accessible from any point in the world could find themselves exposed to potential litigation in any country.[25]

It soon became apparent that the October 1999 draft was unacceptable as it stood. The Hague Conference therefore adopted a new strategy: a series of informal meetings were held (in Washington, The Hague, Basle, Geneva, Ottawa and Edinburgh) to discuss either particular issues such as e-commerce or the intellectual property aspects of the draft Convention, or the more general sticking points.[26] It was also decided that the traditional method of voting on the text was unlikely to produce satisfactory results: putting it bluntly, the European Union countries could probably secure a majority for their preferred solutions but the resulting text would be unacceptable to the United States and possibly other major commercial nations. It was agreed to consider the draft Convention at the Nineteenth Session in two stages, the Session convening in June 2001 as arranged and being adjourned for at least six months before resuming. At the June 2001 meeting, decisions would only be taken by consensus, and where no consensus existed that would simply be noted.

F. The Nineteenth Session, Part I

Commission II of the Nineteenth Session held twenty-two meetings in June 2001. At the first of those meetings, the United States delegation reported its view that the proposed text was unduly weighted against well-developed and reasonable US jurisdictional practices. It stood no chance of acceptance in their country. There were further difficulties over intellectual property and electronic commerce. The road ahead was likely to be difficult, and longer than many had hoped.

---

[25] There is a running sub-theme in the discussions, asking just how important consumer litigation against foreign corporations is in actual practice; and whether e-commerce will change the existing pattern.

[26] The results are reflected in the Permanent Bureau's *Informational Note on the work of the informal meetings held since October 1999 to consider and develop drafts on outstanding items*, Preliminary Document No 15 of May 2001.

The outcome of the meetings was an Interim Text, a detailed and in some respects profoundly depressing document, which at many points notes the absence of consensus. These include the basis of jurisdiction in contracts in general and consumer contracts in particular, employment contracts (not even discussed in June 2001), the possibility of activity jurisdiction in contract and tort, exclusive jurisdiction, intellectual property issues, and the extent of the list of prohibited grounds of jurisdiction.

As at some of the earlier rounds in the process, while progress was made, it was mainly on the less important issues; for example, a quite inordinate amount of time was devoted to the proposal to delete the words 'or delict' from the Article on tort. Overall full agreement was reached on only three of the forty or so draft Articles. Some settled matters turned out to be open questions after all: should the basic connecting factor be the 'habitual residence' or simply the 'residence' of the defendant?

Shortly before the end of the June 2001 meeting, a Working Paper was presented by the delegations of Argentina, Australia, New Zealand, and Norway suggesting the abandonment of the ambitious target so far aimed at in the work at The Hague.[27] It proposed in essence the conclusion of a limited Convention, including only those matters on which there was consensus, but with regular reviews with a view to building on the initial Convention over time. This was an expression of the frustration felt by many delegations, to which the Norwegian delegation had earlier given expression.

Delegations were in no position to take decisions on this proposal, but a few days later the Commission of the Conference dealing with General Affairs and Policy was able to take a view of the state of the work. The Commission reaffirmed the great importance it attached to the Judgments Project, but felt that the second part of the Diplomatic Session could not be held before the end of 2002 and that this Session should be prepared for at a further meeting of the Commission on General Affairs and Policy in early 2002. That meeting would examine whether conditions were met for a successful conclusion of the negotiations, including sufficient agreement on the way to approach critical areas where consensus is still lacking, a result-oriented method of negotiation (in effect the question of majority voting or consensus-seeking), and a schedule for any future negotiations.

---

[27] Working Paper No 97 of 18 June 2001.

Consultations with Governments have already made it seem likely that the meeting of the Commission on General Affairs and Policy will be postponed until later in 2002.

G. Reflections on the Process

Standing back from the detail, what factors have led to the present fairly unpromising situation? The foregoing account has hinted at some of the frustrations felt along the way, and a range of further factors can be identified, in no particular priority order.

One is simply that the meetings held by the Hague Conference are very large. There may be over fifty delegations, from Member and non-Member States, inter-governmental and non-governmental organizations, with the right to speak. The largest delegations may have over a dozen members, though only one or two will have places at the table. In practice there has been a notable increase in the use of small informal groups, supplementing the traditionally prolonged coffee and tea breaks at The Hague. But it remains a major task to make progress in such a large group.

A phenomenon which until recently remained off the official record is the existence of 'blocs' of States which seek to prepare a common position. This has long been the case amongst the European Union Member States, but the coming into effect of the Treaty of Amsterdam led to change in practice, which reflected a serious dispute between the Member States and the institutions in Brussels as to where competence lay. In the event, a joint competence shared by the Union and its Member States seems to have emerged, but the presidency of the Union acted as an acknowledged spokesman for EU countries at the June 2001 meeting. There was not too tight a whip on the delegations from the EU Member States, but some delegations seemed to feel themselves less free to suggest new solutions to problems emerging, perhaps unexpectedly, in debate.

A major factor is what might be termed the 'constitutionalization' of issues. For a leading State to announce that its Constitution precludes a certain solution naturally casts a shadow over debate. Some civil law countries played that card in the early debates about *forum non conveniens* on the ground that a judge could not escape his constitutional duty to judge. Those constitutional difficulties were later re-assessed: perhaps it was not so absolute a bar after all. The United States' position on Due Process is a much more serious, because so wide-ranging, an example of the phenomenon.

Coupled with that is the issue of ratification. In many countries, a Government which has the political will to ratify can almost invariably secure the necessary approval from the legislature. That is far from being the case in the United States. For that very reason, the US delegation had to engage in a much more thorough consultative process than any other, and the opinions in business lobbies and amongst other interest-groups were a major factor in forming the delegation's assessment of the prospects for the work at The Hague.

As has been seen, the sheer passage of time meant that new issues arose during the 1990s, and there was an understandable wish to produce a demonstrably modern and up-to-date text. The reality is that lawyers and policy-makers everywhere are still far from resolving the issues presented by e-commerce and the Internet generally, and to try to solve those issues in the middle of negotiating a global convention on jurisdiction and judgments was an unrealistically ambitious task.

There was an underlying political reality which could scarcely be mentioned in the polite diplomatic and technical exchanges. The European Union Member States are anxious to retain their own, well-developed, rules as between themselves, by some special provision in any Convention text. The value of a Hague Convention would be found largely in the addition of countries such as the United States, Canada, China, Japan, Australia, and New Zealand to the club of countries with enhanced capacity for the enforcement of judgments. Because of its particular legal tradition, the inclusion of the United States is probably the hardest to achieve. The unspoken issue at The Hague can be expressed in two questions: (a) how far are other countries willing to go to accommodate the needs of the United States; and (b) would the United States in the end ratify the Convention, even if most of (or even all) their legal concerns were met?

H. Implications for the Other Common Law Countries

Whether or not something emerges from the last decade of effort, there seem to be implications for English and indeed Commonwealth practice. When the Brussels Convention was being considered by the United Kingdom, an important question was whether or not to retain, in dealings with non-Convention countries and especially other Commonwealth countries, the existing rules on jurisdiction and the recognition of judgments. One factor which led to the decision to retain those rules was the fact that the law and practice in many

Commonwealth jurisdictions still reflects the common law principles incorporated into legislation originally enacted in the United Kingdom.

The familiar features of Commonwealth practice as to jurisdiction are:

(a) the rule that the courts of a country have jurisdiction if the writ[28] or other originating process is served on the defendant while he is present within the territorial jurisdiction;

(b) the ability of the courts to assume jurisdiction in certain other cases, usually defined in Rules of Court having statutory authority, but in each case as a matter of discretion exercised having regard to the reality of the link between the facts of the case and the forum State; in such cases the writ (or notice of it) may be served outside the territorial jurisdiction; and

(c) the power of the courts to disclaim jurisdiction, or to decline to exercise jurisdiction, again as a matter of discretion on the grounds of *forum non conveniens*.

The basic rule, that jurisdiction depends upon service of the writ within the territorial jurisdiction, is much criticized. Service serves a vital procedural purpose, that of putting the defendant upon notice of the claim being brought against him, and every legal system makes some provision to that end. But there is a distinct logical leap in moving from the proposition that service is a necessary procedural step to that which makes it a sufficient basis for jurisdiction. As a basis for jurisdiction, it is widely regarded as exorbitant, and its use was excluded in Brussels and Lugano texts.

Similarly, the statute books of most Commonwealth countries contain Acts derived directly or indirectly from either or both of two United Kingdom statutes, the Administration of Justice Act 1920 and the Foreign Judgments (Reciprocal Enforcement) Act 1933. The principal features of the Commonwealth position were reviewed in a full report for Law Ministers[29] in the mid-1970s, and the position is thought to have changed relatively little. It was found:

(a) that the effect of the legislation in each country generally depended on the designation of reciprocating States, a process which was to some extent haphazard;

(b) that the legislation provided for the registration of judgments where the country of origin was regarded as having a proper claim to jurisdiction on

---

[28] 'Claim form' in the current (English) Civil Procedure rules..

[29] By the present author and Professor K W Patchett.

criteria set out in the Act; these were almost always narrower than the bases upon which the state requested to enforce the judgment would itself claim jurisdiction: in particular, a judgment granted after service of process outside the country of origin would *not* be recognized, even though almost all Commonwealth countries would assert jurisdiction on that same basis.

The jurisdictional criteria for the recognition of a judgment given in an action *in personam* now seem notably old-fashioned. International legal opinion has moved on, and the rising tide of international litigation has given much greater experience and suggested new insights. For example, patterns in international trade were once much influenced by imperial factors, so that a common law country found itself trading largely with countries sharing the same legal tradition. That is no longer the case, and there is much more practical exposure to civil law ideas.

In any of the major Commonwealth countries, including the United Kingdom, the problem is not an obvious one. Law reform, as Peter North or indeed any Law Commissioner will tell you, is a frustrating business when Governments seem not to appreciate the need to act promptly (or at all) to implement the admirable and far-sighted proposals of law reform bodies. The United Kingdom has in place primary legislation and a whole range of bilateral implementing agreements as to the recognition of foreign judgments with Commonwealth countries. The judges have wide discretion in accepting or declining jurisdiction in particular cases. So there is little political pressure to set about reform: it seems not to matter overmuch if the basic rules are increasingly indefensible. And the torrent of paper emerging from Brussels gives the relevant Government departments in the United Kingdom quite enough to do, thank you!

Were the Hague Conference, against the odds as it now seems, to produce a new Convention, it would be important for the common law jurisdictions of the Commonwealth to take counsel together, perhaps through the triennial meetings of Law Ministers, about its ratification and the handling of the transitional phase.

Were the Hague Judgments Project to prove abortive, or to produce a minimal result, what then? Since 1977, the Commonwealth Law Ministers have agreed (largely on the basis of a suggestion made in the report already referred to) to refrain from seeking to develop a Commonwealth capacity in private international law, preferring to work with the Hague Conference. The conclusion of the Hague Child Abduction Convention, a Canadian initiative which led to one of the most successful products of the Hague Conference, reinforced that policy. It may be that the policy will have to be reviewed. It would seem to be at least worth exploring whether Commonwealth countries could find common ground, amongst all the options considered in the Hague process, for the formulation of an intra-Commonwealth Convention or Scheme on jurisdiction and the recognition and enforcement of judgments in civil and commercial matters. That could provide a realistic twenty-first century basis for co-operation between countries which have so much of a shared legal tradition.

12

MAKING ENGLISH PRIVATE INTERNATIONAL LAW

C G J Morse[*]

Sir Peter North has pointed out on several occasions that one of the most significant changes in private international law in the twentieth century is the replacement of rules largely developed in the common law with rules contained in statutes.[1] Sir Peter has been prominent in these changes, not least through his work as a Law Commissioner, and has explained the influences and agencies which have led to them.[2] Sir Peter has also been author or co-author of six editions of what is now Cheshire and North's *Private International Law*. The influential nature of that work is well known,[3] but almost as well known is the observation of its original author, Professor Cheshire, that

---

[*] Professor of Law, King's College London. Parts of this paper were delivered to a staff seminar at the Faculty of Law, Hong Kong University in April, 1999. I am grateful to the Faculty for its invitation and hospitality.

[1] See, most recently North, (2001) 50 ICLQ 477. See also (1981) 6 Dalhousie L J 417, reprinted in *Essays in Private International Law* (1993) 230; (1982) 46 *RabelsZ* 490; (1990) 220 *Recueil des cours*, 1, 13, 25; Cheshire and North, *Private International Law* (13th edn, 1999), p 19.

[2] North, (2001) 50 ICLQ 477.

[3] Eg '. . . it will be difficult to find an English decision on a doubtful or controversial point of private international law in which the judges do not refer to Dr Cheshire's Private International Law—now Cheshire and North . . .'. Kahn-Freund, *General Problems of Private International Law* (1976), p 134. See also Graveson (1962) 78 LQR 337, 347.

Of all the departments of English law, Private International Law offers the freest scope to the mere jurist. It is the perfect antithesis to such a topic as real property law. It is not overloaded with detailed rules, it has been only lightly touched by the paralysing hand of the Parliamentary draftsman . . .[4]

Private International Law, continued Professor Cheshire,

presents a golden opportunity, perhaps the last opportunity for the judiciary to show that a homogenous and scientifically constructed body of law, suitable to the changing needs of society, can be evolved without the aid of the legislature, and, though the task must necessarily be performed by the judges, there seems no reason why the jurist should stand aside in cloistered inactivity.[5]

Given Sir Peter North's involvement with both the legislative development of private international law and *Cheshire*, it seems appropriate to offer some thoughts on the relative merits of judicial and legislative development of private international law. Given the extent of statutory intervention[6] such a debate might be thought to have only an historical character. But the debate still flares up from time to time, most recently in the proceedings leading to the enactment of Part III of the Private International Law (Miscellaneous Provisions) Act 1995.[7] And, more generally, an examination of this debate, in the context of private international law, may make a modest contribution to the more wide-ranging question as to the proper relationship between common law and statute in the legal system.[8]

A. The 'Superiority' of Common Law: Historical Remarks

Professor Jeremy Waldron has persuasively argued

that legislation and legislatures have a bad name in legal and political philosophy, a name sufficiently disreputable to cast doubt on their credentials as respectable sources of law . . . There is nothing about legislatures or legislation in modern philosophical jurisprudence remotely comparable to the discussion of judicial decision-making. No one seems to have seen the need for a theory or

---

[4] Cheshire, *Private International Law* (1935), p vii.
[5] ibid, p viii.
[6] For an earlier contribution, see Nott (1984) 33 ICLQ 437.
[7] See below, pp 293–302.
[8] See Pound (1908) 21 Harvard L Rev 383; Beatson (1997) 56 CLJ 391; Zimmermann (1997) 56 CLJ 315; Beatson (2001) 117 LQR 291. For discussion of the wider aspects of this relationship, see Ewing (2000) 38 Alberta L Rev 708.

ideal-type that would do for legislation what Ronald Dworkin's model judge, Hercules, purports to do for adjudicative reasoning.[9]

In a sense, this view reflects, at a jurisprudential level, the ancient, but traditional view that somehow the common law was superior to legislation. Blackstone taught that

> The common law of England has fared like other venerable edifices of antiquity, which rash and unexperienced workmen have ventured to new-dress and refine, with all the range of modern improvement. Hence frequently its symmetry has been destroyed, its proportions distorted, and its majestic simplicity exchanged for specious embellishments and fantastic novelties. For, to say the truth, almost all the perplexed questions, almost all the niceties, intricacies, and delays (which have sometimes disgraced the English, as well as other, courts of justice) owe their original not to the common law itself, but to innovations that have been made in it by acts of parliament: 'overladen (as Sir Edward Coke expresses it) with provisoes and additions, and many times on a sudden penned or corrected by men of none or very little judgment in law'.[10]

Academically, this kind of attitude continues in the nineteenth century. Thus, for Pollock the common law has 'genius',[11] and 'Our Lady the common law is a very wise old lady',[12] but 'Parliament generally changes the law for the worse and . . . the business of the judge is to keep the mischief of its interference within the narrowest possible bounds'.[13] Dicey proclaimed that 'Judicial legislation aims to a far greater extent than do enactments passed by Parliament, at the maintenance of the logic or the symmetry of the law'[14] and that it was 'quite

---

[9] Jeremy Waldron, *The Dignity of Legislation* (1999), p 1.

[10] Blackstone, *Commentaries on the Laws of England* (1765–1769), Vol 1, p 10 (the reference is to the Facsimile of the First Edition published in 1979). Blackstone, nonetheless, believed that where 'the common law and a statute differ, the common law gives place to the statute': ibid, p 89. In the seventeenth century, Coke proclaimed the dominance of the common law to the extent of claiming it had power to declare invalid a statute which infringed its fundamental principles: *Bonham's Case* (1610) 8 Co Rep 114. 'Coke worshipped the common law ('the perfection of reason', as he said of it) and the courts in which it was administered'. See Kiralfy, *Potter's Historical Introduction to English Law* (4th edn, 1958), p 288. Coke's contemporary, Bacon, was sceptical of statutory law. 'In all sciences, they are the soundest that keep close to particulars; and sure I am there are more doubts that rise upon our statutes, which are a text law, than upon the common law, which is no text law'. Spedding, Ellis and Heath (eds), *The Works of Francis Bacon* (1857–1874), Vol 13, p 67, quoted in Shapiro (1980) 24 Am J Leg Hist 330, 337.

[11] Pollock, *The Genius of the Common Law* (1912).

[12] De Wolfe Howe (ed), *Pollock-Holmes Letters*, Vol ii, p 165.

[13] Pollock, *Essays in Jurisprudence and Ethics* (1882), p 85. To be fair to Pollock it must be said that his reverence for the common law did not preclude his involvement in codification statutes: see below, pp 278–280.

[14] Dicey, *Law and Public Opinion in England During the Nineteenth Century* (2nd edn, 1914), p 365. Note the reference to 'symmetry' which echoes Blackstone (above, text at n 10).

possible that judicial conceptions of utility or the public interest may some-times arise above the ideas prevalent at a particular era'.[15] Further, of course, statutes were interpreted by judges, who themselves created what were thought to be the relevant rules.[16] In the early years of the twentieth century a highly in-fluential American Professor of Law, when reviewing *Dicey's Law and Public Opinion in England During the Nineteenth Century* queried the sense in which Dicey used the term law and said: 'As commonly used by lawyers, the word means law as administered by courts of justice in suits between litigating par-ties, but here it is clearly not used in that sense, but in the sense of legislation'.[17] Virtually the only well known resistance to the 'superiority' of the common law came from Bentham who described it, variously, as 'dog law'[18] and as 'An as-semblage of fictitious regulations feigned after the image of those real ones that compose the Statute Law',[19] and who, by the intemperate nature of his lan-guage, may have made his arguments, at least at the time, appear somewhat less convincing to many than they actually were.[20]

It is of course obvious that the origins of English private international law must be found in the common law as administered by the courts. In terms of English legal history, these origins, for reasons which need not detain us here, are com-paratively recent,[21] with vestiges to be found in the later part of the eighteenth century[22] and more rapid development as a result of changing social and eco-nomic conditions in the nineteenth century.[23] No English treatise on private international law was published until that of Westlake in 1858.[24]

---

[15] Dicey, *Law and Public Opinion in England During the Nineteenth Century*, p 366.

[16] Excessive reliance on the so called 'literal' rule of interpretation might be thought to display a distrust of legislation. For consideration of whether 'an attitude of antipathy towards legislative innovation is a fundamental common law principle', see Pound (1908) 21 Harvard L Rev 383.

[17] Langdell (1906) 19 Harvard L Rev 151.

[18] Bentham, *Truth v Avery* in Bowring (ed) *The Works of Jeremy Bentham* Vol 5, p 231.

[19] Bentham, *A Comment on the Commentaries* in Burns and Hart (eds), *Collected Works of Jeremy Bentham* (1977), p 120.

[20] See Graveson, 'The Restless Spirit of English Law', in Keeton and Schwarzenberger (eds), *Jeremy Bentham and the Law* (1948), pp 101, 111.

[21] See Sack, 'Conflicts of Laws in the History of the English Law', in *Law: A Century of Progress* (1835–1935), Vol 3, p 342.

[22] See, eg, *Pipon v Pipon* (1744) Amb 25; *Penn v Baltimore* (1750) 1 Ves Sen 444; *Scrimshire v Scrimshire* (1752) 2 Hagg Con 395; *Robinson v Bland* (1760) 1 Wm Bl 256; *Solomons v Ross* (1764) 1 Hy Bl 131 n; *Mostyn v Fabrigas* (1774) 1 Cowp 169; *Holman v Johnson* (1775) 1 Cowp 341. Recognition of foreign judgments dates from at least 1607: *Wier's Case* (1607) 1 Roll Abr 530 K12. See Cheshire and North, *Private International Law* (13th edn, 1999), p 17.

[23] Dicey and Morris, *The Conflict of Laws* (13th edn, 2000), p 7.

[24] Westlake, *A Treatise on Private International Law* (1858).

Consequently, English courts turned to foreign legal writers for assistance. Indeed in his inaugural lecture as Vinerian Professor in 1883, Dicey claimed (possibly with the overstatement allowed to an inaugurand) that the 'vast field of so-called private international law has been mapped out in England by three or four rules derived from *Huber* and by the doctrines expounded in *Story's Conflict of Laws*'.[25] Westlake's treatise introduced English lawyers to the work of Savigny, described as 'the founder of modern private international law'[26] and whose ideas, at least in the methodological context, are reflected in English practice today.[27]

The English treatises to appear in the nineteenth century were those of Westlake,[28] Foote,[29] and Dicey.[30] Of Dicey's work more will be said later.[31] Westlake's purpose was to reduce to intelligible propositions a subject that was 'incomplete and chaotic',[32] the rules of which were of a 'fragmentary character'.[33] Twenty years later, Foote maintained that private international law 'was to be collected from the judicial decisions of many nations and from the writings of many jurists',[34] and since the 'English decisions . . . still remain a more or less chaotic mass',[35] his object was 'to reduce into order the mass of materials which has accumulated'.[36]

The works of Westlake and Foote were thus clearly directed at putting some order into which was seen as relative chaos. But there is no suggestion that such order could be achieved through legislative intervention, as opposed to the propositional wisdom of the text-writer who could express the 'English view in

---

[25] Dicey, *Can English Law be taught at The Universities?* (1883) 24 (italics in original).

[26] Kahn-Freund, *General Problems of Private International Law* (1976), p 142.

[27] Cheshire and North, *Private International Law* (11th edn, 1987), p 23; Juenger, *Choice of Law and Multistate Justice* (1993), p 40.

[28] Above n 24. Three editions were published in the nineteenth century. The last edition (7th edn, by Bentwich) appeared in 1925.

[29] Foote, *A Concise Treatise on Private International Jurisprudence* (1878) (2nd edn, 1891) (3rd edn, 1904). The last edition (5th edn, by Bellot) appeared in 1925.

[30] Dicey, *A Digest of The Law of England with reference to The Conflict of Laws* (1896).

[31] See pp 282–285 below.

[32] Dicey (1912) 28 LQR 341, reviewing the 5th edition of Westlake's book.

[33] Ibid.

[34] Foote, *A Concise Treatise on Private International Jurisprudence* (1878), Preface (p ix in 3rd edn. where the Preface to the first edition is reprinted).

[35] ibid, p x. See also Preface to 5th edn (1925), p iii ('more or less chaotic mass of English decisions').

[36] ibid.

a series of propositions or topics'[37] supported by authorities and followed by discussion.[38] The 'statute book', said Westlake, was 'almost entirely blank on the head of foreign laws and judgments'.[39] Foote, who at the end of each chapter of his book summarized the state of the law in a series of propositions derived from the earlier discussion in the chapter, went out of his way to say that the summaries 'are not in any way intended, it is almost unnecessary to say, as an attempt at codification. No branch of jurisprudence is perhaps less adapted to such treatment'.[40]

B. Codification

Given the undeveloped state of English private international law in the nineteenth century, it is hardly surprising that the subject received little attention from the legislator. The one product of change to result from purely Parliamentary attention, the Wills Act 1861, was so badly drafted as to suggest that the development of the subject should indeed be left to the judges.[41] Private international law was not, however, entirely impervious to the 'codification movement' which existed, without much success, it has to be added, in the nineteenth century.

The seminal influence on the codification movement was the work of Thomas Babington Macaulay, later Lord Macaulay, in producing, almost single-handedly[42], the Indian Penal Code in 1837.[43] This work acknowledgedly influenced

---

[37] Westlake, *Private International Law* (4th edn, 1905), p vi.

[38] The need to create order out of chaos is also seen in Story's manuscript 'Digest of Law' held in the Harvard Law Library: see Nadelmann, 'Joseph Story's Contribution to American Conflicts Law: A Comment,' in *Conflict of Laws: International and Interstate, Selected Essays* (1972), pp 21, 25. Much of that Digest (reproduced, ibid, p 41) which is concerned with the conflict of laws reads like a codification.

[39] Westlake, above, n 37, p 7.

[40] Foote, above, n 34, p x. The summaries are reprinted at the end of the book in continuous form. The summaries were all omitted from the 5th edn of Foote's work, edited by Bellot, who proclaimed, p iv, somewhat disdainfully, that they were 'not really required by the practitioner' and would be made 'available to students under a separate cover'.

[41] See Dicey and Morris, *The Conflict of Laws* (13th edn, 2000), p 1032.

[42] *Dictionary of National Biography* (1893) Vol. xxxiv, p 413. Before achieving eminence as historian and literary figure, Macaulay had been called to the Bar, but despite joining the Northern Circuit, he 'never obtained or apparently desired to obtain any business': ibid, p 411. His work in India was carried out in his capacity as a member of the Supreme Council of India.

[43] For discussion, see Smith in Gordon and Fergus (eds) *Legal History in the Making: Proceedings of the Ninth British Legal History Conference, Glasgow,* 1990 (1991), p 145.

the attitude of two scholars who promoted the cause of codification in the field of commercial law, namely Sir Frederick Pollock[44] and Sir Mackenzie Chalmers.[45] For Pollock and Chalmers, codification involved the reduction into legislative form of existing law, (with some supplementation in the case of unresolved points), both common law and statute. As Pollock put it, 'the vagueness of case law and the discontinuity of statute law constantly react upon one another, each confusion making the other worse, so that the whole result is far more than would be given by the simple addition of the two'.[46] For Chalmers a code produced 'a statement under the authority of the legislature, and on a systematic plan, of the whole of the general principles applicable to any given branch of the law'.[47] In the commercial context, codification served the aims of a man of business whose object

> is not to get a scientific decision on a particular point, but to avoid litigation altogether. On the whole, he would rather have a somewhat inconvenient rule clearly stated than a more convenient rule worked out by a series of protracted and expensive litigations, pending which he does not know how to act. A judge deciding a disputed question of law always reminds me of a great surgeon performing an operation. The surgeon proceeds calmly with the use of his knife, and pays no attention to the blood which spurts from every vein of the patient on the operating table. So, too, the judge calmly proceeds to apply his precedents to the case before him, regardless of the costs which spurt from every pocket of the unfortunate litigant.[48]

Both Pollock and Chalmers, of course, recognized that even if an area of law had been codified, there was still an important role for the common law. It is obvious that a code will require interpretation by the courts.[49] No codification was likely to be complete.[50] Codes do not abolish 'difficult cases'[51] or necessarily

---

[44] See Pollock, *A Digest of the Law of Partnership* (1877) p iv; *A Digest of the Law of Partnership* (5th edn, 1890), p iii.

[45] See Chalmers (1903) 19 LQR 10. Chalmers was, after call to the Bar, and at various times in his career a civil servant, parliamentary draftsman and County Court judge, and was strongly supported in his codification work by Lord Herschell variously Solicitor-General and Lord Chancellor. As a civil servant Chalmers had worked in India: see *Dictionary of National Biography* (1922–30), p 166. And see below, n 62.

[46] *Essays in Jurisprudence and Ethics* (1882), p 82.

[47] (1886) 2 LQR 125.

[48] (1903) 19 LQR 10, 13.

[49] Chalmers (1886) 2 LQR 125, 131; (1903) 19 LQR 10, 17.

[50] ibid; Pollock, *A Digest of the Law of Partnership* (1877), p xii.

[51] Pollock, *A Digest of the Law of Partnership* (5th edn, 1890), p vii. See also *A Digest of the Law of Partnership* (1877), p xiii.

make those difficult cases less difficult.[52] As Chalmers eloquently put it: 'I think you may compare a code to a building, and the common law to the atmosphere which surrounds that building, and which penetrates every chink and crevice where the bricks and mortar are not'.[53] Legislation, whether it is aimed at codification or the promotion of reforms, can clearly never fully achieve either aim without the support of the common law.

Pollock's work on codification played, as is well known, an important role in the enactment of the Partnership Act 1890.[54] Chalmers' work was directly responsible for three statutes of the greatest commercial importance, the Bills of Exchange Act 1882, the Sale of Goods Act 1893, and the Marine Insurance Act 1906. The first and last of Chalmers' productions survive today in much the same form as he originally produced them.[55] What it is intended to emphasize here, however, is the methodology which both Pollock and Chalmers adopted in order to give effect to their codificatory aims, though for convenience (and because it had an impact on the evolution of private international law) the primary focus will be upon Chalmers' efforts in relation to bills of exchange.

The idea of codifying the law of negotiable instruments was first suggested to him, said Chalmers, 'by Sir Fitz-James Stephen's Digest of the Law of Evidence and Mr Pollock's Digest of the Law of Partnership'.[56] It was also suggested to him by work he had carried out on the Indian Penal Code of 1860.[57] He accordingly set out to produce a Digest of the law which was to be found in 'some 2,500 cases and 17 statutory enactments'.[58] Where there was a dearth of English authority on a point, he made recourse to American decisions and to the usages of bankers and merchants.[59] The resulting Digest[60] set out the law in the form of Chapters and numbered articles, which are subject, where

---

[52] See Pollock, *A Digest of the Law of Partnership* (1877), p iv; *A Digest of the Law of Partnership* (5th edn, 1890), p iii.

[53] (1903) 19 LQR 10.

[54] See the description in Pollock, *A Digest of the Law of Partnership* (5th edn, 1890), pp v–viii.

[55] Sale of goods has moved on somewhat.

[56] (1886) 2 LQR 125, 126. Stephen had admired Macaulay's work on the Indian Penal Code and was said to have spoken in the highest terms 'of the extraordinary command of the subject possessed by a man whose whole experience as an English lawyer was confined to a single prosecution of a boy for "stealing a parcel of cocks" ': *Dictionary of National Biography* (1893) Vol xxxiv, pp 410, 413. Pollock adopted the 'Digest approach' in his *Digest of the Law of Partnership* (1877) acknowledging his wish to follow the example set by Stephen.

[57] (1903) 19 LQR 10, 11.

[58] (1886) 2 LQR 125, 126.

[59] ibid.

[60] *A Digest of the Law of Bills of Exchange, Promissory Notes and Cheques* (1878).

relevant to 'exceptions', which broadly correspond to provisos that one might find in legislation.[61] Articles and exceptions are, where necessary, made subject to 'explanations' which, in effect, are comments which the author found necessary to expand or explain a point. In conclusion, an Article may be the subject of an illustration designed to illuminate its operation.[62] The *Digest*, in effect, formed a ready-made Parliamentary Bill which after some amendment by a Select Committee both of the House of Commons and the House of Lords, eventually became the 1882 Act.[63] Section 72 of that Act codified some of the conflict of laws' rules relating to bills of exchange, in a form which still exists today. Section 72 is not a complete codification—for example it contains no special rules relating to capacity or to the proprietary aspects of bills.[64] The conflict rules that it does contain have been said to be the 'least satisfactory portions of the statute. Chalmers was a specialist in commercial law, a very great expert in that field, but his understanding of the conflict of laws did not match his mastery of mercantile law'.[65] The nub of this criticism stems from the view that since private international law was relatively undeveloped in England at the time Chalmers produced his Digest, the conflict rules of section 72 constituted a 'premature' codification when looked at in the context of subsequent developments in the English private international law of contract, and, most particularly, the 'proper law' doctrine.[66] Be that as it may, the learned editor who revived Chalmers' book in 1991, has vigorously defended the section[67] and it has been applied, comparatively recently, by the Court of Appeal without adverse comment.[68] The

---

[61] (1903) 19 LQR 10, 11–12.

[62] ibid. This technique derives from Macaulay who inserted such illustrations into his draft Indian Penal Code (but they were excluded from the enacted version). The illustrations were derived from decided cases.

[63] For a description of the legislative process see Chalmers (1886) 2 LQR 125; (1903) 19 LQR 10. Chalmers adopted the Digest technique in relation to sale of goods (see Chalmers, *The Sale of Goods, including the Factors Act, 1889* (1890) which commented on the Sale of Goods Bill) and in relation to marine insurance (see Chalmers and Owen, *A Digest of the Law Relating to Marine Insurance* (1901) which was a commentary on the clauses of the Marine Insurance Bill, then in the process of passage through Parliament).

[64] See Dicey and Morris, *The Conflict of Laws* (13th edn, 2000), p 1430.

[65] Kahn-Freund, *General Problems of Private International Law* (1978), pp 132–133.

[66] ibid; Chalmers and Guest *On Bills of Exchange, Cheques and Promissory Notes* (15th edn, 1998), pp 561–562, 569–570.

[67] Chalmers and Guest *On Bills of Exchange, Cheques and Promissory Notes*, above n 66.

[68] *G & H Montage v Irvani* [1990] 1 WLR 667. In this case, a majority of the Court of Appeal concluded that the relevant instrument, an *aval*, was an indorsement within the meaning of the 1882 Act. Mustill L J did not accept this but nevertheless applied the rule contained in section 72(2) by way of analogy.

section has also, it should be said, given rise to comparatively few reported decisions[69] as to its interpretation since its enactment.

C. Dicey on the Conflict of Laws

There is a good deal of evidence to suggest that Dicey was influenced, at least in the context of what one might describe as his work on private law, by the nineteenth century flirtation with codification. First, he appeared to hold Macaulay[70] in high regard. In his inaugural lecture, Dicey described Macaulay as one of 'three men of genius'[71] who, in the previous thirty years, had given 'a new impulse to the study of law. Macaulay has created a new type of codification. As an historian he is certainly not the head of a school; as a reformer, as a codifier of the law he is the parent not only of legislative codes which may possibly survive the memory of his history, but all the unauthorised though invaluable digests of English law such as Mr Chalmers' *Law of Bills of Exchange* or Sir James Stephen's *Digest of Criminal Law.*'[72]

Secondly, Dicey displayed a strong tendency, perhaps even a compunction, to systematize, at least in the context of private law. Thus in arguing the case that English law could be taught in the universities, he pointed out that in that forum 'the chaotic mass of English law' could be brought into 'some sort of form' and be 'exhibited as a model of the clear and orderly arrangement of legal rules and conceptions'.[73] At the university could be learnt 'the habit of analysing and defining legal conceptions'.[74] 'It is hardly too much to predict', he added,

> that till the terminology of the law has been reviewed and settled, as it has been in other countries, under the influence of professional teaching, England will never possess a *code* at all worthy of the merits of English law…The first duty of

---

[69] Cf Chalmers (1886) 2 LQR 125, 131 ('During the last year I have tried at least two cases a week arising on bills and notes, but I have never had occasion yet to construe any section of the Act').

[70] See above nn 42, 43.

[71] *Can English Law Be Taught at The Universities?* (1883), p 26.

[72] ibid. See also Dicey (1930–32) 4 CLJ 286, 302 ('Macaulay was a lawyer. He was a codifier of rare originality; his illustrative genius has fixed the form of all our Indian Codes'). Dicey delivered the substance of this article as a Public Lecture on Blackstone's Commentaries at All Souls College Oxford in 1901.

[73] *Can English Law Be Taught at The Universities?* (1883), p 18.

[74] ibid, p 19.

the competent teacher is to impress upon himself and upon his pupils that law can be *digested* into a set of rules and exceptions . . .[75]

The desire to systematize has, perhaps, a natural link to codification, emphasized, in Dicey's case, by his support for the work of Chalmers and Stephen. Dicey's first book, published in 1870, *A Treatise on the Rules for the Selection of the Parties to an Action*, purported to state the law on this topic in the form of rules and exceptions which were derived from existing case law or legislation.[76] Of more direct relevance to private international law was the publication, in 1879, of *The Law of Domicil as a Branch of the Law of England Stated in the Form of Rules*. This volume purported to state the law of domicile in the form of rules and exceptions which encapsulated the case law and legislation, with comment, where relevant, which was designed to further elucidate the law as so stated. Such a presentation could, said Dicey, 'constitute . . . a *code* of what may be termed the English law of domicil'[77] which might 'at once *codify* and explain a branch of English law which specifically needs systematic treatment'.[78]

The Rule, Exception, Comment approach was continued by Dicey, most notoriously, in his *Digest of the Law of England with Reference to the Conflict of Laws*, published in 1896.[79] Dicey's *Digest*, described by Sir Otto Kahn-Freund, as being presented in 'code-form' and as an example of 'private codification',[80] has exerted considerable influence over the development of English private international law in the century or so since it was originally published. 'The unparalleled role played' by the book, wrote Sir Otto Kahn-Freund,

> was not only due to the accuracy of his [Dicey's] thought and the precision of his style. Nor was it only due to his unswerving loyalty to the English principle of precedent and his extreme caution in making any statement not strictly

---

[75] ibid, 20 (emphasis added).

[76] Dicey's aim was to 'reduce it [the law of parties] to systematic form'. See *A Treatise on the Rules for the Selection of the Parties to an Action* (1870), p iv.

[77] *The Law of Domicil as a Branch of the Law of England Stated in the Form of Rules* (1879), p v (emphasis added).

[78] ibid, p vi. (emphasis added).

[79] Westlake, in reviewing Dicey's book said that though 'Prof Dicey calls his work a Digest its nature is rather that of a treatise, for the law digested is classified under the rules which the author has drawn up in order to express what he considers to be its principles, and not under the subjects that would have formed the classification of a digest as commonly understood.' See (1896) 12 LQR 397. In the Preface to *The Conflict of Laws*, p v, Dicey describes his book, variously, as a 'digest' and a 'treatise' and given that his book on parties was described as a 'treatise', it is not clear that the distinction between the two types of text was particularly important to him.

[80] *General Problems of Private International Law* (1976), pp 130, 134.

supported by judicial authority. *It was due to the form he had chosen for its presentation.*[81]

The preface to *The Conflict of Laws* contains no allusions to codes and codification such as are found in the earlier work on domicile.[82] The author merely says that the principles of the conflict of laws 'are exhibited in the form of systematically arranged Rules and Exceptions . . .'.[83] It may well be that by the time he completed his book, Dicey had become less enamoured of the methodology he had adopted than he was when he began the task.[84] Four years after completing the book, he wrote that his 'faith in digests'[85] had declined.

Yet even when his faith had been stronger, just after the publication of his book on domicile, Dicey had written to Oliver Wendell Holmes: 'I know of no branch of law which is so exclusively of judicial manufacture; and I am coming more and more to the belief that judge-made law is in quality, almost always better than statute law'.[86] His preference for judicial law-making continued after the publication of *The Conflict of Laws*.[87] If Dicey is, therefore, to be classified as a 'codifier' it is in the sense of one who reproduces, in propositional form, the existing state of the law, derived largely from the decisions of courts. It needs to be noted, however, that Dicey's technique was not entirely static and reproductive. Towards the end of the nineteenth century, there was still much of English private international law which was unclear or uncertain and which had not been elucidated by judicial decision. If a point was uncertain Dicey would, nonetheless, proffer a Rule followed by a printed query (replaced in later editions with the expression '*semble*'). He was, in this way, not only able to tell courts what the law was, but also how to develop or evolve it in the requisite area.[88]

---

[81] *General Problems of Private International Law*, 133 (emphasis added).
[82] Above, n 79.
[83] p v.
[84] Apparently, Dicey found the task of producing the book (which took some 14 years) extremely laborious, commenting in a letter he wrote to James Bryce in 1894 'I wish less of my time had been given to this horrible conflict of laws.' The letter is quoted in Cosgrove, *The Rule of Law: Albert Venn Dicey, Victorian Jurist* (1980) 164. The book was a professional success but Dicey is said by one of his biographers to have taken a less than positive view of it: ibid, p 165.
[85] See J H C Morris, biographical note in Dicey and Morris, *The Conflict of Laws* (13th edn, 2000), p xvii.
[86] Quoted in Cosgrove, above n 84, pp 42–43.
[87] See, eg, *Law and Public Opinion in England in the Nineteenth Century* (2nd edn, 1914), pp 363, 364, 365, 366, 368.
[88] Kahn-Freund, *General Problems of Private International Law* (1978), pp 133–134.

Dicey's methodology does not appeal to everyone and, from time to time, reviewers have questioned its retention.[89] Dr J H C Morris, who revived the book as General Editor of the sixth edition, was of the view that the rule-based treatment of the subject was useful to the practitioner,[90] and it has undoubtedly been influential on the practice of the English courts.[91] This influence led one commentator to describe Dicey's *Conflict of Laws* as a 'major defect in this subject'. [92] 'The danger of the book', he said, 'lies in the great respect paid to it by the courts, who are prone to take for granted the theories of Dicey on the points in question'.[93] Were it not for its rule-based style, it is possible to speculate that the influence of the book would have been much less obvious.

It can be reasonably contended that the 'quasi-legislative' style of *Dicey*, the link thereof to nineteenth century ideas of codification, and the influence which that style has had, establishes, at least historically, a strong 'legislative' influence in the development of English private international law.[94] As Lord Wilberforce has put it '. . . the rules are very clear. They are almost statutory in form . . . You have a clear statement just as you might get in a statute'.[95]

D. Case Law versus Legislation

The legislative development of private international law has been resisted in recent years by a number of distinguished lawyers. Despite what he said about *Dicey*, referred to above,[96] Lord Wilberforce has also said that the

---

[89] See, eg, Lando (1998) 47 ICLQ 394. Westlake doubted whether Dicey's methodology was not 'better suited to legislation than to exposition, whether a more connected manner of writing and a less formal arrangement, which need not be less precise or accurate, would not conduct a student more easily into the heart of a subject.' Westlake (1896) 12 LQR 397.

[90] See North (1988) LXXIV Proceedings of the British Academy 443, 460.

[91] For some 'classic' cases discussing Dicey's rules, see *Re Bankes* [1902] Ch 333; *Ralli Bros v Compania Naviera Sota y Aznar* [1920] 2 KB 287; *Luther v Sagor* [1921] 3 KB 532; *Republica de Guatemala v Nunez* [1927] 1 KB 669; *Re Askew* [1930] 2 Ch 259; *Re Paine* [1940] Ch 46; *The Tolten* [1946] P 135.

[92] Foster (1935) BYIL 84, 102.

[93] ibid, 103. Cf the view of Lord Goff referring to Dicey and Morris, *The Conflict of Laws* as 'that prince of legal textbooks': *Hansard,* HL Vol 515, col 1482, February 15, 1990.

[94] The technique of Dicey was the model expressly followed in the American Restatement of the Law. See Yntema (1951) 4 ILQ 1, 2.

[95] *Minutes of Evidence taken before the Special Public Bill Committee on the Private International Law (Miscellaneous) Provisions) Bill, 16 January, 1995* in HL Paper 36 (1995) 7. Lord Wilberforce is not, however, particularly enamoured of statutory intervention in private international law: see below, n 97.

[96] ibid.

subject of conflict of laws is essentially one which ought to be left to the judges. It has been developed by the judges over the years and, on the whole, the judges have done a very good job. There are very few cases where injustice has been seen to be done. One does not want this part of the law frozen into the lapidary phrases of the Parliamentary draftsmen, however well drafted they may appear to be. It is better to leave it to the judges.[97]

Another vociferous and distinguished critic of the legislative trend was the late Dr F A Mann. Whereas Cheshire had thought the hand of the Parliamentary draftsmen could induce mere paralysis in private international law, whereas Lord Wilberforce saw it as merely freezing the law in stone (something of a mixed metaphor), Dr Mann appears to have thought that treatment by the legislator would automatically place the law on the intellectual equivalent of a life-support machine. In commenting on the Contracts (Applicable Law) Act 1990, which implemented in the United Kingdom the Rome (EEC) Convention on the Law Applicable to Contractual Obligations 1980, the day of whose entry into force 'many lawyers and traders will remember with sadness',[98] he had this to say:

> The Act replaces one of the great achievements of the English judiciary during the last 140 years or so, an achievement which produced an effective private international law of contracts, was recognized and followed in practically the whole world and has not at any time or anywhere led to dissatisfaction or to a demand for reform . . . [T]he Act substitutes statutory rules for judicially developed experience and thus creates problems of statutory interpretation, where formerly there existed flexible and fruitful judicial evolution based on argument and derived from principles, precedents and experience. This is particularly so where, as in the present case, the statute adopts, among other peculiarities, the odious method of interpretation which has become fashionable on the Continent and involves reference to reports by two continental academics (see s 3(3)); their distinction is not in doubt, but their familiarity with and experience of the common law and the requirements of practical men is likely to be minimal. The statute, therefore, involves a break not only with English tradition, but also with the law and the development in the countries of the Commonwealth where in the past the English doctrine of the proper law was almost invariably followed and thus represented a cultural and intellectual tie of considerable strength. Why was it thought right to abandon it in order to assist certain Continental countries to improve their law?[99]

---

[97] *Hansard*, HL 16 December 1994, col 840.
[98] (1991) 107 LQR 353. The dark day was 1 April 1991.
[99] (1991) 107 LQR 353, 353–354.

Here, Dr Mann does not exactly conceal his dislike (a) for legislation, in general[100] and (b) the Rome Convention on the Law Applicable to Contractual Obligations 1980,[101] in particular. Elsewhere he had said that the Convention involved the substitution of an allegedly 'clear, firm, statutory basis' for the 'well-established, yet flexible and largely identical judge-made rules prevailing in England as well as in most other countries',[102] leading to 'the replacement of a sound and trusted instrument by the hazards of statutory interpretation'.[103]

Coming from such distinguished sources, these comments deserve the greatest respect. But what are the arguments against legislative action in private international law and how substantial are they?

The first argument seems, essentially, a historical one. The subject has been developed by judges over the years. As this is how it has always been, it is how it always should remain. From time to time, however, the law needs to respond to considerations which judges cannot easily respond to (eg, the need to harmonize law in the European Union) or the law may need to respond more quickly to a particular issue than the gradual process of case law can accommodate (eg, the development of electronic commerce).

The second argument is that judges on the whole have done a good job. This is undoubtedly true in many areas of private international law, perhaps particularly in the context of contracts, the example focussed on by Dr Mann. But it is not necessarily true in all areas of private international law and is particularly untrue of the judicial contribution to the development of choice of law rules in tort, as will be shown below.[104]

---

[100] He was equally critical of the codification contained in the Swiss Private International Law Act 1987: see (1989) 38 ICLQ 715.

[101] He described the Convention as one of the 'most unnecessary, useless and, indeed, unfortunate attempts at unification or harmonization of the law that has ever been undertaken'. (1983) 32 ICLQ 265.

[102] ibid, 266 adding that the Convention is a 'misconceived initiative . . . likely to corrupt our present law' and productive of 'insecurity and irritation all over the world'.

[103] ibid.

[104] See HL Paper 36, *Written Evidence Taken before the Special Public Bill Committee on the Private International Law (Miscellaneous Provisions) Bill*, memorandum from Professor Anton ('tort/delict in the conflict of laws is the paradigm instance of the failure of the judges to develop an adequate and principled set of rules in the conflict of laws'). In the United States, conflict of laws has been largely judge made, and judicially it has been said that 'the law on "choice of law" in the various states and in the federal courts is a veritable jungle, which, if the law can be found out, leads not to a "rule of action" but a reign of chaos': *Re Paris Air Crash of March 3, 1974*, 399 F Supp 732, 739 (1975). See also *Himes v Stalker*, 416 NYS, 2d 986, 991 (1979): 'While the

The third argument, inferentially, is that the legislator will always do a bad job. But this, surely, cannot be by necessary implication. There is good legislation and bad legislation just as there is good case law and bad case law.

The fourth argument is that legislation must necessarily freeze, petrify, or ossify the law, must necessarily render the law inflexible and incapable of proper judicial development as a consequence. But the force of this argument depends upon the nature of the legislative style and the approach taken to interpretation. As to style, in the case of the Contracts (Applicable Law) Act 1990, it can hardly be said that the provisions of the Convention which it implements suffer from the vice of inflexibility.[105] And even in purely domestic legislation it is possible to advance flexible statutory solutions: the main provisions of Part III of the Private International Law (Miscellaneous Provisions) Act 1995, discussed below, are a good example of this. Within a flexible statutory framework, there can be plenty of scope for development of the law through creative judicial interpretation which seeks to give effect to legislative policy.[106] While statutory interpretation may be a different process to that of judicial evolution, statutory interpretation is, nonetheless, a standard part of the judicial function and can hardly be thought of as a process alien to the judiciary. It may also be

legal academicians continue to enjoy a Bacchanalian revelry of law review delights and the Appellate Courts attempt to soothsay whether the majority, or the concurring, or the dissenting opinion of the last Court of Appeals determination should be followed, and the trial courts wallow in the legal quagmire and seek to divine an initial decision that hopefully will pass muster with its respective Appellate Division and if not will merit approval of the Court of Appeals, the unfortunate litigant in the tort conflict problem pays for appeal upon appeal.' I am indebted to Juenger, *Choice of Law and Multistate Justice* (1993), p 110 for this reference. See also, ibid, 121–123. The chaotic state of choice of law has led to discussion and some advocacy of legislative solutions. See Leflar (1977) 44 Tenn L Rev 951; Reese (1987) 35 Am J Comp L 395; Trautman (1981) 32 Hastings LJ 1612; Sedler (1981) 32 Hastings LJ 1628; Petersen (1990) 38 Am J Comp L 423; Kramer (1991) 89 Mich L Rev 2134; Gottesman (1991) 80 Georgetown L J 1. Louisiana enacted a new codification of private international law in 1991, effective from 1 January 1992; for discussion, see Symeonides (1993) 57 *RabelsZ* 460. In the late nineteenth century the American Jurist, David Dudley Field produced his *Outlines of an International Code* on private international law: see Juenger in Erauw and Laurent (eds), *Liber Memorialis François Laurent* (1989), p 837. The approach taken in the *First American Restatement of the Law of Conflict of Laws* (1934) and that of *the Second Restatement* (1971) might also be seen 'as an example of an attempt to reduce private international law to the form of a Code', Kahn-Freund, *General Problems of Private International Law* (1976), p 134.

[105] Particularly in so far as where the parties have not chosen the law to govern the contract, the applicable law will be that of the country with which the contract is 'most closely connected.' This test is very similar to the 'closest and most real connection' test adopted in the common law.

[106] See *Pepper v Hart* [1993] AC 593 at 635 where Lord Browne-Wilkinson refers to the 'purposive approach to construction now adopted by the courts in order to give effect to the true intentions of the legislature'.

true that statutory interpretation is beset with hazards. But so is case law. That there are hazards from time to time in a particular mode of law making does not mean that mode of law making is always inappropriate.

The fifth argument appears to be that judges working with argument, principles, precedent and experience are in a better position or, perhaps, are better qualified to develop the law than is the legislator. But is this really so? Judges hear 'argument': but it is argument rooted in support of the respective positions of the parties before the court and which is likely to obscure the broader considerations of public interest to which the judicial ruling may give rise. 'Principles' may be obscure, vague and point in different contradictory directions. 'Precedents' (if they exist) may be old and seriously lacking in modern relevance. It has always been something of a mystery to the present writer that, for example, tort choice-of-law rules forming the basis of the law, either currently (in whole or in part) or in the recent past, in Australia, Canada, England, Hong Kong, New Zealand, and Nigeria were established in the nineteenth century in a case the facts of which arose out of the actions of a colonial governor in suppressing a rebellion in then colonial Jamaica.[107] Such facts are not the stuff of modern tort law.

The sixth argument appears to be that the legislative process is incapable of adequately embracing the relevant considerations which should lie behind the development of the law. But is this really so? A piece of legislation may originate with a law reform body (eg, the Law Commission in England) where the case for and against reform will have been examined in detail, where the various options for reform will have been examined in detail, and where formal consultation on proposals takes place within the legal or commercial communities and such other interested constituencies as might be appropriate to the matter in question. If Government decides to proceed with proposals, these and the draft legislation which accompanies them will be subject to the scrutiny and debate of the parliamentary process, often leading to amendments and change even in the area of private international law, a subject, it must be

---

[107] *Phillips v Eyre* (1870) LR 6 QB 1. For Australia, see, eg, *McKain v RW Miller & Co (South Australia) Pty Ltd* (1991) 104 ALR 257, now overruled, at least in part, by *John Pfeiffer Pty Ltd v Rogerson* (2000) 172 ALR 623. For Canada, see *McLean v Pettigrew* [1945] 2 DLR 65, now overruled by *Tolofson v Jensen* (1994) 120 DLR (4th) 289. For England, the effect of the *Phillips v Eyre* rule is preserved for defamation cases by Private International Law (Miscellaneous Provisions) Act 1995, ss 10, 13. For Hong Kong, see *Red Sea Insurance Co Ltd v Bouygues SA* [1995] 1 AC 190. For New Zealand, see *Richards v McLean* [1973] 1 NZLR 521. For Nigeria, see *Ajakaiye v Adedeji* [1990] 7 NWLR 192.

admitted, which one does not often associate with political controversy.[108] Conventions emanating from the European Union (*contra* Dr F A Mann) are drawn up by experts and informed by input from Ministries of Justice or relevant government departments. When the House of Lords decided, judicially, that a court could give judgment in a currency other than sterling, Lord Simon dissented, saying, 'I do not think that this is a law reform which should or can be properly imposed by judges; it is, on the contrary, essentially a decision which demands a far wider range of review than is available to courts following our traditional and valuable adversary system—the sort of review compassed by an interdepartmental committee'.[109] And even Lord Wilberforce has expressed the view that the nature of the rule that English courts will not take jurisdiction over actions concerning title to foreign land was such that change, if it was to come, should come from a legislative rather than judicial source.[110]

None of the critics of the legislative trend have been able to point to anything particular about private international law which makes it an inappropriate subject for legislative intervention. Nor, in the present view, have they made out the case in support of the supposed advantages of judicial development. No one would support a view that judicial development is inappropriate. But it is suggested that legislative development is also appropriate and that even where legislation exists there is proper scope for judicial development within legislative parameters.

E. The Nature of Legislative Activity in Private International Law

In the first edition of his student textbook, published in 1971, Dr J H C Morris had this to say:

---

[108] Although there was adverse comment bordering on hysteria in the press concerning application of the original version of Part III of the Private International Law (Miscellaneous Provisions) Bill in the context of defamation: see below, nn 164–169. Implementation of the Rome Convention on the Law Applicable to Contractual Obligations 1980 in the Contracts (Applicable Law) Act 1990 gave rise to correspondence in *The Times*: see F A Mann, *The Times*, 4 December 1989; North, *The Times*, 19 December 1989.

[109] *Miliangos v George Frank (Textiles) Ltd* [1976] AC 443 at 480. In a letter considered amongst *Written Evidence Taken before the Special Public Bill Committee on the Private International Law (Miscellaneous Provisions) Bill*, HL Paper 36, 55, Lord Simon, in contrast, remarked that 'considerations indicate clearly that private international law is a sphere where the development of the law is preferably left to the courts'!

[110] *Hesperides Hotels v Aegean Turkish Holidays Ltd* [1979] AC 509 at 537.

The main sources of the English conflict of laws are the decisions of the courts, statutes, and the opinions of jurists. Statutes are placed second in this list because there can be no doubt that judicial decisions are by far the most important source. Parliament has intervened only on rare occasions to remedy some glaring injustice, to implement some international convention or (on one occasion only) to codify a very small part of the subject. However, the activities of the Law Commission . . . seem likely to lead to greater parliamentary intervention in the conflict of laws than in the past.[111]

By the time of publication of the second edition of the book in 1980 statutes had replaced the decisions of the courts at the head of the list. This was because

there can be no doubt that they have become, potentially at any rate, by far the most important source, and their importance seems likely to increase rather than to diminish in the future. Until the middle of the twentieth century, Parliamentary intervention in the conflict of laws was haphazard, sporadic and (compared with the mass of case law) slight and unimportant.[112]

Just two years later Dr North felt able to say that 'Private International law is an area where creeping codification has crept so silently that few people other than those directly involved have even noticed that it is happening'.[113] By 1995 the same commentator stated:

Virtually all our rules relating to the jurisdiction of the courts and recognition of judgments are dealt with by either primary or secondary legislation: the whole of the law on state immunity, all of the rules relating to choice of law in contract, virtually all the family law rules including aspects of marriage law, the whole of the law on matrimonial causes, the law on adoption, the law on custody, on abduction, the law on trusts . . . [T]he balance has been tipped almost completely the other way and the only major areas of law whose private international law rules are not statutory . . . are torts and some areas of the law of property.[114]

So what are the motives for, and nature of, this legislative activity? To the extent that legislation arises out of domestic concerns, the impetus is often a report of the Law Commission which may recommend legislation[115] and include a draft

---

[111] Morris, *The Conflict of Laws* (1971), p 7.
[112] Morris, *The Conflict of Laws* (2nd edn, 1980), pp 7–8. See also Dicey and Morris, *The Conflict of Laws* (10th edn, 1980), p 7.
[113] North (1982) 46 *RabelsZ* 490, 520.
[114] See HL Paper 36, *Minutes of Evidence taken before the Special Public Bill Committee on the Private International Law (Miscellaneous Provisions) Bill* 38. Dr North was responding to a question from Lord Wilberforce which asserted that private international law was still largely judge-made.
[115] As was the case in relation to choice of law in tort: see Law Com No 193 (1990). For general discussion of the work of the Law Commission in the field of private international law, see North (2001) 50 ICLQ 477.

bill which may (or may not) see the light of day as drafted.[116] Of increasing importance, however, is the impetus provided by international Conventions to which the United Kingdom becomes a party. Two of the most important of these Conventions came onto the scene as a consequence of the United Kingdom's membership of the European Union,[117] but the United Kingdom has also implemented, by legislation, Conventions produced under the auspices of the Hague Conference on Private International Law.[118] Additionally European Union legislation may contain direct material on aspects of private international law,[119] or otherwise have cross-border implications which may need to be catered for through conflict of laws rules. The impetus for legislative activity in the last respect is very much reflective of the particular agenda of the European Union from time to time.[120]

The legislative 'style' of these various sources is, of course, by no means identical. Traditionally, domestic English legislation has been written in a somewhat detailed style with a view, perhaps, that it is likely to be interpreted literally. However, this style is no longer universal and more generalised statutory provisions are now appearing written in language which is apt for the early twenty-first century rather than for the beginning of the nineteenth century.[121] International Conventions are usually incorporated into United Kingdom law in an implementing statute, the English text of the relevant Convention appearing as a Schedule to the Act.[122] The style of these conventions is more rem-

---

[116] The Law Commissions' draft bill on choice of law in tort was somewhat different to the Bill eventually introduced into Parliament.

[117] Civil Jurisdiction and Judgments Act 1982, implementing the Brussels Convention on jurisdiction and the enforcement of judgments in civil and commercial matters; Contracts (Applicable Law) Act 1990, implementing Rome Convention on the Law Applicable to Contractual Obligations. The Brussels Convention is replaced (except in relation to Denmark) by Council Regulation (EC) No 44/2001 of 22 December 2000 on Jurisdiction and the Recognition and Enforcement of Judgments in Civil and Commercial Matters [2001] OJ L12/1, which entered into force on 1 March 2002.

[118] Eg, Wills Act 1963; Recognition of Trusts Act 1987.

[119] See, eg, the choice of law rules for insurance contracts covering risks situated within the territories of the EU Member States derived from directives implemented in England, originally, in Insurance Companies Act 1982, as amended. See now Financial Services and Markets Act 2000 (Law Applicable to Contracts of Insurance) Regulations 2001, SI 2001 No 2635, made under Financial Services and Markets Act 2000, s 424(3).

[120] See EC Treaty, Arts 94–97, 293.

[121] Part III of the Private International Law (Miscellaneous Provisions) Act 1995 is a good example.

[122] This is the method adopted in the Conventions referred to in n 116, above. In the Wills Act 1963 the relevant Convention is translated into English statutory language. The latter technique

iniscent of a continental code than an English statute: they are written in broader more generalized language (perhaps more reminiscent of Dicey's rules than of English legislative technique). The language has a modern ring to it. Conventions do not necessarily give rise to fewer questions of interpretation than do statutes, but many of the problems of interpretation to which they do give rise are different to those encountered in interpreting domestic statutes. In particular, it is important in interpreting Conventions to keep in mind the need for uniformity in application in the various states that sign up for them.[123] More direct EU legislation again seems to be written in the civilian style: implementing (secondary) legislation invariably largely reproduces the language of, eg, the Directive concerned.[124]

Each of these legislative styles is capable of producing sound and effective rules of private international law. This is not to say that they always do so: there are bound to be gaps, poor draftsmanship, and, from time to time, mistakes. But none of these particular vices is endemic in legislative activity: the occasional lapse in standards cannot be allowed to condemn the activity as a whole.

F. Case Law versus Legislation: A 'Case' Study

The relative merits of judicial and legislative development of private international law can usefully be explored by reference to the English choice of law rules for torts. Until 1995 these rules were entirely judge-made.[125] But, in 1995, after a lengthy process of examination by the Law Commission these rules were largely placed on a statutory footing.[126]

---

can give rise to difficulties of interpretation. See, eg, Recognition of Divorces and Legal Separation Act 1971, discussed in North, *The Private International Law of Matrimonial Causes in the British Isles and the Republic of Ireland* (1977), Chaps 10 and 11.

[123] Cf Rome Convention, Art 18.

[124] See, eg, Commercial Agents (Council Directive) Regulations 1993, SI 1993 No 3053, as amended by SI 1993 No 3173 and SI 1998 No 2868 (which amends the conflict of laws' rule contained in the original regulations). The Directive which is implemented in this legislation contained no conflict of laws rules.

[125] For discussion see Dicey and Morris, *The Conflict of Laws* (11th edn, 1987), Chap 35.

[126] Private International Law (Miscellaneous Provisions) Act 1995, Part III. For the Law Commission's work, see Law Commission Working Paper No 87, *Private International Law: Choice of Law in Tort and Delict* (1984), discussed by Fawcett (1985) 48 MLR 439; Law Com No 193, *Private International Law: Choice of Law in Tort and Delict* (1990), criticized by Carter (1991) 107 LQR 405.

In the debate on the Bill that became the Private International Law (Miscellaneous Provisions) Act 1995, Lord Wilberforce had this to say:

> I suggest to your Lordships that statutory intervention in this area, or any area, is only justified if one has certain conditions fulfilled. For example, the first is where the common law has given rise to injustice which it is feared may continue to exist; secondly, where the law is seen to be too complex or uncertain in its application; or thirdly where the reform of the law is thought to be necessary for some international reason to bring us into line with an international convention with other countries.[127]

Analysis against these desiderata can immediately dismiss the third reason for legislative intervention, since there is no international convention in this area to which the United Kingdom is required to accede.[128] Analysis against the first two desiderata requires a brief elucidation of the position reached by the common law.

By 1994, it appears to have been accepted that the state of the law was accurately set forth in Dicey and Morris:

> (1) As a general rule, an act done in a foreign country is a tort and actionable as such in England only if it is both:
>   (a) actionable as a tort according to English law, or, in other words, is an act which if done in England would be a tort; and
>   (b) actionable according to the law of the foreign country where it was done.
> (2) But a particular issue between the parties may be governed by the law of the country which with respect to that issue has the most significant relationship with the occurrence and the parties.[129]

Clause (1) of this Rule states the now notorious principle of 'double actionability', according to which the defendant's conduct must not only be civilly actionable by the law of the country where it occurred, but must also be such that were the conduct to have occurred in England, it would have given rise to a claim in tort according to English notions of tort law. This part of the rule dates back to a famous pronouncement by Willes J in 1870,[130] receiving the

---

[127] *Hansard*, HL 6 December 1994, cols 842–843.

[128] Future developments in the EU may give rise to such a convention, currently known as 'Rome II'.

[129] Dicey and Morris, *The Conflict of Laws* (12th edn, 1993), Rule 203. The case which ultimately approved this formula, courtesy of Hong Kong, is *Red Sea Insurance Co v Bouygues SA* [1995] 1 AC 190, PC.

[130] *Phillips v Eyre* (1870) LR 6 QB1. Clause (1)(a) is usually said to be derived from *The Halley* (1868) LR 2 PC 193.

imprimatur of the House of Lords (including Lord Wilberforce) in 1971.[131] Clause (2) of the Rule is of more dubious origin. It is said to be based on the views of Lords Wilberforce and Hodson in *Boys v Chaplin*,[132] but this outcome can only be supported by indulging in the most muscle-stretching intellectual gymnastics. More likely, clause (2) is the child of Dr J H C Morris who legitimated this offspring by incorporating it into *Dicey and Morris*, thereby ensuring its eventual acceptance by respectable legal opinion.[133] Clause (2), of course, only establishes an *exception* to clause (1). It enables displacement, in an appropriate case, of either the law of the country where the tort was committed in favour of the sole application of the law of the forum,[134] or the law of the forum in favour of the sole application of the law of the country in which the tort was committed.[135]

Lord Wilberforce was of the view that this rule had produced injustice in only one case,[136] and that was a Scottish one.[137] But is this view sustainable? Clause (1)(a) of the Rule, in effect, generally admits only conduct which constitutes a tort by English standards to be successfully sued upon in an English court, thereby excluding torts such as invasion of privacy and unfair competition. It is likely that there have been countless instances where potential claimants have been advised that, on the basis of the clause, their claim will fail. Even if injustice is not perceived in reported cases (and there are, admittedly, relatively few of these) that does not mean that serious injustice may not have been perpetrated upon those who have been correctly advised on the basis of the Rule. Secondly, the general rule requires satisfaction of two systems of law: it imposes a double hurdle, the reasons for which, to put it mildly, are not obvious. Thirdly, there is no obvious reason why essentially foreign liabilities should always be tested against the template of English tort law.

---

[131] *Boys v Chaplin* [1971] AC 356. In a sense this case provides a conclusive argument *against* judicial development of the law in this area. The five opinions reach the same result but appear to do so by reference to five different lines of reasoning.

[132] ibid. See Dicey and Morris, *The Conflict of Laws* (12th edn, 1993), 1497.

[133] Morris had advocated application of the 'proper law of the tort,' the law with which the events which gave rise to the claim had the closest and most real connection: see (1951) 64 Harvard L Rev 881. Clause (2) is also strongly influenced by what became section 145 of the *American Restatement Second on the Conflict of Laws*.

[134] As in *Boys v Chaplin*, above.

[135] As in *Red Sea Insurance Co v Bouygues SA,* above. See also *Pearce v Ove Arup Partnership Ltd* [2000] Ch 403, CA.

[136] *Hansard*, HL 6 December 1994, col 841.

[137] *McElroy v McAllister* 1949 SC 110 which, admittedly, gave rise to a grave injustice.

Lord Wilberforce was also of the view that the law in this area was neither uncertain or complex except to the extent that such uncertainty or complexity was inevitably propagated by the infinite variety of cases which may have to be considered.[138]

> When one considers that there are 175 countries in the world with different nationalities, and the numbers are multiplied, one can see the numbers of varied cases against the hundreds of thousands of cases which may occur. You cannot cater for them all in a few phrases.[139]

But the common law was, and is, uncertain. Historically, it had been uncertain and an inevitable deterrent, as such, to claims. And uncertainty remains. Thus, for example, it is not undoubtedly clear when the exception to clause (1) may be invoked, what factors will operate to trigger it, and whether it can be invoked in favour of a system of law which is neither the law of the forum nor the law of the country where the tort was committed. And does not clause (2) purport to cater for Lord Wilberforce's 'hundreds of thousands of cases'[140] in a few phrases? It surely does and does so in far fewer phrases than those contained in Part III of the 1995 Act! Judicial application of clause (2) involved mere tinkering with clause (1). If you tinker with something its vices will remain though perhaps not in such stark a form. And the vices of clause (1), particularly clause (1)(a), undoubtedly remain and it is insufficient to say that 'as the law has been perfectly well adjusted by the judges, it is not in any further need of reform'.[141] As Sir Peter North has put it: 'It seems clear, I fear, that the judges have led us right into the middle of the swamp. It is now for Parliament relying on some (though not all) of the signposts provided by the Law Commissions, to be our guide to firmer ground'.[142]

So how effective has been statutory reform? It is suggested that, apart from one or two drafting aberrations and one fairly serious miscalculation of policy, Part III of the 1995 Act provides a sound statutory framework within which the courts are given plenty of scope to develop this area of the law in a rational and effective fashion.[143]

---

[138] *Hansard*, HL 6 December 1994, col 841.
[139] ibid.
[140] ibid.
[141] ibid.
[142] North (1991) 42 N I LQ 183 reprinted in *Essays in Private International Law* (1993), 71, 88.
[143] For a full discussion, see Dicey and Morris, *The Conflict of Laws* (13th edn, 2000), Chap 35.

The nub of Part III of the Act is a general rule accompanied by a rule of displacement. The general rule is that the applicable law is the law of the country in which the events constituting the tort in question occur.[144] Where the elements of those events occur in different countries, the applicable law under the general rule is to be taken as being (a) for a cause of action in respect of personal injury[145] caused to an individual or death resulting from personal injury, the law of the country where the individual was when he sustained the injury; (b) for a cause of action in respect of damage to property, the law of the country where the property was when it was damaged; and (c) in any other case, the law of the country in which the most significant element or elements of those events occurred.[146]

It will be immediately noticed that under this general rule there is no reference to a requirement of actionability by the law of the forum.[147] The sole reference, to put it rather generally, is to the law of the country where the tort is committed. Where all the relevant events occur in one country we are provided with a single rule which in the ordinary case will be a straightforward rule to apply (whether by lawyers or non-lawyers, eg, insurers). This approach satisfies the requirements of certainty. Where the elements which together constitute the tort occur in different countries, the position is inevitably more difficult.[148] Here again, however, Part III of the Act aims to supply a solution for what are thought to be likely to be the most common types of claim, *viz* torts causing personal injury or death and torts causing damage to property. At the very least, in regard to the former group, since individuals are involved, a simple rule for the ordinary case is necessary to avoid costly litigation.[149] The rule for the latter group of cases is also likely to be sufficiently clear to avoid unnecessary litigation.[150] The third aspect of the general rule provides a 'sweep-up' principle for all other torts. This is inevitably more uncertain than the other two, not least because of the variety of torts which may arise. However, the central goal of the provision is clear: we have a clear statutory outline within which the courts can operate in the light of the circumstances of the case.

---

[144] s 11(1).
[145] Which includes disease or any impairment of physical or mental condition: s 11(3).
[146] s 11(2).
[147] Although this is preserved in cases of defamation: ss 10, 13, discussed below.
[148] As it was at common law as well.
[149] It is possible, of course, to conceive of cases in which it is difficult to identify the country where an individual is when personal injury is suffered.
[150] There may, however, be some cases where it is not easy to determine where property is when it is damaged.

If, however, the law of the place of commission of a tort were to apply uniquely in every case, the rule would undoubtedly suffer from the vice of inflexibility.[151] Accordingly, it was necessary to enact a 'rule of displacement' which could lead to the general rule being displaced in favour of another law in an appropriate case. According to section 12 of the Act:

> (1) If it appears, in all the circumstances, from a comparison of—
>   (a) the significance of the factors which connect a tort . . . with the country whose law would be the applicable law under the general rule: and
>   (b) the significance of any factors connecting the tort . . . with another country,
>   that it is substantially more appropriate for the applicable law for determining the issues arising in the case, or any of those issues, to be the law of the other country, the general rule is displaced and the applicable law for determining those issues or that issue (as the case may be) is the law of that other country.
> (2) The factors that may be taken into account as connecting a tort . . . with a country for the purposes of this section include, in particular, factors relating to the parties, to any of the events which constitute the tort . . . in question or to any of the circumstances or consequences of those events.

This rule, it must be admitted, is of a somewhat slippery quality. It contains language which is judgmental in nature—'significance,' 'substantially' 'appropriate', in particular—on which views are legitimately capable of being different. Further, the factors in sub-section (2) are not exclusive—other factors may be relevant—and are stated in terms which almost enable any factor deemed relevant to be taken into account. Nonetheless, the section taken as a whole may be thought to provide a clear statutory framework in which courts can operate to deal effectively with the more 'unusual' case, as opposed to the ordinary case. That the rule of displacement is for the unusual case may be indicated by the threshold requirement built in to the rule. It must be 'substantially more appropriate' for the law of a country other than that which is indicated by the general rule to be the applicable law. The policy is clear. Section 12 contains a real exception to be applied in truly exceptional cases.[152] Departure from the general rule is not to be the 'norm.' If this policy is borne in mind, the judgmental quality of the language used in the section is more justifiable. That language must cater for Lord Wilberforce's 'hundreds of thousands of cases'. It can

---

[151] Which was also a criticism of the double actionability rule before an exception to it was recognized.
[152] For an example, see *Edmunds v Simmonds* [2001] 1 WLR 1003. Cf *Hulse v Chambers* [2001] 1 WLR 2386; *Roerig v Valiant Trawlers Ltd* [2002] 1 All ER 961, CA.

only do so through broad and flexible terminology. But in so far as the section creates a clear framework with a clear policy objective, the parameters within which the courts can operate are also reasonably clear.

That the fact that choice-of-law rules have been placed on a statutory footing does not preclude judicial activity in this area can be seen in other sections of the Act as well. Thus it will still be necessary for an issue to be classified as an issue in tort for the relevant provisions of the Act to apply.[153] At this point we can advert to one of the drafting aberrations in the Act. The relevant sub-section says that the 'characterization for the purposes of private international law of issues arising in a claim as issues relating to tort . . . is a matter for the courts of the forum.' This of course is a glaring insight into the obvious since it must of necessity be the case that the court trying the case classify the issue. Without too much artifice,[154] however, an intelligible meaning can be given to the sub-section.

First, the sub-section[155] must not be construed as requiring what is 'tort' or an 'issue in tort' to be characterized according to the forum's domestic law concepts of such questions. Such an approach is not mandated by the wording of the provision and would, indeed, conflict with the general policy of Part III of the Act in abolishing the first branch of the rule of double actionability, thereby permitting torts which were not actionable as such by English tort law to be the subject of a claim in England. Secondly, the presence in the sub-section of the expression 'for the purposes of private international law' explicitly relates to the context in which the process of characterization is to be effected. And in that context, the context of private international law, it is well established that English courts may take a broader view, inspired by the international dimension

---

[153] s 9(2).

[154] More artifice is required to reconcile ss 9(6) and 14(2). The former provision says that the new choice of law rules apply even in cases where a tort is committed in the forum state. The latter provision says that the new choice of law rules only apply in cases where the common law choice of rules would have applied had they not been abolished. Unfortunately it had been held at common law that choice of law rules did not apply to torts committed in England, such torts being governed exclusively by English law: *Metall und Rohstoff A G v Donaldson, Lufkin & Jenrette Inc* [1990] QB 391. This appears to create a complete contradiction between ss 9(6) and 14(2). On how it might be avoided see Morse (1996) 45 ICLQ 888, 890. Cf Cheshire and North, *Private International Law* (13th edn, 1999), 625–626. Part III of the 1995 Act has, nonetheless, been applied without question to a tort found to have been committed in England: see *Roerig v Valiant Trawlers Ltd* [2002] 1 All ER 961, CA.

[155] For discussion, see Dicey and Morris, *The Conflict of Laws* (13th edn, 2000), pp 1517–1531; Cheshire and North, *Private International Law* (13th edn, 1999), pp 618–622.

of the problem, of a particular concept than they would take if the problem was purely domestic in character.[156] Approaching the question of characterisation in an 'internationalist' spirit should enable the courts to resolve any issues which arise in the light of the explicit policy contained in Part III of the 1995 Act.[157] Reference can, of course, be made to common law authorities where they provide appropriate analogies,[158] but such authorities should not be construed as establishing that the process of characterization is governed by the forum's domestic tort law. Other provisions of Part III of the 1995 Act may require a court to make a direct inquiry into common law rules. As a result of section 14(3)(b) those aspects of damages which were regarded, at common law, as procedural will continue to be governed by the law of the forum whereas those aspects of damages which are regarded as substantive will be governed by the law applicable to the tort.[159] In the first reported decision on Part III it appears to have been said that issues of quantification of damages could be governed by the applicable (in that case English) law but it was also stated that (and this is an *obiter dictum*) that the preferred view was that quantification of damages are a matter for the law of the forum.[160] Subsequent cases have squarely characterized the issue of quantification as a procedural one.[161] Finally one might mention that some of the doubts and uncertainties described above which surround the common law choice-of law-rules[162] may necessitate continued inquiries on behalf of the courts since these choice of law rules will continue to apply to defamation and related claims.[163] The existence of the foregoing issues is hardly sufficient to demonstrate judicial redundancy in the development of choice of law in tort.

Mention of defamation and related claims draws attention to what proved to be a controversial feature of Part III of the 1995 Act. The principal reason for the exclusion of defamation and related claims (as defined in section 13[164]) and

---

[156] Eg, *De Nicols v Curlier* [1900] AC 21; *Re Bonacina* [1912] 2 Ch 394; *Re Maldonado's Estate* [1954] P 223; *Phrantzes v Argenti* [1960] 2 QB 19.

[157] See Cheshire and North, above, n 155.

[158] See Dicey and Morris, above, n 155.

[159] For discussion, see Dicey and Morris, *The Conflict of Laws* (13th edn, 2000), pp 1532–1533.

[160] *Edmunds v Simmonds* [2001] 1 WLR 1003.

[161] *Hulse v Chambers* [2001] 1 WLR 2386; *Roerig v Valiant Trawlers Ltd* [2002] 1 All ER 961, CA.

[162] Above, nn 140–142.

[163] 1995 Act, ss 10, 13.

[164] Which can itself give rise to difficulties of interpretation which may require judicial attention: see Dicey and Morris, *The Conflict of Laws* (13th edn, 2000), pp 1561–1562; Briggs (1995) LMCLQ 519.

the reference of such claims to the common law choice-of-law rules (section 10) appears to have been a fear that freedom of expression, and particularly freedom of expression by the press, would be prejudiced by the application of the new choice-of-law rules.[165] Under the new choice-of-law rules, so the argument appears to have gone, the abolition of the common law requirement that the tort had to the actionable as such by the law of the forum, would mean that the press would be exposed to liabilities for defamation and related claims under a foreign law when, for example, the statement of which a plaintiff complained would attract some form of privilege or other defence under English law.[166]

Arguments of these kinds were expressed in hysterical form in certain sections of the press. According to the London *Evening Standard* 'the most obvious and dangerous implication of the Bill is that it will open the floodgates to highly dubious, speculative libel actions against British newspapers from abroad . . . Parliament must stamp hard on this pointless, wasteful and deeply dangerous Bill'.[167] In more measured, but equally unsupporting words, a distinguished lawyer who sits in the House of Lords took the view that 'it would be quite wrong for the freedom of the press in this country and elsewhere to be chilled or restricted by applying in English courts the laws of foreign countries which are far more repressive of freedom of expression. I hope your Lordships will think that there is nothing narrowly nationalistic about my saying so'.[168]

Whether these sentiments justified these exclusions is highly questionable. There is a ready tool for securing the non-application of foreign laws which unduly restrict freedom of speech, namely the concept of public policy which is enshrined is section 14(3)(a)(i) of the Act. According to one proponent of the exclusion of defamation 'it is invidious for a judge to have to find, and to say that he has found, the law of another country to be so objectionable that it offends English . . . public policy . . . I suggest that this is a recipe for a divisive jurisprudence'.[169] The problem with this comment is, of course, that instead of allowing judges to act openly in rejecting the sub-standard laws of a foreign country, it permits the judge to conceal what is being done by allowing the

---

[165] *Hansard* HL, 6 December 1994, cols 830–831; *The Times*, 19 January 1995.

[166] Proponents of this view would be wise to bear in mind that English libel judgments have been denied recognition in the United States because of a conflict with the First Amendment of the US Constitution: see *Bachchan v India Abroad Publications*, 58 NYS 2d 661 (1992); *Telnikoff v Matrusevitch*, 702 A 2d 230 (1997).

[167] *Evening Standard*, 19 January 1995.

[168] *Hansard*, HL 6 December 1995, col 839, *per* Lord Lester of Herne Hill.

[169] ibid.

judge to hide behind the first branch of the rule of double actionability. How does this encourage a non-divisive jurisprudence?

G. Conclusion

Although the statutory reforms of the English choice of law rules for torts are not perfect, they do illustrate how private international law can be developed by legislative activity and that there is nothing especially particular about private international law which requires that its sound development be left entirely to the courts. However, it is equally clear that the legislature cannot be exclusively entrusted with the task and that legislative and judicial development must go together. To compartmentalize common law and statute and to adopt what Professor Beatson has described as the 'oil and water' approach[170] ignores the important and complementary roles which each source can play in the making of private international law.

---

[170] Beatson (1997) 56 CLJ 291; (2001) 117 LQR 247.

13

DECLINING JURISDICTION UNDER THE BRUSSELS I REGULATION 2001 AND THE PRELIMINARY DRAFT HAGUE JUDGMENTS CONVENTION: A COMPARISON

Peter Nygh [*]

[*] Visiting Professor of Law, University of New South Wales, Sydney, Australia. Co-reporter (with Fausto Pocar) of the Diplomatic Conference on a Draft Convention on Jurisdiction and Recognition of Foreign Judgments in Civil and Commercial Matters.

A. What do We Mean by Declining Jurisdiction?

For the purposes of this article, a court can be said to decline jurisdiction when it refuses to exercise a jurisdiction that the plaintiff has regularly invoked under the law of the forum.[1] This is quite distinct from the situation where a court finds that it lacks jurisdiction. There are four situations in which courts can decline jurisdiction:[2]

- where there are parallel or concurrent proceedings pending between the same parties concerning the same subject matter in different jurisdictions at the same time (*lis pendens*);
- where there exist related proceedings arising out of the same sub-stratum of fact and raising the same issues, even though the parties and the claims raised by them in each proceeding may not entirely coincide;
- where the forum in which a party has commenced an action, although it has jurisdiction under its normal rules, is 'clearly inappropriate',[3] or where another forum is 'clearly more appropriate'[4] to try the particular dispute (*forum non conveniens*); and
- where the parties have validly agreed that another court shall have jurisdiction in respect of their dispute or have validly agreed to submit that dispute to arbitration and the forum under its law has a discretion whether or not to give effect to that agreement.[5]

Since both the Brussels I Regulation 2001[6] and the Hague Preliminary Draft Convention of October 1999[7] provide for the exclusive jurisdiction of the chosen forum, unless the parties agree otherwise, the situation arising under the

---

[1] *Voth v Manildra Flour Mills Pty Ltd* (1990) 171 CLR 538 at 558 *per* Mason CJ, Deane, Dawson and Gaudron JJ. See also , Fawcett (ed), *Declining Jurisdiction in Private International Law* (OUP, 1995), p 2.

[2] See Fawcett, n 1 above, p 2.

[3] This is the formula adopted by the High Court of Australia in *Voth v Manildra Flour Mills Pty Ltd* (1990) 171 CLR 538. It only applies in Australian courts.

[4] This is the formula adopted by the House of Lords in *Spiliada Maritime Corporation v Cansulex Ltd* [1987] AC 460 and followed in many Commonwealth jurisdictions other than Australia, see Cheshire and North, *Private International Law* (13th edn 1999), p 335.

[5] If the forum has no discretion, but must stay the proceedings brought in breach of a valid choice of forum agreement, it has no jurisdiction: see Brussels I Regulation 2001, Art 23; UN Convention on Recognition and Enforcement of Foreign Arbitral Awards 1958 (the 'New York Arbitration Convention') Art II.3.

[6] Council Regulation (EC) No 44 / 2001 of 22 December 2000 on Jurisdiction and Recognition of Foreign Judgments in Civil and Commercial Matters.

[7] Preliminary Draft Convention on Jurisdiction and Recognition of Foreign Judgments

last heading under both instruments will be one of lack of jurisdiction rather than of declining jurisdiction and requires no further discussion in this paper.

B. Do We Need to Regulate the Circumstances in Which National Courts Decline Jurisdiction?

It is true, as we shall see, that common lawyers generally have managed quite well without a strict rule of *lis pendens* and civil lawyers have managed to survive so far without *forum non conveniens*. But it would seem that some mechanism, be it the one or the other or an amalgam of the two, is required. At some stage or another, the issue of conflicting jurisdictions and possibly conflicting judgments has to be faced. It can, of course, be postponed to the very end when the forum is asked to enforce one of several conflicting judgments obtained between the same parties in relation to the same dispute. If there was no contrary provision in national or conventional law, the judgment first obtained should prevail through the mechanism of *res judicata*.[8] One could even argue that this is an appropriate mechanism in a global market economy: let the most efficient court prevail. But the natural inclination in that case would be to favour one's own.[9] Thus, the Hague Convention on the Jurisdiction and Recognition of Foreign Judgments in Civil and Commercial Matters 1971[10] in Article 5(3)(b) permitted the State addressed to refuse enforcement of a parallel judgment rendered in another Member State, if proceedings between the same parties based on the same facts and having the same purpose had resulted in a decision of a court of the State addressed. There was no requirement that the local decision result from proceedings having priority in time or even that the local judgment be rendered prior to the foreign judgment.[11]

---

in Civil and Commercial Matters adopted by the Special Commission on 30 October 1999.

[8] This appears to be the prevailing approach in the United States: see, *Laker Airways Ltd v Sabena*, 731 F 2d 909 at 928 (DC Cir 1984) followed in *Ingersoll Milling Machine Co v Granger*, 833 F 2d 680 (7th Cir 1987) (stay of US proceedings not granted until court presented with Belgian judgment).

[9] See Fawcett, n 1 above at p 42.

[10] This Convention never entered into effect.

[11] Art 20 of the 1971 Convention did provide for the dismissal or stay of one of the concurrent actions, but imposed no obligation to do so nor did it provide that the first action should prevail over the later.

Another possible solution is by unilateral action: one of the courts involved in parallel litigation can either stay the action before it or seek to restrain a party from proceeding in the foreign court through the so-called anti-suit injunction. But this is the law of the jungle: national courts are often reluctant to stay local actions and sometimes too ready to restrain foreign proceedings. This may lead to an undignified contest between courts. An example of this can be seen in the litigation between Akai Pty Ltd, an Australian subsidiary of a Japanese corporation, and The People's Insurance Co, a Singapore corporation, concerning their contract of insurance. They had agreed in their negotiations on England as the chosen forum for any disputes arising out of their relationship. The High Court of Australia by majority (Gaudron, Gummow, and Kirby JJ) on the application of the insured, held the choice to be invalid because its effect was to avoid the application of the consumer-protective provisions of the Australian Insurance Contracts Act 1984.[12] But in the English proceedings the insurer counterclaimed for a declaration of non-liability and sought an anti-suit injunction restraining Akai Pty Ltd from proceeding with its litigation in Australia.[13] The English court refused to stay the counterclaim and granted the injunction. Thus, despite the decision of the High Court of Australia, a single judge of the High Court in England determined that the Australian proceedings ought to be terminated. Since it is most unlikely that an English court will apply a mandatory Australian statute in a case where neither the proper law nor the forum is Australian,[14] the likely result, if the litigation in each country were to proceed, is conflicting judgments in favour of the party having the carriage of the matter in Australia and England respectively. It will also mean that upon attempts to enforce any resulting judgment, the Australian courts are likely to deny recognition to the English judgment by reason of public policy and the English courts will deny recognition of a judgment pronounced in defiance of a choice of court agreement.[15]

It follows that regulation of this aspect of the law at the international level is

---

[12] *Akai Pty Ltd v People's Insurance Co Ltd* (1996) 188 CLR 418. The High Court at the time of hearing was aware of the English proceedings instituted at the same time by Akai in that country, ibid at 448, but still held that the 'overwhelming balance of considerations' favoured the Australian forum.

[13] *Akai Pty Ltd v People's Insurance Ltd* [1998] 1 Lloyd's Rep 90 at 108.

[14] ibid at 98–100 *per* Thomas J.

[15] Civil Jurisdiction and Judgments Act 1982 (UK) s 32. See also, Dicey and Morris, para 14-091. As regards enforcement in Singapore, this was left to the courts of that country to decide: [1998] 1 Lloyd's Rep 90 at 108 *per* Thomas J.

highly desirable if one wants to promote certainty and predictability for international trade. There should not be any room for the protection of local interests. International co-operation should not only promote the proper allocation of jurisdiction between courts and discourage improper forum shopping, but also reduce the unnecessary incidence of concurrent jurisdiction and the risk of irreconcilable judgments.[16] The purpose of this paper is to investigate how the Brussels I Regulation and the Hague Draft Convention have sought to resolve that issue.

C. Brussels and The Hague

Certainly the question of preventing parallel litigation was very much in the minds of the drafters of the original Brussels Convention on Jurisdiction and Recognition of Foreign Judgments in Civil and Commercial Matters of 1968 (the 'Brussels Convention')[17] and of those engaged in the drafting in The Hague of a worldwide Convention on Jurisdiction and Foreign Judgments in Civil and Commercial Matters.[18] The Brussels Convention has now been replaced (except as regards Denmark) by the Council Regulation (EC) No 44/2001 of 22 December 2000 on Jurisdiction and Recognition of Foreign Judgments in Civil and Commercial Matters (the 'Brussels I Regulation').[19] That Regulation entered into force, except as to Denmark,[20] on 1 March 2002.[21]

The Hague and Brussels have for many decades had a symbiotic relationship. This is particularly marked in the area of recognition and enforcement of judg-

---

[16] See the Preamble to the Leuven/London Principles of the International Law Association in *Report of the 69th Conference of the ILA*, London, July 2000, 137 at para 48.

[17] Reference should also be made to the 1988 Lugano Convention on Jurisdiction and Recognition of Foreign Judgments in Civil and Commercial Matters (the 'Lugano Convention'). Since the provisions of the Conventions that are relevant to the discussion in this article are the same, it is not necessary to repeat references to the Lugano Convention.

[18] This project that has been going since 1992 in some form or other, is not yet completed. The Special Commission that sat from 1997 until 1999 did on 30 October 1999 produce a Preliminary Draft Convention but this document has no particular status until and unless the Diplomatic Conference of the 19th Session completes the work. Following the completion of the First Part of that Session in June 2001, the future of the project is, at the time of writing, uncertain.

[19] [2001] OJ L12/1.

[20] Regulation Art 1(3).

[21] Regulation Art 76.

ments. The Hague Conference on Private International Law was first in the field in drafting the Convention on the Recognition and Enforcement of Judgments in Civil and Commercial Matters and the Supplementary Protocol thereto, which were completed at the Extraordinary Session in 1966. Those instruments did not have to deal with parallel litigation since they established a so-called 'single' Convention,[22] but the Protocol did in Article 4 set out a list of prohibited jurisdictions. Recognition and enforcement of a judgment based only on one or more of the grounds specified in Article 4 had to be refused. This practice of listing specifically heads of jurisdiction that were objectionable reappeared in Article 3 of the Brussels Convention in 1968, even though it was arguably unnecessary since that Convention purported to define exclusively those heads of jurisdiction that were permissible.[23]

Mechanisms for dealing with parallel and related proceedings were first inserted in the Brussels Convention of 1968.[24] The Hague Preliminary Draft Convention of October 1999 seeks to regulate parallel proceedings, but does not deal with related proceedings. Instead it creates another and linked mechanism based on the common law principle of *forum non conveniens* to supplement the principle of *lis pendens*. When the Brussels Convention was revised as the Brussels I Regulation 2001 the Hague version of *forum non conveniens* was not adopted. The mechanisms adopted by the Brussels I Regulation on the one hand and the Hague Draft on the other appear therefore to be quite different with the former appearing to prefer certainty and the latter flexibility. The purpose of this article is to explore the advantages and disadvantages of each of the systems. In writing this I am aware of the uncertain status that the Hague Preliminary Draft Convention has at the moment.[25] However, the ideas and concepts that it represents will persist and have to be considered at some future stage, even if present negotiations do not produce an immediate result.

---

[22] It did deal in Art 5(3) with the question of parallel judgments and it is notable that in subparagraph a) recognition and enforcement could be refused in the case where parallel proceedings were pending in the State addressed and 'those proceedings were the first to be instituted'. Those proceedings need not have resulted in a judgment: but see Art 5(3)(b). This compares with the common law position where it is the priority of the judgment that is decisive: *Vervaeke v Smith* [1983] 1 AC 145; *Showlag v Mansour* [1995] 1 AC 431.

[23] Now duly 'demoted' to Annex I of the Brussels I Regulation as examples of situations where courts of Member States should not exercise jurisdiction over a defendant domiciled in a Member State: Art 3(2).

[24] But see the provisions of Art 20 of the 1971 Convention referred to in n 11, above.

[25] See 18 above.

D. The Regulation of Forum Choice

The proliferation of jurisdictional bases in most national legal systems has given plaintiffs a wide choice of fora. It is not suggested here that 'forum shopping' is inherently immoral or even undesirable. As the late Fritz Juenger has pointed out, the plaintiff is entitled, within reasonable limits, to select the forum that will supply the best means of recovery.[26] It is also increasingly recognized that a plaintiff who has suffered harm at his place of habitual residence as the result of a trans-national tort, should be able to sue the defendant in the plaintiff's forum. Thus, the well-known decision of the European Court of Justice in *Handelskwekerij Bier v Mines de Potasse d'Alsace*[27] was an obvious policy decision to expand the options available to a plaintiff. In deciding that 'the place where the harmful event occurred' could, at the plaintiff's option be either the place where the initiating act was done by the defendant or the place where the plaintiff suffered the resultant damage, the Court acknowledged that it would not be appropriate to confine the plaintiff to the place of the initiating act—a place that most commonly would coincide with the defendant's residence. In the result the Dutch plaintiff in *Bier's* case availed itself of the opportunity offered and brought suit in the District Court of Rotterdam.[28]

Not all jurisdictional options are benign. Virtually all legal systems have exorbitant grounds of jurisdiction that permit plaintiffs to bring suit 'at home' despite the absence of any serious link between the subject matter of the dispute and the forum. The jurisdiction of French courts under Article 14 of the French Civil Code based on the French nationality of the plaintiff is perhaps the most notorious of these, but jurisdiction based on the presence within the forum of assets of the defendant that are unrelated to the dispute and the common law 'tag' jurisdiction can be equally obnoxious.

However, it is not usually the existence of exorbitant jurisdiction that causes problems. The availability of a wide choice of fora for plaintiffs, whether proper or improper, has created situations where the defendant may be placed at a serious disadvantage. Furthermore, the defendant to one action in relation to a dispute, may choose to become the plaintiff in another forum. This may be

---

[26] Juenger, 'What is Wrong with Forum Shopping?' (1994) 16 Syd LR 1.

[27] [1976] ECR 1736.

[28] See note Verheul (1978) 9 NYIL 331. By consent the court applied Dutch law: District Court, Rotterdam 8 January 1979: note Duintjer Tebbens (1979) 28 NILR 63.

because the defendant in the first action may have a counterclaim or related action against the plaintiff in the first action arising out of the same sub-stratum of fact, or the defendant in the first action may seek a declaration that it has no liability to the plaintiff in relation to the dispute (the so-called 'negative declaration') in another forum that it considers more favourable.

Thus the invocation of an exorbitant jurisdiction is not necessarily the reason why jurisdiction may be declined. The contest may lie between two jurisdictions that in themselves are entirely appropriate.[29] Similarly, a jurisdiction need not be exorbitant in order to be inappropriate: in *McShannon v Rockware Glass Ltd*[30] the House of Lords declined English jurisdiction even though the defendant was an English company.[31] In the most recent decision in *Lubbe v Cape plc*[32] the House of Lords acknowledged that South Africa was a clearly more appropriate forum than the English forum where the defendant companies were resident, but refused a stay on the ground 'that substantial justice would not be done in the more appropriate South African forum'.[33] It follows conversely that a jurisdiction that is exorbitant may, in certain, admittedly rare, circumstances be viewed as 'appropriate'. Thus 'tag' jurisdiction has at times been justified on the basis that this allows the plaintiff to invoke a forum to obtain justice when his action is time-barred in the 'natural' forum.[34]

E. *Lis Pendens*

(1) *The Common Law Position*

Although the term '*lis alibi pendens*' is known to common lawyers, it has a quite different meaning than '*lis pendens*' in the civil law. For the common lawyers the existence of parallel litigation between the same parties with respect to the same subject matter did not by itself have any particular consequences on the exercise of either jurisdiction.[35] An English court might decide that the existence of such litigation was vexatious and oppressive. In that case it could stay or restrain either the first or the second action in time. In one of the earliest

---

[29] See *CSR Ltd v Cigna Insurance Australia Ltd* (1997) 189 CLR 345.
[30] [1978] AC 795.
[31] See also *Re Harrods (Buenos Aires) Ltd* [1992] Ch 272.
[32] [2000] 1 WLR 1545.
[33] ibid at 1556 *per* Lord Bingham of Cornhill.
[34] As in *Evers v Firth* (1986) 10 NSWLR 22.
[35] See Fawcett, n 1 above, p 29.

English decisions, *Bushby v Munday*,[36] the English court restrained by the use of an anti-suit injunction the first action brought in Scotland in favour of the second English suit. But the existence of parallel litigation even if brought by the same plaintiff, was not seen as necessarily bad. In *Cohen v Rothfield* Scrutton LJ said: 'It is not prima facie vexatious for the same plaintiff to commence two actions relating to the same subject matter, one in England and one abroad . . .'.[37] *Lis alibi pendens* was no more than a factual description of a situation in which an English court could interfere 'whenever there is oppression and vexation to prevent the administration of justice being perverted to an unjust end'.[38] In practice the courts only intervened where the plaintiff's action in bringing suit could be described as malicious. In that case it made little difference if only one proceeding or multiple proceedings were pending.[39]

The High Court of Australia, in *Henry v Henry*[40] did for a moment appear to embrace *lis alibi pendens* as a separate doctrine, or at least as a distinct subspecies of *forum non conveniens*, when it declared in that case: 'the problems which arise if the identical issue or the same controversy is to be litigated in different countries which have jurisdiction with respect to the matter are such . . . that, *prima facie*, the continuation of one or the other should be seen as vexatious or oppressive within the *Voth* sense of the words'.[41] This passage at least seems to suggest that the existence of parallel litigation raises the presumption that one of the actions is brought in an inappropriate forum.[42]

The reference to *Voth* in this passage relates to the earlier decision of the High Court in *Voth v Manildra Flour Mills Pty Ltd*[43] where the words 'oppressive and vexatious' were explained in an objective sense rather than as words that require some degree of malice on the part of the person initiating the action. Nor was the passage confined to a situation where one party as plaintiff had initiated

---

[36] (1821) 56 ER 908 (5 Madd 297).
[37] (1919) 1 KB 410 at 414.
[38] *McHenry v Lewis* (1882) 22 Ch D 397 at 408 *per* Bowen LJ.
[39] As in *Egbert v Short* [1907] 2 Ch 205, where the plaintiff, an American, served the defendant, a resident of India on leave in England, with a writ concerning events that had occurred in India, one day before the defendant was to embark on his return voyage to India. Compare *Baroda v Wildenstein* [1973] 2 QB 282, where there was a similar ambush of a foreign defendant by a foreign plaintiff, but the Court of Appeal held that the action was not 'vexatious' because the plaintiff was entitled to take advantage of the superior English civil procedure!
[40] (1996) 185 CLR 571.
[41] ibid at 591 *per* Dawson, Gaudron, Mc Hugh, and Gummow JJ.
[42] See the remarks of Lord Diplock in *The Abidin Daver* [1984] AC 398 at 411–2.
[43] (1990) 171 CLR 538.

multiple litigation. In *Henry v Henry* each party (husband and wife) had initiated proceedings in the forum that each considered most favourable to his or her cause. The clear inference from the passage is that the majority considered a *lis pendens* situation to be clearly undesirable and were calling for action to prevent it. At the same time, their Honours did not embrace a 'first come, best served' principle of preference. At most, the priority of the proceedings was a factor to be considered among other considerations usually relevant to *forum non conveniens*.[44]

However, in *CSR Ltd v Cigna Insurance Australia Ltd*[45] the High Court appears to have retreated to the nineteenth century approach that there was nothing inherently wrong with parallel litigation unless there was no additional advantage to be gained by bringing proceedings in the foreign or the local court.[46] In other words, *prima facie* the continuation of one or the other is not vexatious or oppressive. Something more—the lack of a legitimate juridical advantage—has to be shown, before it becomes so. Yet, later on in the judgment, the majority in the *CSR* case repeats the passage cited above from *Henry v Henry* without suggesting that it has been abandoned or qualified. How are the two statements to be reconciled?

One answer may be that in the earlier passage in the *CSR* case, the Court was merely making the point that foreign parallel proceedings should not be restrained by anti-suit injunction merely because they are parallel proceedings. It is well established that the forum should be more cautious in restraining foreign proceedings than in restraining its own.[47] The existence of the foreign parallel proceedings is therefore a factor to be considered in granting a stay of the local proceedings on *forum non conveniens* grounds. That issue will be further explained below. It is sufficient to note at this stage that the decisions in *Henry v Henry* and *CSR Ltd v Cigna Insurance Australia Ltd* have not altered the basic proposition, as noted by Fawcett in his General Report in *Declining Jurisdiction in Private International Law*, that the common law treats *lis alibi pendens* as nothing more than an aspect of *forum non conveniens*.[48]

---

[44] (1996) 185 CLR 571 at 592.

[45] (1997) 189 CLR 345.

[46] ibid at 393 *per* Dawson, Toohey, Gaudron, McHugh, Gummow, and Kirby JJ. Their Honours specifically referred to *Peruvian Guano Co v Bockwoldt* (1883) 23 Ch D 225 as having continuing significance: ibid.

[47] *Société Nationale Industrielle Aerospatiale v Lee Kui Jak* [1987] AC 871 at 895–6.

[48] See, Fawcett, n 1 above, p 29. It is dubious whether it can even be described as an 'important facet'.

(2) Lis Pendens *in the Civil Law*

Although the strict rule of *lis pendens* presently found in Article 27 of the Brussels Regulation is viewed as an essentially civil law doctrine, the research by Fawcett has shown that it does not have a particularly ancient pedigree in civil law systems. It does have its precedents in the domestic law of the various Member States, but it took some time to translate to international litigation.[49] It is probably fair to say that Article 21 of the original Brussels Convention transformed a principle established in the domestic law of some of the Member States into an international rule.

(3) *The Brussels Provisions*

In its original form Article 21 of the Brussels Convention provided that in the case of proceedings involving the same cause of action and the same parties, any court other than the court first seised shall of its own motion decline jurisdiction in favour of the first court. That absolute rule was only qualified in the case where the jurisdiction of the first court was contested. In that case the second court had a discretion to stay its proceedings until the jurisdiction of the first court was established. The provision was slightly modified in 1989 and now reads in the version appearing as Article 27 of the Brussels I Regulation:

1. Where proceedings involving the same cause of action and between the same parties are brought in the courts of different Member States, any court other than the court first seised shall of its own motion stay its proceedings until such time as the jurisdiction of the court first seised is established.
2. Where the jurisdiction of the court first seised is established, any court other than the court first seised shall decline jurisdiction in favour of that court.

There is therefore no longer the risk of a gap in the case where the court first seised feels compelled to refuse jurisdiction, even though it was not contested at the time the second proceedings were brought. The parties are therefore assured of a forum in either the court first seised or in a court subsequently seised.[50]

---

[49] This appears to have been the situation in France: see national report by Gaudemet-Tallon in Fawcett, n 1 above, pp 180–1. In some countries it was barely known or applied with flexibility, see for Finland, Klami in Fawcett, p 171 and for Greece, it appears to be only of domestic significance, ibid Kargados and Moustaika at pp 248–9. In Belgium international *lis pendens* only operates by force of treaty: ibid Fallon at pp 107–110. In Italy the principle was applied more restrictively (if at all) in international cases as opposed to domestic cases: ibid, Trocker, pp 281–294. See also, Baumgartner, 'Related Actions', *ZZPInt* 3 (1998) 203, 204–5.

[50] This follows the concerns expressed in the *Jenard-Møller Report on the Lugano Convention* [1988] OJ C189/60 at p 78, para 64.

It is not the purpose of this paper to analyse in any detail the jurisprudence relating to this provision. It suffices to say that the words 'involving the same cause of action and between the same parties' have been broadly interpreted to cover situations where the claims are based on the same factual situation or contractual or other relationship and concern the same legal issues, even if in the strict sense the causes of action and the relief sought are different.[51] Most relevantly this means that an action seeking to establish liability for the breach of a contractual or other obligation and an action seeking a declaration in respect of the same event that no liability has arisen out of it ('negative declaration') fall within the scope of Article 21.[52] Needless to say, this allows a potential defendant to select the forum by proceeding first with an action for a negative declaration. The forum selected as a result of the jockeying for the most advantageous position may not always be the most appropriate forum. But, even if it were willing, the forum first seised cannot cede jurisdiction to the court second seised. Nor can it decline jurisdiction if it is properly seised under the Convention or Regulation.

Another problem that has arisen in relation to the Brussels Convention is the lack of uniformity as regards the date of commencement of proceedings under national law. The European Court of Justice in *Zelger v Salinitri (No 2)*[53] declined to give an autonomous interpretation on when a court could be considered to be seised of a matter, leaving this issue to be determined by the national law of the forum. However, national law is divided between those who favour the date on which proceedings are filed in court and those who favour the date of service of proceedings. As regards the latter, there is a further complication: is service on the defendant effected when the documents are delivered to the defendant, or when they are delivered to the public official charged in some countries with the service of process? Finally, in some countries service must be effected before the documents can be filed in the court registry.[54]

---

[51] *Gubisch Maschinenfabrik KG v Palumbo* [1987] ECR 4861; *The Tatry* [1994] ECR 1–5493; compare *Henry v Henry* (1996) 185 CLR 571 at 591–2 where there was held to be a coincidence of the subject matter in controversy—the marital relationship—where one party sought a divorce and financial settlement and the other a decree of judicial separation.

[52] *The Tatry*, n 51 above. See also *Overseas Union Insurance v New Hampshire Insurance* [1991] ECR I-3317.

[53] [1984] ECR 2397.

[54] See Møller, 'The date upon which a Finnish and a Swedish Court becomes seised for the purposes of the European Judgments Convention', in *E Pluribus Unum:Liber Amicorum Georges A L Droz* (1996), pp 219–233.

That problem has now been dealt with by including the following provision in Article 30 of the Brussels I Regulation:

> For the purposes of this Section, a court shall be deemed to be seised:
> 1. at the time when the document instituting the proceedings or an equivalent document is lodged with the court, provided that the plaintiff has not subsequently failed to take steps he was required to take to have service effected on the defendant, or
> 2. if the document has to be served before being lodged with the court, at the time when it is received by the authority responsible for service, provided that the plaintiff has not subsequently failed to take the steps he was required to take to have the document lodged with the court.

(4) The Leuven-London Principles

The Committee of the International Law Association on International Civil and Commercial Litigation considered the issue of declining jurisdiction at its meetings between 1997 and 2000. The Committee's membership consists of scholars and practitioners from both the common law and civil law traditions, both within and outside Europe. It developed certain principles, known as the Leuven-London Principles on Declining and Referring Jurisdiction in International Litigation[55] that were accepted at the 69th Conference of the International Law Association in London in July 2000.[56] As the title of its document indicates, the Committee sought to couple the principles upon which jurisdiction was to be declined with an assurance that the claims brought by the plaintiff would, in such a case, be referred to another court that not only had jurisdiction but would assume it. This is, of course, the principle that has been a part of Article 21 of the Brussels Convention since 1989.

The Committee considered but rejected a proposal to subsume the notion of *lis pendens* in a general rule of referring jurisdiction on grounds similar to *forum non conveniens*[57]—the common law approach. It saw merit in maintaining *lis pendens* as a separate rule. Thus as a primary principle the approach found in Article 21 of the Brussels Convention was to be maintained: the court second seised has to defer to the court first seised by suspending its proceedings until

---

[55] The reference to Leuven reflects the fact that the Committee formulated the Principles at its meeting in Leuven, Belgium, in November 1998. They were ultimately approved in London.

[56] See *Report of the 69th Conference*, London, 2000, p 137.

[57] The term '*forum non conveniens*' is not used in the Principles. They use the words 'referral of proceedings'. The reason is twofold: to avoid the use of a term which has different meanings in common law countries and to stress that its function is not merely to decline jurisdiction but to refer the matter to another court that will assume jurisdiction.

such time that the court first seised has established its jurisdiction and not declined it. If the first court assumes jurisdiction, the second court must terminate the proceedings before it. But, unlike the Brussels Convention, the Committee proposes that the court first seised have the opportunity to refer the matter to a court subsequently seised in accordance with the principles proposed by it in relation to referring jurisdiction generally. In the latter case, the court subsequently seised need not terminate its proceedings.[58]

The principles upon which referral is to take place generally under the Committee's proposals will be discussed below. The point to be stressed here is that the major departure from the Brussels prototype is the ability of the court first seised (and only that court) to refer the matter to a court subsequently seised (and only such a court). The court first seised retains primacy and is in charge.

(5) The Preliminary Draft Convention

The Preliminary Draft Convention adopts an approach similar to that recommended by the ILA Committee, as described above. By sheer coincidence the provision for *lis pendens* is also found in an Article 21. As recommended by the ILA Committee it is closely linked with the proposal for a more general discretion to decline jurisdiction in Article 22 as part of a compromise package.[59] The first two paragraphs of Article 21 repeat in substance the language now found in Article 23 of the Brussels I Regulation and Article 30 of the Regulation has its counterpart in Article 21(5) of the Preliminary Draft. With one important exception, referred to below, the provision is likely to bear the same meaning as its prototype.[60]

The major differences are:

• Under the Hague proposals the suspension of proceedings in the court subsequently seised lasts until it is presented with a judgment by the court first seised that is entitled to recognition under the Convention.[61] Under the Brussels I Regulation the proceedings in the second court must be terminated as soon as the first court has established its jurisdiction. Furthermore,

---

[58] Leuven-London Principles, Principle 4.1. See also *Report* , n 56 above, pp 158–9, paras 60 to 62.

[59] See Nygh and Pocar, *Preliminary Draft Convention on Jurisdiction and Foreign Judgments in Civil and Commercial Matters*, August 2000, p 85.

[60] ibid, p 85.

[61] Preliminary Draft Convention Art 21(2). A similar provision appears in the Swiss Private International Law Statute Art 9(3).

under the Hague draft the court subsequently seised may resume the suspended proceedings 'if the plaintiff in the court first seised has failed to take the necessary steps to bring the proceedings to a decision on the merits or if that court has not rendered such a decision within a reasonable time'.[62] This provision further narrows the risk of a 'gap' developing whereby both fora are immobilized.

- In contrast with both the Brussels I Regulation and the Leuven-London Principles, the Preliminary Draft not only deprives an action for a negative declaration (an action where 'the plaintiff seeks a determination that it has no obligation to the defendant') of the status of a parallel *lis*, but it also reverses the priority between the fora. If an action is brought for a negative declaration in the court first seised and an action seeking substantive relief is brought in the court second seised, it is the court first seised that must suspend the proceedings.[63]

- Finally, but most importantly, the Hague proposals follow the Leuven-London Principles in providing that the court first seised may yield its primacy to the court second seised if it determines that the latter court 'is clearly more appropriate to resolve the dispute, under the conditions specified in Article 22'.[64] As in the Leuven-London proposals that option is only open to the forum first seised and can only be exercised in favour of the forum second seised. Each forum must be a court of a Contracting State.[65]

F. Related Actions

(1) Common Law

This is another area that is unknown to the common law as such, although the existence of a related action can be an important factor in determining whether a forum is clearly more appropriate. The existence in England of a very similar action involving the same defendants and arising out of the same facts (the '*Cambridgeshire* factor') was an important consideration in *Spiliada Maritime*

---

[62] ibid, Art 21(3). See, Swiss Private International Law Statute Art 9(1) which mandates suspension only 'if it is to be expected that the foreign court will, within a reasonable time, render a judgment recognisable in Switzerland'. A resumption of the original proceedings in the case of delay is also foreseen in Principle 5.8 of the Leuven-London Principles.

[63] ibid, Art 21(6). See Nygh and Pocar, n 59 above, pp 87–8.

[64] ibid, Art 21(7). See, Nygh and Pocar, n 59 above, p 88.

[65] ibid, Art 2(1)(c).

Corp v Cansulex Ltd[66] leading to the conclusion that England was the more appropriate forum in that case. Since the plaintiffs in each case were different and apparently not connected, it is probably incorrect to describe the two actions as 'related', but the connection would only have been the stronger if they had been related.

However, the notion of 'related proceedings' as a distinct concept has some support in Australian case law and legislation. A situation of related actions is found in the Australian case of *CSR Ltd v Cigna Insurance Australia Ltd*.[67] In this case actions were pending in the United States and in New South Wales. The substratum of the actions was the same: they flowed out of the attempt by CSR Ltd, an Australian company, to recover indemnity from its insurers, Cigna Corporation, a US corporation, in respect of claims made in the United States for damage suffered through inhalation by workmen there of asbestos mined by CSR Ltd in Australia and exported by it to the United States. CSR Ltd and its US subsidiary commenced the first proceedings in the United States against Cigna Corporation and other insurers seeking indemnity, the payment of damages and statutory treble damages for violation of the US Sherman Act. Subsequently, Cigna Corporation's Australian subsidiary, Cigna Insurance Australia Ltd, brought action in New South Wales against CSR Ltd and its US subsidiary, seeking an anti-suit injunction restraining the US proceedings as well as a negative declaration that they owed no obligations under the relevant policies to indemnify CSR Ltd either in respect of the US claims or in respect of similar claims made against CSR Ltd in Australia. The High Court pointed out that the subject matter of each set of litigation was not the same, saying:

> There is not the same correspondence of subject matter in this case. As already indicated, the NSW proceedings. but not the US proceedings, extend to the Australian asbestos claims, as well as the American asbestos claims. More importantly, the US proceedings, but not the NSW proceedings, involve claims for damages against Cigna Corporation. And the parties accept that one of those claims, namely the claim for statutory treble damages under the Sherman Act, cannot be pursued in the NSW proceedings.[68]

---

[66] [1987] AC 640.
[67] (1997) 189 CLR 345.
[68] ibid at 399 *per* Dawson, Toohey, Gaudron, McHugh, Gummow, and Kirby JJ. At 401 the same judges point out that the Supreme Court of New South Wales could not deal with the Sherman claims instituted by CSR in the US.

It was the last-mentioned consideration that led the High Court to conclude upon consideration of the issues in dispute in both proceedings that New South Wales was a 'clearly inappropriate forum' for the litigation of the matters in dispute between the parties in the United States. The Court stayed the NSW proceedings and refused to restrain the US proceedings thereby referring the parties to the US as the sole forum. Although the Court did not say so expressly, it is clear that the ability of the US court to deal with all issues was an important consideration.[69] Thus, the real test was one of the more appropriate forum and that is the forum able to deal with all the issues in dispute between the parties.

Under the Australian cross-vesting legislation a proceeding may be transferred as between the Supreme Courts of the States and Territories of Australia and from the Federal and Family Courts of Australia to the Supreme Courts on the ground, *inter alia*, that the relevant proceeding arises out of, or is related to, another proceeding pending in the transferee court and it is more appropriate that the matter be dealt with in that court.[70] It is generally not relevant whether the transferring court is the one second seised or first seised.[71] Neither at common law or by statute is any definition of 'related action' provided. In so far as the Australian courts have sought to apply the provision they have stressed the degree of impact that the one set of proceedings might have upon the other, if they were successful.[72] This would certainly cover, but possibly be wider, than a test based on the risk of irreconcilable judgments. However, as the use of the words 'it is more appropriate' indicates, essentially the test is one of *forum conveniens*. The Australian provision is unique in that it permits the transfer of the

---

[69] The ostensible and more debatable reason given was that the proceedings in NSW had been commenced 'with the dominant purpose of preventing another party from pursuing remedies available in the courts of another country and not available in this country', ibid at 401. In effect, the Court saw the application for the negative declaration as an attempt to conceal the true purpose of stopping the US proceedings: ibid. But the liability of the insurer was a real issue in the proceedings. See further, Nygh and Davies, *Conflict of Laws in Australia*, 7th edn, 2002) para 7.22.

[70] See, Jurisdiction of Courts (Cross-vesting) Act 1987 (Cth) s 5(2)(i) and parallel legislation in each of the States and self-governing Territories. The attempt to cross-vest State jurisdiction in federal courts was held to be invalid on constitutional grounds by the High Court in *Re Wakim, ex parte McNulty* (1999) 198 CLR 511. For the interpretation of this provision, see Nygh and Davies, n 69 above, para 6.10.

[71] Thus in *Re Hamilton-Irvine and the Companies Act 1985* (1990) 94 ALR 428 it is unclear whether Mr Hamilton-Irvine or his wife first commenced proceedings.

[72] *Bell Group Ltd (in liq) v Westpac Banking Corp* (2000) 173 ALR 427 at 464 *per* Carr J (Federal Court of Australia).

actual file and in that the transferee court will have jurisdiction to hear and determine the transferred matter even though otherwise jurisdiction would be lacking.[73]

(2) The Brussels Convention and Regulation

Although provisions with respect to related actions are found in the domestic legislation of some of the Member States, it seems that there was no provision at the transnational level before Article 22 of the Brussels Convention was enacted in 1968.[74] Article 22 has now been re-enacted as Article 28 of the Brussels I Regulation. In so doing the opportunity has been taken to rectify an anomaly in the original text.[75] It is therefore best to confine discussion to Article 28. Paragraph 1 of that provision gives a discretion to the court subsequently seised in related proceedings to stay its proceedings. Presumably, this is the same power that common law courts have inherently to temporarily stay proceedings to allow another court either at first instance or on appeal to determine issues that may be relevant (or even raise cause of action or issue estoppel) to the proceedings before it.[76] More important is paragraph 2 that gives an additional discretion to the court subsequently seised in cases where the related proceedings are pending at first instance, 'to decline jurisdiction if the court first seised has jurisdiction over the actions in question and its law permits the consolidation thereof'.

It will be seen that only the court first seised can hear the consolidated proceedings. The fact that a court subsequently seised may be the more appropriate forum is irrelevant. 'Related proceedings' are defined in paragraph 3 'where they are so closely connected that it is expedient to hear and determine them together to avoid the risk of irreconcilable judgments resulting from separate proceedings'. The word 'irreconcilable' has been broadly interpreted by the European Court of Justice in *The Tatry*[77] as involving 'a risk of conflicting decisions, without necessarily involving the risk of giving rise to mutually exclusive legal consequences'. This interpretation is still considerably narrower than the Australian query whether a decision in the one proceeding will have an im-

---

[73] Jurisdiction of Courts (Cross-vesting) Act 1987 (Cth) s 4 and parallel legislation in each State and self-governing Territory.

[74] See Baumgartner, 'Related Actions' (1998) *ZZPInt* 3 203, 206–9.

[75] See Briggs and Rees, *Civil Jurisdiction and Judgments* (2nd edn, 1997), para 2.217.

[76] See *Sterling Pharmaceuticals Pty Ltd v Boots & Co (Aust) Pty Ltd* (1992) 34 FCR 287 at 294 *per* Lockhart J (Australian proceedings in trade mark infringement stayed pending determination of similar issues between the same parties in New Zealand).

[77] [1994] ECR I-5439 at 5482, para 5.

pact on the outcome of the other. It is clear however that proceedings can be 'related' if the subject matter of the litigation is the same although the parties differ, and where the parties are the same, but the subject matter differs.[78] This is similar to the common law position.[79]

(3) The Leuven-London Principles

The Leuven-London Principles propose an important liberalisation of the provisions now found in Article 28 of the Brussels I Regulation. Principle 4.2 proposes that either court should be able to suspend or terminate the related proceedings before it and refer the matter to the alternative court in accordance with the procedure laid down in Principle 5. The latter Principle will be more fully discussed in relation to the general power of referral. It is sufficient to note at this stage that this Principle seeks to ensure that the matter to be referred will actually be dealt with by the alternative court and within a reasonable time. As with Article 27, it is a precondition for referral that the transferee court has jurisdiction in respect of the proceedings[80] and that the actions can be consolidated there.[81]

The Leuven-London Principles are a considerable advance on the relative rigidity still found in Article 28 of the Brussels I Regulation. They come close in effect to the provisions of the Australian cross-vesting legislation that have operated successfully despite the constitutional hurdles erected by the High Court. The Principles do not define what is meant by 'related actions'. This is not surprising since they merely state basic principles and do not purport to provide a legislative code. Should a definition be considered necessary, the Australian 'impact test', as discussed above, may be appropriate. Nor do they state which jurisdiction is to be preferred. It is a fair inference that this should be the jurisdiction that will have jurisdiction in respect of all claims[82] and, if both are able to do so, the jurisdiction that is more appropriate in dealing with the litigation having regard to the convenience of the parties, the balance of juridical advantage and the applicable law.

---

[78] ibid and see Briggs and Rees, n 75 above, para 2.215.
[79] See, the so-called *Cambridgeshire* factor in *Spiliada Maritime Corp v Cansulex Ltd* where the plaintiffs differed but the claims arose out of the same incident and were made against the same defendant, and *CSR Ltd v Cigna Insurance Australia Ltd* as discussed above, n 67.
[80] See Principle 5.1(a).
[81] See Principle 4.2.
[82] This may resolve the issue in many cases, see *CSR Ltd v Cigna Insurance Australia Ltd*, n 67 above. Of course, even if a court is able to deal with all claims, this does not exclude that it may be an inappropriate forum on other grounds.

(4) The Preliminary Draft Convention

The Preliminary Draft Convention makes no reference to 'related actions' nor was any proposal for such a provision the subject of serious discussion. It may therefore still arise if and when the Draft Convention is to be completed.

One issue that should be then considered is whether a separate provision will be really necessary. As mentioned earlier, the common law has treated the existence of related actions as a factor in determining whether another forum is clearly more appropriate. The Australian cross-vesting legislation has basically adopted the same approach although at a more demanding level. The provisions of Article 22 of the Preliminary Draft Convention, to be discussed below, certainly do not exclude the existence of related actions as a factor in determining whether jurisdiction should be declined. In any event, it would be advisable to include specific reference to the existence of related actions in the list of factors to be considered that presently appears in Article 22(2).

G. General Grounds for Declining Jurisdiction

(1) Forum Non Conveniens

The common law principle of *forum non conveniens* offers courts a discretionary mechanism to decline jurisdiction in cases where the plaintiff has commenced proceedings in an inappropriate forum. Although the mechanism has only come into frequent use during the last two decades, it has much earlier antecedents. It started with the statutory discretion that English courts had to exercise in deciding whether or not to grant leave to serve a defendant out of the jurisdiction under what was then known as Order 11 of the Rules of the Supreme Court.[83] As early as 1885 it was said that an English court 'must consider seriously whether it would be a convenient forum to try the rights and obligations of a foreigner, who, at common law, owes no allegiance or obedience to the court'.[84] This discretion did not exist in cases where the defendant was served within the jurisdiction.[85] Although it was relatively rare, jurisdiction was at times declined in cases where the connection between England and the alleged wrong was slight and the matter could be more effectively dealt with

---

[83] Those provisions are now found in the Civil Procedure Rules, Pt 6.
[84] *Société Générale de Paris v Dreyfus Bros* (1885) 29 Ch D 239 at 242–3 *per* Pearson LJ.
[85] See, eg, *Maharanee of Baroda v Wildenstein* [1972] 1 QB 282.

by a foreign court.[86] However, even if the connection with England was slight, a plaintiff would not be sent away if it was unlikely that he would obtain justice in the otherwise more appropriate forum.[87]

The House of Lords in *Spiliada Maritime Corporation v Cansulex Ltd*[88] extended this discretion to the non-statutory bases of jurisdiction, in other words, to persons who did at common law owe allegiance to English courts. In so doing the House of Lords adopted as part of English law the Scottish formulation of *forum non conveniens* as arising where: 'there is some other tribunal, having competent jurisdiction, in which the case may be tried more suitably for the interests of all the parties and for the ends of justice'.[89] This involves an inquiry at two stages. The first stage inquires whether 'there is another available forum which is clearly or distinctly more appropriate than the English forum'.[90] The word 'available forum' refers to a forum that has jurisdiction in respect of the parties and the subject matter but the House of Lords in *Lubbe v Cape plc* held that such jurisdiction can be conferred by the submission of the defendant. It need not exist independently.[91] The determination of which is the 'clearly more appropriate forum' involves connecting factors, such as the residence and place of business of each of the parties, the availability of the evidence, and the applicable law. It is normally for the defendant to establish that such a forum exists.

If the answer to the first inquiry is positive, the need for making a second inquiry may arise. This is whether 'there are circumstances by reason of which justice requires that a stay should nevertheless not be granted'.[92] A stay has been refused in cases where the plaintiff would be regarded as an enemy in the

---

[86] *Kroch v Rossell & Cie* [1937] 1 All ER 725; *Rosler v Hilbery* [1925] Ch 250. In New Zealand, see *Eyre v Nationwide News Ltd* [1967] NZLR 851.

[87] *Oppenheimer v Louis Rosenthal & Co AG* [1937] 1 All ER 23 (Jewish employee at London branch office dismissed in breach of contract by Nazi controllers of German company).

[88] [1987] 1 AC 460 at 474 *per* Lord Goff of Chieveley.

[89] ibid, citing Lord Kinnear in *Sim v Robinow* [1892] 19 R 665 at 668. For the origins of the principle in Scots law, see: Anton, *Private International Law* (1st edn, 1967), pp 148–154.

[90] [1987] 1 AC 460 at 477.

[91] See *Lubbe v Cape plc* [2000] 1 WLR 1545 at 1562–66 *per* Lord Hope of Craighead. But this proposition is not generally accepted: see Dicey and Morris at para 12–123 (written before the House of Lords decision in *Lubbe*) and see also, *CSR Ltd v Cigna Insurance Australia Ltd* (1997) 189 CLR 345 at 401 *per* Dawson, Toohey, Gaudron, McHugh, Gummow, and Kirby JJ who considered it relevant that the US parent company, Cigna Corporation, was not within the jurisdiction of the Supreme Court of New South Wales, except through submission.

[92] [1987] 1 AC 460 at 478.

foreign court,[93] or where the alternative forum was a country with inadequate or no provision for legal aid[94] or where legal services generally were underdeveloped.[95] In this inquiry the onus rests on the plaintiff resisting the stay.

The High Court of Australia rejected the *Spiliada* test in *Voth v Manildra Flour Mills Pty Ltd.*[96] Instead, it adopted a single inquiry: whether the forum chosen by the plaintiff is 'clearly inappropriate' in the sense that it was in an objective sense oppressive and vexatious to the defendant to continue the proceedings in that particular forum.[97]

The advantage that their Honours saw in the single inquiry was that it made it unnecessary to compare fora in order to determine which was the more appropriate and that there was no need for the second inquiry into the needs of justice. Indeed their Honours appear to suggest that if the chosen forum is 'clearly inappropriate', the fact that another forum is not available is not relevant.[98]

This 'pure' approach was abandoned by the majority of the Court in *Henry v Henry*[99] where the Court was faced with a *lis pendens* situation. Only Brennan CJ maintained the position that the only question was whether the Australian forum was 'clearly inappropriate'.[100] He agreed with the majority that it was because the parties to this marital dispute had never lived in, or even visited, Australia as husband and wife nor did they have any matrimonial assets there. The question of whether another forum was available to resolve their dispute was for him of no relevance. However, the majority did compare the alternative fora and decided, in effect, that the foreign forum was 'more appropriate' because of its greater connection with the marriage and the prior institution of proceedings there. It is therefore necessary in Australia to draw a distinction between the 'single forum' situation where a theoretical alternative forum may not be considered, and the 'multiple fora' situation where the proceedings in both places must be considered and, as in fact occurred in *CSR Ltd v Cigna*

---

[93] *Mohammed v Bank of Kuwait and Middle East KSC* [1996] 1 WLR 1483.
[94] *Connelly v RTZ plc* [1998] AC 854.
[95] *Lubbe v Cape plc* [2000] 1 WLR 1545.
[96] (1991) 171 CLR 538.
[97] ibid at 557–8 per Mason CJ, Deane, Dawson, and Gaudron JJ. Their Honours endorsed the remarks on this point made by Deane J in *Oceanic Sun Line Special Shipping Co Inc v Fay* (1988) 165 CLR 197 at 247.
[98] ibid at 558–9.
[99] (1996) 185 CLR 571.
[100] ibid at 558–9.

Insurance Australia Ltd,[101] the Australian forum, although 'appropriate' in respect of the proceedings actually before it, can become 'clearly inappropriate' because it can not deal with all matters in issue between the parties.[102] In the latter case the Australian forum becomes 'clearly inappropriate' because the foreign forum is 'clearly more appropriate'. This is, of course, playing with words and the High Court may in the future have to decide whether it can continue to justify this.

The notion of *forum non conveniens* developed separately in the United States.[103] Professor Weintraub has formulated the current policy as follows:

> Under the doctrine of *forum non conveniens*, a court may decline to exercise its jurisdiction if the court finds that it is a 'seriously inconvenient' forum and that the interests of the parties and of the public will be best served by remitting the plaintiff to another, more convenient, forum that is available to him.[104]

Like the *Spiliada* test, the US test is based on a comparison of fora and requires that there be another more appropriate forum available with jurisdiction over the parties and subject matter. The US test appears to require a finding that the forum selected by the plaintiff be 'seriously inconvenient' whereas under the *Spiliada* test that is not necessary. Under the latter test the forum selected by the plaintiff need not be 'inappropriate' provided the alternative forum is 'clearly more appropriate'.[105] But the major difference lies in the 'public interest' consideration.

Although adumbrated by the US Supreme Court as early as 1947,[106] it was further developed by that Court in *Piper Aircraft Co v Reyno*[107] into a rule whereby jurisdiction can be declined by the jurisdiction of the residence of a US defendant if the plaintiff is a foreigner and the relevant events giving rise to the litigation have taken place in the plaintiff's country of residence. That rule was explicitly based on a fear of a flood of foreign litigation: 'The American courts, which are already extremely attractive to foreign plaintiffs, would become even

---

[101] (1997) 189 CLR 345.
[102] ibid at 400–1.
[103] For the historical background, see Del Luca and Zaphiriou, United States Report in Fawcett (ed), *Declining Jurisdiction in Private International Law* (OUP, 1995), pp 401, 403–7.
[104] Weintraub, *Commentary on the Conflict of Laws* (3rd edn, 1986), p 213.
[105] See *Connelly v RTZ Corp plc* [1998] AC 854 at 873 *per* Lord Goff of Chieveley (suing at the place of residence of defendant cannot be inappropriate).
[106] *Gulf Oil Corp v Gilbert*, 330 US 501, 508–9 (1947).
[107] 454 US 235 (1981).

more attractive. The flow of litigation into the United States would increase and further congest already crowded courts'.[108] This consideration would not necessarily apply to US plaintiffs suing foreign defendants in US courts. It is the foreign plaintiff whose interests demand 'less deference' than the US one.[109] The fact that the remedy provided in the alternative forum was less favourable to the plaintiff was no objection, unless 'the remedy provided by the alternative forum is so clearly inadequate or unsatisfactory that it is no remedy at all'. In such a case dismissal would not be 'in the interests of justice'.[110] Although the test of 'the interests of justice' is formulated in the same manner as in England, its application in the United States has been very different.

The public interest factor was used most prominently to decline jurisdiction in the *Bhopal* case[111] despite the submissions by the Indian government that its legal system was not equipped to deal with mass tort claims. It has also been successfully invoked in other cases where foreign plaintiffs brought suit in the United States against United States defendants in respect of consumer, industrial and environmental claims arising out of the practices of those companies and/or their subsidiaries abroad.[112] The fact that the legal systems in some of those countries were so inadequate as to render any remedy meaningless, does not appear to have perturbed the US courts at all.[113]

In England and Australia, on the other hand, the courts have rejected any notion of a 'public interest factor'.[114] A foreign plaintiff is not to be treated with any less deference than a local plaintiff.

---

[108] 454 US 235 (1981) at 252 per Marshall J.

[109] ibid at 256.

[110] ibid at 254.

[111] *In re Union Carbide Corporation Gas Plant Disaster at Bhopal, India, in December 1984*, 634 F Supp 842 (SDNY 1986); aff'd 809 F 2d 195 (2d Cir). The Indian Government represented the individual plaintiffs before the US court.

[112] See, *Stangvik v Shiley Inc*, 819 P 2d 14 (Cal 1991); *Delgado v Shell Oil Co*, 890 F Suppl 1324 (SD Tex 1995); *Polanco v H B Fuller Co*, 941 F Suppl 1512 (D Minn 1996); *Iragori v United Tech Corp*, 46 F Suppl 2d 159 (D Conn 1999) (where interestingly the plaintiff, although a US citizen, was denied 'deference' because of long-term residence abroad); *Jota v Texaco Inc*, 157 F 3d 153 (2d Cir 1998).

[113] See, for a critical discussion of the US practice: C M Marlowe, 'International Forum Non Conveniens', (2001) 32 Inter-American LR 295. Referring a plaintiff to a judicial system where he may not be afforded adequate legal representation may be a violation of the right to 'a fair and public hearing within a reasonable time' in relation to his civil rights under Art 6(1) of the European Convention on Human Rights: see the remarks by Lord Bingham of Cornhill in *Lubbe v Cape plc* [2000] 1 WLR 1545 at 1561. See also: the UN Convention on Civil and Political Rights 1966, Art 14.

[114] *Lubbe v Cape plc* [2000] 1 WLR 1545 at 1561 *per* Lord Bingham of Cornhill, at 1566–7

(2) The Brussels Convention and Regulation

The idea of *forum non conveniens* is not known to the civil law as such. Indeed, to some civil lawyers the very idea that a judge can decline to exercise a jurisdiction the law has vested in him, is offensive. This does not mean, as Fawcett has pointed out, that civil law courts do not have a discretion in some cases to decline jurisdiction on the basis of insufficient connection with the forum. But this is often disguised as a lack of jurisdiction as opposed to a discretion to decline to exercise it.[115]

It is therefore not surprising that the original Brussels Convention of 1968 made no provision for declining jurisdiction on the ground of *forum non conveniens*. Indeed, as I have shown, the notion was only partially developed in England at the time and even later when the United Kingdom acceded to the Community. But it was also not accepted as part of the revision that resulted in the Brussels I Regulation 2001.

(3) The Leuven-London Principles

The ILA Committee in the drafting of its Principles sought to meet some of the concerns expressed by civil lawyers, notably that the common law notion of *forum non conveniens* gave courts too much discretion and could result in a plaintiff being denied access to a court that would hear the complaint. The Committee decided to avoid use of the term '*forum non conveniens*' and its accompanying common law baggage. Instead it refers to 'Other grounds for referral'. This is not a semantic change. What the Committee aims at is the referral of the proceedings to the more appropriate forum, rather than their simple dismissal or stay leaving the plaintiff to find another court. Thus, the opening sentence of Principle 4.3 reads:

> An originating court shall decline jurisdiction and refer the matter to an alternative court where it is satisfied that the alternative court is the manifestly more appropriate forum for the determination of the merits of the matter, taking into account the interests of all of the parties, without discrimination on grounds of nationality.

The protocol to be followed in referring the matter to another court is laid down in Principle 5. Most important among the conditions to be satisfied is

---

per Lord Hope of Craighead; *Voth v Manildra Flour Mills Pty Ltd* (1990) 171 CLR 538 at 561 per Mason CJ, Deane, Dawson, and Gaudron JJ. See also: *James Hardie & Co v Grigor* (1998) 45 NSWLR 20 (NSW CA).

[115] See, Fawcett, n 1 above, pp 24–7.

that laid down in Principle 5.1 which requires the applicant for a referral to satisfy the originating court that the alternative court:

(a) has and will exercise jurisdiction over the matter; and
(b) is likely to render its judgment on the merits within a reasonable time.

Under Principle 5.7 the applicant is obliged to promptly inform the originating court that the alternative court has assumed jurisdiction and shall cooperate with any consequential order the originating court may wish to make, including an order to terminate the proceedings in the originating court. If the alternative court does not assume jurisdiction for any reason, then under Principle 5.8 the originating court may assume jurisdiction.

This goes much further than the common law notion of *forum non conveniens* discussed above. Although the common law notion requires satisfaction that in principle an alternative forum is available, the courts do not normally wait to see whether in fact the alternative forum will exercise jurisdiction effectively and promptly.[116] In other respects Principle 4.3 reflects the reasoning in *Spiliada*. Thus, it looks for the manifestly more appropriate forum rather than inquires into the inappropriateness of the initial forum seised. It does not specifically refer in the text or in the Commentary to the 'needs of justice', but it is implicit in the reference to 'the interests of all the parties' that the plaintiff cannot be referred to a forum that would deny it justice.[117]

Another important provision is found in Principle 5.3. That provision encourages the parties and the originating court to consider appropriate terms of referral on issues such as the applicant's submission to the alternative court and the possible waiver of a defence based on time-bars.

Very important is the direction that the interests of the parties must be considered 'without discrimination on the ground of nationality'. There are two aspects here: firstly it is the interests of the parties, not that of the court, that must be considered. Secondly, there must be equal deference given to the interests of a foreign and a local plaintiff. In other words, there is no place for the approach taken by the US Supreme Court described above.

---

[116] Thus an undertaking to submit to a foreign court does not by itself confer jurisdiction on that court nor may it accept it, see Dicey and Morris, para 12–023. The foreign court may also be ill-equipped to deal with the litigation: see particularly the US cases referred to in n 112 above.
[117] *Mohammed v Bank of Kuwait and the Middle East KSC* [1996] 1 WLR 1483 at 1495 *per* Evans LJ. If there is a separate test that looks at 'substantial justice', then obviously one must use it, see Cheshire and North, pp 336–7. But the omission of such a separate test does not mean that the issue becomes irrelevant.

Principle 4.3 also sets out in a non-hierarchical and non-exhaustive manner some of the factors that the referring court shall take into consideration in coming to its decision. It refers to the convenience of the parties and their witnesses, the balance of advantage afforded by the law, procedure and practice of each jurisdiction to each of the parties, and the applicable law. This sweeps all relevant factors together in a single stage inquiry, as in the Australian approach. But it also directs attention to the enforceability of any resulting judgment. That issue was considered by the High Court of Australia in *Henry v Henry*[118] where the majority judgment pointed out that it was not only enforceability in the referring forum that was important, but also enforceability in any third country where assets were situated.[119]

Finally the Principle refers to 'the efficient operation of the judicial system of the respective jurisdictions'. This is explained in the commentary as including 'both the extent to which the respective systems will decide the dispute effectively, and the impact which hearing the dispute will have on the efficient operation of the respective systems'.[120] This raises a sensitive issue: to what extent it is legitimate for a court to pass judgment on a foreign judicial system? In *Voth v Manildra Flour Mills Pty Ltd*, the High Court saw as a merit of the sole inquiry that it would avoid such invidious comparisons.[121] They thought that this might be inevitable under the *Spiliada* inquiry. But in *Lubbe v Cape plc* the House of Lords and the courts below were careful not to make such comparisons.[122] However, they did make a comparison between the ability of the respective legal services as a whole, such as the ability to fund litigation by indigent plaintiffs and the ability to handle complex litigation, in favour of the English system.[123] The risk, of course, is that a judgment may be made about a foreign legal system on dubious evidence. This happened recently in the child abduction case of *JLM v Director General, NSW Dept of Community Services*[124] where the majority judgment in the High Court appears to have given weight

---

[118] (1996) 185 CLR 571 at 592.

[119] In *Henry v Henry*, although the choice of forum lay between Australia and Monaco, it was understood that a substantial part of the assets of the respondent husband was situated in Switzerland, ibid, at 582–3.

[120] *Report of the 69th Conference*, pp 161–2, para 69.

[121] (1990) 171 CLR 538 at 556–7 *per* Mason CJ, Deane, Dawson, and Gaudron JJ.

[122] [2000] 1 WLR 1545 at 1559 *per* Lord Bingham of Cornhill. The same point was made by Lord Goff of Chieveley in *Spiliada* [1987] 1 AC 460 at 482 and in *Connelly v RTZ Corp* [1998] AC 854 at 872.

[123] ibid at 1557–9 *per* Lord Bingham of Cornhill.

[124] (2001) 180 ALR 402.

to the allegation made by the abducting parent, not supported by any admissible evidence, that Mexican judges were corrupt.[125]

Consideration was given in framing the ILA Principles to incorporate the proposition that the court of the domicile of the defendant should never be able to decline jurisdiction. But the ILA Committee on International Civil and Commercial Litigation did not think that the possibility of declining jurisdiction in cases brought in the defendant's domicile should be entirely eliminated.[126] This possibility was also not excluded in the Hague Preliminary Draft Convention.[127] The main difficulty is that both in the Brussels I Regulation and in the Hague Preliminary Draft Convention the domicile of a corporation is defined in such terms as to give the plaintiff a potential choice of at least three different fora.[128] The possibility that one of those fora might in the circumstances of the particular case be 'clearly inappropriate' cannot be excluded.

(4) The Preliminary Draft Convention

The Preliminary Draft Convention in Article 22 is clearly influenced by the proposals in what later became known as the Leuven-London Principles.[129] Like those Principles they avoid the use of the term *'forum non conveniens'* and are designed to ensure not only that there is another court available in theory but that it will actually assume jurisdiction. It follows the recommendation of the Principles in that Article 22 requires suspension at the first instance and only allows the actual declining of jurisdiction when the court of the other State assumes jurisdiction. If the court of the other State decides not to assume jurisdiction, the first court must proceed with the case, as is also foreseen by the Principles. This will overcome the problem of the undertaking to submit given by a defendant seeking referral to another forum where no independent basis for jurisdiction is available. The alternative court will only have jurisdiction if the defendant actually does submit and that submission is accepted as a basis for exercising jurisdiction by the alternative forum.

---

[125] ibid at 421 para [73] *per* Gaudron, Gummow, and Hayne JJ.
[126] N 120, above, para 67.
[127] See *Report by Peter Nygh and Fausto Pocar on the Preliminary Draft Convention*, August 2000, p 90.
[128] See Brussels I Regulation Art 60; Preliminary Draft Convention Art 3.2.
[129] The crucial meeting in Leuven took place in November 1998 and the final shape of the principles were approved in Milan in early October 1999 just before the final meeting of the Special Commission that resulted in the Preliminary Draft Convention on 30 October 1999. However, the Principles were approved by the ILA as a whole in July 2000.

As recommended by the Principles, the first court must have regard to certain considerations including the convenience of the parties and the availability of the evidence, as well as the applicable limitation or prescription periods and the possibility of obtaining recognition and enforcement of any decision. Unlike the Principles, Article 22 does not make specific provision for the imposition of conditions of referral such as the waiver of limitation bars, but undoubtedly they could be given and considered in determining whether this particular factor is still relevant to the determination. As recommended by the Principles, there is a direction to the first court not to discriminate on the basis of nationality or habitual residence of the parties. This may not altogether eliminate the relevance of the 'crowded docket', but that 'public interest factor' must be applied in a non-discriminatory manner.

On the other hand, Article 22 is more stringent than the Principles in defining the circumstances in which jurisdiction can be declined. It requires satisfaction on the part of the originating court that it is a clearly inappropriate forum and that the other forum is clearly more appropriate to resolve the issue. This repeats the American test, but without the 'public interest' consideration that in many cases has led US courts to conclude that the forum chosen by a foreign plaintiff is 'inconvenient'. In fact it will mean that in most cases a defendant who is sued at the place of habitual residence or on most other authorized grounds of jurisdiction under the Convention cannot complain of that jurisdiction being 'clearly inappropriate' even if there is another more appropriate forum available. It is only where that connection is slight or inconsequential, such as a minor publication locally in a multi-State dissemination of defamatory material or a minor aspect of the performance of a contract for the sale of goods or the supply of services in a particular country as compared with other places of performance, that the issue will be relevant at all.

There is no specific provision in Article 22 for a refusal of a referral on the grounds of possible denial of justice. But, it is submitted, that this is clearly implicit in the notion of a 'clearly more appropriate forum'. It is hard to see how a forum where one of the parties cannot obtain justice (and that goes for the defendant also) can be described as 'appropriate'.

On the whole the provisions of Article 22 are in accordance with the Leuven-London Principles in that they stress referral of jurisdiction rather than the dismissal of proceedings and seek to do so in a responsible internationalist manner without discrimination against foreign plaintiffs.

H. Conclusion

One can only agree with the conclusion reached by Fawcett in his General Report in *Declining Jurisdiction in Private International Law* that: 'Parallel proceedings at home and abroad are undesirable and should not be allowed to continue'.[130] It is also preferable that such proceedings be prevented as early as possible without provoking a 'race to judgment'. Nor should such a race necessarily be replaced with a 'race to the courthouse'.

This makes it essential to reach international agreement and to encourage international co-operation at the judicial level. Principle 5.2 of the Leuven-London Principles provides that 'the originating court may communicate directly with the alternative court on any application for referral' and encourages States to permit its courts to take part in such communications. Of course, the parties to the dispute should be consulted before communication is initiated. Unilateral action, such as the issue of an anti-suit injunction (or its dreadful progeny—the anti-anti-suit injunction) should be avoided.[131]

Such international agreement should aim at referral of jurisdiction rather than dismissal of jurisdiction. In other words, the plaintiff should not be left to scramble for another forum. The jurisdiction of the referring court should not be terminated unless:

• the alternative court not only has jurisdiction, but actually assumes it;
• the alternative court proceeds to deal with the proceedings without undue delay; and
• the judgment of the alternative court will be recognized and enforced in those jurisdictions where enforcement is likely to take place.

Ideally therefore, the jurisdiction of the referring court should remain suspended until and unless a judgment entitled to recognition and enforcement is produced to it. Until that time the referring court should retain the power to resume the hearing if the proceedings in the alternative forum do not proceed satisfactorily.

While a rule that gives priority to the proceedings first instituted can be de-

---

[130] See n 1 above, p 67.
[131] See the Leuven-London Principles No 7 which would bar the use of anti-suit injunctions between judicial systems applying the Principles with the possible exception of the case of a breach of an exclusive jurisdiction clause, see *Report of the 69th Conference*, pp 165–7.

fended on the grounds of ease of applying and predictability, it should not be an absolute rule. There should be flexibility allowing the court first seised to refer the proceedings to a court subsequently seised. In so doing priority should be given to the court that is seised of the substantive dispute, rather than an application for a declaration of no liability. Other considerations are the well-known trio of balance of convenience, balance of legal advantage and the applicable law.

There is a need for a *lis pendens* rule subject to the flexibility described above. To make this effective, the court subsequently seised must suspend proceedings of its own motion as soon as it becomes aware of the *lis pendens* to allow an application for transfer to be made to the court first seised. The court first seised will have the power to make the final determination for, unless it does so, the court subsequently seised will not have jurisdiction.

There is also a need to provide for a consolidation of related actions in the one forum, be it the forum first seised or subsequently seised. There cannot in this case be any priority of time, although it may be desirable for pragmatic purposes to allow the court first seised to determine its attitude first. In the case of refusal, the court subsequently seised could still refer the matter. Related actions should be defined by their impact on each other both as regards the conduct of the proceedings (such as similar evidence) or as regards the likely decisions (such as the avoidance of incompatible conclusions of fact or of law). Related actions are likely to arise where the parties are the same though the claims differ or where the subject of the dispute and the defendant are the same, though the plaintiffs may differ. It is also desirable to treat this category separately and not as a part of *forum non conveniens* or similar considerations.

What is left is the single forum situation where no similar or related action is pending in any alternative court. It may be questioned whether it is at all necessary to deal with this situation. In many cases one might expect that the party seeking referral of the proceedings to an alternative forum, will start proceedings there. But, as *Lubbe v Cape plc*[132] shows, that may not always possible: the defendant may not have a counter-claim (other than the generally undesirable application for a declaration of no liability)[133] or may be outside the jurisdiction

---

[132] [2000] 1 WLR 1545, where it was stated at 1550, that since 1989 the defendant had had no presence anywhere in South Africa and had no assets in that country.
[133] As the decision of the High Court in *CSR Ltd v Cigna Insurance Australia Ltd* (1997) 189 CLR 345 shows that will place it immediately at a disadvantage.

of the alternative court unless it submits to proceedings an unwilling plaintiff is unlikely to institute there. Hence, there is also room for a power of referral in this situation provided the three conditions referred to above, can be satisfied, if not at the time of hearing the application, then as soon as possible after suspension of the initial proceedings is granted by the originating court.

14

NATIONAL PRIVATE INTERNATIONAL LAW AND INTERNATIONAL INSTRUMENTS

Kurt Siehr *

A. Problems

During the last fifty years many European countries enacted national statutes on private international law (PIL).[1] So did several countries in the

---

* Professor of Law, University of Zurich, Faculty of Law.
[1] This was done in Austria (1978), Croatia (1982), Czechoslovakia (1963), Estonia (1994), Germany (1986, 1997, 1999), Hungary (1979), Italy (1995), Liechtenstein (1996), Lithuania

Americas,[2] in Africa,[3] and Asia.[4] Some of these statutes on private international law are very comprehensive consisting of 200 or almost 200 sections covering the law of international civil procedure (jurisdiction, recognition of foreign judgments) and provisions on the applicable law.[5] Other enactments are considerably shorter and are laconic leaving many problems to be answered by the courts. This codification movement can be compared with the situation one hundred years before when the codification of private law in civil codes also led to legislation on private international law.[6] Does this codification trend indicate that private international law becomes petrified in national statutes and thereby sacrifices international dimensions to domestic peculiarities and traditions? I shall try to show that the answer to my questions is far from being affirmative. Many national rules are shaped according to international models, in particular to international conventions. This hidden harmonization can be demonstrated on various levels of different intensity.

(2000), Poland (1965), Portugal (1966), Romania (1992), Russia (1996), Slovenia (1999), Spain (1981), Switzerland (1987), Turkey (1982), Yugoslavia (1982). Many of these codifications are reproduced in the original language and in German translation in: Wolfgang Riering (ed), *IPR-Gesetze in Europa* (Bern/München 1997).

[2] Costa Rica (1986), Cuba (1975,1987), Ecuador (1970), Guatemala (1989), Louisiana (1991), Paraguay (1985), Peru (1984), Quebec (1991), Venezuela (1998). See the original version of the statutes on private international law of these states in: J Kropholler/H Krüger/W Riering/J Samtleben/K Siehr (eds), *Außereuropäische IPR-Gesetze* (Hamburg/Würzburg 1999).

[3] Algeria (1975), Angola (1966), Burkina Faso, (1989), Burundi (1980), Central African Republic (1965), Congo [Brazaville] (1984), Gabon (1972), Libya (1954), Madagascar (1962), Mauretania (1989), Mozambique (1967), Ruanda (1988), Senegal (1972), Somalia (1973), Sudan (1971), Togo, (1980), Chad (1967). Tunisia (1998). The statutes of these states can be found in the collection of Kropholler/Krüger/Riering/Samtleben/Siehr (n 2 above).

[4] Afghanistan (1977), Bahrain (1971), China (1986–1988), Korea (1962), Iraq (1951), Japan (1989), Yemen (1992), Jordan (1977), Kazakstan (1963, 1969, 1982), Kuwait (1961), Mongolia (1973, 1994), Philippines (1987), Taiwan (1953), Uzbekistan (1997), Vietnam (1986, 1996). The statutes of these states can be found in: Kropholler/Krüger/Riering/Samtleben/Siehr (n 2 above).

[5] The Swiss Federal Statute on Private International Law of 1987, English translation in (1989) 37 Am J Comp L 193 with introduction by S C Symeonides, and in (1990) 29 Int Legal Materials 1244, consists of 200 sections, the Romanian Statute on Private International Law of 1992 has 183 sections.

[6] See the codification of private international law in Argentina (1869), Chile (1855), Germany (1896), Italy (1865), Japan (1898), Spain (1889) and Switzerland (1891).

B. Impacts of International Instruments

(1) Reference to International Conventions

For almost fifty years several international instruments on matters of private international law have been conceived as exhaustive pieces of legislation leaving no room for national legislation. They do not require any reciprocity and even apply if members of non-Contracting States are involved or if the law of such a State governs the case. Therefore some national legislators abstained from formulating identical or different domestic rules of private international law and instead made reference to international Conventions. As an example of such a reference there is Article 83(1) of the Swiss Statute on Private International Law (Swiss PIL Statute).[7] This states that 'Maintenance obligations between parent and child are governed by the Hague Convention of 2 October 1973 on the Law Applicable to Maintenance Obligations'. Similar references are made to four other Hague Conventions[8] and to the New York Convention of 1958 on the Recognition and Enforcement of Foreign Arbitral Awards.[9]

The Italian PIL Statute of 1995[10] decided to pursue the same method and refers to the EEC Conventions of Brussels[11] (Article 3(2)) and of Rome[12] (Article 57), to two Hague Conventions (Articles 42(1) and 45)[13] and to the Geneva Conventions of 1930/31 on the Law Applicable to Bills of Exchange and Cheques[14] (Article 59(1)). Also the Austrian codification refers to the

---

[7] See the English translations of the Swiss Statute of Private International Law at n 5 above.

[8] References are made to Convention of 1961 on the Jurisdiction of Authorities and the Law Applicable in Matter of the Protection of Minors (Art 85 (1)), to the Convention of 1961 on the Conflict of Laws Relating to the Form of Testamentary Dispositions (Art 93 (1)), to the Convention of 1955 on the Law Applicable to International Sale of Goods (Art 118 (1)) and to the Convention of 1971 on the Law Applicable to Traffic Accidents (Art 134). The Hague Conventions are collected in the publication of the Hague Conference on Private International Law: *Recueil des Conventions, Collection of Conventions* (1951–1996) (The Hague 1996).

[9] 330 UNTS 3, 38.

[10] See the English translation in (1996) 35 Int Legal Materials 765 with introduction by A Giardina.

[11] Brussels Convention of 27 October 1968/29 November 1996 on Jurisdiction and the Enforcement of Judgments in Civil and Commercial Matters [1972] OJL99/32, [1982] OJL388/1.

[12] Rome Convention of 19 June 1980 on the Law Applicable to Contractual Obligations, [1980] OJL266/1.

[13] Hague Conventions of 1961 on the Protection of Minors (Art 42) and of 1973 on Maintenance (Art 45), *Recueil* (n 8 above) nos X and XXIV.

[14] See 143 LNTS 257, 317, 337 and 143 LNTS 7, 355, 407.

Rome Convention of 1980 (§ 35(1)) and therefore abrogated conflicting private international law conflicts rules.[15]

I do not want to give an exhaustive list of similar phenomena in other jurisdictions.[16] Suffice to say that national codifications of private international law are not any more as national as they used to be one hundred years before. Modern statutes refer to international Conventions and refrain from formulating competing domestic rules and thereby provide for an efficient integration of Conventions into the corpus of national law sources.

(2) Extension of International Conventions

The reference to international Conventions in national codifications of private international law is a useful instrument for integrating different sources of law into this specific sector of law, which is not known or praised as a subject matter of lucid transparency and easy accessibility. Another shortcoming of this field of law is eliminated by national codifications: the incompleteness of international Conventions.

Application as to Matters

The Hague Convention of 1961 on the Conflict of Laws Relating to the Form of Testamentary Dispositions[17] is limited to testamentary dispositions and does not cover the form of other dispositions *mortis causa,* eg, of contracts of succession (Erbvertrag) or the testamentary dispositions in a marriage contract (institution contractuelle). Article 93(2) of the Swiss Statute of Private International Law extends the application of the Hague Convention to the 'form of any other disposition *mortis causa*'. Article 26(3) of the German Introductory Statute to the BGB (EGBGB) does the same.[18] Such extensions easily 'amend' some sources of law which, in the international arena of diplomatic conferences, could not be finalized in every detail.

---

[15] The original version of the Austrian Federal Statute of 15 June 1978 on Private International Law is translated into English in (1980) 28 Am J Comp L 22 with article by E Palmer.

[16] See, eg, the Dutch draft of a PIL Statute in K Boele-Woelki/M J De Rooij (eds), *Internationaal Privaatrecht Verdragen & Wetten* (Nijmegen 1996) 2.

[17] See *Recueil* (n 8 above) no XI.

[18] See the English translation in: (1988) 27 Int Legal Materials 16 with introduction by G Wegen.

Application as to Persons

It was rather late during the last century that it became common for Hague Conventions on the law applicable to draft instruments valid *erga omnes*, ie, for all persons irrespective of their nationality and without requiring that the law governing must be the law of a Contracting State. An example of such restrictions is the Hague Convention of 1961 on the Protection of Minors.[19] There are two restrictions as to the minors covered by this instrument. It applies only to minors being minors according to their law of nationality as well as according to the law of their habitual residence (Article 12). The other restriction is that of Article 13(1): The minor must be habitually resident in a Contracting State. The Italian and the Swiss Statutes on Private International Law extend the Hague Convention to

- minors being minors only according to Swiss law (Article 85(2) Swiss PIL Statute) or only according to their national law (Article 42(2) Italian PIL Statute),
- minors wherever they are habitually resident [Article 42(2) Italian Statute, Article 85(2) Swiss PIL Statute),
- to all adult persons (Article 85 (2) Swiss PIL Statute).

These extensions are remarkable in several respects. Forty years ago, when the Hague Convention of 1961 was adopted by the 1960 Ninth Session of the Hague Conference the delegates were not ready to agree on a clear definition of a minor person. Yet this was easily done more than thirty years later at the 1996 Eighteenth Session of the Hague Conference when the revised Convention on the Protection of Minors was adopted.[20] Even more dramatic is the second extension to all minors wherever habitually resident. In 1960 many Member States of the Hague Conference supported vigorously the principle of nationality and were anxious to preserve as much of this principle as possible. Therefore they limited the Hague Convention on the Protection of Minors to children habitually resident in a Contracting State and even provided a potential reservation whereby the Convention could be limited to minors being nationals of a Contracting State (Article 13 (3)). That Switzerland did not make

---

[19] See *Recueil* (n 8 above) no X.

[20] See Hague Convention of 10 October 1996 on jurisdiction, applicable law, recognition, enforcement, and co-operation in respect of parental responsibility and measures for the protection of children in: Recueil (n 8 above) no XXXIV. Art 2 of the 1996 Convention reads: 'This convention applies to children from the moment of their birth until they reach the age of 18 years'.

this reservation can easily be explained by the Swiss tradition of favouring the principle of domicile or habitual residence. The interesting extension is that of Italy which, being the trustee of the Mancinian principle of nationality, rather late (1995) ratified the 1961 Hague Minors Convention and is now ready to subscribe, at least partially, to the principle of habitual residence. The same happened in Austria, another partisan of the nationality principle, when it gave up the reservation made under Article 13(3) of the Convention.

The last extension to adult persons proved to be an incentive for the Hague Convention of 2001 on the Protection of Adults.[21]

Clarification of Instruments

Nothing is perfect, neither international instruments nor national legislation. But the *lex posterior* may clarify uncertainties which have arisen as to the field of application of the *lex prior*. Under the Hague Maintenance Convention of 1973 it is unclear whether it also covers any of the costs of delivery of the child.[22] Therefore Article 83 Swiss PIL Statute refers to the Convention in paragraph 1 and expressly states in paragraph 2 that the cost of delivery is also governed by the law applicable to claims for maintenance of the child.

Another clarification is provided by Article 118(2) of the Swiss PIL Statute. It provides that the Hague Sales Convention of 1955[23] does not apply to consumer sales. This seems to be a national derogation from internationally accepted and assumed obligations. This impression is misleading. The exception only verbalizes the common opinion of the Hague Conference and the Member States of the Conference that the 1955 Hague Sales Convention is limited to commercial sales[24] and it was for this reason that the Hague Conference tried to prepare a draft Convention on the law applicable to international consumer sales.[25]

---

[21] The English version of this Convention is reproduced in: (2000) 64 *Rabels Zeitschrift für ausländisches und internationales Privatrecht* 752.

[22] See M Verwilghen, 'Explanatory Report', in *Actes et documents de la Douzième session 2 au 21 octobre 1972,* vol IV (The Hague 1975) 384, 390 et seq, 433 et seq.

[23] Hague Convention of 15 June 1955 on the Law Applicable to International Sale of Goods, *Recueil* (n 8 above) no III.

[24] See Acte final of the 14th Session, Part C: 'Declaration and Recommendation relating to the scope of the Convention on the law applicable to international sale of goods, concluded June 15th, 1955', in *Actes et documents de la Quatorzième session 6 au 25 octobre 1980,* vol II (The Hague 1982) II-177, II-180.

[25] See Draft Convention on the law applicable to certain consumer sales, in *Actes et documents* (n 24 above) II-178.

(3) Incorporation of International Conventions

The German 1986 amendment to the EGBGB does not refer to the Rome Convention or Hague Conventions. It incorporates these Conventions as if they were of national origin. The Rome Convention does not apply in Germany directly[26] although normally every self-executing convention applies directly in Germany as soon as Parliament has approved the instrument. Germany wanted to incorporate the Rome Convention as a body of national conflicts rules. As a result there is Article 27 et seq of the EGBGB. The German solution cannot be recommended as a model. Conflicts rules of international origin have to be interpreted according to international standards. They should not be dressed in national costumes, thereby giving the impression of that they are of domestic vintage. Germany would have been better to make short references to international Conventions.[27] The new Italian Statute of 1995 on Private International Law did not copy the German example, but instead refers in Article 57 to the Rome Convention.

(4) Domestic Adaptation to International Conventions

Switzerland not being a Member State of the European Union could not refer to the 1980 Rome Convention, which has not entered into force in Switzerland. Yet, Switzerland did not want to deviate too much from the common European model of rules governing international contracts. Therefore Articles 116 et seq of the Swiss PIL Statute on international contracts are very similar to those contained in the Rome Convention. Such an approach was chosen for mainly two reasons. Firstly, the idea of applying the law of the State in which the characteristically performing party to a contract is habitually resident, is of Swiss origin. Adolf Schnitzer (1889–1989) developed this approach,[28] the Swiss Federal Court followed[29] and the Rome Convention

---

[26] Art 1(2) of the Act of 25 July 1986, approving the Rome Convention, in [1986] II *Bundesgesetzblatt* 809.

[27] Kurt Siehr, 'Multilaterale Staatsverträge *erga omnes* und deren Inkorporation in nationale IPR-Kodifikationen—Vor- und Nachteile einer solchen Rezeption', in (1986) 27 *Berichte der Deutschen Gesellschaft für Völkerrecht* 45–146.

[28] Adolf F Schnitzer, *Handbuch des internationalen Privatrechts* (4th edn Basel 1958) 642 et seq, id, 'Les contrats internationaux en droit international privé suisse' in (1968-I) 123 *Recueil des cours* 541, 571 et seq.

[29] See Swiss Federal Court: 10 June 1952, 78 II Entscheidungen des Schweizerischen Bundesgerichts (BGE) 190, 191; 31 August 1953, 78 II BGE 295, 298; 21 October 1955, 81 II BGE 391, 394.

accepted the same solution.[30] The other reason for the Swiss approach is that it is very sensible to adopt commonly accepted rules in a highly internationalized field of commerce where uniformity is very important and where small countries can make use of court decisions and precedents of their more populous European neighbours.

The same tendency can be observed in some other European States, which are not Member States of the European Union. The codifications of the Czech Republic, the Slovakian Republic (§ 10), of Hungary (§ 25), Poland (Article 27), and Romania (Articles 77 et seq) also, expressly or tacitly, accept the principle of characteristic performance.[31]

(5) Reception of International Conventions

What do courts do if they do not get any guidance from national statutes or precedents? In the Netherlands courts turned to international conventions and applied them although not yet ratified by the national parliament.[32] By such a voluntary judge-made reception of international Conventions Dutch private international law became very international and avoided any provinciality.

(6) Intermediate Summary

During the last forty years many States in Europe and overseas codified rules on private international law. Unlike the codification movement at the end of the nineteenth century, the modern codifications of PIL did not copy any national model. Instead they looked at international conventions and tried to keep pace with supra- and international developments as manifested in international instruments on private international law. National legislators did not only copy these instruments or refer to them, they also extended them in several respects. The result of this international orientation of legislators is a remarkable similarity of national codifications in several respects. They do not cherish local niceties, they try to be as cosmopolitan as possible.

---

[30] See M. Giuliano/P Lagarde, 'Report on the Convention on the law applicable to contractual obligations' [1980] OJ C 282/1, art 282/21 (comment no 3 to Art 4 of the Rome Convention).

[31] The codifications of Central and East European countries are reproduced in Riering (n 1 above).

[32] Hans Ulrich Jessurun d'Oliveira 'Die Freiheit des niederländischen Richters bei der Entwicklung des Internationalen Privatrechts', (1975) 39 *Rabels Zeitschrift für ausländisches und internationales Privatrecht* 224–252.

C. Special Problems

(1) Interpretation of International Instruments

National pieces of legislation form part of domestic legal traditions, culture, and understanding. Courts apply the domestic canons of interpretation and construction and thereby contribute to a rather provincial conception of law and policy. If this were true even of private international law, this field of law, which is concerned with trying to avoid conflicts, coordinating competing legal systems and adapting foreign law to domestic needs, these goals could not be achieved at all. Therefore it is often emphasized that private international law should be interpreted differently. It should be construed 'kollisionsnorm-gerecht', ie, functionally according to the needs of conflicts rules.[33] In many jurisdictions such a method of interpretation is recognized in theory and practice. Even more than that has to be done. Conflicts rules originating in international instruments should be construed according to internationally accepted rules of uniform interpretation along the line of Article 18 of the Rome Convention of 1980. This provides that 'regard shall be had to their [the rules] international character and to the desirability of achieving uniformity in their interpretation and application.' This rule on uniform interpretation has also been transferred to the EGBGB as Article 36.

(2) Interpretation of Unilaterally Harmonized Law

A special problem has arisen in Switzerland where the 1961 Hague Convention on the Protection of Minors has been extended to all children, wherever they are habitually resident, and to all adult persons: Article 85(2) Swiss PIL Statute. In cases covered by the unilateral extension of the 1961 Convention the Convention should be applied—as is statutorily provided—'sinngemäss', 'par analogie' or 'per analogia', translated into English as 'by analogy'. What does this mean? Should the Convention be applied as if it were binding or should it be adjusted to special or general needs? The answer has to be given in the crucial situation of Articles 4 and 7 of the 1961 Convention. Under Article 4(1) the courts and authorities of the minor's national State have jurisdiction to take measures of protection and these measures have to be recognized in every Contracting State, as provided in Article 7 of the 1961 Convention. Do these provisions also apply to cases not covered by the

---

[33] K Siehr, *Internationales Privatrecht* (Heidelberg 2001) 432 et seq.

Convention but which should be solved 'by analogy' to the Convention? It is generally accepted that a literal application of the Convention is not required.[34] There are two choices which may be made. On the one hand, any head of jurisdiction deviating too much from the principle of domicile or habitual residence should not be exercised and foreign decisions of such national *fora* should not be recognized. The other choice is to take into account the new Draft Conventions of 1996 and 2001 on the Protection of Children (1996)[35] and of Adults (2001).[36] The application 'by analogy' should take into account the new Draft Conventions because they reflect the correct answers to the modern policies of protection of minors and adults.[37] I have advocated such a prospective interpretation of the 1961 Convention 'by analogy'.

(3) Parallel Interpretation of Domestic and International Law

A key problem of private international law is the interpretation of domestic conflict rules. In order to avoid any narrowly conceived provincial construction several different approaches are possible.

International Approach

Of course, national versions of international models should be interpreted according to the international model. This is done in the Swiss international law of contractual obligations (Articles 116 et seq Swiss PIL Statute) because they are drafted along the lines of the Rome Convention.[38]

In other less obvious cases the same international approach is also chosen. Article 113 Swiss PIL Statute provides a special head of jurisdiction at the place of performance. Here the question has to be answered as to where the place of performance is to be located. The *Tessili* case of the European Court of Justice decided that the law governing the dispute should fix the place of performance.[39] Some Swiss courts favoured this approach also for Article 113 Swiss

---

[34] See J Schwander, in H Honsell, N P Vogt and A K Schnyder (eds), *Internationales Privatrecht* (Basel 1996) Art 85 IPRG, marginal notes 62 *et seq.*
[35] See n 20 above.
[36] See n. 20 above.
[37] In Support of such a 'prospective' interpretation K Siehr in A Heini, M Keller, K Siehr, F Vischer and P Volken (eds), *IPRG-Kommentar* (2d edn Zürich 2002) Art 85 IPRG, marginal notes 2 and 79.
[38] See B(4) above.
[39] Case 12/76 *Tessili v Dunlop*, [1976] ECR 1473, [1977] CMLR 1, 26, ECJ.

PIL Statute[40] and thereby achieved harmony between the Brussels Convention and Swiss domestic conflicts law.

More courage is necessary for a third kind of international interpretation or adaptation. The Hague Child Abduction Convention only applies to children abducted from States being States Parties of the Hague Convention.[41] But what should domestic courts do if a child was abducted from a non-contracting country? Because such a State has no central authority to be designated under the rules of the Hague Convention, cooperation between States may be more difficult than in Convention cases. But should the attitude towards illegal child abductions be different from those arising under the Hague Convention? Hardly! Therefore it has been advocated[42] and even practised[43] that the same principles of quick return proceedings and return order apply in non-Convention cases.

(4) Coordinating Interpretation

Considerations of public policy of every forum may interfere with the idea of achieving international harmony by the uniform interpretation of international instruments or of provisions copying such instruments. Such a tension is well known to everybody who tries to coordinate Article 5 of the Rome Convention on consumer contracts with Article 7 of the same Convention on mandatory rules of the respective forum. The problem may be described like this: Article 5 is limited to specific consumer contracts which are concluded under special circumstances mentioned in paragraph (2), and Article 7(2) makes a reservation in favour of mandatory rules of every forum. If every forum rule protecting consumers was qualified as a mandatory rule under Article 7(2) Rome Convention, the provision of Article 5 Rome Convention would in effect be extended to all consumer contracts and the limitation to 'passive' consumers would be abandoned. Therefore Article 7(2) Rome

---

[40] Court of Appeal Basel 7 November 1990, 1991 *Basler Juristische Mitteilungen* 191, 192 et seq.; contra: Commercial Court Zurich 9 January 1996, (1996) 95 *Blätter für Zürcherische Rechtsprechung* no 96 at 300 et seq.

[41] Convention of 25 October 1980 on the Civil Aspects of International Child Abduction, *Recueil* (n 8 above) no XXVIII.

[42] Tobias Helms, 'Zivilrechtliche Aspekte internationaler Kindesentführungen—Der Rückführungs-mechanismus und seine Erstreckung auf vom Übereinkommen nicht erfaßte Sachverhalte', in 2000 *Jahrbuch Junger Zivilrechtswissenschaftler* 267–280 at 273 et seq (2001).

[43] See, the following decisions of the English Court of Appeal: eg, *G v G (Minors)* [1991] 2 FLR 506, CA; *D v D (Child Abduction: Non-Convention Country)* [1994] 1 FLR 137, CA.

Convention should be interpreted restrictively and be limited to general provisions of mandatory application.[44]

D. Common Problems Originating in Substantive Law

(1) Equality of Husband and Wife, Father and Mother

Pasquale Stanislao Mancini (1817–1888) introduced the principle of nationality into private international law. The reason for this is well known. Unified Italy (1861) felt responsible for all Italians wherever they live and the 'italianità' was the same denominator of national identity as it was the Hellenism in early nineteenth century when Greece was liberated (1830).[45] Since then the principle of nationality and the principle of domicile divide several systems of conflict of laws.

What originated in public law, was preserved as 'national heritage' in private international law and constantly defended as a firm dogma melted in modern times under the influence of substantive law of equality of husband and wife, father and mother. As soon as there was a 'mariage mixte' of different nationalities it was not possible any more under the equality principle to apply the national law of the husband or father. A common connecting factor had to be found and it was found in the common habitual residence. The same was true in the field of parent and child. The father's national law should not govern this relationship but the law at the child's habitual residence. Finally the principle of nationality will not vanish because its partisans will become less dogmatic or pass away. It will disappear because of values of substantive law[46] and, perhaps of European law because in the European Union there should be no discrimination because of nationality (Article 12 (2) EC Treaty, Amsterdam version of 1997).

(2) Welfare and Equal Treatment of Children

Even before the 1989 UN Convention on the Rights of the Child was approved, national constitutions and statutes provided for the improvement and

---

[44] See the discussion of this problem in Siehr (n 33 above) § 26.
[45] It is for this reason that the Greek king was called King of the Hellenes. See M L Smith, *Ionian Vision Greece in Asia Minor, 1919–1922* (London 1998) 3.
[46] See D Henrich, 'Abschied vom Staatsangehörigkeitsprinzip ?' in *Festschrift für Hans Stoll* (Tübingen 2001) 437.

revision of family law relating to the field of parent and child. Influenced by this, several legislators also revised their PIL codifications in this respect. The division of legitimate and illegitimate children was abolished[47] and the welfare of the child was also recognized in private international law as a guiding principle.[48]

(3) Private and Party Autonomy

Private autonomy is well recognized everywhere as freedom of contract and freedom to contract. This idea of autonomy was also extended to private international law as party autonomy in contractual relations[49] and spread to several other areas, especially to the field of matrimonial property law[50] and to the field of succession. The testator should be free to make a choice between the law of his last domicile and the law of his last nationality.[51] Also in this respect the antagonism between the principle of nationality and the principle of domicile can be mitigated.

E. Summary

Many European countries have codified their private international law in recent years. This seems to be a forceful and postmodern centripetal movement in the direction of national peculiarities and traditions and a menace to any harmonization or unification of private international law. This evaluation of first impression is corrected on looking more carefully. National codifications copy international treaties, refer to them and even extend their field of application. In several instances courts take international instruments as a model for the solution of questions not answered by codification. Hence modern codifications of private international law serve as a useful intermediary between national legislation and international treaty making. These national codifications are pacemakers for future harmonization or unification of conflicts law. They are no obstacle to greater uniformity in Europe private international law.

---

[47] This was done not only in former Socialist countries but also in Germany (1997) and Switzerland (1997).

[48] See Preamble and Art 22 of the 1996 Hague Convention on the Protection of Children (n 20 above).

[49] Peter Nygh, *Autonomy in International Contracts* (Oxford 1999).

[50] See, eg § 19 Austrian PIL Statute, Art 15(2) German EGBGB, Art 30 (1) Italian PIL Statute, Art 52, Swiss PIL Statute.

[51] See., eg, Art 90 (2) Swiss PIL Statute.

INDEX